GEORGE WASHINGTON WILLIAMS

Fraternally Yours,

Geo. W. Williams.

Williams the historian

"Not as a blind panegyrist of my race, nor as a partisan apologist, but from a love '*for the truth of history*,' I have striven to record the truth, the whole truth, and nothing but the truth." Williams, *History of the Negro Race*.

GEORGE WASHINGTON WILLIAMS

A Biography

JOHN HOPE FRANKLIN

The University of Chicago Press
Chicago and London

John Hope Franklin is the James B. Duke Professor of History at Duke University. He is the author of *Racial Equality in America* (1976) and *Reconstruction after the Civil War* (1961), both published by the University of Chicago Press.

The University of Chicago Press, Chicago 60637
The University of Chicago Press, Ltd., London
© 1985 by The University of Chicago
All rights reserved. Published 1985
Printed in the United States of America

94 93 92 91 90 89 88 87 86 85   5 4 3 2

Library of Congress Cataloging in Publication Data
Franklin, John Hope, 1915–
    George Washington Williams, a biography.

    Bibliography: p. 333
    Includes index.
        1. Williams, George Washington, 1849–1891.
2. Afro-Americans—Biography.   I. Title.
E185.97.W695F74   1985   973′.0496024 [B]   85-5800
ISBN 0-226-26083-6

To
William Edward Burghardt DuBois
Carter Godwin Woodson
Charles Harris Wesley
Rayford Whittingham Logan

Warm admirers of George Washington Williams and able
contributors to several fields in which he labored

Contents

Appendixes

Illustrations

Acknowledgments

Over the years I have become indebted to many institutions and people in the preparation of this work. I have attempted to keep lists of such institutions and people, but thirty-nine years have not been kind either to those lists or to my memory. If I have omitted some names, it was through inadvertence rather than a lack of gratitude. A simple expression of deep gratitude to those who have helped seems quite inadequate, except for the fact that they all seem to have been rewarded, to some extent, by the satisfaction and pleasure they derived from the act of assisting in various ways. Among the institutions to which I am grateful are the Andover Newton Theological School, the American Antiquarian Society, Arents Research Library of Syracuse University, Atlanta University Library, Baptist Missionary Society of London, Blackpool Public Library, Boston Public Library, British Library, University of Chicago Library, Cincinnati Historical Society, University of Cincinnati Archives, Clark University Archives, Duke University Library, Fisk University Library, Houghton Library of Harvard University, Library of Congress, London School of Economics Library, Martin L. King Library of the District of Columbia, Massachusetts Historical Society, Moorland-Spingarn Research Center of Howard University, National Archives and Record Service, North Carolina Central University Library, University of North Carolina Library, Ohio Historical Society, Public Library of Columbus and Franklin County, Ohio, Public Record Office of Great Britain, Royal Archives of Belgium, Rutherford B. Hayes Library, St. Catherine's House (London), Schomburg Center for Research in Black Culture, School of Oriental and African Studies of London, Stanford University Library, *Times* of London Library, Tulane University Library, Virginia Union University Library, Western Reserve Historical Society, Warden's Office of the Layton Cemetery (Blackpool, England), and Yale University Library.

Numerous colleagues, associates, and friends have given generously of their time, talents, and resources. In some special way, each of them has contributed significantly to this work. Carter G. Woodson, Director of the Association for the Study of Negro Life and History, started me out on this venture and offered encouragement until his death in 1950. Henry P. Slaughter placed at my disposal the few Williams papers in his possession. Charles H. Wesley gave me Woodson's notes on Williams and made valuable suggestions regarding possible sources. Rayford W. Logan, who had done much basic research on the period in which Williams lived, shared with me his vast knowledge of that period. When she was at the Moorland-Spingarn Research Center, Dorothy B. Porter was alert to my needs and came up with some critical documents and information that made it possible for me to move to the next stage. Michael Winston, her successor, was equally cooperative and supportive.

The Reverend François Bontinck of the University of Kinshasa shared with me his intimate knowledge of the Congo and his extensive acquaintance with Williams's activities there. The Honorable Jules Marchal, the Belgian Ambassador to Niger, read the manuscript, offered many valuable suggestions, and provided me with a large number of clippings from the Belgian and French press. Charles A. Johnson also read the manuscript and made helpful suggestions and criticisms. Over the years Hunt Hawkins and I have exchanged information on Williams and his contemporaries, to my great benefit. John Blassingame sent many "care packages," culled from the Frederick Douglass Papers Project at Yale University and containing much information on nineteenth-century Afro-Americans that I would not have known about from other sources.

There were others affiliated with institutions who did much to facilitate my research. Among them were Nancy Burkett and John Hench of the American Antiquarian Society, Robert L. Clarke of the National Archives and Record Service, Gale Peterson of the Cincinnati Historical Society, John Fleming and Gary Hess of the Ohio Historical Society, Mildred Vannorsdall of the Chicago Public Library, Dorothy deFlandre of the United States Educational Foundation in Belgium, Thomas A. Duckenfield, Clerk of the Superior Court of the District of Columbia, Ann Allen Shockley of the Fisk University Library, Ellis E. O'Neal, Jr., of the Library of the Andover Newton Theological School, Lee Alexander and Annette Phinazee of the Atlanta University Library, Jean Blackwell Hutson of the Schomburg Center for Research in Black

Culture, Dwayne Cox of the University of Louisville, Alan Bryant of the Blackpool Town Hall, Gordon Phillips of the *Times* of London Archives, John Mulrooney of the West Lancashire *Evening Gazette*, the Reverend B. Amey of the Baptist Missionary Society of London, H.G. Pearson of the Office of the Home Secretary of the United Kingdom, the Reverend Wilbur A. Page of the Union Baptist Church of Cincinnati, and the Reverend Michael E. Haynes of the Twelfth Baptist Church of Boston.

In the course of their own research, many scholars passed on to me information that proved valuable to this study. Among them were William Banks, Joseph Boromé, Randall Burkett, Philip Butcher, James Cassada, William Cohen, Clarence Contee, Roger Daniels, William E. Farrison, Willard B. Gatewood, David Gerber, Adelaide Cromwell Gulliver, Herbert Gutman, Judith Gutman, Vincent Harding, Louis Harlan, John Higginson, Anthony Cromwell Hill, Maldwyn Jones, William Leuchtenberg, Leon Litwack, Edna McKenzie, Pearl McNeil, Paul McStallworth, August Meier, Ruth Miller, Nell Painter, James Patterson, Benjamin Quarles, George Shepperson, Philip A. M. Taylor, Walter Williams. Friends and colleagues who have offered assistance, suggestions, observations, and support in many other ways are numerous and, in some cases, nameless. Among those one can name are Allen Ballard, John Cell, John Coatsworth, Harlan Davidson, Helen G. Edmonds, Abraham S. Eisenstadt, Anne Paige Ewing, Neil Harris, David Hellwig, Emory A. Johnson, Barry Karl, Arthur Mann, Betty Torrey Oldham, Charles A. Ray, James Rogers, Otey Scruggs, and Hannah Bowman Watkins.

My research assistants often discovered information and produced results that would have eluded persons less able or less diligent. One can only remark that this task would have been infinitely more difficult, perhaps even impossible, without their help, which far exceeded their obligation. They are Richard P. Fuke, Loren Schweninger, Joseph Castrovinci, Robert Bloomberg, Michael Lanza, and Patrick Thompson. Scores of students have been helpful in providing leads, bits of information, and ways of looking at material and interpreting it. At the risk of omitting some, I am obliged to mention Eric Anderson, Richard Estrada, Hayward Farrar, David Feingold, Paul Finkelman, Frances R. Keller, Genna Rae McNeil, Robert Morris, Alfred A. Moss, Jr., Michael Perman, Howard Rabinowitz, Rodney Ross, Juliet E. K. Walker.

From time to time, I have needed and received technical assistance. Cherie Maiden performed a herculean task in translating a large file of Belgian and French newspapers. My Senegalese son, Bouna S. Ndiaye, helped in translations and interceded in securing the assistance of Joe Muwonge, who constructed a map of Europe and Africa. My son, John

Whittington Franklin, assisted in translating, served as my interpreter in Zaire, and performed various tasks in Washington. Inge Johnson was of immense help in translating German texts. Hortense Creuzot, Gertrude Johnson, and Nancy Helmy did typing and secretarial work at various stages of the project. My secretary and personal assistant for more than twenty years, Margaret Fitzsimmons, not only typed several drafts of the manuscript but also assisted in the research and served as a gifted and discriminating editor.

Among those who supported this project very generously were Kenneth and Harle Montgomery, the John Simon Guggenheim Memorial Foundation, the Center for Advanced Study in the Behavioral Sciences, and the National Humanities Center. While I was doing the research and writing this book, the institutions with which I have been affiliated have been generous in granting leaves of absence and released time as well as research and secretarial assistance, without which I would have been unable to complete the task. These are North Carolina Central University, Howard University, Brooklyn College, Cambridge University, the University of Chicago, and Duke University.

My wife, Aurelia, has been a constant companion and a source of inspiration and encouragement—from Bedford Springs to Kinshasa to Blackpool. While I am deeply grateful and more to all who had a part in this undertaking, I assume full responsibility for its defects and deficiencies.

JOHN HOPE FRANKLIN

Independence Day
1984

Introduction

Stalking George Washington Williams

It was almost forty years ago that I had the experience, but I remember it as distinctly as if it were yesterday. In the spring of 1945 I was just beginning to work on a book that was to be called *From Slavery to Freedom: A History of Negro Americans*. A good way to begin, I thought, was to read the shelves in the library of North Carolina College at Durham, where I was teaching, to see what, if anything, had been written on the subject, aside from Carter G. Woodson's *The Negro in Our History*, published in 1922. To my astonishment, my eyes fell on a two-volume work, *A History of the Negro Race in America from 1619 to 1880; Negroes as Slaves, as Soldiers, and as Citizens*, by George Washington Williams. I discovered that the work had been published in 1882 by a reputable publisher, G.P. Putnam's Sons, was about one thousand pages long, and, beginning with African civilization, covered virtually every aspect of the Afro-American experience in the New World. I saw that it was carefully researched—with plenty of footnotes—logically organized, and well written. Upon examining the card catalogue I learned that Williams was the author of still another work, *A History of Negro Troops in the War of the Rebellion*, published in 1887 by Harper and Brothers.

Among the many things I later learned was that Williams was destined for a life of adventure and excitement almost from the time of his birth in 1849 in Bedford Springs, Pennsylvania. With virtually no education, he ran away from home in 1864—at fourteen years of age—and joined the Union Army. After the Civil War, during which he saw action in various battles, he went to Mexico and fought with the forces that overthrew Maximilian. Returning to the United States, he enlisted in the Tenth Cavalry, one of the four all-Negro units of the regular

United States Army, from which he received a medical discharge in 1868.

Williams received a first-rate education at the Newton Theological Institution; semiliterate as an entrant, he became a polished writer and speaker within five years. At the age of twenty-five, following his graduation and marriage, he was installed as pastor of the Twelfth Baptist church in Boston. The following year, he went with his wife and young son (born in Boston earlier that year) to Washington, where he edited *The Commoner*. Soon afterward he settled in Cincinnati, pursuing a varied career as pastor; columnist for the Cincinnati *Commercial*; lawyer, after studying with President William Howard Taft's father; first black member of the state legislature; and historian of his race.

In 1890 Williams went to study conditions in the Belgian Congo under the patronage of the railroad magnate, Collis P. Huntington. After an extensive tour of the country, he wrote an *Open Letter* to King Leopold II, assailing him for his inhuman policies in the Congo. Although he had written a report to President Benjamin Harrison, at the president's request, there was little reaction in the United States to his attacks on King Leopold. Williams then went to England with his English "fiancée" (he was separated from his wife), intending to write a lengthy work on Africa. Illness overtook him, however, and he died in Blackpool at forty-one years of age.

Williams had a wide acquaintanceship among important personages in various parts of the world. He had at least one lengthy interview in Brussels with King Leopold II. He knew Sir William Mackinnon, a British shipping magnate, and George Grenfell, the British missionary. In the United States he met and talked with Presidents Rutherford B. Hayes, Grover Cleveland, and Benjamin Harrison. Senator George F. Hoar of Massachusetts was one of his staunchest supporters. In Ohio he counted Governor Charles Foster, Senator John Sherman, Judge Alphonso Taft, Murat Halstead (editor of the Cincinnati *Commercial*), and Senator Charles Fleischmann among his friends. He also had contact with such literary figures as Henry Wadsworth Longfellow, George Bancroft, and George Washington Cable.

He knew Frederick Douglass; Congressman John Mercer Langston; T. Thomas Fortune, editor of the New York *Freeman*; Richard T. Greener, an early black graduate of Harvard; Robert Terrell, the first black judge in the District of Columbia; and such leading black Bostonians as Judge George L. Ruffin, the civic leader James M. Trotter, and Lewis Hayden, abolitionist and legislator. It would be my good fortune to find, from time to time, correspondence between Williams and his many acquaintances that would greatly assist me in putting together the missing pieces of the Williams story.

Although I had never had a course in Afro-American history, I reproached myself for not having heard of this man and learned of the many events in his remarkable life. I wondered then, as I have many times since, why this historian of the Negro race had dropped into complete obscurity. I knew enough about the period in which he lived to realize that his obscurity was the result, at least in part, of social forces at work in this country in the late nineteenth century. Those forces dictated that Afro-Americans were not to be remembered for their constructive contributions to society, for their involvement in the literary history of the country, or for their revelations of the rape of Africa by Europeans and Americans. If Williams was unknown in the two generations that separated me from him since his death in 1891, I was determined that I would do what I could to repair the situation.

Fortunately there was a sketch of Williams in the *Dictionary of American Biography,* and I devoured it immediately, not knowing at the time that it was replete with factual errors. Shortly thereafter, when in Washington, I called on Dr. Carter G. Woodson, the founder and executive director of the Association for the Study of Negro Life and History. I asked Dr. Woodson about George Washington Williams. To my pleasant surprise he said he knew something of Williams although he was too young to have known him personally. He told me a few things about him and said that if I wrote a paper on Williams he would invite me to read it at the annual fall meeting of the association. He then said that he believed Mrs. Williams was still living, and in Washington. I could hardly accept the fact that anyone widowed in 1891 would still be alive in 1945! Shortly after I returned to Durham, however, I received word from Dr. Woodson that it was indeed the case. He gave me Mrs. Williams's address, whereupon I wrote her immediately. Within a few weeks I heard from one Henry P. Slaughter that, alas, Mrs. Williams had died on May 15, at ninety-two years of age, and that he had what letters and materials of George Washington Williams the widow had possessed. He indicated to me that he would be pleased to have me examine the materials.

Since I had accepted Dr. Woodson's invitation to write a paper on Williams, I did not have much time. As soon as I could arrange it, I went to Washington and was received graciously by Henry P. Slaughter, who brought out the small bundle of letters (less than a dozen) and three notebooks containing the diary that Williams kept while in Africa in 1890 and 1891. Slaughter was himself a remarkable man. As a minor civil servant in the federal government, he had spent much of his spare time and most of his resources collecting materials—manuscripts, books, pamphlets, newspapers—by and about Negroes. In 1945 his collection was, perhaps, the finest of its kind in private hands. His three-story townhouse had been converted into a library, with bookshelves running the length of the house on every floor. It was cluttered beyond description. Slaughter permitted me to read the letters from Williams to his wife, from which I took notes. He showed me the diary, suggesting I take it back to North Carolina, but I declined because I did not want the responsibility for its safety. That is something I have regretted to this day. Since the diary dealt with his trip to Africa, I did not need it at the time. I merely wanted to concentrate on his career as a historian.

In the autumn of 1945 I read a paper before the Association for the Study of Negro Life and History entitled "George Washington Williams, Historian." In the following January it was published in the *Journal of Negro History.* Except for the brief sketch in the *Dictionary of American Biography,* it was the first piece on Williams to appear since his death. It added something to what the author of the article in the DAB wrote, but I am now depressed by the number of factual errors I made and by the things I did not then know about Williams. Nevertheless, I had been able to fill in a sufficient number of details to give some idea of what manner of man Williams was.

In order for Williams's life to be reconstructed, almost all the information on his activities had to be dredged up by painstaking efforts. There were no Williams papers except for the few letters and the African diary in the possession of Henry P. Slaughter. And after my initial examination of the letters, I had the misfortune not to be able to look at any of that material again. Each time I visited Washington, I would call on Slaughter and ask to see the Williams diary. Each time he stalled. Finally, he shocked me by declaring that he was planning to do a biography of Williams himself and therefore preferred not to let me see the materials again. I was not worried about competition from Slaughter, for he was already seventy-nine and unlikely to complete the work. But I did wonder why he did not want me to examine the material.

Shortly thereafter, Slaughter sold his entire collection to Atlanta University. I rushed to Atlanta and requested to see the Williams diary but was informed that there was no Williams material at all in the collection. I was crushed, for by this time the desire to see the diary had become almost an obsession. I began to wonder if I, or anyone else, could do a biography of Williams without seeing it. The one consolation I had came from my surmise as to what had happened to the Williams manuscripts. When I visited Slaughter, I saw piles of newspapers from which he planned to take clippings but never did. I suspect that when some of that clutter was hauled away as trash, the Williams material went with it. My conclusion has been tentatively confirmed by more than thirty-five years of fruitless searching for the diaries.

I knew almost nothing of the early life of Williams until one day, at Howard University, I discovered a letter he wrote in March 1869—when he was nineteen years old—to General Oliver Otis Howard seeking admission to that university. It was a long letter, full of misspellings and other errors to be sure, telling the general about his early life, his drifting from one town to another with his parents, his service in the army during the Civil War, and his burning desire to secure an education and be of service to his people. This letter opened up new leads to his life with his parents and siblings at his birthplace in Bedford Springs, his army career, and his training for the ministry. In 1874, as a fundraising project during his pastorate in Boston, Williams wrote a history of the Twelfth Baptist Church. I found a printed copy and learned a great deal not only about the history and importance of the church but also about Williams's Boston years as a student and as a pastor.

It was almost impossible to learn anything about the year Williams spent in Washington after he left Boston in 1875. He went to the capital to found a newspaper, *The Commoner*, which would succeed the *New National Era*, a paper published by Frederick Douglass that had folded during the panic of 1873. It was an important time in Washington, for it was in the midst of the Reconstruction era, when the fate of Negro Americans was being decided in the Congress. There was nothing about Williams in the Douglass papers and very little in the daily press. I searched everywhere for the newspaper that Williams allegedly edited, but there were no copies at the Library of Congress and the other likely places. It was not even listed in the *Union List of Newspapers*.

That period in his life remained a blank until my research assistant told me he had seen a reference to a newspaper, *The Commoner*, that was in the library of the American Antiquarian Society in Worcester, Massachusetts. I would not allow myself to believe that this was the *Commoner* edited by Williams. I wrote the society, almost casually, inquiring about the newspaper, its editor, and its contents. I was surprised and delighted to receive a reply saying that the paper in their collection was edited by the Reverend George Washington Williams, that they had what they thought was a full run—about six months—and that they would send it to me on microfilm if I cared to examine it. It turned out to be a treasure trove, for Williams had been the editor, publisher, columnist, reporter, and just about everything else. In it I learned much about his interests, values, views on numerous subjects from religion to Reconstruction, and relations with others.

From the time Williams went to Cincinnati in 1875, he became more and more visible, and material on his Ohio years is relatively abundant. Shortly after his arrival in Cincinnati, Murat Halstead, editor of the Cincinnati *Commercial*, invited him to write a column for the paper. Many of his columns were autobiographical, and are especially informative on his years in the United States Army and his service with the republican forces in Mexico. As an active member of the Republican party in Ohio, he made numerous speeches, some of which were reported in the daily press. Williams himself became a candidate for public office and the center of much attention not only in Cincinnati but across the state as well. As a successful candidate for the legislature in 1879, he was able to place his name and his work in the public record for posterity to examine.

When he left the legislature in 1881, Williams decided to devote full time to his history of the Negro race in America. Indeed, he had already begun while a member of the state legislature. One of the benefits one derives from researching a problem for a long time is that people get to know about it and often share relevant information. At a meeting of the board of the Chicago Public Library, a staff member who had done her doctoral work in Ohio libraries offered me a list of the books Williams borrowed from the Ohio State Library while in the legislature in 1880. The list is filled with works on general history, histories of the United States, military history, and books out of which Williams could have pieced together some information about blacks.

Since Williams indicated in the preface to his *History of the Negro Race* his indebtedness to librarians in many parts of the country, I directed inquiries to those libraries. In each—the American Antiquarian Society, the Boston Athanaeum, the Massachusetts Historical Society, etc.—there were records of his having done research, of having used manuscripts, of having requested services from time to time. There were also, unfortunately, records of his not having paid for all of the manuscript copying he engaged clerks at the libraries to do for him.

Once Williams had gained considerable attention through the publication of his first major work, he was never altogether invisible again. Newspapers and letters tell of his leaving Ohio and settling in Boston, where he was admitted to the bar on the motion of a resident lawyer. After a few months he returned to Washington, presumably to begin research on a history of Reconstruction. He had not cut his ties with politics, however, and, soon after his arrival, President Chester Arthur appointed him United States minister to Haiti. But although the Senate had confirmed him before the president left office on March 4, 1885, and the outgoing secretary of state had given him his commission, the new secretary of state would not permit him to take up his post.

I knew of the Haitian appointment too but lacked some of the reasons for his not taking office until I discovered a full file on the matter in the papers of the Department of State housed in the National Archives. It was here that I found the details of his appointment and confirmation, the numerous objections to him voiced in the black community, and the department's own findings regarding Williams's conduct the previous summer. When the incoming Cleveland administration refused to permit him to take up his duties in Port-au-Prince, Williams sued the United States for his salary. The details of the case were reported in the decision of the United States Court of Claims, which upheld the position of the Department of State. Having done just about all that he could to advance himself in the United States, he turned his attention to Africa.

The African phase of Williams's career is in many ways the most interesting; it was also by far the most complicated to reconstruct. There was almost nothing to go on. I knew that Williams went to the Congo early in 1890, and in due course I was able to locate the *Open Letter* that he wrote to the king of the Belgians. I found two other important documents, a report to the president of the United States and a report on the problem of building a railroad through the Congo. These three documents told me much, but not nearly enough. How did Williams get to the Congo? He was certainly not a man of wealth despite his predilection for fine hotels and restaurants. Whom did he see in Africa, and what did they think of his venture? Did anyone from Europe know him and have any connection with his African venture? These and many other questions plagued me for years.

Gradually I acquired information that led me to some of the answers. I worked the libraries of Belgium and secured considerable information about the part played by the king; I also found references to Williams suggesting he was an imposter or a blackmailer. In England I learned much in the Public Record Office and other libraries. For example, the Baptist Missionary Society of Britain maintained missions in the Congo in the early 1890s, and the missionaries sent full reports to the London office about problems they encountered and even about people who visited them. One frequent visitor was Williams. Before he wrote his *Open Letter* to King Leopold, the Baptist Missionary Society in London already knew what Williams thought of the king and his policies. The missionaries' reports are housed in the society's library in London.

Williams's *Open Letter*, the first public criticism of the Belgian monarch, created quite a stir in Brussels. A special session of the parliament was called for the purpose of praising Leopold's policies and, by indirection, criticizing Williams for his temerity in speaking ill of the king. In the course of studying this aspect of Williams's life, I discovered that the best vantage point from which to watch developments in Brussels was not in the Belgian capital or in Washington (for the United States minister to Brussels took almost no notice of the matter), but in London. The British minister to Belgium, Lord Vivian, watched events very closely and sent reports almost daily to the Foreign Office in London. These reports provided much information not only about the proceedings in Brussels but also about Vivian's view of Leopold's Congo policies.

I still did not know how Williams got to the Congo, who financed the trip, what his day-to-day experiences were, and why he wrote a report on the Congo railway. For years I fretted over these questions and reproached myself for not having taken that diary when it was offered to me in 1945. Then, one day I recalled a sentence from the ill-fated diary. It went something like this, "Today, I wrote Mr. Huntington." Perhaps this was Collis P. Huntington, president of the Southern Pacific Railroad, who might have had an interest in a railroad in the Congo. I knew he was a trustee of Hampton Institute and had expressed an interest in Africa. I inquired about the Huntington papers at the Huntington Library, at the Stanford University Library, at the Museum at Norfolk, and at Syracuse University. There was no encouragement from any of these places, but Syracuse's discouragement acted as a spur. The people at Syracuse told me their Huntington collection was so large that they did not know what they had, and it would be years before they could organize and catalog the manuscripts.

A few years later I was in the vicinity of Syracuse and decided to visit the Arents Research Library there. The librarians were cordial, but reminded me of what they had written to me. When I found that the letters were arranged by year, I started going through beginning with January 1890. There must have been a half dozen boxes of letters sent to Collis P. Huntington the first three days of the year 1890 from all sorts of people asking for railroad passes or for a renewal of the passes they already had. Then, although these were *incoming* letters, I came across an *outgoing* letter written by Huntington on January 7, 1890, to George W. Williams, who was in Brussels. In two or three sentences the letter told me all that I wanted to know. It read, "I enclose herewith my check on London and Westminster Bank . . . for £100. . . . I hope all will go well with you in your new field of work, and shall await with interest your first letter giving impressions of the Congo Country." Huntington did not have to wait until Williams reached the Congo to receive reports. Williams began writing from the Canary Islands, and from that point on until Williams sailed from Egypt for England almost a year later, his letters to Huntington constitute a veritable diary. He shared with his benefactor all his experiences. It was at this point that I began to feel I no longer needed the diary that Slaughter presumably lost.

Williams's death outside the United States without any relatives at his bedside turned out, ironically, to be a favor to posterity. On instructions from London, the United States consul at Liverpool went to Blackpool and took charge. He made an inventory of Williams's personal effects, arranged for the funeral and the interment, and sent Mrs. Williams in Washington certain personal effects, including three notebooks containing her husband's African diary. The consul also made daily reports to the secretary of state; and it is in these reports that I learned, for example, that Williams was engaged to an Englishwoman. It was rumored that he met Alice Fryer en route from Egypt to England in the spring of 1891. I was unable to confirm this until November 1983, when I found in the Public Record Office in England the passenger list of SS *Golconda*. It shows that Miss Fryer boarded the ship at Madras, India, and Williams at Ismailia.

In 1975, my wife and I were visiting England and decided to go to Blackpool to see what we could learn about Williams's last days. On my first morning there I went to the Blackpool Town Hall and encountered Alan Bryant, the director of the Blackpool Tourist Bureau. I told him the story of Williams and how he came to die in Blackpool. Bryant expressed great interest though he regretted that Williams had died in Blackpool, since that town is known as a popular resort. Even so, he volunteered to help in every way that he could. He called the local newspaper, which sent over a reporter who wished to interview me as well as to escort me to the newspaper office where I could read the newspapers for August 1891.

During our fruitful conversations I wondered aloud if Williams was buried in the vicinity. In less than five minutes, Bryant's secretary produced the following information: The funeral was held in the local Baptist church, just across the square, on August 5, 1891, the services conducted by the Reverend Samuel Pelling. Williams was buried in the Layton Cemetery, a mile from the town square, Section F., Grave 123.

That afternoon at 2:30, on the thirtieth anniversary of my first acquaintance with George W. Williams, two reporters and a photographer, the warden of the cemetery, my wife, and I formed a procession to his grave. I laid a wreath on the unmarked grave of the man whose career I had followed for so long. The grave is no longer unmarked. Now he sleeps beneath a black granite slab on which are engraved the words "George Washington Williams, Afro-American Historian, 1849–1891."

Stalking George Washington Williams has been worth every minute I have spent on it, and not merely for the joy of the sleuthing. It is also because the search brought to light an American of extraordinary achievement.

GEORGE WASHINGTON WILLIAMS

· 1 ·

Soldier and Student

In the middle years of the nineteenth century, several roads ran from Virginia northward, through the mountains and Maryland into Pennsylvania. More Virginians than one might imagine, white and black, traveled these roads, lured by the many attractions that Pennsylvania had to offer. For whites there were new business opportunities as well as rest and recreation. For blacks there was freedom for the runaway slaves and better treatment for those already free. Just a mile south of the village of Bedford, a mineral spring had been discovered in 1796; in the years that followed, Bedford Springs, Pennsylvania, became known far and wide as a place of relief for the weary and afflicted.[1]

The springs, along with the strategic location of the village as a trading post, made Bedford Springs an attractive place for settlers as well as visitors. Virginians brought their agricultural produce and traded with Pennsylvanians and other Easterners who were headed west. There were always iron ore and its products that Virginians could purchase if they planned to return to their native state. Those who remained could seek out those new opportunities that had been heralded by the boosters of western Pennsylvania.

As white Virginians began to visit Bedford Springs, some brought their slaves to attend them as they took the waters. Although Pennsylvania had freed its slaves and some of its citizens held strong antislavery views, the state tolerated its free-spending slaveholding visitors. In 1821 a Pennsylvania judge held that it was no violation of the state's law for a Virginia slaveholder to bring his slave to the Springs, since it was frequented "principally and in great numbers" by Southerners accustomed to being attended by their slaves.[2] The feeling against slavery was not as strong in the Bedford area as it was among the residents of the eastern part of the state, in the vicinity of Philadelphia. In any case,

Pennsylvanians rationalized their position by telling themselves that the Southern slaveholders were only sojourners, who would soon return with their slaves to their plantations.

Some Virginia free blacks came to the Springs on their own, for there was work there—among Virginia whites who did not bring their slaves, and in the nearby coal mines. In 1849, when Thomas O. B. Carter of Fauquier County, Virginia, freed his forty slaves, they all settled just south of Bedford.[3] A few years earlier a young Virginia free Negro, Thomas Williams, had left his native home to seek his fortune in Bedford. His father was thought to be a wealthy white planter, but when and how Thomas secured his freedom is not known.[4] Apparently he was illiterate and had no skills. Consequently he joined most of the other free blacks of Bedford, who were day laborers. The exceptions in the borough and township of Bedford in 1850, with a Negro population of 195, were one barber, one farmer, one shoemaker, and one Methodist minister.[5] Sometime before 1846 Thomas Williams met and married Ellen Rouse, later described by her oldest son as a "genuine Pennsylvania Dutch Girl," perhaps the younger sister of Eli Rouse, a mulatto barber of Bedford.[6] In 1846 their first child, Margaret, was born, and three years later, on October 16, 1849, their first son. They named him George Washington. In due course others would follow: John in 1852, Thomas in 1855, and Harry in 1860.[7]

Within a year of George's birth, the family moved to Johnstown, where thirty-five-year-old Thomas secured a job in boating. These were Pennsylvania's canal days, and an ambitious man like Thomas Williams would not be denied a decent living for himself and his family.[8] There were even fewer blacks in Johnstown, only twenty-five, than there had been in Bedford; and the opportunities were neither as adequate nor as healthy as the Williams family would have desired. Soon Thomas fell in with a crowd of "bad boatmen" and became a heavy drinker. The care of the children was left to their mother, while Thomas, according to his son George, became more and more irresponsible. Soon Ellen and the children went to live with her mother in Newcastle, north of Pittsburgh.[9] Chastened by his wife's departure, Thomas soon followed; and he settled down to serve as a minister of the African church as well as a barber. By 1860 he owned real estate valued at $500 and personal property worth $100.[10]

The education of the Williams children was, at best, scant. George said that his father never took any interest in their education. With Thomas often away from home, Ellen was compelled to go out to work. George, then in his early teens, became "wicked and wild," and no one could do anything with him. He was placed in a house of refuge where he was to learn a trade, presumably that of a barber. For the first time in his life he became interested in religion. He was, as he put it, "learning about Jesus," until he was let out. Although he did not forget his teachers, he soon forgot his books.[11] As a young teenager, George was more interested in adventure than in education; and he seemed willing to follow anything if it was sufficiently exciting.

Western Pennsylvanians, black and white, were caught up in the excitement of the Civil War. At the very beginning of the war, army enlistments among white volunteers were heavy; and when blacks were given the opportunity to bear arms late in 1862, they also offered their services. Although not yet fifteen years old in the summer of 1864, Williams later said that his "Hart Burned with Eager Joy to meet the Planter on the Field of Battle to prove our Human Cherater [Character]."[12] Since he was under age, he was unable to convince the enlistment officers that he was eligible, whereupon he went to Meadville in northwestern Pennsylvania, set his age up, and enlisted under an assumed name.

It is virtually impossible to follow the Civil War military career of George Washington Williams because we cannot ascertain what name he used. After his death, many years after the war, his widow was unsuccessful in her application for a pension because she lacked that information. She thought he might have served under the name of William Steward or Charles Steward, both of whom were in the Second Division of the Twenty-fifth Army Corps, in which Williams stated in 1877 he had served.[13] Both William Steward and Charles Steward, each claiming to have been born in Alabama, enlisted in Meadville, Pennsylvania, on August 30, 1864.[14] Physical descriptions of the two men differ significantly. William Steward, in 1865, gave his age as twenty-two. He was five feet, four and one-half inches, tall. His complexion was described as yellow, his hair and eyes black. He could not write his name. Charles Steward, also in 1865, gave his age as nineteen. His complexion was described as dark, his hair and eyes black.[15] He could sign his name, and when the pension office compared his signature with that of George W. Williams in 1867, the similarity was striking. William Steward was discharged from Co. C., 41st U.S. Colored Troops on December 12, 1865. Charles Steward was listed as a deserter from Co. C. of the 41st U.S. Colored Troops, near Brownsville, Texas, on October 31, 1865.[16] When George W. Williams reenlisted (under his own name) in the United States Army in 1867, the endorsement on his enlistment paper read, "3rd Enlistment; last served in Co. C., 41st U.S.C. Infantry; discharged December 7, 1865."[17]

George Williams was closer in physical description to William Steward than to Charles Steward. In 1867, George was described as being five feet, seven inches, tall, with a light mulatto complexion, blue eyes, and dark hair. It is unlikely, however, that in 1864, at a few months short of fifteen, he could have passed for twenty-one, the age claimed by William Steward. Nor is it likely that George could not sign his name, for he had spent some time in school. His signature on a letter written in 1869, when he had received no further training, was about as legible as it ever would be. Charles Steward, on the other hand, though his physical description does not fit George, gave his age as eighteen—a closer match than William Steward.[18] Thus, either Charles Steward, who deserted in Texas in October 1865, or William Steward, who was discharged in Texas in December 1865, could in fact have been George W. Williams. Williams was certainly in Texas late that year and, as we shall see, went on to Mexico for another adventure.

By Williams's own account, he entered the army in 1864 and saw service until the war's end. He served for a while in the Tenth Army Corps, commanded by Major-General D. B. Birney, and was on Birney's staff all through the campaign before Richmond and Petersburg.[19] In September 1864, when he had been in the army for only a brief time, Williams was wounded in the assault on Fort Harrison, some five miles from Richmond.[20] He recovered quickly and was soon in the thick of the fight again. When the Negro troops were consolidated, Williams was placed in the Second Division of the Twenty-fifth Army Corps. He saw action during the closing days of the war at Hatcher's Run, Five Forks, and at various points along the sixteen-mile battle line to Petersburg, and was present when that well-defended town fell on April 2, 1865. Later, Williams would rejoice that he was involved in the final battles of the Civil War.[21]

In the month following the close of the war, the Twenty-fifth Army Corps was stationed at Camp Lincoln, near City Point, Virginia. Then came the orders moving the corps to Texas. At Fortress Monroe, on May 18, the corps transferred to the U.S. mail steamship *Illinois*. While some of the men were sorely disappointed, Williams was delighted at the opportunity for more adventure. Furthermore, the weather was pleasant and the thirty-one-day voyage to Port Isabel, Texas, was pleasant. There were a well-stocked bar, a brass and string band, and a glee club "that discoursed sweet music every evening."[22]

Williams had never experienced such intense heat as he found on the Island of Brazos, where the soldiers were stationed in the summer of 1865. "As far as the eye could reach there was nothing but sand, and not a drop of fresh water to be had," he recalled years later.[23] They were tormented, moreover, by a hurricane and numerous sandstorms. Consequently, Williams welcomed the orders to move to the Rio Grande, twelve miles from its mouth, and on to Brownsville, twenty-five miles farther. Troops were then dispatched along the border to various points such as Cortina's Ranch, Edenburg, and Ringgold Barracks.

It is at this point that Williams (alias Charles Steward) may well have deserted. In an 1877 article he wrote: "Some of the men had served out their time of enlistment, the time of others was almost out, while others had to serve until the spring of 1866. As soon as their time expired they were 'mustered out.' Some remained in Texas, others went to Mexico, and still others went home." Williams did not say whether he had been mustered out. "When our time was out," he recalled, "naturally being fond of adventure, we crossed the river at the celebrated Cortina's ranch, a few miles above Brownsville." Williams then reported to the headquarters of General Espinosa, who commanded the republican forces at that time laying siege to Matamoras.

It is unlikely that Williams knew who Emperor Maximilian was or that this hapless puppet of Napoleon III, supported only by French soldiers, was already unpopular with virtually every segment of the Mexican population, which feared he would destroy its republican form of government. Nor is it likely that Williams knew or even cared that the United States, invoking the Monroe Doctrine, had demanded the withdrawal of the French troops from Mexico. Even so, he and most other American soldiers of fortune pleased their own country by fighting on the republican side, which was committed to the overthrow of Maximilian's government.

Williams obviously made a favorable impression on General Espinosa, who welcomed any soldier from the United States who would "lend his sword to the cause of the Republic of Mexico." Williams received a commission as lieutenant in the First Battery from the State of Tamaulipas. By this time he had picked up some Spanish and, perhaps, some understanding of what the fight was all about. He had also acquired the reputation, quite by accident, of being a "good gunner." In subsequent months the republicans did battle with the "Imperials" at several points along the river and in neighboring towns. During the winter there was drilling, hunting, and reading; but there was also time to visit such cities as Aguayo, Monterey, and Querétaro. In the spring of 1867, just before the final march that resulted in the overthrow and execution of Maximilian, Williams returned to the United States to have his last fling at military life in his own country.[24]

By the time Williams returned to his Pennsylvania home in 1867, most of the Civil War soldiers had returned to civilian life. Those that remained—a mere skeleton force of 20,111 by the middle of 1867—had been deployed in the former Confederate states or sent to the posts on the frontier.[25] For a young black male with no education and few marketable skills, the army appeared to be one of the most attractive of the few options open to him. Within a few months after his return from Mexico, Williams took up that option.

Meanwhile, the United States had taken some significant steps toward regularizing the place of Afro-Americans in the armed forces. During the Civil War, arrangements depended on day-to-day conditions, the attitudes of military leaders, and the evolving uncertain policy of President Lincoln. Under these circumstances it is remarkable that the United States Army between 1863 and 1865 included more than 180,000 blacks. Once the war was over, the federal government, compelled to formulate some sort of policy regarding the freedmen, also had to dispose of the problem of what to do with Negro soldiers. This disposition took the form of legislation on July 28, 1866, authorizing six regiments of Negro troops, two of cavalry and four of infantry, to serve in the regular peacetime army.[26]

Williams enlisted in the regular army on August 29, 1867. "A few months at home with books," he later said, "made us long for the outdoor, lively exhilarating exercise of military life."[27] He went down to Pittsburgh from his home in Newcastle and signed up for a period of five years with Captain H. Haymond of the Twenty-seventh Infantry.[28] Assigned to Company L of the Tenth Cavalry, he reported for duty at Carlisle Barracks in early September. Within a few weeks he was "honored" with the position of drill sergeant. He remained at Carlisle until the Ninth and Tenth Regiments were almost up to strength. Then, with about one hundred recruits in his charge, he was ordered to deliver them to General Benjamin H. Grierson at Fort Riley, Kansas. After a "tedious" journey of four days, the young noncommissioned officer arrived at the fort, which, he said, was "about the geographical center of the country and one of the healthiest spots in the west."[29]

Williams had made a good impression at Carlisle Barracks, and he took with him to Fort Riley a letter from the commanding officer to General Grierson. Writing with warmth of the soldierly qualities of the eighteen-year-old drill sergeant, the officer recommended him for the highest position to be filled. Williams was also acquainted with Major Samuel L. Woodward on Grierson's staff. Small wonder that he was promoted to sergeant major and assigned the task of fitting out the companies for marching orders. Williams congratulated himself that his life "would flow merrily away at headquarters, with but little to do, far away from the Indian's deadly arrow."[30]

Once the companies were fully equipped, Williams was subject to reassignment. One of the officers "who had done noble service in the 'Curbstone Brigade' " was "thirsting for Indian blood" and wanted Williams assigned to him. Williams had no desire to leave his comfortable post, especially to follow the lead of one who was "as ignorant of cavalry as the late Henry Wilson, who could not get his regiment off of Boston Common."[31] Nevertheless, Williams received orders to report to the officer and be prepared to leave within two weeks. Three companies of the Tenth Cavalry, D, E, and L, were assigned to the Indian Territory. Thus Williams took up his duties in the vicinity of Fort Arbuckle, where he was to remain until he received his discharge in September 1868.

We know few details of Williams's activities during the year he was with the Tenth Cavalry on the plains and in the Indian Territory. There was little or no fighting in the environs of Fort Arbuckle, but there was plenty of work to keep the troops busy. Bootleggers, cattle and horse thieves, and bandits made life dangerous for well-intentioned civilians. They hoped the soldiers would provide a measure of security. The principal work of Companies D, E, and L was in rebuilding Fort Arbuckle, in which they made considerable progress in the fall and winter of 1867–68. Relief parties went out to provide protection or assistance to some beleagured group, but it is not certain that Williams ever participated.[32]

Even off-duty soldiers could get into real trouble, either by becoming involved in some of the treacherous activities easily found on the frontier or merely by searching for adventure to relieve the boredom. On the morning of 19 May 1868, Williams received a gunshot wound "through the inferior lobe of the left lung." A board of investigation, consisting of two first lieutenants and one second lieutenant, was appointed to meet that same afternoon to make a thorough inquiry into the circumstances of the shooting.[33] Meanwhile, Williams was confined to the hospital for the remainder of his time in the army.

In the papers for Fort Arbuckle for this period there is no report of the board of investigation. If it made a finding, it might have been in a phrase included in the explanation of Williams's disability at the time of his discharge, September 4, 1868. After indicating that Williams had been unfit for duty for sixty days, the Certificate of Disability for Discharge explained that he "Received a Gun shot wound thro the left Lung May 19, 1868—*not in line of duty* rendering him unfit to perform the duties of a soldier."[34] If Williams was in any way involved in conduct unbecoming a soldier, the official records do not reveal it. R. H. Pratt of the Tenth Cavalry, who as a first lieutenant had been on the board of investigation to look into the shooting, later became superintendent of the Indian Industrial School at Carlisle, Pennsylvania. In his report of 1890 he recalled his days with the Tenth Cavalry and singled out Williams for praise.[35] Ten years later, Major George W. Ford, who succeeded Williams as first sergeant of Troop L, recalled the reason for Williams's discharge but said nothing to suggest misconduct. In any case, the official discharge papers contain no hint of dishonor.[36]

When Williams was discharged from the United States Army, he had not yet reached his nineteenth birthday. But he had experienced more than many of his contemporaries even in the excitement-filled years of the 1860s. He had fought in the Civil War and had been wounded. He had helped the Mexicans save their republican form of government. And he had given a year to maintaining order on the Indian frontier. His several brushes with death, especially the one at Fort Arbuckle, must have been sobering experiences. Later he would claim that he left the army because in the Indian Territory he became convinced that killing people was not the calling of a Christian.[37] No doubt he did not want to get killed either.

Upon his discharge, Williams went to St. Louis, where he formalized his religious position by joining a Baptist church whose pastor was the Reverend Henry White. He then spent some time in Hannibal, Missouri; there, in pursuit of his goal to become "a servent of the Lord," he was licensed as a Baptist minister. Several months later, Williams went up the Mississippi River to Quincy, Illinois, where, in his words, God left him "in the keeping of a good Herald of the Cross," Andrew Pleasant.[38] While living in Quincy in 1869, Williams learned of the founding of Howard University the previous year. He thereupon wrote a long, autobiographical letter to General Oliver Otis Howard requesting admission to the new institution. Since he was seeking to prepare himself "to Do His Will," he was willing—like so many Negro soldiers returning from the war—to work part-time while studying. If admitted, he would, he said, "prove my Self Worthy of all Expences may Be given." On receipt, the letter was endorsed with the words (presumably General Howard's) "Answer favorably, if qualified."[39]

Williams apparently possessed the requisite qualifications, for within a few weeks he had enrolled as a student at Howard University. Upon his arrival in Washington he did not delay making direct contact with the Civil War general who was the first commissioner of the Freedmen's Bureau and the founder of the university that bore his name. On April 23, 1869, General Howard served as a witness for Williams's unsuccessful application to secure a disability pension based on the gunshot wound he allegedly received "while engaged in action with the Indians near Fort Arbuckle, Indian Territory."[40]

One supposes that Williams did not find at Howard University what he was looking for. The records do not show that he was a student during the academic year 1869–70. On September 9, 1870, however, Williams appeared before the faculty of the Newton Theological Institution near Boston and was examined. He stated that in 1869 he had been licensed to preach by the Baptist church in Hannibal, Missouri, a short distance down the river from Quincy, Illinois. He also indicated that he had studied in 1869 at the Wayland Seminary, a Baptist institution in Washington devoted to the training of ministers.[41]

Williams was obviously not prepared to begin theological studies, and the faculty mercifully admitted him as a general student.[42] Because of the postwar demand for ministers and because of the limited number of available men with collegiate training, Newton introduced in 1869 the two-year English course for general students.[43] Of the fourteen students admitted by faculty examination on September 9, 1870, nine were graduates of Amherst, Brown, and Colby and were admitted to study theology. Williams and four others were classified as general students. They were to "receive English-Exegesis from the several professors," and Professor Ezra Palmer Gould was to tutor them on the life of Christ.[44] Of the other four, two had entered with some collegiate training; after a probationary period of three months these two were transferred to the theological program, graduating with their class in 1873. The third received the English diploma in 1872 but did not remain at Newton; the fourth dropped out during his first year.[45]

Williams completed the English course on schedule and in 1872 was admitted to the theological program, a three-year curriculum, which he completed in two years. In the first year, called the junior year, the subjects covered were biblical interpretation of the Old and New Testaments, theology, and homiletics. In the second or middle year the courses were theology, Hebrew interpretation, Greek interpretation, and homiletics. Senior year courses included homiletics, church history, more interpretation of the Old and New Testaments, and elocution.[46] It is not clear how Williams completed the three-year course in two years. One may assume that his performance was superior and that his professors encouraged him to complete the work as rapidly as possible. And since Williams had no visible means of support, one may also assume that he was supported by the institution or some of its benefactors.

During the years that Williams was a student at Newton, the institution was a leader in the training of Baptist ministers. Its physical

appearance underwent significant change with the erection of several
new buildings and the refurbishing of some older structures. Even more
important, it had a strong faculty, some of whom had achieved distinction in their fields. Alvah Hovey, the president and professor of theology
and Christian ethics, was one of the most influential Baptist leaders in
the country. His *Outlines of Christian Theology* (1861) was widely used
in churches and religious training institutions. Galusha Anderson, professor of church polity, homiletics, and pastoral duties, was one of the
most outspoken members of the clergy against slavery. He was to have a
distinguished future as president of the old University of Chicago and as
a professor in the Divinity School of the new University of Chicago.
Others were young Ezra Palmer Gould, who tutored Williams on the
life of Christ, and Herman Lincoln, professor of church history, who
exposed Williams to his first formal courses in history.[47]

On June 10, 1874, Williams graduated in a class of twenty-six men.
Only three other members of the class did not have collegiate training;
most had attended such institutions as Harvard, Amherst, Brown,
Washington University, Colby College, and the University of Vermont.[48] When Williams went to Newton in 1870 he was semiliterate at
best. By the time he graduated, he had fully caught up with his class-
mates.

At the commencement exercises Williams was one of twelve graduates selected to address the audience. He chose as his subject, "Early
Christianity in Africa."[49] It was a ten-minute survey of the beginnings of
Christianity in Africa with special attention to the great African church
leaders: Athanasius, Origen, Cyprian, Tertullian, and Augustine.

> Paganism had been met and conquered. The church had passed
> through a baptism of blood, and was now wholly consecrated to the
> cause of its Great Head. Here Christianity flourished; here it
> brought forth rich fruit in the lives of its tenacious adherents. Here
> the acorn had become the sturdy oak, under which the soldiers of
> the cross pitched their tents.

Williams hastened to point out that only a "narrow belt" of Africa had
been reached by Christianity and that, indeed, vast portions of that
continent were still unknown. One of the reasons for this was the
preoccupation of Europeans and Americans with the slave trade.

> For nearly three centuries Africa has been robbed of her sable sons.
> For nearly three centuries they have toiled in bondage, unrequited
> in this youthful republic of the west. They have grown from a small

company to be an exceedingly great people—five millions in number no longer chattel, they are human beings; no longer bondsmen, they are free men, with almost every civil disability removed. . . . With his Saxon brother, the African slakes his insatiable thirstings for knowledge at the same fountain. . . . The Negro of this country can turn to his Saxon brothers, and say, as Joseph said to his brethren who wickedly sold him, "As for you, ye meant it unto evil, but God meant it unto good, that we, after learning your arts and sciences, might return to Egypt and deliver the rest of our brethren who are yet in the house of bondage." That day will come![50]

The twenty-four-year-old graduate, with the help of his mentors, had transformed himself in the short span of four years from an uninformed, raw youth to a well-educated man with a felicitous writing style and a refinement that reflected itself in his bearing and his manners. The transformation was remarkable, but these new assets would place an enormous burden on one whose very speed in acquiring them had left little time in which to ponder their effective and successful use.

Successful Clergyman

Despite his meager academic background, which required him to devote much time to his studies, Williams somehow found time for numerous civic and social activities during his years at Newton. Although a member of the Baptist church in Watertown, Massachusetts, he early made contact with the Negro community in Boston. There were only nineteen blacks in Watertown as late as 1875, when the black population of Newton stood at 130. Boston, on the other hand, had a viable black community—almost five thousand in 1875. Blacks had attended school for years before the Civil War, and in 1855 they won admission to the public schools. They had published volumes of poetry and fragments of history, and they had organized charitable, fraternal, and religious institutions. They had been admitted to the bar even before 1865. There were outstanding black leaders such as William C. Nell, the author; George L. Ruffin, the lawyer; and James Still, the physician. To a young, ambitious student of theology, Boston appeared to be the place of opportunity.[1]

Williams made the most of what Boston had to offer, and became a well-known figure there. In November 1873, when "the colored citizens of Boston held a meeting . . . to protest . . . the general mistreatment of blacks in the South," Williams was present and spoke. Two weeks before a convention was to meet in Washington to urge passage of the civil rights bill, Williams sent a letter to a Washington paper expressing the hope that the call would be heard "by every colored man throughout the land!" He spoke of black men's contribution to the development of the country through "unrequited toil" and how, "as defenders of the Union" during the Civil War, they helped to save it. A day earlier, Williams had spoken with the bill's sponsor, Charles Sumner, who said that "every colored leader ought to be at the convention."[2]

Shortly before the convention assembled in Washington, Williams had been there on personal business. Already he was establishing contact with Negro leaders in various parts of the country. Although urged to attend the convention by such worthies as J. Sella Martin, a Washington labor leader and writer, and James M. Trotter, a Boston civic leader and author, he was unable to do so.[3] His studies at Newton and his church work kept him in Boston during the convention in December 1873. In absentia, however, he made his debut on the national scene. When it was suggested that a letter from Williams that had appeared in the *New National Era* be read to the convention, a Massachusetts delegate objected, stating that Williams was opposed to civil rights. The minutes of the convention do not indicate whether or not the Williams letter was read, but when Williams learned of the incident he was outraged. In another letter to the *New National Era*, he said, "As far as civil rights is concerned, my heart, my brain, and my pen have been busy in its behalf. . . . I cannot think of a man in Boston so cowardly, so unnatural, so unprincipled as to charge me with treachery to the cause of human justice and free citizenship!" He pointed to his war record "dampened by my own blood" and to other ways in which he had served the "righteous cause." He closed by declaring that never "by word, influence, or act" had he opposed civil rights or any other measure designed to bring "the rights, privileges, and immunities for which we have so long prayed, fought, and looked!"[4] It was never made clear why the delegate had questioned William's commitment to civil rights.

Even as a student, Williams traveled widely. During the summer of 1873 he took a trip through several Southern states, returning by way of Chicago. During the autumn of that year he was in Washington. Perhaps it was on his visit to Chicago in 1873 that he met Sarah A. Sterrett, whose father, Theodore, was an early resident and a barber in that city.[5] There ensued a courtship that culminated in marriage the following year. In the spring of 1874, while waiting to graduate, Williams married twenty-one-year-old Sarah in Chicago on June 2. The Reverend D. B. Cheney, pastor of the Baptist church to which the Sterretts belonged, performed the ceremony.[6] The newlyweds arrived in Newton Centre in time for the commencement exercises the following week.

On the day following graduation, Williams was ordained into the Baptist ministry at the church in Watertown of which he had been a member since his first year at Newton. In the afternoon of June 11, 1874, he was called before the church council; and in the evening of the same day he was ordained. Three of his professors participated in the ordination. Galusha Anderson, who had taken up the pastorate of

Brooklyn's Strong Place Baptist Church in 1873, delivered the sermon. Oakman Sprague Stearns, Williams's teacher in biblical interpretation, gave the charge, and Samuel Lunt Caldwell, professor of church history, offered the prayer of ordination. The pastor, Granville S. Abbott, offered a prayer and led in extending the hand of fellowship to Williams.[7]

"I can never forget the tenderness with which my dear pastor spoke his hearty and all-embracing fellowship," Williams declared. "And how can I forget the happy home I found for four years among the good friends of Watertown." Williams singled out William A. Blodgett, "whose devotion to and care for me are worthy of more explicit mention," and the "never tiring charities of the Marches and Gilkey." They were, indeed, his New England family, who would "never be forgotten."[8] But they were already a part of his past, of his years of preparation for the Christian ministry that now awaited him.

While still a student at Newton, Williams had developed a close connection with the Twelfth Baptist Church in Boston. Perhaps the outstanding religious institution in Boston's black community, the Twelfth Baptist had grown out of the First Independent Church in the 1840s. A small group of Boston Negroes, interested in building a church of real importance, invited Leonard A. Grimes of New Bedford to lead them. Grimes, a Virginia free Negro, had migrated to Massachusetts in 1840. Eight years later he joined the twenty-three people who organized the Twelfth Baptist Church. In the following decade, the church had numerous difficulties, not the least of which was the flight to Canada of some of its members after the passage of the Fugitive Slave Act in 1850. Its remaining members joined Grimes in supporting fugitive slaves in every way possible and in opening its doors to such abolitionists as William Lloyd Garrison, Wendell Phillips, and Frederick Douglass. By 1860 there were 246 members, and by the end of the Civil War the membership of what was referred to as "the fugitive slaves' church" had increased to 300.[9]

On arriving in Boston in June 1870, Williams had joined the Twelfth Baptist Church, but he transferred his membership to Watertown when he was admitted to Newton.[10] He maintained his contacts in Boston, however, not only because he greatly admired Leonard Grimes and learned much from him but also because of his desire to cultivate friendships with some of the leading blacks of Boston who attended Twelfth Baptist. Grimes, Williams said, was "a leader of excellent judgment, a pastor of tender sympathies, and a father who loved them with all the strength of truly manly affection." One of the first men Williams met was George L. Ruffin, clerk of the church and a member of the Massachusetts legislature, who became a close friend and adviser.[11] Williams went to the Boston church whenever the opportunity arose.

When Leonard Grimes died suddenly on March 14, 1873, the city of Boston was shocked, and the members of his congregation were not prepared for that eventuality. He was the only pastor they had ever had, and there was no assistant pastor. For two months the pulpit was filled by the Reverend Mark Solon, but he left for Europe in May. The trustees then turned to Williams, who preached for two Sundays but then left on a long-planned trip to the South and Midwest. During the summer months, a former chaplain by the name of Carlton served as acting minister. The church had not forgotten Williams, however, and it may be assumed that Williams kept the church in mind, for the officers knew how to get in touch with him. In August 1873 Williams was in Chicago, living on Third Avenue, just a block from Sarah Sterrett's home, when he received the following communication from George L. Ruffin, the church clerk:

> At a special meeting of the 12th Baptist Church, it was voted that you be invited to fill the pulpit of that society for eight months, from September, 1873. It was also voted that the salary be fixed at the rate of $50 per month; and I was instructed to inform you of this action, and request an early reply.

There was never any doubt as to what the reply would be. Williams returned "rested from a vacation of three months," and on the first Sunday in September he began his duties. Thus, while still a student who had not yet reached his twenty-fourth birthday, George Washington Williams became the acting pastor of a congregation of almost seven hundred members. If the church regarded this as a period of probation for Williams, it must have been satisfied. Although he traveled during the year, was becoming more involved in public affairs, and completed his final year at Newton,[12] he did not neglect his duties at Twelfth Baptist. The church steadily increased in members, and the prayer meetings were well attended and full of interest. Obviously the members were fully satisfied with Williams's performance, for on April 4, 1874, they invited him "to take the pastoral charge of the church and become the leader of this flock." They were certain, they declared, that "from what we have seen of your ministrations among us during the past few months, the well-begun work of . . . Bro. Grimes . . . will receive no detriment at your hands; but will be carried forward to the extent of your ability."

The end of the search for a leader to fill the post that had been vacant for more than a year was the occasion for a celebration. George and Sarah Williams were the honorees at several celebrations. The formal installation occurred on June 24 before a large crowd. Dr. George C. Lorimer, the distinguished pastor of Boston's Tremont Temple, preached the sermon, and the Reverend Daniel C. Eddy, pastor of the Harvard Street Baptist Church of Boston, gave the charge to the new pastor. The Reverend Rollin H. Neale, who had spoken at the ordination of Leonard Grimes and at the meeting of Baptist ministers when Grimes died, gave the charge to the church. Other local ministers offered prayers and read scriptures. The new pastor gave the benediction.[13]

On June 26, the Friday following the installation, the members tendered their pastor and his wife an elaborate reception. While there were the customary prayers and hymn singing, the focus of attention was on their new leader and his bride. George L. Ruffin, graduate of the Harvard Law School and easily the most distinguished member of the church, gave the address of welcome. He was especially pleased that Williams, by training and point of view, represented a new type in the black ministry. "We welcome the day that brings to our pulpits an educated ministry, to lead the people in righteous ways," he said. Williams responded with a brief talk in which he thanked the members and indicated the importance of the work in which all of them needed to be engaged.

One of the members, Elijah W. Smith, had written a poem for the occasion; and it was read with great feeling by Josephine St. Pierre Ruffin, the wife of the church clerk. In obvious reference to the recent nuptials were the following lines:

> Bless thou the handmaiden whose lot
> Is Woven with his own;
>
> Grant that the buds of love's young dream
> In perfect flowers be blown:
>
> And should their bark, on life's broad sea,
> By angry waves be stayed,
>
> Say to them, from the tempest cloud,
> "'Tis I, be not afraid!"

Williams delivered his first sermon as the regular pastor of the Twelfth Baptist Church on 28 June 1874. He recalled the numerous ways that Leonard Grimes assisted him when he arrived in Boston four years earlier. He reminded the members that the church had called

Grimes when he was "in the freshness of his manhood" and kept him "until almost every member could call him father. Now you have taken me in the freshness of young manhood, to carry forward the work he loved and engaged in for so many years." Williams then spoke on the nature of the church's mission, which was to seek the lost. It was a work in which the laity as well as the clergy should be engaged. And the Christian "was not simply to pray for the conversion of sinners but for his own growth in grace."

One of the first things that Williams did was to write a history of the church. His standards were high, and he insisted that nothing could have induced him to write it hastily over the summer months, "save the hope that it may be the means of serving the church financially, for which it was written, and bring its pressing wants before the benevolent public." Williams was convinced that there was much work to do in Boston and that the public would support his efforts. Speaking to the Newton alumni at commencement in 1874, Galusha Anderson said that the only thing he regretted was that Williams had chosen Boston, instead of the South, "where he would find a larger field." In his history of the Twelfth Baptist, Williams argued that Boston was an important field. "A healthy, vigorous, intelligent church, here in the very centre of benevolent activities, will do much to temper the giving of those who are disposed to aid our needy brethren of the South."

The history was well written, despite the haste, and provides invaluable information on the early years of the church and of the character and work of Leonard Grimes. Its seven chapters gave attention to such matters as "The Origin of the Church," "The Church and the Anti-Slavery Party," and "The Church During and After the Rebellion." It included the program of the installation services of June 24 and the text of the introductory sermon by Williams on June 28. It gave the members their first opportunity to have a retrospective look at their church; and it provided posterity with an important source of information on a pioneering Negro institution. It is not clear, however, that the work achieved the desired results. Despite Williams's acquaintance with such worthies as George C. Lorimer and Daniel C. Eddy, there is no evidence that Boston's religious philanthropists were touched by the pastor's fervent appeal.

With a membership of seven hundred and accommodations for only five hundred, there was an urgent need to enlarge the church building. The reporter who described the church as "uncomfortably crowded every Sunday" apparently agreed. Even more to the point was the assertion that the church was flourishing under the ministry of Williams, who appeared to be "well fitted for his sacred work."[14] In the autumn of

1874 the membership stood at 774. A year later there were 849 members.[15]

Williams undoubtedly felt that by projecting himself into community activities he was promoting the Twelfth Baptist Church. It may also be assumed that the "flourishing" condition was not enough to occupy all the time and attention of a man of boundless energy who had been able to lead the church and travel about the country while completing his final year at Newton. Thus, when the Negro citizens of Boston became concerned over "the recent murders and outrages upon the peaceful colored citizens of the South," Williams was active in calling a mass meeting for September 2, 1874. He was joined in the call by some of Boston's leading blacks, including James M. Trotter, Lewis Hayden, and George L. Ruffin. Williams presided and, after a short address, introduced William Wells Brown, the principal speaker. The resolutions adopted by the meeting condemned the outrages and the White Man's League Movement, called for a special session of Congress to deal with the problem, and requested the president to use his powers to suppress the disturbances.[16] Brown and his listeners were especially anxious for Congress to take some favorable action on the pending civil rights bill, which had been getting nowhere even before its sponsor, Charles Sumner, died the previous March.[17]

After that meeting of the Negro citizens of Boston, Williams sailed for New Brunswick, perhaps on a brief vacation, during which he completed his history of the Twelfth Baptist. He wrote his friend James M. Trotter that America's pride was inevitably limited, even as she boasted that there was not "a single slave under her stars and stripes. . . . Are there not many political slaves in America?" He wondered what Negroes should do as they witnessed the betrayal of American principles by so many. They had no choice, he said, but to work to make the Republican party live up to its declared principles. This, despite the resolutions censuring the Republican party which Williams submitted at the meeting on 2 September. In commenting on a "very ill-spirited editorial" on the meeting which he saw just before he sailed from Boston, Williams said that the resolutions were "the true convictions of, if not a wise, an honest heart. . . . I am determined to stand by the Republican party, and have that party stand by me."[18]

In the autumn of 1874, Williams began to manifest a more specific interest in politics, not by running for public office but by letting his name be presented as a candidate for chaplain of the Massachusetts House of Representative.[19] While the more prominent members of the Massachusetts clergy did not seek the office, the less well-known and younger ministers saw the chaplaincy as an opportunity to increase their visibility and influence. Consequently, the lobbying on behalf of the various candidates was very lively. Two days before the election Elijah W. Smith—a member of Twelfth Baptish Church and the poet at Williams's installation services—wrote a letter to the *Evening Transcript* in support of his pastor's candidacy, part of which reads:

> There is an "eternal fitness" in human affairs, and it seems to us that the election of Mr. Williams would do much to disabuse the public mind in distant parts of the country in regard to the position of Massachusetts on . . . civil rights. . . . What an opportunity presents itself in this case for Massachusetts to place herself in her true light! What an opportunity it will furnish for her sons, wherever on the broad domain protected by the stars and stripes they may be located, when asked, "How stands Massachusetts on the question of equal rights for all men?" to reply, in the language of Daniel Webster, "Look at her, and see where she stands!"[20]

It would take much more than the eloquent advocacy of Twelfth Baptist's poet laureate to secure the chaplaincy for his pastor. There were four active candidates; and when the House took the vote on 6 January 1875, Williams, the only black candidate, was second with 55 votes, preceded by the Reverend J. W. Hamilton with 88. The third and fourth candidates had 28 and 22 votes respectively. Since the House, with 210 members, required that the victor have the support of at least one-half of the members, no one was elected. The House then voted to postpone indefinitely the election of a chaplain and authorized the speaker to invite each day some member of the clergy to open the House with prayer.[21]

The tradition of the House having its own chaplain was so strong that the members were not satisfied with the ad hoc arrangement. Upon reconsideration, the House voted to retain the incumbent, the Reverend Robert Seymour of Boston's Ruggles Street Baptist Church, as chaplain. Seymour's candidacy was advocated by some of the members because the election of one who had not been a candidate "would be a proper rebuke to the unseemly lobbying on behalf of the candidates this year."[22] Thus, Williams's first bid for elective office was unsuccessful, but he had succeeded in adding a considerable number of legislators to his list of supporters.

Sumner's civil rights bill passed in March 1875, just before the Democrats took control of the House. It was a time of rejoicing for Negro Americans throughout the country.[23] Black Bostonians were as delighted as any over the federal law supporting equal treatment of all persons regardless of race. While the bill was under consideration Williams had expressed his fervent hope that it would be passed. "If we fail to get civil rights during this Administration, it will be forever buried beyond the realm of possibilities," he had said.[24] Now that it had become law, he shared the happiness of his fellow blacks over the prospects of enjoying equal protection of the laws. He would soon share with them the despair over the nonenforcement of the Civil Rights Act.[25]

When Williams became pastor of Boston's Twelfth Baptist Church, he seemed committed to holding the post indefinitely. In his introductory sermon, he said, "I feel deeply the importance of my position, the dignity of my calling, and my weakness and imperfection. But one thought comforts and urges me into this vast field; and that is: 'Lo, I am with you always, even unto the end of the world. . . .' This is the grand thought that lifts me up; Christ is to be my sufficiency." In that same sermon, he stated some of the major concerns that he could not ignore and that, one day, would take him from Boston and eventually from the ministry. "As a minister of the Gospel, as a member of that great race whose future, as yet, is beyond the interpretation of human wisdom, and as one whose life is laid upon the altar of the common interests of my people, I cannot be insensible to their interests, whenever or wherever presented." Speaking of Africa, he said, "My heart loves that land, and my soul is proud of it. It has been the dream of my youth that that country would be saved by the colored people of this country. And my heart is more hopeful today than at any previous period."[26]

Within months, Williams was preparing to leave Twelfth Baptist, despite its flourishing condition. The papers of Boston broke the news on July 2, 1875, that Williams had resigned his pastorate, effective October 1. There was no discussion of the matter and no indication of the reasons.[27] One does not suppose that any serious misunderstanding developed between Williams and the officers of the church, for several years later, when Williams returned to Massachusetts and became a resident, the relations between him and his old friends at Twelfth Baptist were most cordial (see below, chapter 10). It may be assumed that Williams concluded that the challenges and opportunities were greater elsewhere than in Boston.

Once he had resigned Williams began to articulate his plans, which must have been claiming some of his attention for months. In a letter to Henry Wadsworth Longfellow, whom he had not met, he spoke of his intention to publish a journal in Washington, D.C.

> The time has come when the Negro must do something. . . . This is
> a plastic period. The Negro will begin to make history. What

manner of history will it be? That is the question. . . . To this end I
go to Washington and edit a journal. It will be their teacher, their
friend, their mirror. As a teacher it will discuss educational and
social problems; as a friend it will lead them from the political arena
to the firm foundations of enlightened citizenship and nobler manhood; as a mirror it will reflect the virtue, genius, and industry of
the emancipated millions of this country.[28]

Williams requested Longfellow to receive him, which the poet
promptly did. While there is no record of their conversation, Longfellow apparently approved the idea of a journal. A few days later Williams
thanked his new friend and asked for some words of commendation. "A
letter from you would tend to swell my subscription list and would
greatly cheer my young heart in this noble work."[29] There is reason to
doubt that Longfellow complied, however, for no letter from the poet
appears among the letters of endorsement that Williams later
published.[30]

If the members of the Twelfth Baptist Church were disappointed
with the brief tenure of their pastor, they did not show it publicly. But
there is no record of an elaborate farewell; his departure was as uncere-
monious as his resignation. Long before October 1, the effective date of
his resignation, Williams was busy with the plans for his new journal.

·3·

Editor and Publisher

When Williams set for himself the task of founding a journal to serve the black community and to speak for it, he was following a well-established tradition. In 1827 John B. Russwurm and Samuel E. Cornish had launched *Freedom's Journal*, the first Negro newspaper, with a clear statement of their objectives. "We wish to plead our own cause. Too long have others spoken for us," they declared.[1] *Freedom's Journal* was one of twenty-four Negro newspapers that appeared before the Civil War; the best known of these was the *North Star*, edited by Frederick Douglass and later called *Frederick Douglass's Paper*. Douglass dedicated his paper "to the cause of our long oppressed and plundered fellow countrymen," who "must help each other if we would succeed."[2]

After the Civil War, black newspapers could scarcely survive, despite the fact that they could now be published and distributed in the South. The rate of illiteracy was so high, and the pressures of the postwar adjustment of freedmen to their new status so great, that newspapers enjoyed no high priority in the black community. Thus, in 1870, there were only about ten newspapers serving that community.[3] The outstanding paper of the post-Civil War years was the *New Era*, and once again the moving force behind the venture was Frederick Douglass. The paper made its appearance in Washington on January 13, 1870, under the editorship of J. Sella Martin, with Douglass as corresponding editor. When the paper began to falter later that year, Douglass purchased a one-half interest in it, renamed it the *New National Era*, and became the editor. Although he was busy with a dozen major activities, Douglass regarded the newspaper as an important force that would assist in "the removal of the hardships and wrongs which continue to be the lot of the colored people of this country."[4]

Before the year ended, Douglass had purchased the remaining one-half interest in the *New National Era* and its printing plant as well. He did as much as his busy schedule would allow in managing the affairs of the paper. It was not enough, however. Along with the general failure of the economy in 1873–74, the *New National Era* failed. Douglass invested another $10,000 in the paper and turned it over to his sons. But it became impossible to collect either from subscribers or from advertisers. With some support from the Republican party, for which it spoke, the paper "staggered along until September, 1874, when it finally passed out of existence."[5]

Williams doubtless knew of the demise of the *New National Era* and of the void it left. He had appeared in its columns on several occasions during the last two years of its life, writing letters to the editor, reporting events in Boston, and seeking information from readers.[6] There was now no Negro newspaper in the nation's capital, and no really important Negro newspaper anywhere.[7] The significant papers of the late nineteenth century, such as the Chicago *Conservator*, the Washington *Bee*, the Cleveland *Gazette*, the New York *Globe*, the Richmond *Planet*, and the Philadelphia *Tribune*, would emerge later, primarily in the 1880s. The time seemed ripe to launch a newspaper to speak for the black community, as Russwurm's *Freedom's Journal* had attempted to do almost a half-century earlier.

National events during Williams's ministry at Twelfth Baptist had much to do with his decision to edit a newspaper. The elections of November 1874 had placed the control of the House of Representatives in the hands of the Democrats, a party that Williams abhorred. The struggle for a civil rights bill had finally ended with its passage in March 1875; but, with the country losing interest in the plight of Negroes, any hope for its enforcement was unrealistic. And there was violence. The so-called Grant Parish (Louisiana) massacre of April 13, 1873, had a profound effect on Williams.[8] He later said that reading about that incident, in which seventy blacks were killed, and other "numerous unprovoked murders" convinced him that a journal was needed to tell the world of such miscarriages of justice.[9]

During that year, Williams did much thinking and talking about a journal. He discussed it with various Negro leaders in Boston, who apparently encouraged him as his plans began to take shape. On June 29, 1875, several days before the announcement of his resignation from Twelfth Baptist, Williams went to Washington to explore possibilities there. He talked at length with Frederick Douglass and "communed with him freely upon the necessity and methods of establishing a journal."[10] Williams subsequently called on some of the leading black men of Washington and sought their views. They all encouraged him to move ahead.

At one of Washington's Independence Day celebrations held on July 5, Williams heard Douglass and another of the nation's greatest black orators, John Mercer Langston (who had just resigned as dean of the Law School and vice president of Howard University).[11] As no reporter was present, Williams was asked to write for publication an article on the proceedings. For Williams it was both an exciting moment and "the dawning of a new era." Langston and Douglass pointed out the need for blacks to move toward independent manhood. Yet there was no journal to spread the news to the black community. Williams decided "then and there" to publish a newspaper regardless of the sacrifice or the cost. Returning from the celebration, he rode with "our friend, Mr. Douglass, meditating upon the subject nearest our heart."[12]

Douglass had invested at least $20,000 in the *New National Era*, which had the benefit of his extensive journalistic experience and the wise leadership of J. Sella Martin. Yet the newspaper had failed. This did not diminish Douglass's belief in the importance of a Negro journal or his optimistic view of the possibilities of success. He was less clear on what was needed for success. Little seems to have been said, however, about the difficulties of building a black readership.

Williams spent the next few days working up interest in a meeting that several leaders had called to consider establishing a journal. On the evening of July 12, 1875, a group of "the most prominent men of the city and of the country" assembled in the lecture room of Washington's Fifteenth Street Presbyterian Church. After Douglass declined to take the chair, Langston agreed to preside. Pointing out that it was useless for blacks "to try to edge in with the whites," Langston said that a paper devoted to the interests of the Negro race should be established and supported. He then called on Williams to explain his mission to the audience.[13]

In his address, described as "eloquent" by a local reporter, Williams anticipated and refuted any objections to establishing a journal in Washington. To the claim that blacks were not a reading people, he asserted that educational statistics revealed increased literacy the last decade. To those who pleaded insufficient capital, Williams replied that the greatest journals in the country had started in humble circumstances and won their way to fortune, and that "another one could be started in the same way." If some would argue that there was no need for a Negro journal because freedom had brought with it the opportunity for integration, Williams replied that no one would argue that Negro churches were no longer necessary, and "journals were as necessary to the people as their churches." Whites no longer took a personal interest in blacks, who were now expected to walk on their own feet.

According to Williams, a journal would be "a powerful agent for REORGANIZING THE RACE." It would develop an independent spirit and teach self-government. He proposed to edit a paper, he said, "devoted to the colored people, politics, arts and the events of the day." Regarding his own qualifications the twenty-five-year-old Williams said that he had made a study of journalism "for years." He had waited a long time for this opportunity and was willing "to sacrifice everything in the enter-prise because duty urged him." He asked the audience to help in the cause, give him their sympathy and support, and do all they could to make the journal a power.

Douglass then said that he was impressed with Williams's range of vision and decided ability. He agreed that blacks needed a paper of their own. As the bayonet had been an instrument to work out their eman-cipation, the press would be an instrument to protect their liberties. He moved the appointment of a business committee " to arrange a suitable expression." The chair appointed Douglass, J. P. Sampson, and M. M. Holland to the committee, which withdrew for consultation. In the interim others made speeches warmly supporting the new enterprise.

The committee, with Douglass as the spokesman, offered a set of resolutions endorsing the Williams proposal. They spoke of the "chilling shadow of slavery" that interfered with the freedom and enfranchise-ment of all blacks. A well-conducted weekly journal "of commanding size, devoted to our common cause, owned and edited by men of our class, published here in the capital of the nation, would be a powerful instrument for destroying prejudice against our race and promoting manly ambition and self-respect among ourselves." They had heard with satisfaction Williams's proposal "to establish such a journal in Washington" and would do what they could "to make the proposed enterprise a success." Before adopting the resolution, Douglass empha-sized that this was a grave matter that deserved the group's most careful deliberation. Perhaps remembering his own journalistic misadven-tures, he said that the failure of the project would be disastrous.

Several speeches supported the project and none opposed it. The resolutions were adopted unanimously. After speaking warmly and at length in support of the enterprise, Langston called for the names of those who would contribute to the journal each month for the next six months. Douglass pledged $10 per month, as did Langston and C. C. Crusoe; others pledged $5.00, $2.50, and $2.00. A total of $43.50 per month was pledged by those assembled.[14] The group also gave Williams a letter stating that he had authority "to represent the sentiment and views of the leading men of this District and other sections of the country in relation to a national paper which shall represent the colored race."

From mid-July, Williams had the double task of getting out a sample issue of the paper and working up support for the undertaking in various parts of the country. In a sense, they were twin projects; and he experienced difficulty in trying to accomplish one before accomplishing the other. Heartened by the support of the Washington leaders and armed with their letter of endorsement, Williams returned to Boston, where he immediately won the enthusiastic support of the venerable abolitionist crusader, William Lloyd Garrison. After congratulating Williams and wishing him well, Garrison indicated that there was still much work to do to bring about full justice for Negro Americans. He warned Williams, moreover, that in view of previous failures of similar enterprises he should be careful lest he suffer "pecuniary embarrassment" that would necessitate a speedy suspension of the journal. The main reliance of the editor, Garrison cautioned, must ultimately be upon an adequate list of paying subscribers and not upon the aid of supporters such as he received at the Washington meeting.[15]

Although his resignation from the Twelfth Baptist Church would not be effective until October 1, church members saw little of Williams during the remaining weeks of his pastorate. In August he was in the Midwest, preaching at the Croghan Street Baptist Church in Detroit; and he was making plans to have a meeting in that city within two weeks in the interest of his proposed journal.[16] A few days later he was back in Washington putting the final touches on a specimen issue of the paper. This would give him a better argument for urging support in Boston, Detroit, and various communities in the South that he planned to visit.

On September 4, 1875, the specimen issue of *The Commoner* appeared, bearing on its masthead "Rev. George W. Williams, Editor and Proprietor." It was a four-page, seven-column paper, which undertook to show its readers what they could expect in the future. In the prospectus, Williams asserted his determination to make *The Commoner* the equal of any weekly journal in the United States. It would be "to the colored people of the country a guide, teacher, defender, and mirror." To that end there would be departments that would cover all interests of Negro Americans: political, educational, agricultural, home, religious, and scientific. For Washingtonians it would carry city news, and from all over the country there would be correspondents and contributors, black and white, providing news and commentary for the journal. In the editorial columns Williams would discuss "all questions that affect the public good in their proper relations to the people at large and in the proper spirit." He would publish nothing that would furnish the occasion for personal acrimony or strife. And at times there would be poetry. (Verses entitled "Hail to Thee, 'Commoner' " were written by Elijah W. Smith, the poet of the Twelfth Baptist Church, for the specimen issue of *The Commoner*.) Williams called for 10,000 subscribers to come forward and pay in advance $2.50 per year. He also suggested that subscription clubs be organized with reduced rates according to the size of the clubs.

In this first issue Williams printed letters from distinguished leaders to indicate the kind of support he enjoyed. In addition to a warm letter of support from Garrison there were communications from Wendell Phillips and Frederick Douglass. As a general rule, Phillips did not approve of anything that was separated on the basis of race. Because of the determination of many Americans to insult the Negro and deny him the protection of the Reconstruction Amendments, however, it was "absolutely necessary that he should have churches and journals devoted entirely to the welfare of his race." Phillips hoped that the black man would let the world know that he knew his duty by supporting journals like *The Commoner*.

The sentiments that Douglass expressed went beyond those he set forth at the July meeting in Washington that endorsed the proposed journal. He now emphasized the importance of success in all efforts made by black people. "Failure on our part is but another name for ruin, for it involves the loss of all. . . . We have to show, and keep on showing, that a dark skin does not necessarily becloud or degrade the intellect it covers." He thought that the present was "just the time, and Washington is just the place," for the establishment of *The Commoner*.

> The fact that others have failed in similar efforts should not discourage us now. . . . I am happy in the assurance that you have not rushed thoughtlessly into this enterprise; . . . and have entered upon your work conscious of its gravity, and with your whole heart, from absolute choice. I shall hail your proposed journal, *The Commoner*, with grateful sentiments and hope. . . . You know our people, their situation and wants. You are a ready writer and a fluent speaker. Go forth, then, without cant, without pretense of any kind and with all honesty of heart and life.[17]

Armed with the blessings of men like Garrison, Phillips, and Douglass and with ample copies of the specimen issue of *The Commoner*, Williams was prepared to go forth and secure additional support before beginning weekly publication. Ten days after the issue appeared, he was back in Detroit, where he held a meeting of prospective subscribers. Many of the leaders of the Negro community were present. Williams emphasized the importance of having a paper to defend the rights and privileges of Negro Americans, to "show up the Southern disturbances in their true colors, and teach [Negroes] the duties which devolve upon them." A committee then commended *The Commoner* "to the patronage of all intelligent colored people as a fit and able exponent of their political and social necessities and the manner in which they should be met." Before the meeting adjourned, "a number of subscriptions" were taken.[18]

Williams hoped he would find generous and enthusiastic support for *The Commoner* in the South. Consequently, in the early fall of 1875 he spent six weeks traveling and speaking in Southern cities. He had become a professional lecturer and hoped to earn sufficient funds to provide for him and his family while soliciting subscriptions and other forms of support for the newspaper. Already he had important contacts, which facilitated visits and lectures in several places.

From Detroit, Williams went south, spending some time in Alabama before going to New Orleans at the end of September. In the Crescent City he was the guest of P. B. S. Pinchback, a former lieutenant governor and claimant of a seat in the United States Senate. In the following weeks Williams had a firsthand, close-up introduction to Southern racial practices and the collapse of Reconstruction that made it difficult for him to focus on his principal mission. Although the laws of Louisiana permitted white and black children to attend the same schools, strict racial segregation was generally the rule. Even racially integrated examinations for admission to high schools were the cause of consternation on the part of white parents, who withdrew their children. Violence or the threat of violence seemed to be everywhere. "The religion of this section is the revolver and rifle," Williams said.[19] He learned a great deal about Louisiana politics. How much support he garnered in New Orleans for his journal remains unclear.

Leaving New Orleans on October 2, Williams arrived in Jackson, Mississippi, the following day. His host was James Hill, the Mississippi secretary of state. In those early days of October, the whole area was in a feverish state of excitement. Opposition to the Republican Reconstruction program had increased to the point where violence had replaced mostly peaceful forms of rivalry. There were riots and murders of blacks at Water Valley, Louisville, Macon, Vicksburg, and Yazoo City. In the village of Clinton, near Jackson, violence erupted on September 4 during a political debate; and the incident in which two whites and two blacks were killed led to four days of slaughter of black and white radical leaders, fatalities reaching somewhere between thirty-five and fifty. The reign of terror continued for a month or more, culminating in the murder on Christmas Day of Charles Caldwell, Clinton's most respected black leader, and his brother.[20]

The "Clinton butchery" was still the chief topic of conversation when Williams reached Jackson a month later. He talked with several men about the general political situation; and he sought and gained an interview with Governor Adelbert Ames. The state's chief executive had taken official notice of the violence by issuing a proclamation calling on all extralegal armed bodies to disband. Governor Ames told Williams that these groups, largely White Liners, were determined to disrupt Republican political gatherings, that they were well armed and disciplined, and that the state did not have the military strength to execute his proclamation. He had appealed to President Grant for federal assistance, but upon the advice of Mississippi's Senator James L. Alcorn and Attorney General Edwards Pierrepont, the president declined to send any aid.[21] Only the nation's sole black senator, Blanche K. Bruce of Mississippi, urged the president to send troops to his beleagured state.

The Mississippi disorders were a shattering experience for Williams. He had not imagined that conditions could be so wretched or that the white Democrats, in their determination to overthrow the Reconstruction government, could be so ruthless. "It is impossible for Eastern men to understand the political situation here," Williams remarked bitterly. "They complain when a call for United States troops is made, pronounce the Republicans of the South cowards, and charge Republicans and Negroes with bringing about disorder and bloodshed." If they were to visit Mississippi and spend *"only a few days"* they would not howl so much about the 'outrage mill.' "[22]

On October 4, Williams gave a lecture on "The Agencies of Race Organization" in the hall of the Mississippi House of Representatives. The meeting was called to order by General Alexander Warner, chairman of the state Republican Executive Committee, who then called on James Hill, the secretary of state, to preside. Williams began his speech by commenting on the absence of women, for whom he had a special message, and on the small size of the audience—which, under the circumstances, should have been no surprise to him. The principal argument of the lecture, which he would deliver many times, was that the future progress and well-being of Negroes depended on their ability to overcome political, moral, and intellectual obstacles. They must realize that the politics of party influence could do nothing for them and that they must work out their own salvation.[23]

The lecture was well received, and the large number of White Liners, whose presence was reported by Williams, apparently found no reason to complain.[24] Williams prudently restricted his censure of conditions in Mississippi to his letters to Wendell Phillips and other friends in faraway places. The editor of the *Daily Pilot*, where a full account of the lecture appeared, said that he wished it "could be read and pondered by every man who desires the elevation of the negro race to the highest state of civilization of which it is susceptible." Undoubtedly the editor, as well as the White Liners, were pleased with Williams's lack of emphasis on politics. Indeed, the editor concluded, "Williams is the most intellectual negro on the continent, and if he will continue to eschew partisan politics in his lectures, will effect great good for his race."[25]

It is not possible to know how many stops Williams made after he left Jackson, but he was back in Washington in time for the appearance of the first regular issue of *The Commoner*, Saturday, November 6, 1875. If the specimen issue was calculated to attract readers and support, the first regular issue was not. The front page of this new journal of the race was without a single article of particular interest to a Negro readership. There was a long poem, "Darling Dorel," about a German princess; a quite lengthy story, "Farmer Brill's Pleasure," concerning some new experiences of a European yeoman; and an article on "The Wrongs of Red Men." Elsewhere there were letters congratulating Williams on the venture; praise from General Oliver Otis Howard, whose letter of good wishes was carried; and a piece by Williams himself, vowing that he would go on using "Reverend" before his name to indicate his continuing spiritual and professional commitments.

The second issue, appearing on November 13, was little better than the first. This time the poem was "How the Leaves Came Down," followed by "A Tale of India, 1857," and a piece on "The Turkish Insurrections." There were a few pieces of special interest to blacks, such as the article covering the oration on Charles Sumner by Richard T. Greener, the first black graduate of Harvard; one on the ill-fated Freedmen's Savings and Trust Company that had closed in 1874; and some local news items from Washington, Richmond, and Charleston. The interests of the editor in Republican politics and in the problems of Reconstruction were reflected in his discussion of the importance of resuming a policy of specie payment and his report on the continuing revolution in Mississippi. In this and succeeding issues, moreover, Williams argued vehemently that P.B.S. Pinchback's 1873 election to the United States Senate by the Louisiana legislature was legal in every respect and that he should be seated.[26]

While Williams continued to print enthusiastic letters of support from a variety of people in several parts of the country, there is no way of knowing how many subscribers he was gaining or how much genuine support he actually received. Richard T. Greener, who was teaching in South Carolina, sent an impressive list of subscribers, including Judge Jonathan J. Wright of the South Carolina Supreme Court and Francis L. Cardozo, the state treasurer; but he was rather casual in giving Williams the option of billing each subscriber or having him make the collections. Subscribers were increasing, to be sure, but one cannot be certain that subscription revenues were increasing. Nor is there any way of knowing if the men who pledged certain amounts to support *The Commoner* honored their pledges. Since Williams had praise for Douglass and Langston throughout the life of the paper, one may assume that they remained in good standing.[27] But what of the others who made those pledges on the night of July 12, 1875?

Williams would not complain, even if things were not going well. He was the perennial optimist whose pride would not permit him to reveal to the public the problems he was facing. He reprinted the "Prospectus" in each issue and continued to call for ten thousand subscribers. That, he argued, was the only way that *The Commoner* could become an effective national voice. In the issue of November 20, there is a hint of anxiety in an article by the editor under the title, "What is Necessary to the Success of A Paper?" Williams said that capital, though necessary, *is not all*. The editor, the managers of a paper, must do their part; but there is a great deal to be done by the people. *They* must support a paper." Everyone is saying that the paper should succeed, and "every person we meet will bid us 'God-speed'; but what more do they do?" The many papers begun by blacks that had failed should be "a warning and a stimulus to all those who desire to see a national journal permanently established."

For the time being Williams seemed willing to settle for something less than a national journal. He had gone to Washington because he believed a strong base for support was located there. Consequently, as national support foundered, he turned to the Negroes of the District of Columbia and appealed for help.

> There are 45,000 Colored Americans in this District. About 5,000 of them claim to be educated—more or less. Therefore, it would appear that at least one-fifth of them could and would gladly subscribe for a paper edited by men of their own nationality. . . .
>
> Some men say, "When I have seen, after three or four months that you have succeeded, then I will subscribe." Suppose we were

to walk into a dry-goods store or a hotel and say, "When you have
been in existence for three or four months, and succeed, then the
people will begin to patronize you." How absurd such an idea is. If a
hotel, dry-goods store or a newspaper is a necessity in a community, why should the people put them on probation?[28]

It is not clear just how much assistance Williams had in handling the
paper's editorial and business affairs. Only his own name appeared on
the masthead or in the editorial columns. Many years later, "Bruce
Grit" (pseudonym for journalist James E. Bruce) recalled that Howard
L. Smith was the city editor for *The Commoner.*[29] If that was so, one may
assume that Williams and Smith were the sole occupants of the editorial
offices at 1410 New York Avenue, Northwest. Inadequate help may
explain why there was not greater focus on the Negro community in the
articles and why many of them were merely lifted from other sources.
Williams was not alone in this practice, which in nineteenth-century
journalism was not regarded as plagiarism. But Williams needed to be
innovative and imaginative if he was to have any chance of capturing the
support of his special audience. Despite typographical errors, the paper
was fairly well edited, and contained a considerable number of adver-
tisements (a few of which were inverted). Even so, a leading Washington daily said that "its mechanical execution is in a very high order of the
typographical art."[30]

While Williams was well received by both races in the South during
his tour in September and October 1875, one doubts that the whites
would have been as cordial to him as the editor of the Jackson *Daily Pilot*
had been if he had returned in December. As the real significance and
tragedy of the events transpiring in the South made their impact upon
Williams, he became more bitter about what was happening to blacks
there. He took the initiative in calling a meeting to support the claims of
P.B.S. Pinchback to a seat in the Senate.[31] He bemoaned the atrocities
perpetrated by White Liners against would-be Negro voters in Columbus and Port Gibson, Mississippi, and declared that their treatment
was quite typical of the state. The more he heard about them, the more
strident he became, calling White Liners clayeaters, nutcrackers, and
cut-throats and declaring that the Bourbons delighted in reminiscing
about the time that they could "with impunity flog a Negro to death just
for amusement."[32] By December 1875, the pledge offered in September
that there would be no bitterness in the pages of *The Commoner* had
clearly been broken.

By mid-December 1875, one could well wonder how Williams was
making ends meet. He continued to advertise his services as a lecturer

for any church or society, adding the words "For terms, address the editor." He had a few takers. On November 23 he addressed Labour Council 27 in Hillsdale, D.C., but since it was for the benefit of the poor, the lecturer's fee might have been rather modest. The following evening he delivered his favorite lecture, "The Agencies of Race Organization," before the faculty and students of Howard University. The faculty called it "very able and interesting" and expressed its "hearty approbation of the sentiments contained therein."[33] There is reason to believe that those two performances, added to whatever he could take from the paper's income, did not provide an adequate living for the young editor and his family. Sarah, a seamstress and hairdresser, doubtless worked to support herself and their son George, less than one year old.

In the issue of December 18, Williams announced that there would be no holiday issue of the paper. "We take this little respite to move, go west after our family, and attend to some other business of importance," he explained. He urged the agents, meanwhile, to enlarge their list of subscribers, and said that he hoped soon to enlarge the paper. After wishing the readers a Merry Christmas, he said that he hoped to "visit them again through *The Commoner* on the 1st proximo." Yet it could hardly be a coincidence that the two poems on the first page of that issue were entitled, "Farewell" and "Good-bye":

> Farewell? Nay, nay! Unblessed I cannot leave
>   thee
> Denied; I plead against thy queenly power,
> And importune, though importuning
>   grieves thee—
> Yield me this blessing in this bitter hour! . . .
>
>   . . .
> Sweet is rest; but by all showing
>   Toil is nigh.
> We must go. Alas! The going
>   Say "goodbye."

There was no issue of *The Commoner* "on the 1st proximo" or at any later date. After eight issues Williams was unable to continue. As he had complained more than once, there were too many well-wishers who had not subscribed and too many subscribers who had not paid. One cannot even speculate on the extent of his arrears with the rent or with R. Beresford, the printer on Seventh Street, who had put out all eight issues of *The Commoner*. Later some would imply that Williams made personal use of the money he received for subscriptions; but there is every reason to doubt that there were even sufficient funds to pay the debts incurred by *The Commoner*. The assets of the paper were never of any real consequence; and Williams could hardly be blamed if he withdrew funds for travel and other expenses.

Living from day to day as he did, always hoping that the morrow would bring an avalanche of prepaid subscriptions and advertising revenue, Williams could not plan and announce the paper's demise any more than he could plan the next four issues. The best he could do was to announce the forthcoming issue and sit back and hope. He had to take steps, however, to provide for himself, his wife, and his young son, born during Williams's pastorate in Boston. Consequently, on December 22, 1875, he took a job with the Post Office Department in Washington.[34] We do not know whether, or where, he "went west after his family." If his wife and son were already with her people in Chicago, they may as well have remained there, for in February 1876 the erstwhile editor of *The Commoner* would himself become a Midwesterner.

The failure of *The Commoner* was a painful repetition of the fate of black newspapers for more than a half-century. Despite Williams's claims, the black reading public that would place a black newspaper high on its list of priorities was very small. Those readers who were inclined to support a black newspaper might well find *The Commoner*— and others like it—inadequate in serving their interests and needs. Articles on the resumption of specie payment or even articles attacking the White Liners could have very limited interest even to the most likely subscribers, the black men and women of Washington. *The Commoner* did not have the resources to sustain itself while prospective readers made up their minds and a favorable reputation could be built. For Williams, *The Commoner* was a valuable experience, but it was not the answer to his almost desperate desire to distinguish himself and to perform an important service for his people.

·4·

A Star in the Midwest

Williams held his job in the Post Office Department for a mere two months. On February 10, 1876, he was called to the pastorate of the Union Baptist Church of Cincinnati; and on Sunday, February 20, he preached his first sermon there. He was no stranger to the Midwest. He had lived briefly in Illinois after receiving his army discharge in 1868. He had visited Chicago several times and met and married Sarah there. He had first visited Cincinnati in 1873, while still a student at Newton. In June of that year he preached at the Zion Church and two days later delivered a lecture on Toussaint L'Ouverture. The reporter, who described him as "an intelligent, refined young man, without ostentation or presumption," indicated that Williams was "very favorably impressed with our city and expresses a desire to remain a while with us."[1]

In the post–Civil War years, Cincinnati was a growing metropolis, whose breweries, meat-packing plants, and other industries provided an economic base that attracted black and white alike. In 1860, with a population of 161,044, the 3,731 blacks made up 2.3% of the total. By 1870, when the total population had grown to 210,335, blacks numbered 5,896, or 2.7%.[2] The vitality of Cincinnati's black community manifested itself in the multiplicity of flourishing institutions—churches, fraternal orders, rescue missions, literary societies, and political clubs. As in other communities, the church was the most important and most powerful institution; and as blacks migrated into Cincinnati in the post–Civil War years, it was the church that received them first and gave them a sense of belonging and of involvement. Baptist and Methodist churches were well established before the war, and by 1876 there were seven Negro Baptist churches in the city.[3]

Union Baptist was the oldest Negro Baptist church in Cincinnati and the second oldest in the state. In 1831, fourteen blacks who had been members of the white Enon Baptist Church organized "The Colored Branch of the Enon Baptist Church." This was the first step toward independence, the second coming in 1835 when they adopted the name "African Union Baptist Church." Soon they had their own pastor and officers, but they maintained their connection with Enon and in 1840 acquired the Baker Street property of the mother church at a bargain price. Five years later it was incorporated by the Ohio General Assembly as the Union Baptist Church of Cincinnati. In 1864 it moved to a building at Mound and Richmond Streets, which it purchased for $12,000. It spent $8,000 on remodeling the structure, repaired the parsonage, and purchased a sixteen-acre tract for a cemetery.[4] For many years it had been the most popular and the most progressive church in the Negro community; and its choir enjoyed a sufficient reputation that even strangers were often attracted to the church to hear it. This was the institution to which Williams was invited early in 1876.

The installation of Williams at Cincinnati's Union Baptist Church was at least as auspicious as the one at Boston's Twelfth Baptist. Printed invitations for the services on March 2, 1876, went out to certain people whose presence was especially desired, but, as a local newspaper pointed out, it was not to be an exclusive affair "as the doors and seats are open to all."[5] On the appointed evening, some nine hundred people assembled, "all standing room being occupied." The Reverend Samuel W. Duncan, pastor of the prestigious white Ninth Street Baptist Church, preached the installation sermon; the Reverend S. K. Leavitt, pastor of the venerable First Baptist Church, delivered "a very eloquent and interesting address upon the duties of a pastor"; and the Reverend Joseph Emery, for twenty-five years the leader of the Union Baptist Church's Sabbath School, offered the principal prayer.[6] The choir sang several times.

The high point of the evening was the brief address by the new pastor. He spoke of his earnest desire to serve the church in every way, "spiritually and otherwise." Already Williams had developed into an excellent speaker; and he impressed his audience not only with what he said but how he said it "with a voice of unusual depth and fullness."[7]

If the Negro Baptist churches of Cincinnati had prospered in the past, in 1876 Williams thought this was no longer so. It was well known that Union Baptist had suffered some misfortune under Williams's predecessor, the Reverend James H. Magee. This setback was generally regarded as temporary, and it was believed that things would go well under Williams. Nine months after he took over the pastorate, however, Williams concluded that all of Cincinnati's Negro Baptist churches, including Union, were in a "perishing condition. Not a single edifice is

one-third filled on the Sabbath," Williams complained, "and the for-
lorn, dilapidated looks of the houses, inside and out, is a sad picture of
the religious condition of the people who occasionally meet in them." In
the preceding five years no church had held a revival, and there had
been no growth in membership. All were in debt, with obligations
ranging from $100 to $6,000.

Such a sad state called for radical reform Williams contended, and his
proposals were doubtless shocking to the pastors and perhaps their
memberships. He called for a merger of the seven churches into not
more than two, "one church in the 'East End' and the other in the 'West
End'! Then each church could afford to support a first-class pastor and
contribute to a mission station somewhere near the river." He was
convinced that the salvation of the churches lay in consolidation. He
suggested that the oldest of them—Union Baptist—issue a call for a
convention of all the Negro Baptists of the city. The wisest would come
as messenger-delegates who would discuss every aspect of the problem.
The old names of the churches should be given up, "for there is nothing
in them"; dues should be reduced and, if paid, they could support the
new organizations handsomely.

In what was fast becoming a Williams trademark, he concluded his
statement on the churches with a ringing appeal:

> Let the colored Baptists rise up and say that they will seize the
> scepter that is passing from them; that they will discharge their
> whole duty in this matter, and a cause once illustrious and powerful
> will again rise in glory more resplendent, in beauty more gorgeous,
> in piety more robust, in goodness more efficient, in unity more
> indissoluble, in peace more abiding, and in joy more unspeakable
> and full of glory.[8]

Williams had not reckoned with the matter of the vested interests
represented in the leadership in each of the seven churches. There was,
for example, the insecurity that all of them felt, especially the smaller
ones, at the possibility of being completely absorbed by the larger
groups. Nor had he taken fully into account the emotional attachments
that the origin and history of the several churches provided for each set
of communicants.

For the moment, at least, Williams's principal interest was in
strengthening Union Baptist Church. There was no immediate call for a
revival, in whose revitalizing influence and impact he had much faith;
and he did not appeal to the more affluent white community for support,
as he had done in Boston. Nonetheless, Union began to prosper, and

once again it enjoyed the popularity and the membership that it had lost in the previous decade. One thing Williams did was instill in the membership a sense of pride in their church and an appreciation of its past. When Union celebrated its forty-fifth anniversary in July 1876, Williams devoted his sermon to the history of the church. The founders of Union Baptist Church were heroes, he said, "who in their day were compelled to contend not only with the ordinary obstacles which beset the way of all attempting a new departure, but likewise with the strong prejudice of the time." He paid tribute to his predecessors in the pastorate and called on the members to maintain the best traditions of the church by working for the social and moral elevation of the people.

Comments by one paper, the *Commercial*, were not calculated to increase his popularity among his fellow black clergymen. The reporter covering the anniversary celebration asserted that few clergymen in the city could rival "the young colored divine as a speaker, or preach a sermon marked by such natural eloquence and originality of interest as characterize his address." Then, moving on to Williams's immediate competitors, the reporter contended that he was a man "of considerably higher culture than the pastors of colored congregations are usually endowed with."[9] Such comments, even if deserved, would make it more difficult for Williams to gain the friendship and cooperation of his peers.

Before conducting a revival at Union Baptist Church, Williams offered a series of four Wednesday evening lectures. The public announcement that they would begin on Wednesday, December 20, 1876, did not indicate the subject matter.[10] It is safe to assume, however, that Williams drew on his well-developed repertoire, which included "Advent of the Colored Soldier" and "Toussaint L'Ouverture." Thus, while other churches were holding midweek prayer meetings, Williams was attempting to provide his members with some aspects of Afro-American life and history. After a brief illness, during which time the lectures were suspended, Williams gave his well-practiced lecture "The Agencies of Race Organization" on January 31, 1877.[11] The following month Williams celebrated the first anniversary of his pastorate at Union. To a large audience composed of whites as well as blacks, Williams opened the long-awaited revival by reviewing the previous year's work and challenging the members to greater achievements in the following year.[12]

The sheer variety and volume of activity in Cincinnati—religious, cultural, civic, and political—must have been stimulating for a man of Williams's interests. It was not long before he was a part of many secular activities. In that centennial year of the independence of the United States, Williams was one of Cincinnati's principal celebrants. At Avondale, a largely black section of the city, he was the orator of the day on July 4. His address, "The American Negro, from 1776 to 1876," laid the groundwork for the history of his race he was to write some years later (see chapter 8 below). In the lengthy address, Williams recounted the role of blacks in the War for Independence, through slavery and the Civil War, and during Reconstruction. After commenting on the relation of the Negro to the future of the country, he closed with these words:

> And when another hundred years are settled upon the gracious brow of the nation, may it be seen as now, that eternal peace and prosperity shine in her youthful countenance, and cast their healthful beams upon all her adopted sons, irrespective of color or nationality.[13]

Problems of Reconstruction continued to agitate Williams, as they had when he was editor of *The Commoner*; but he was also worried about problems of discrimination in Cincinnati and elsewhere in Ohio and about the general condition of his 63,000 fellow blacks in the state. And there was ample cause for concern. In January 1868, the legislature rescinded its earlier ratification of the Fourteenth Amendment. In the following year the legislature refused to ratify the Fifteenth Amendment. It was not until that amendment became a part of the Constitution in 1870 that Ohio blacks gained the ballot.[14] When Congress passed the Civil Rights Act in 1875, the Cincinnati *Daily Enquirer* polled the city's leading innkeepers. Only one said that he was willing to obey the law. Another planned to circumvent the law by separating blacks from whites both in sleeping quarters and dining facilities.[15] The record of the state regarding the rights enjoyed by blacks was not an enviable one. There was much to be done if Ohio blacks were to have equal protection of the laws.

Williams almost immediately began a round of activities that soon brought him to the attention of large numbers of Cincinnati citizens, black and white. In August 1876 he became a member of the executive committee of the Colored Protective Association, the purpose of which was to secure for blacks the rights denied them in Cincinnati and "this section of the country."[16] In the following week, a group of Cincinnati blacks met to protest the riot that had occurred on July 8 in Hamburg, South Carolina, in which five Negroes were shot in cold blood. Williams, then in Yellow Springs, could not be present because of illness but sent a message applauding the move on the part of Cincinnati Negroes to "record their protest against the Hamburg massacre."[17] In

September he spoke at length at a meeting called to discuss the financial plight of the Colored Orphan Asylum at Avondale. He said that if the three or four thousand members of the seven Baptist churches were to contribute twenty-five to fifty cents per capita, the asylum would not only be relieved of its indebtedness but would have a permanent operating fund as well.[18] There is no record that the group even considered this suggestion.

In his newly chosen home city, Williams was thus making his mark as an energetic pastor, an eloquent spokesman for worthy causes, and an imaginative leader in religious and civic affairs. Nine months after his arrival, the Cincinnati *Daily Enquirer*, featured Williams in its section "Among the Colored Folks." The reporter who interviewed him found him in his study "hard at work with books scattered about in plenteous numbers." The article was full of inaccuracies, for example: "Horace Greeley made him an army correspondent" while an officer in a Negro regiment; "Later he became political editor of the National Republican"; and "Mr. Williams is a graduate of Harvard University."[19]

Doubtless these flagrant misrepresentations were provided by Williams. Had he taken exception to the material in the article, he would surely have demanded a correction as he was to do on numerous occasions in the future. Despite the remarkable talent that Williams possessed and his flair for calling attention to himself, he apparently thought his considerable achievements were not enough. When only twenty-seven years old, Williams began to make claims for himself that were patently false. In time they would run the gamut from his age to his education to his writings.

The reporter's October interview with Williams may have had something to do with his very satisfactory relationship with the *Commercial* which began in December 1876 and continued for some two years. The *Commercial*, an old, established journal in Cincinnati, was by this time under the firm control of Murat Halstead, an innovative and even adventurous writer and editor. He had covered the execution of John Brown, had written brilliant firsthand accounts of the military operations in the Civil War and the Franco-Prussian War, and had joined a small group of influential Republican editors who supported the presidential candidacy of fellow journalist Horace Greeley in 1872.[20]

We do not know how and when Williams met Halstead, or under what conditions Williams began to write for the *Commercial*. Perhaps Halstead merely gave Williams the privilege of writing for the *Commercial* when he saw fit, paying him for any items accepted for publication, an arrangement similar to the one that T. Thomas Fortune was to have with the New York *Sun* in 1887.[21] In any case, on December 3, 1876,

Williams became a regular contributor to the Cincinnati *Commercial*. Writing under the pseudonym "Aristides," Williams presumably sought to emulate Aristides Publius Aelius, the second-century Greek rhetorician and sophist whose writings are remembered for their eloquence and correctness of style. The Williams columns generally appeared once a week, occasionally on successive days. Eschewing politics, in which he was becoming deeply interested, Williams chose to write on religious, cultural, military, and racial topics. Some of his columns were autobiographical. Others treated local and state civic matters, such as the orphanage in Cincinnati and the soldiers' home near Dayton. He wrote at least four engrossing pieces on "Business Colored Men of Cincinnati" and one on "Colored Chicagoans."

Some of the articles were highly critical of local Negroes, such as the one on "The Colored Baptists of Cincinnati."[22] Others, like "Our Colored Fellow Citizens," were critical of local whites and lamented the bleak conditions and lack of opportunities for blacks in Cincinnati. "There isn't a colored man or woman in Cincinnati employed as a clerk in any bank, store, or business house of any kind," he complained. Nor was there a single black man or woman employed as a copyist or messenger in any dry-goods store, telegraph office, printing office, police force, fire department, or the street railroad company. "There are no openings for our educated youth. They graduate from year to year, but what hope have they of getting employment? None whatever. So our schools are training a large company of boys and girls—for what? To seek employment in vain; to knock at the doors of places of business only to be turned away."[23]

Not all the pieces by Aristides were so grim. In the spring of 1878 he reported on the joyous rendition of the cantata *Esther* in "Music among the Colored People." Williams recalled that as pastor of the Union Baptist Church he had done much to encourage musical activity among the young people. At his suggestion the church had purchased an organ and reorganized and enlarged the choir. This ultimately led to the rigorous study and rehearsal of the cantata and the renting of costumes as well as a commodious church at Sixth and Broadway. The choir and guest soloists rendered it twice in one week. Williams, fancying himself a music critic, wrote that the excellent acting of the person in the role of Esther "apologized for the thickness of her voice at times" and that Charles Bentley as Haman "was in perfect sympathy with the character he was taking . . . sang a pure tenor, and enthused the entire audience." He wished them much success in their Louisville appearance in "One of the greatest Music Festivals ever given by colored people."[24]

The only article by Aristides dealing directly with politics did not purport to express Williams's own views. Early in 1877, when in Chicago, Williams called on Joseph Medill, editor of the *Tribune*. Williams reported the conversation that ensued as an interview by Aristides. To a question about the Southern policy of the newly elected president, Rutherford B. Hayes, Medill answered that the restoration of peace was the most important matter before the country. He praised the president's expressed policy of withdrawing troops from the South, although he was not prepared to see Southern Republican officials deserted. At the prompting of Williams, Medill said that Negroes should make friends with the Conservatives and cast their vote for the party that would give them protection. Medill thought that regimes such as the Kellogg government in Louisiana, which had acknowledged numerous political murders that it had not been able to prevent, should step aside and yield to a government that could protect all citizens, black and white. This is the only extant example of a Williams article in the form of an interview; and in it he demonstrates considerable skill as an interviewer.[25]

The last article by Aristides appeared on November 24, 1878, by which time Williams was one of Cincinnati's best-known citizens. To his prominence as a clergyman, civic leader, and columnist, must be added his increasing activity and influence in Republican Party circles. Blacks in Cincinnati had never wielded much political influence, not only because of their small numbers but also because of their preoccupation with survival. Yet they had shown some political awareness as early as 1870, when they voted with the Protestants in supporting religious instruction in the schools, which the Catholics opposed. They succeeded in using their political strength to elect to the school board a slim majority that favored the use of the Protestant Bible.[26] As their numbers grew and as their leaders saw the value of organizing them politically, it appeared that blacks could become an important force in the political life of the city.

Such a possibility did not escape a man of Williams's sensitivities and ambitions. He had been in the city less than two months when he made the first move to become the spokesman for Negro Republicans. In April 1876, a group of Cincinnati blacks called a meeting at Zion Church to consider the recommendation made at a recent National Colored Convention in Nashville that blacks should leave the Republican party. Williams was unable to attend, but he sent a lengthy letter that proved to be the most important statement at the meeting. He was not surprised that the Nashville meeting was "badly wanting in unity of political sentiment" because of the "unsettled state of our national politics, the revolutionary oscillations in Southern politics, the triumphs of terrorism, and the palpable mistakes of our own party—its sins of omission and of commission." Williams did not agree that Negroes should quit the Republican party. Even if those in the South found it impossible to function as Republicans, they should not embrace the Democrats. On the other hand, "a mere inexorable, automatic, blind holding to our party will not save it. We must strain every tension of body and mind to secure the best men as leaders. We must show that we are the formidable enemies of any man, white or black, who does not carry into the discharge of his political duties the highest qualities of virtue and ability. Primitive Republicanism in its letter and spirit must be resuscitated."[27]

If Williams was fairly strong in his allegiance to the Republican party in April, that loyalty had all but disappeared by midsummer. In denying a report from Oxford, Ohio, that he had made a rousing speech there for the Republican candidate, Rutherford B. Hayes, Williams declared he was not in sympathy with either the Republican or the Democratic party.

> When I say that the Democratic party is unworthy of the countenance, confidence and support of the American voters, I state a truth that is as broad as the universe. And when I say that the Republican party has played the part of the hypocrite, has misused its power, squandered the hard earnings of the people, has failed to punish the guilty and protect the emancipated . . . when I state these facts, with thousands of terrible facts unstated, every honest man, in whatever party, must assent to the unvarnished truth.

Thinking no doubt of the Liberal Republicans in 1872, Williams expressed the hope that the best citizens would once again attempt to organize a third party "working for the good of the American people."[28]

While the sentiments that Williams expressed were excessive and would be modified almost immediately, they threw him into the midst of a controversy that merely added to his prominence. A reader berated him as an ingrate for attacking a party that had poured out the blood of its sons "to rescue him and his race from the bonds of slavery." Williams replied that he had not been a slave and that he too had poured out his blood to rescue his brothers from slavery. He made a distinction, he said, between the Republican party and Republican principles, and when the party returned to "a faithful and honest discharge of those noble theories laid down by the men who brought it into existence," no man would be more faithful than Williams himself.[29]

These views brought praise from the editor of the *Commercial*, a

Liberal Republican in 1872, who added that Williams was not fully appreciated by the black community, including his own congregation, which preferred "red hot exhortations of the old-fashioned camp-meeting type, interspersed with slang, and emphasized by violent stamping and shouting." The editor said that Williams's political independence was offensive to many members of his congregation, who had even called a meeting for his ouster. Williams expressed appreciation for the *Commercial*'s kind mention of him but pointed out that the editor was in error about the feelings of his congregation toward him. When he was out of the city, a group (actually the Protective Association) had held a meeting at his church. Someone had objected to Williams being on the executive committee, offering the wild and inaccurate accusation that he was a Democrat. "I am not in any trouble with my church," Williams assured the editor. "I am not a Democrat, but of earnest Republican faith, and trust that our party will be worthy of the victory of which its principles are worthy, though it has not done its whole duty to my race. All I desire is to keep out of politics, and preach the everlasting Gospel of Peace."[30]

Even as he made this eloquent reaffirmation of his commitment to the church, Williams must have been entertaining doubts about his future in that institution. Some would charge that blind ambition was what led him into politics, while others would insist that external pressures pushed him in, much against his will. In any case, toward the end of October 1876 he made his formal political debut at a mass meeting of Negro Republicans at Hopkins Hall. Among the speakers were Peter H. Clark, former editor and school principal, and Colonel Robert Harlan, member of the Republican State Central Committee and trustee of the Colored Orphan Asylum. It was Williams, "a speaker of large ability and larger promise," who captivated the audience. He said that the clergy should remain out of politics as a rule, but "when the storm clouds thicken and darken our National sky, when the hand of treason is at the throat of the Nation; when the temple of justice, humanity, and equality is about to be desecrated by traitors . . . I would be false to the great issues of this hour . . . if I did not lend my pen, my voice, my soul to the cause of the illustrious Republican party, led by those sagacious and patriotic gentlemen—Rutherford B. Hayes and William A. Wheeler."

Williams spoke at great length, indeed for more than an hour. He spoke of the unrepentant South, "more rebellious today than she ever was," and of a Democratic party "with a Southern head and a Northern tail." Then followed the classic statement of the case against the Democratic party, a proslavery party that Negroes would never be able to trust, and one that was inclined to repudiate public obligations, thus striking "terror and consternation in the English and German money market." He praised Hayes, who stumped the state with Peter Clark in support of the Reconstruction Amendments. "He believes in the colored man, and desires to see him have all the rights accorded to other men." Reminding his audience that this was the Centennial year, "rich in memory of the good and the great," Williams asked his audience to renew their commitment to freedom and equality so that all the grand achievements of the century would not be trampled under the heel of treason and disunion.[31]

With this address, Williams became an active Republican politician who would work assiduously for the party and expect the usual party rewards. Although he continued to refrain from political subjects in his newspaper column, he was not so disciplined in his other activities. At one of the regular meetings of a Cincinnati Sunday School, Williams offered a resolution to congratulate President Grant for his support of Sunday Schools and to thank him for his "willingness and promptness to protect our people at the South when wronged and throw about them the mantle of justice and citizenship."[32] This sentiment was clearly contradictory to the information that Williams collected on his Southern trip in 1875 and indicates the extent to which he had resolved to play the political game for all that it was worth.

If Williams was attentive to the outgoing president, he had no intention of neglecting the incoming one. On February 20, 1877, even before the problems connected with the disputed presidential election of the previous November had been fully resolved, Williams already was seeking an appointment with Rutherford B. Hayes. He sent a telegram to Hayes, still in the governor's mansion in Columbus, asking him if he could see him that same evening.[33] There was no reply, and on the following day Williams wrote to Hayes, introducing himself as a Massachusetts man who had been a pastor in Cincinnati for one year. He told Hayes that he had visited the South and was informed about conditions there. The sooner color lines were obliterated "by a broad and far reaching policy the better it will be for the entire country." Williams hoped to discuss these matters with Hayes some evening in the quiet of the governor's home.[34] There is no evidence that the meeting materialized, however.

Once Hayes was in the White House, Williams made an all-out effort to secure presidential favor. His Sabbath School, under the leadership of the Reverend Joseph Emery, expressed to the president their "unqualified approbation of the course of our esteemed and honored chief Magistrate." The group said that they believed his Southern policy would prove a blessing to white and black alike.[35] Williams followed up this expression with a personal letter to the president, a covering letter to the president's secretary, and a statement that he was distributing to the "Colored Voters of the South." Williams assured the president that although he got another man to sign it with him, "to save myself from the charge of presumption," he himself had written every line of it. And he had sent three thousand copies to the South. The piece was an outpouring of sympathy for the sufferings that black Southerners had endured. Williams told them that he understood the tottering Republican state governments in the South, but Northerners and Southerners alike had urged the president not to interfere. Williams assured black Southerners that in obeying that voice, the president had exacted a promise from the new regimes in the South that they would respect the new Amendments. The president was committed to support and enforce the Constitution, "and the nation will not soon forget his solemn pledges." Williams assured his readers that if the Southern promises were broken, the president would adopt measures "adequate to accomplish what has not been reached through measures of pacification."[36]

In his own letter to the president, Williams was not long in coming to the point. He was virtually without pride as he told the president that he was without employment and without funds.[37] "I am praying and hoping for you to appoint me to a Consulship! Beside the endorsement of some white gentlemen, your personal friends, I am endorsed by the colored men of this city and state.[38] I shall wait patiently and prayerfully. Please remember a young man who has served his country and party with fidelity, and who desires an opportunity to do good."[39] The appointment to a consulship did not materialize, and Williams would have to wait another year before a federal appointment came through (see chapter 11 below).

Williams accepted his failure with resignation and renewed ambivalence toward the Republican party and its leaders. He took exception to the claim of the Cincinnati *Enquirer* that Hayes had appointed more Negroes to office than any of his predecessors. He insisted that Grant had made a larger number of Negro appointments, many of them to important offices. "I do not like to see President Hayes get any more credit than belongs to him," he fretted. He further complained that the president "has been four months appointing four colored men." Regarding the news that the president had offered the Haitian post to John Mercer Langston, Williams reminded the *Enquirer* that two Ohio blacks, James Poindexter and Alfred J. Anderson, were candidates for the post and were well endorsed by Democrats and Republicans, black and white.[40] He complained that Langston, a graduate of Oberlin, could no longer be considered an Ohioan. "If the President desires to recognize the 15,000 colored voters in this state he can do it in a much handsomer way than by appointing a man from this state who is not identified with the interests of its people."[41]

Williams was not prepared for a complete break with the president and the party, although he was apparently willing to turn his back on Langston. Obviously he was piqued because he himself had failed to secure an appointment. But he did not want to burn his bridges. Thus, when a group of black Cincinnati Republicans met on July 20, 1877, to discuss and possibly to condemn Hayes's Southern policy, Williams (who had not been a party to calling the meeting) attended. The sentiment seemed to favor a resolution of censure until Williams spoke. He criticized those who belonged to the party merely for personal gain. He did not come to condemn the president's Southern policy, "so called," or to criticize him for withdrawing troops from Louisiana and South Carolina. It was proper, of course, for Negroes of Hamilton County to stand up for their rights, but broader principles were involved than jobs or even troops in the South. Principles of political independence and integrity were at least as important. Peter Clark spoke along similar lines, and the resolution that was adopted did little more than express attachment to the Republican party.[42]

For the moment, Williams had lowered his sights. He could not command influence or respect in Washington until he had a strong political base in Cincinnati. This involved seizing control of the political machinery in the black community and using the power of that apparatus to lift him to national attention. He could gain much satisfaction from the manner in which his remarks at the July 20 meeting on Hayes's Southern policy affected the content of the resolutions. Building a strong base might even involve standing for a public elective office. That would surely test his local strength, which, if considerable, could perhaps be translated into national attention. The time was at hand, and no one saw more clearly the opportunity than George Washington Williams.

Republican Yeoman

Although Williams at the meeting on July 20 had deflected the plan of many blacks to denounce Hayes's Southern policy, he saw in their very displeasure an opportunity to turn the situation to political advantage. If they were willing to express their unhappiness by becoming more active politically, Williams could benefit. If the Republicans became aware of blacks' discontent, they might be willing to take steps to mollify them. Peter Clark, one of the Republican stalwarts in Cincinnati's black community, had already become sufficiently disillusioned to accept nomination on the Socialist Labor party ticket for state school commissioner.[1] An even deeper defection, with others joining the Democratic ranks, would really hurt the Republicans, especially when "political instability and narrow margins of victory in presidential and gubernatorial elections highlighted the importance of Ohio's . . . black voters."[2]

A local reporter asked Williams what he thought of Peter Clark's candidacy on the "Workingmen's" (Socialist Labor party) ticket. Williams replied that the nomination had been made to "catch all the colored vote, not alone in Hamilton County, but this state, but in that I think they are mistaken." He said that while some of Clark's friends would vote for him, many would vote the Republican ticket. He left the reporter guessing when he said, "Even though a Republican myself, and believing in Republican principles, I would vote any ticket that would protect the interests of my color." He declared his dissatisfaction with the manner in which the party had treated his people. Only five had received appointments in the county in the past seventeen years. Surely they deserved more consideration in view of all they had done. He insisted that the better class of whites in the South, most of whom were Democrats, "want colored people to have their rights. . . . There's

Kentucky, she is a Democratic State: see what she has done, she has many colored men holding office."[3]

Clearly the Republicans were apprehensive; therefore, Negroes, by working together, could force the party to make concessions. On August 20, 1877, just before the Hamilton County Republican convention met to name its slate of candidates for the fall elections, the black Independent Union Club held a meeting to agree on candidates to recommend. Sixty or seventy members and about 150 spectators were present. The club agreed to recommend William Jones as a candidate for the legislature and Jesse Fossett for justice of the peace. Then a group from the Eighteenth Ward, in which Williams was vice-president of the Republican Club, moved that Williams should also be recommended as a candidate for the legislature. This created considerable confusion, during which the matter was referred to the committee on resolutions, which took no action.[4]

When the Republican convention met on Wednesday, August 22, the black delegates were determined their group should receive some recognition for its loyalty and service. No one, however, nominated William Jones, on whom the Independent Union Club had agreed. Instead, Charles Bell, editor of the defunct *Colored Citizen*, presented the name of George W. Williams, who garnered 216 votes, the largest number received by any candidate, with only 192 needed for nomination. A reporter from the Democratic paper remarked rather unkindly, "Cuffee showed his teeth and Cuffee got a bone, not from love but from fear."[5] In response to loud calls, Williams went to the stage and said,

> I rise simply to tender my sincere thanks for the honor you have conferred upon me in nominating me as one of your Representatives in the Legislature of Ohio. I heartily thank you, for myself, for the colored people, and for the Republican Party. I take this as an earnest of the feeling that has ever been in the Republican Party for the colored man (Applause). And I simply desire to say . . . that I shall do all in my power to carry this State for the Republican Party, and endeavor to lead the 3,000 colored voters of this county, and the 15,000 in the State of Ohio, under the standard of the good old Republican Party, that has a history replete with acts of Patriotism.[6]

Williams returned to his seat amid loud applause, but he must have been sobered to read in the *Enquirer* the following morning that he was nominated only because he and his people threatened to "bolt" if he failed to secure it. More ominously, the newspaper declared that "while the convention was compelled to take him, the Republican voters of the county will not be, and will not." Although these were grudging remarks from a Democratic paper, it seemed clear that Williams would have to work very hard even to make a decent showing at the polls. A few days later, at a meeting of Negro Republicans called to ratify the actions of the recent convention, Williams explained that he could not decline the nomination when the party as well as the people expressed a strong desire to have him run. He called for party unity and urged the members to be vigilant and earnest. He was certain that if they were, they would receive a handsome majority at the polls in October.[7]

Even as he realized that he needed a strong local political base, Williams never considered being a local ward heeler. He would work locally, of course, but as a party man he would not be confined to Cincinnati or Hamilton County. In his speech to the Negro Republicans in Cincinnati he announced that he would open the campaign the following week in Xenia, two counties away and more than fifty miles from where he was running for office.

The Xenia speech of September 3 was well covered by the Republican press of Cincinnati. As a spokesman for the Ohio Republican Committee, Williams dealt with issues that were not confined to Hamilton County but were of concern to the state and nation. First, he had praise for the Republican party and rejected the view that it had been in power too long. Quality of service to the people rather than length of tenure should be the criterion for continuing a party in power. "I am willing to see the Republican Party remain in power til 1960, providing it serves the people faithfully and well." Second, he reminded his audience that the real test of whether a party deserved support was to be found in what it would do about the great issues of the day: the Southern question, civil service reform, the financial question, and labor. The record of the two parties left no doubt in Williams's mind that the Republican position deserved the support of the people.

While he gave some attention to specific issues, Williams was most effective in his general indictment of the Democrats—the principles and not the men—and in his fulsome praise of the Republicans. A lengthy tirade against the Democrats began: "When the righteous spirit of the Puritans rose in opposition to the cruelties of slavery, it was the Democratic Party that with one hand strangled a free press, and with the other bribed courts and crushed out free expression." He began his lengthy statement on the virtues of the Republican party by saying that it had "a glorious record. It was born in the days when the South ruled the country with a rod of iron. It was rocked in the cradle of political storms. Its infancy was passed in obscurity and sorrow; but in its youth it went forth as young David to challenge, fight, and slay the Goliath of slavery." He argued that if there were things wrong with the party it was because of the men in it and not because of the principles. "Let no colored man flatter himself that he is so far removed from a condition of servitude that he may vote for the Democratic party with impunity. If the Democracy gets the Federal Government in 1880, they will not hesitate to expunge the amendments from the Constitution and strip the colored voter of every vestige of citizenship." It was the duty, he concluded, of every man, black and white, to vote the Republican ticket in October, "the whole Republican ticket, and nothing but the Republican ticket."[8]

During the campaign there were the usual efforts to discredit or embarrass the candidates; and Williams, an unusually visible target, could not expect to escape such designs. Early in September it was rumored that in a letter to Richard M. Bishop, the Democratic candidate for governor, Williams had offered to stump the state for the Democrats. There was so much talk about the matter that a reporter from the *Commercial* called on Williams to get his response. Williams said that he was acquainted with Bishop, "a very estimable gentleman," and that he had had two recent conversations with him on political matters. In one of these talks, Williams said, he told Bishop, in answer to a specific question, that there was some dissatisfaction among blacks but that they would follow the decisions made by the county and state conventions. He read him some excerpts of a speech he was to deliver in Dayton, and Bishop was so pleased with what he said that he suggested the speech be printed. Halstead, editor of the *Commercial*, thought it "too heavy" for the newspaper. At the suggestion that it be printed as a pamphlet, Williams got some estimates of the cost and sent them to Bishop in a letter. It subsequently appeared as a pamphlet, but the record does not indicate whether Bishop had a role in its publication.

The other conversation between Bishop and Williams involved the proposed establishment of an independent Negro newspaper. Williams had sought the support of blacks and whites, Republicans and Democrats, including Bishop. When the requisite amount of money was not subscribed, the matter was dropped. Williams concluded the interview by saying, "Mr. Bishop never made any proposition to me; I never made any to him. He never asked me to support him; I never promised him my support. . . . Some persons are trying to make political capital on which to do business during the campaign. That is all."[9]

There can be no doubt that Williams had experienced some disenchantment with the Republicans and had said some harsh things about them. It was therefore a source of considerable embarrassment to him to be reminded by the *Enquirer*, the Democratic newspaper, of his attack on the Republican party just weeks before his nomination. On August 5, 1877, Williams had said, "I would be destitute of honor, veracity, and conscience were I to urge the perpetuation of a party that has displayed such gross ignorance and imbecility."[10] The *Enquirer* further reminded Williams that in his letter to Bishop he had said that the cost of printing his pamphlet would be $35. "If you will have it published, it will serve as a good campaign document for you." He also allegedly proposed to publish an independent campaign paper that would cost $350 to launch. "I have obtained a subscription of $250 and want you to subscribe the other $100, as the paper will be a benefit to you," he was reported to have written Bishop.

The *Enquirer's* account of the Williams-Bishop relationship infuriated Williams. And he was even more agitated when he read of a reporter's interview with Bishop carried in *Volksblatt*, a local German-language newspaper, in which Bishop made damaging remarks about Williams. He took two steps to vindicate himself. One was to challenge Bishop to a joint public discussion of the "political questions before us."[11] Doubtless the letter and the Dayton speech would come up. The Democratic gubernatorial candidate clearly saw that he could gain nothing by engaging in a debate with a Republican legislative candidate, and a black one at that![12] Bishop appears to have ignored the challenge. With regard to the Bishop interview, Williams dispatched another letter to Bishop thanking him for his kind references to him but expressing consternation for Bishop's withholding the text of Williams's letter to him "as if it were an act of charity on your part." This was particularly regrettable, since he had given the *Enquirer* "a choice passage" from the letter.

> There is nothing in my letter that I have not uttered in public again and again. There was no plot to sell out, no offer to support either yourself or the party you represent. As an independent man I have spoken my sentiments without fear. . . . "Let the colored man think act and vote for himself." The garbled extracts in the *Enquirer* of yesterday do me great injustice. . . . And now sir, I most respectfully request you to furnish a *true copy* of my letter to the press. . . . And if you fail to make it public, *just as I wrote it*, you must be responsible for the reflections you have already cast upon my character.[13]

In a letter to the editor of the *Commercial*, Williams observed that "the *Enquirer* is attacking me again. It maintains its hard earned reputa-

tion of perverting the truth." Then Williams proceeded to state to the
Commercial and its readers, whose confidence he hoped to retain, what
he had said to Bishop and the *Enquirer.* He insisted that he would
continue to maintain his independence, even if it meant criticizing the
Republican party. "I have been working for the Republican party and
my race for fourteen years, and in all this time I have been true. I have
had sense enough to see its mistakes and courage to say so without
wincing." Whatever he said or did was in the interest of his people and
"the good old Republican party."[14]

In Cincinnati and in various parts of the state, Williams remained
busy with his speaking engagements. Already regarded as one of the
ablest and most eloquent spokesmen for the Republican party, he was in
great demand and usually drew large crowds.[15] When he spoke at St.
Mary's, Ohio, on September 25, an "immense gathering" listened to
him for two hours on "The Fruits of Emancipation." His oration was
described as "masterly, convincing and scholarly, showing rare culture
and superior mind. All who attended were astonished that a colored
man could be so highly educated . . . and many said if Hamilton County
sent Mr. Williams to its Legislature she need not be ashamed of her
Representative. As the Committee said after his nomination that if the
Democrats pitched into the negro, to turn Mr. Williams loose and he
would vindicate his race."[16]

In the final two weeks before the election on October 9, Williams
confined his activities to Hamilton County. On September 28 he spoke
to a large and enthusiastic crowd on the corner of Sixth and Broadway in
Cincinnati. Some thought that the Kentucky Negro Democrat, J. Allen
Ross, would appear and demand equal time since Williams had earlier
rejected his invitation to debate. Ross did not appear; so Williams had
the entire evening to himself and made good use of his "illustrative
anecdotes and touches of sarcasm" as he spoke of the claims and history
of the two parties.[17] The following evening he spoke at Northwestern
Hall, in the Twenty-third Ward, sharing the platform with Benjamin
Butterworth, a distinguished lawyer who would be elected to Congress
the following year, and Ferdinand Vogeler. Three days before the
election Williams made one of his stirring speeches at a Republican
barbecue and rally, after which the audience "went for the roasted ox
and its two companions."[18]

Certain elements in the city—and even in the black community and
in the local Republican party—simply could not accept the fact that a
Negro had become as prominent as Williams. There was a rumor that
many black voters would "scratch" Williams's name because they re-
sented "his prominence as a representative of the colored element."

The *Commercial* ridiculed this attitude, insisting that if elected, Williams would be a credit to his race.[19] There was also a rumor that many white Republicans could not bring themselves to vote for Williams because of his color. The *Enquirer* advised Negroes to visit the German wards, where they would discover that the "professions of love for the down-trodden have been but mere words."[20] Indeed, "An Enthusiastic Colored Republican" confirmed the *Enquirer's* claim. "On visiting the halls and gardens over the 'Rhine,'" he said, "it is nothing uncommon to hear German Republican voters boldly assert they will not vote for a colored man." He added that while Negro Republicans were working zealously for the entire ticket, some white candidates made it clear that they were not working for Williams. He warned the whites that many blacks would wait until the afternoon to vote, and if the whites attempted to defeat Williams, "the guillotine will not fall on him alone."[21]

On Tuesday, October 9, the guillotine fell on all Hamilton County Republican candidates for the legislature. Doubtless the Socialist Labor or Workingmen's party, snaring 20 percent of the vote, hurt the Republicans, who received only 33 percent. The Democrats, with 47 percent, elected all nine of their candidates. There can be no doubt that some Republicans did scratch Williams's name, for with 15,811 votes he ran more than 1,700 votes behind the next lowest vote-getter among the Republicans.[22] Even in his betrayal by fellow Republicans, Williams might derive some consolation from the fact that Republicans in Cincinnati did not perform as shabbily as those in Cleveland. John P. Green, a prominent Negro citizen and former justice of the peace, had been nominated for the legislature by the Cuyahoga County Republicans. The morning after the election, Green was declared elected by a majority of 62 over his nearest opponent, a Democrat. In a recount two days later, 84 of Green's votes were thrown out because the officials could not determine if they were intended for John P. Green or F. W. Green, a Democrat. The victorious white Republican candidates waged no fight for Green and went to the legislature with only one Democratic member of the delegation—the one who defeated Green, the only black candidate.[23]

The election over, Williams left town for awhile. Shortly after his return, the following brief statement appeared in the press: "Rev. George W. Williams will occupy his pulpit just as though nothing had happened in the way of an election."[24] Williams also continued to write his column for the *Commercial*, although there were weeks, even months, during 1877 and 1878 when the column did not appear. There were, moreover, various civic and social activities, such as the Young People's Improvement Circle, the Cincinnati Literary Club, and the orphan asylum. The death on September 16 of Levi Coffin, widely regarded as the "president" of the Underground Railroad, claimed some of Williams's attention following the election. At a meeting called to decide how the black community should be represented at Coffin's funeral, Williams was appointed chairman of a committee to consider some appropriate permanent recognition of Coffin.[25] On October 29 another meeting, this one convened by Williams, adopted a series of resolutions calling for the erection of a monument in honor of Coffin, "one of the bravest, most self-sacrificing, and useful anti-slavery men in the west."[26] It is not known what came of the project. Williams also gave his time to other matters, such as a new Soldiers and Sailors Memorial Association.

But Williams was restless again. The church no longer satisfied him. He still had his eye on a federal appointment, and even in defeat he had served the Republican party well. He was waiting for a message from Washington.

On December 1, 1877, after twenty-two months of service, Williams resigned his pastorate of the Union Baptist Church.[27] Apparently there was no serious dissension in the church, particularly regarding the pastor, for Williams would continue to participate in various activities at Union Baptist. But he would no longer be under the constraints imposed by the pastoral duties of preaching on Sundays, conducting a variety of programs during the week, and ministering to the needs of several hundred communicants. He was now free to lecture, to serve the party in other parts of the state and the nation, and to travel whenever and wherever he pleased. Already a certain wanderlust had begun to seduce Williams, and soon he would yield to it with no sense of obligation to anyone save himself.

Two major projects now began to claim a good deal of Williams's time. One was a proposed newspaper, and the other was the study of law. Williams's experience with *The Commoner* led him to appreciate the power of the press and to a desire to wield that power personally. It will be recalled that in the summer of 1877 he discussed the possibility of launching a newspaper in Cincinnati with several local citizens, including R. A. Bishop, then successfully running for governor. Shortly after he resigned the pastorate, he returned to his objective of editing another paper; and in February his plans had reached the stage where the local press took notice of them. The *Commercial* indicated that Williams would begin publication "about the first of March of a weekly journal devoted especially to the interests of the colored people."[28] Williams's paper has been referred to as the *Western Review* and the *Southwestern Review*.[29] John J. Crittenden McKinley of Louisville was described in one place as "the Kentucky mouthpiece" of Williams's Cincinnati newspaper.[30] The *Southwestern Review* was published for thirteen or fourteen weeks and then folded. No copies are in any public repository.

Williams had doubtless admired lawyers he had met, such as Benjamin Butterworth and Ferdinand Vogeler, and especially the power they wielded and the financial success they enjoyed. At some point in 1877 he became acquainted with Cincinnait's outstanding lawyer, Alphonso Taft, who had returned to Cincinnati from Washington, where he had served in President Grant's cabinet as secretary of war and attorney general. Taft, who combined the successful career of a lawyer with that of a politician and public servant, must have been an ideal model for Williams. Taft seemed willing to do what he could to assist an ambitious young man who was black, a Republican, and obviously very able. There was only one black in Cincinnati with legal training, William Parham, but as superintendent of the city's black schools he was not actively engaged in the practice of law. Taft was willing to take Williams into his office; and in January 1878 he began the study of law in the offices of Taft and Lloyd, hoping to become Cincinnati's premier black member of the bar.[31]

With a lull in political activity, from which Williams received his expenses and perhaps some income, and with his resignation from Union Baptist Church, Williams once more had to confront the grim task of providing for himself and his family. Happily his law tutor had good connections. Taft had long been active in railroad development, and in 1871, as a Superior Court judge, he had upheld the constitutionality of a law by which the city of Cincinnati issued two million dollars in bonds to complete the Cincinnati Southern Railway.[32] Early in 1878, undoubtedly through Taft's recommendations, Williams obtained a job in the auditor's office as secretary of the two-million-dollar fund to build the railroad.[33] It is not clear what his duties were, but to make one's living as a white-collar employee of a major enterprise in the world of transportation must have been gratifying to a man of his ambition and vanity.

The railway was constantly in need of additional funds for construction. In April 1878, the Ohio legislature passed the sixth supplementary act authorizing the city to issue bonds for another two million dollars, provided the qualified voters of Cincinnati ratified it. The sentiment against ratification was fairly strong because some citizens believed the funds were more urgently needed elsewhere.[34]

A few days before the voting, Williams took a trip on the railway. He then turned his public relations talents to a glowing account in the

Commercial for the benefit of those who were not acquainted with this "gigantic enterprise, the destiny of which will be affected by the popular vote on Friday next." After travelling one hundred miles south to the High Bridge on the Kentucky River, Williams pronounced the Cincinnati Southern Railway one of the finest in the country. The grades were numerous and difficult, but gradual, only sixty feet to the mile, "a very great saving to the city." The curves were frequent and sharp, the "most beautiful" that Williams had ever seen—much better than those on the Pennsylvania Central, Boston and Albany, and many other roads. It was in "quite a good state of repair," while the tunnels were "among the finest in the country." As for the bridges, "for grace, strength, durability, length and height, they rank among the best bridges in the world."[35] Despite Williams's superlatives, however, the bond issue lost by a narrow margin of 11,237 to 11,456.[36]

Williams's duties at the Cincinnati Southern Railway and his legal studies did not prevent his remaining active in Republican politics. Indeed, his mentor, Judge Taft, and his superiors at the railway office, most of whom were Republicans, may well have encouraged him. On occasion he could be quite useful. In March 1878, Williams was elected from the first precinct of the Eighteenth Ward as a delegate to the city Republican convention at the end of the month.[37] Williams served on the committee on resolutions and worked behind the scenes on slatemaking. When Alphonso Taft's name was presented for judge of the Superior Court, it was suggested that he was not interested. At that point Williams "mounted a chair, and said that he had learned that, although Mr. Taft was not seeking a nomination, yet if placed on the ticket he would make the race." Whether or not Williams had any privileged information, he could hardly err in promoting Judge Taft's name.[38]

As it turned out, Williams was wrong about Taft's willingness to run, but it was a mistake that benefited him. He was appointed to a committee to inform Taft that the convention had nominated him. After receiving the committee, Taft sent a letter to the convention expressing appreciation for the honor but declining because of the many obligations to which he was committed.[39] One thing he saw, however, was that his protégé was not only active but influential in Republican party circles.

In June, Williams attended the Republican state convention at the Cincinnati Music Hall as a delegate from Hamilton County. Among the other Negro delegates were Cleveland's John P. Green, who had run unsuccessfully for the legislature the previous year, and the venerable James Poindexter of Columbus, one of the vice-presidents of the convention. Williams attracted the most attention, however, by making

himself available to the press and by speaking on the floor of the
convention. He told the *Enquirer* that his thorough canvass of the
delegates led him to believe that, instead of a specific endorsement of
President Hayes's Southern policy and his program for civil service
reform, there would be a resolution declaring his "title to the Presidency good and sufficient."[40] On the convention floor Williams
seconded the name of Judge William White for reelection to the state
supreme court. The Democratic press made much of the point that
White was "the only Judge who had ever remanded a negro to slavery
from an Ohio bench." In his speech Williams took no notice of that.
Instead, he praised the Republican Party and declared that it was
necessary to have members of the judiciary who would protect the
Amendments that Republicans had added to the Constitution. He
believed that Judge White was such a man.[41]

By this time Williams had risen to the point where the party was
willing to reward him in some modest way. Indeed, he obtained an
audience with the president early in August. Within a few days, Amor
Smith, Jr., Collector of Internal Revenue for Cincinnati, offered Williams a job as Internal Revenue storekeeper. This placed Williams in a
dilemma, which he described thus to President Hayes:

> I have had already so many earnest calls to render the party Service
> that I am halting between two opinions—I need the position but
> want to Stump the State. If arrangements could be made by the
> National Committee at Washington to pay me $30.00 per week and
> send me where I could do the most good I would cheerfully forego
> the pleasure and profit of a Federal office until after the fall elec-
> tion. I have a truly missionary spirit. I feel that the harvest is truly
> great but the labourers are few. I think I appreciate the political
> situation in this and in other States, and am willing to add my Small
> influence to the forces at work for the consummation of a glorious
> victory in October.[42]

There is no record of a reply from the president, and, in the absence
of any assurance from the Republican National Committee that it would
add him to its payroll, Williams went to work for the Revenue Service on
September 2, 1878.[43] The new employment seems not to have slowed
down his political activities. Three days after writing the president that
he was anxious to serve the party, Williams was serving on the resolutions and credentials committees of the party's district and county
conventions.[44] Clearly, politics was on his mind much more than his new
job. He wrote his friend John P. Green of Cleveland that he was very

busy preparing his campaign speech. He proposed that Green should have the local authorities invite him to Cleveland, and Williams would, in turn, arrange to have Green come to Cincinnati.[45]

Apparently Green acted on Williams's suggestion, for a week after he had joined the Revenue Service he was in Cleveland to deliver a major address. Williams insisted that he had no interest in digging up the past, but if the leaders of the Democratic Party "refused to accept the olive branch of peace and fraternity, who shall blame me for meeting those issues with the severity of candor and with that frankness and fairness born of honest and intelligent convictions." Williams then described the South as unrepentant, showing "from first to the last, a sulky, insubordinate, rebellious and cruel spirit." The South's interest was not in a perfect union but in a doctrine of nullification that counseled it to disregard the Reconstruction Amendments. And the Democratic party thrived on this disregard for the Constitution and the rights of the people. That was why the party did not deserve the confidence or support of the electorate.[46]

Williams maintained a steady pace until the elections in October. On September 19 he delivered an "eloquent address" to a large audience in Washington Court House. On the following day he was at Circleville, where he "opened up" the Republican campaign.[47] For the final week of the campaign he was in the Cincinnati area, speaking to more than fifteen hundred at a meeting in the Sixth Ward on the first day of October. Other engagements were at Camp Dennison, Avondale, and in the Tenth Ward.[48]

Before the election, Williams had predicted a Republican sweep. His party was sound on the money question, he thought; and since the people wanted a sound monetary policy, they would turn to the Republicans. He was certain that the people of the First District would send Benjamin Butterworth to Congress and General Thomas L. Young would win the Second District.[49] He was correct in both cases. Indeed the results were such a resounding victory for the Republicans that Williams was overcome with joy. He immediately dispatched a telegram to the president saying, "My prediction to you at Dayton is fulfilled."[50] A few days later he again expressed his delight to the president:

> The result in Ohio was all that friends of your Administration could hope for. We are sure that the good people of this State are not in favor of inflation or repudiation; and besides crushing the rag baby, we have annihilated the "side-show" parties and have an open field in which to fight straight through to 1880.

New York, Pennsylvania, Illinois, and Michigan—as well as
Massachusetts, will be aided by our victory. "Let us have peace"
within our party and turning our guns upon the old enemy, victory
in 1880 is sure.[51]

He was understandably less restrained in sharing his delight with his
political comrade, John P. Green. "We have elected the entire Republican ticket with the exception of one Magistrate! Shake Old fellow; [here
were sketched two open hands approaching each other for a shake], and
how is that for high? Republicans jubilant, and Democrats correspondingly despondent." Williams enclosed an order for $18, informing
Green that he had kept $2.00 and wondered if it was satisfactory. This
was apparently in connection with Green's appearance in Cincinnati.
Williams said he had secured this amount from the party secretary, who
could get it from the committee. He was determined that they should
not "beat" his friend Green.[52] The glow of victory was apparent in
everything Williams said; and even persons more modest than he would
have claimed at least some of the credit for putting the Republicans over
the top.

Although there was much to do merely to support a young family and
to make up for the salary and gratuities he no longer received from the
church, Williams was never far from the political arena within the next
few years. He continued to pursue his legal studies in Judge Taft's office;
and shortly after the elections in 1878, he decided to expand his efforts
in that area. One of Cinncinnati's outstanding lawyers was George
Hoadly, of the firm of Hoadly, Jackson, and Johnson, who had been a
professor at the Cincinnati Law School since 1864. Williams could not
have liked Hoadly's politics. As a young man the lawyer was a Democrat, but became a Republican during the sectional crisis, then a Liberal
Republican in 1872, and again a Democrat in 1876. But Williams
admired Hoadly's well-known legal scholarship and wondered how he
could benefit from it. He enlisted the aid of Judge Taft, from whom he
requested a letter of introduction to Hoadly. "State to him," Williams
suggested, "that I am a law student in your office, a Federal officer, and
can only get in to his evening lectures and therefore crave that
privilege."[53] There can be little doubt that Taft complied, for later
Williams was able to assert that he had attended the Hoadly lectures at
the Cincinnati Law School.[54]

Williams seemed unable to escape the feeling that the Republican
party was merely using him to attract blacks to the support of its ticket
with no serious intention of rewarding him with anything as important as
an elective office. He told a reporter from the *Enquirer* that the Repub-

licans feared that he would demand a place on the ticket in 1879; and that is why they were promoting another Negro stalwart, Robert Harland, for county clerk. They would reject Williams because of Harlan's candidacy and then persuade Harlan to withdraw because he could not win. "After having been wounded four times in the war and giving years of faithful service to the party, I was finally rewarded with a store-keepership. However, I intend to resign in a few months and begin the practice of law." He had not yet passed the bar, but expected to go to Columbus shortly "and be passed by the Supreme Court."[55]

Regardless of his feeling about the Republican party's exploiting him, Williams had not given up hope of using it for his own ends. One can assume that at the time of his defeat for the legislature in 1877 Williams was determined to run again. He talked like a candidate the following year; and during the 1879 spring campaign for city offices he worked like a candidate. He wrote letters to the editor denouncing the Democrats and praising the Republicans; and he pleaded with the Negro voters not to touch a Democratic ticket "for love or money, for it is already stained with the blood of the colored man."[56] A local white Democrat called Williams's charge "as mendacious and brazen a statement as ever was made."[57]

The day before the election, Williams was at it again, admonishing Republicans not to be too optimistic, for the "enemy is subtle and adroit and will not hesitate to use any means that will contribute to the success of their ticket." He was especially disturbed over the claim of the Democrats that one of their candidates, Judge M. F. Wilson, had earned the support of blacks because he had often "released colored criminals" and "winked at their public transgressions." Williams argued that if they were guilty of the crimes, then Judge Wilson was wrong in allowing them to go free. His heart ached, he declared, at the very thought that any of his people would vote for a single man on the Democratic ticket.[58]

Williams was delighted with the results of the election. "Republicans of Cincinnati, we have met the enemy and they are ours," he told a cheering crowd gathered to serenade Charles Jacob, the mayor-elect. "We have routed the enemy, horse, foot, and dragoons; and this is the precursor of the victory in Ohio next fall and the victory in 1880."[59] Immediately Williams dispatched a lengthy letter to the *Commercial* expressing delight with the Republican victory and praising Negroes for their support of the party. He vigorously denied the claim of one newspaper that Negroes had voted the Democratic ticket in considerable numbers. White Republicans who had watched the polls supported his contention. Indeed, several signed a statement that in the Eighteenth Ward the black voters were faithful, while the assistant district attorney certified that in the Sixth Ward "there were not more than fifteen colored votes cast against us. . . . Let the white Republicans of Cincinnati treat the true colored voter with that measure of respect that his vote and character claim, and those who are faithless and mercenary with the contempt they so richly merit."[60]

Williams maintained the pace that had kept his name before the public for months—a pace he intended to maintain until he had once again secured nomination for the legislature. In late May he attended the Republican state convention. Seconding the nomination of Alphonso Taft for governor, he gave the audience a sample of his political oratory:

> Representing, as I do, an element in the Republican party of this State and in this Nation, composed of true and loyal men, loyal during the dark days of slavery to the principles of anti-slavery, loyal to the Federal army, . . . a race of men who were loyal even to the shedding of their blood, . . . representing this class of people, I stand here to-day . . . on . . . behalf of a large number of colored voters in this Commonwealth, to second . . . the nomination of . . . that distinguished jurist, that liberal-hearted Christian man, Judge Taft, the only white man in the Cabinet of any President during the last eighteen years who had the manhood, the temerity and humanity to exact . . . the powers of the Constitution of the United States, to protect the black man in the exercise of his constitutional rights (cheers). Give us our standard-bearer in this fight Alphonso Taft, and every black man from the Ohio River to Lake Erie will give you a solid and united voice (applause).[61]

Taft was not nominated. Nonetheless, Williams had served his mentor well as well as himself.

By late spring of 1879 it was generally conceded that Williams would again seek a legislative seat in the fall elections. One of the obstacles was that several politicians, white and black, were promoting Robert Harlan, a fast-talking, high-living Negro Republican, for the post of county clerk. Many held the view that one black on the ticket was quite enough. Thus, Williams *and* Harlan could hardly both be slated, although they were running for different offices.[62] The Democratic *Enquirer* accused the Republicans of plotting to keep both Williams and Harlan off the ticket. The editor cautioned Negro voters that the Republican party was interested only in their votes while seeing to it that they shared in "none of its emoluments."[63]

Even some blacks did not think it possible for two of their race to be on the Republican ticket and were willing to concentrate on one office that seemed to be within their reach. On June 26, some three hundred of them met at Zion Church to consider the matter. The speakers— Miles W. Handy, William Taylor, and others—declared that a place on the legislative ticket was out of the question and that they should press for Harlan to be nominated for county clerk. An inquiring reporter learned from several in attendance that Harlan—although he liked the horses, spent much time at the Saratoga race track, and "was an old sinner"—was popular and would make a good race. Many expressed a dislike for Williams. He was smart, they admitted, but "he knew too well himself that he was a smart man. He appeared to be under the impression that he had been the entire United States army at one time. . . . He was coming too fast as a champion of the colored man. . . . He was too aristocratic to suit them."[64] Some felt, moreover, that he was too much the favorite of certain white men.[65]

It was time for Williams to become more active in his own behalf, lest his silence be interpreted as a surrender to the Harlan forces. He insisted that the meeting of June 26 had more Williams than Harlan supporters and that only after the meeting broke up were the "few" Harlan supporters able to reconvene and express their sentiments.[66] This account was, in turn, bitterly disputed by a Harlan man, Robert V. Troy, who said in a letter to the *Commercial* that Williams had not been present and had been misinformed by "some of his henchmen, who were few and far between." Troy reminded the readers of the *Commercial* that Williams had been severely critical of the party in 1876, had offered to "sell out" to Bishop in 1877, and had been defeated "pretty badly" when he ran for the legislature that same year. By this time it was conceded that Williams and Harlan were opponents for one nomination; and Troy believed that Harlan would poll "a larger vote any day than Mr. Williams."[67]

The Williams candidacy was the most discussed political subject in Hamilton County in the summer of 1879. Newspapers interviewed Williams as well as voters on both sides. There were numerous letters to editors in which citizens expressed their views. There were mass meetings held by Harlan and Williams followers respectively, with opposing groups attempting to infiltrate and capture the meeting of the other group. To one such meeting—called by Harlan—Williams sent a letter, which his supporters sought to have read. Harlan objected on the ground that this was *his* meeting and his interests should be attended to first. The Williams supporters said there was nothing in the letter "in the least prejudicial to the interests of Colonel Harlan," and their point was carried by a vote.

The Williams letter was cordial and gracious, pledging to support Harlan for the county clerkship, and soliciting Harlan's support for his legislative race. If he was defeated for the nomination, Williams promised to "stump the county" for Harlan and the entire ticket. He hoped Harlan would be equally magnanimous if he failed to get the clerkship nomination. One of the Williams men called for the appointment of a resolutions committee that presumably would endorse Williams for the legislature and Harlan for the clerkship. Harlan objected, for after all he had hired the hall and paid the bond for a meeting in his interests and saw no reason why the meeting should consider other matters. A stormy debate followed, and the meeting broke up "in a loud dispute as to who had been endorsed."[68]

When the Republicans of Hamilton County met on Monday, July 28, to nominate candidates for office, speculation persisted as to what would happen to Negro aspirants. Democrats confidently predicted that the whites would snub their black colleagues. Some Republicans thought such predictions not altogether inaccurate. Harlan was unlikely to receive serious consideration for the county clerkship. The real problem seemed to be the disposition of Williams, and it would be understandable if he was lost among some eighty legislative aspirants named on the first ballot. Charles W. Bell, who had nominated Williams at the 1877 convention, was one of the blacks who had been named. He now rose to withdraw his name and then violated the rules of the convention by asking his friends to support Robert Harlan, "a man who will command the solid vote of the colored people, and a man whose integrity cannot be questioned by his political opponents." Another delegate, S. S. Davis, moved that the convention drop the names of all who did not receive one hundred votes on the first ballot. After some debate and over the strenuous objections of some delegates, the motion carried.

On the first ballot, which took more than four hours, many candidates received fewer than a half-dozen votes. The two Negro candidates, Harlan with 144 votes and Williams with 334, survived the first round. It was clear, however, that Williams was the more formidable candidate. Delegate Frank G. Jobson of the Twenty-third Ward moved to drop every person who had received less than 150 votes. Among those who objected was Robert Harlan, who called for a division rather than a voice vote on his motion to lay Jobson's motion on the table. Harlan lost that skirmish, and thus his fight for the nomination ended. On the second ballot, Williams received 419 votes, the lowest number of the nine candidates nominated.[69] On the ticket with him would be L. M. Dayton, Charles C. Davis, Frank Kirchner, Joseph E. Heart, Peter F. Stryker, D. Gano Ray, William H. Hill, and Lewis Voight.

In the face of considerable opposition in the black community and discomfort on the part of many whites, Williams's nomination for the legislature was a signal victory. It was of greater significance than his nomination two years earlier, for then the Republicans had virtually no hope of victory. By 1879 their chances were at least even, and, furthermore, Williams had become more widely known. For the white delegates to place a black on the ticket in 1879 suggests that they recognized the political and oratorical skills of George Washington Williams as an asset and that they were willing to run the risk in order to prove their own commitment to political equality. They had yet to see if they could convince the party's rank and file of the wisdom of their choice.

On the Campaign Trail

The nomination of Williams by the Hamilton County Republican convention was not the occasion for universal rejoicing in either the white or the black community. No sooner had the convention adjourned than various citizens began to express misgivings about the effect of his name on the ticket, and the Democrats resumed their campaign of harassment. On July 30, 1879, an editorial in the Democratic *Enquirer* asserted that there was a "well-defined kick among the Republican managers against WILLIAMS being allowed to remain on the ticket. The only charge they have against MR. WILLIAMS is that he is a 'nigger.' "[1] The editor continued to heckle the Republicans and on the following day said that Williams was "as big a man in brain as Ben Eggleston, but then he is black, and that is what bothers the Republicans."[2] There was also a rumor that Williams would be offered the Haitian mission if he could be persuaded to resign his place on the ticket. "In other words," the *Enquirer* editor asked, "is President Hayes offering diplomatic appointments to prevent ambitious colored men from breaking into our State Legislatures?"[3] The *Enquirer* baited Williams and the Republicans apparently to distract voters from the fact that the Democrats had not even considered the nomination of a black for the legislature.

No doubt there was some unhappiness in the black community, and a part of the white daily press seemed anxious to make the most of it. The Cincinnati *Daily Gazette* said, "If there are George W. Williams colored Republicans hereabouts they should come to the front. The anti-Williams colored Republicans seem to be numerous."[4] Even the Columbus *Dispatch* made some observations on the subject, declaring that "although our colored friend and brother is represented on the Hamilton County Republican ticket, the nomination does not seem to be satisfactory to all the voters of that race." The paper claimed that

Colonel Bob Harlan, the defeated black candidate, had said that Williams must go. It then hauled out charges previously leveled at Williams, citing the letter Williams was alleged to have written to Governor Bishop "offering to sell out to the Democrats," and his 1876 speech at Yellow Springs in which he characterized the Republican party as "a gang of thieves."[5]

The Columbus paper appeared to be getting its information from those sources in Cincinnati, including the *Gazette*, that were opposed to Williams's candidacy. Things were not quite as bad as the opposition claimed or hoped. On August 2, the day on which Harlan left for his regular visit to Saratoga, Harlan and Williams met "in the presence of other prominent colored Republicans and shook hands in reconciliation, Colonel Harlan withdrawing his opposition. . . . Everything is lovely."[6] Meanwhile, Negro voters began to pledge their support to Williams. On August 4 they held an "enthusiastic ratification meeting" at a church in the Second Ward, endorsing the action of the county convention and pledging to support the entire ticket.[7] Another ratification meeting, a few days later in Hibernia Hall, was memorable not only because it endorsed the entire Republican slate but also because of the important personages present. Peter Clark, who had left the Socialist party to return to the Republican ranks, presided and renewed his allegiance to the party.[8] He warned his listeners of the dangers of flirting with the Democratic party in places such as Cincinnati. "As to whether the colored men have not Democratic friends is not to be studied in Ohio. . . . Go South to study Democracy. Go to Congress. The record is written in blood. . . . Go to the bulldozing districts and study Democracy, and then vote the Democratic ticket if you dare." Among the other speakers were Samuel J. Lewis, who called the meeting to order, George H. Jackson, chairman of the Committee on Resolutions, and Miles W. Handy, who urged the voters "to stand not only by Captain Williams but by the whole Republican ticket."[9]

The high point of the evening was an address by the county's black nominee for the state legislature. Following "continued calls . . . he came forward and was enthusiastically greeted." After declaring himself a true Republican and urging everyone to vote the "whole Republican ticket," Williams answered the charges that he had not been a good Republican and was hurting the ticket because of his race. He brushed the latter charge aside by saying, "If there are votes enough in the Republican party to elect eight Representatives, there are enough to elect nine Representatives." On the more serious charge, his alleged transaction with Governor Bishop, Williams denied any wrongdoing. He said that Bishop himself had offered to have the *Enquirer* publish his

Dayton speech on emancipation when Halstead at the *Commercial* found it too long. He had asked Bishop to aid him in starting a newspaper "as I would have asked any friend who was able to assist me."

> But the letter I wrote was no offer to support him or any person on the Democratic ticket. The matter was brought up in the campaign of 1877, and I called upon Governor Bishop to publish my letter. He gave it to the *Times*—just as I had written it—a few brief sentences, that had no reference to selling myself or my party. (cheers) And now I say once and for all time that the man who says I offered to sell out is a liar, and the truth isn't in him. (Loud and long cheers, and cries of "bully.")[10]

Williams also referred to the charge that he ought not to run because two years earlier he paid $150 as a party assessment and then drew on the money for speeches. That was a lie, he declared; the money went "to pay men who worked well and hard at the polls."[11] He had given thought to the suggestion that he withdraw from the ticket and had concluded "If I have the support of the colored people I'll stick. (Cries of 'Stick. We will support you!') But I am too good a Republican to injure my party (cheers)." He declared that if there was a colored man in Hamilton County stronger than he was, "name him and I'll get off the ticket and make a hundred speeches to elect him. (Loud applause)" Thanking his listeners for their "magnificent reception," he urged them to support the party that had stood by the race and made it possible for a colored man to be on the Republican ticket—a party that would, "if united, do more—send him to the Legislature in October."[12]

Williams remained uneasy about white support, however. The local press, especially the *Gazette*, was hostile to him, and the *Enquirer* was not above using him to embarrass its journalistic rivals. Consequently, on August 11 he called a group of white leaders to meet with him at the Lincoln Club. Among those who came were "Deacon" Richard Smith, editor of the *Gazette*, who had urged Williams's withdrawal; General Andrew Hickenlooper, president of the Cincinnati Gas-Light and Coke Company; Amor Smith, for whom Williams worked in the Internal Revenue office; and more than a dozen others "prominent in the counsels of the party . . . with three or four colored men." Williams told them he sought their advice regarding his candidacy, since some claimed he had not brought strength to the ticket.

"Then there was an experience meeting and love feast," the *Commercial* reported. Smith stated the objections to Williams; a man named Wiltsee reported that letters from black citizens of Ohio and communications from Washington, D.C., were favorable to Williams. General Hickenlooper took strong ground in favor of keeping Williams on the ticket and made a motion to that effect, which was carried unanimously, "pledging him the heartiest support of all present."[13]

Rumors that he would withdraw persisted, however. Three days after the Lincoln Club meeting, Richard Smith printed a statement in the *Gazette* that Williams had decided to withdraw in order to canvass the state for the Republican ticket.[14] To put down the rumors once and for all, Williams made his position clear in a letter to the *Gazette*:

> It is the desire of a large majority of the Republican party in this county that I should run. I owe it to my people, to courage, and common sense to make a brave fight for the Legislature. If I meet with no organized opposition in my own party I am confident of my election. No considerations, financial or otherwise, can alter my decision.[15]

After this definitive pronouncement, journalists such as Smith sought to cover their flanks. "It may as well be understood," the *Gazette* observed, "that the opposition to Mr. WILLIAMS is not on account of his color, and that it is not confined to white people; nor is it organized, nor will it be. It is such opposition as any candidate, white or black, might be expected to meet under like circumstances, and is scattering; but there is more of it we apprehend, than there was two years ago when Mr. WILLIAMS fell largely behind the ticket."[16] The *Commercial* was considerably less equivocal about Williams's determination to stick: "Why shouldn't he? He has more brains than nine-tenths of the Representatives sent to Columbus."[17]

The continuing veiled threats that white Republicans would scratch Williams if he remained on the ticket and dark hints that he did not enjoy the support of the black community must have been extremely trying to Williams. Yet he was the most active nominee on the Republican ticket, the *Commercial* for August 22 claimed, and made "more speeches than all the rest of the candidates for the Legislature." In the three weeks following his nomination he appeared in two-thirds of the wards of the city and "made friends wherever he . . . presented himself."

Williams sustained a serious blow in the black community when the respected leader Miles W. Handy made a blistering attack on him in a letter to the *Gazette*. Handy had been at the unity meeting on August 8 and had urged support of Williams and the entire Republican ticket. It appeared that Smith's constant nagging was finally having the desired result. There was, indeed, some disaffection in the black community, as the editor had insisted all along. It must have given Smith much satisfaction to reveal this unhappiness with the Williams candidacy through Handy's letter. Handy predicted that Williams's ungovernable passion for office would "cause history to chronicle another inglorious defeat, if not of the party, certainly of him." He expressed amazement that the convention would accept Williams "on any terms whatever, in view of the damaging letters that have appeared in your issue relative to him, and the many other accusations that have been alleged concerning him, not to say anything of the unanimous opposition . . . against him by the people of color before, during, and I might as well add after the convention."

Handy suggested that the outcome of the convention had been prearranged in order to force a "played out and inefficient candidate to be unmercifully slaughtered at the polls by the votes of honest men. . . . If Geo. W. Williams is defeated—and there is no doubt but that he will be—no one will be to blame but those that gave the boom . . . but when October comes he will be quietly and peacefully laid aside in his political grave until resurrection day." Handy concluded by recalling the alleged acts of Williams in attacking the Republican party in 1876, in seeking to form an alliance with the Democrat R. M. Bishop, and in fraudulently seeking financial support for a newspaper.[18]

Smith could not have been more pleased had he written the Handy letter himself. Indeed, it is strikingly similar to pieces in the *Gazette* he had been writing for weeks about Williams. While Handy had not been among the rabid supporters of Williams, he had not openly opposed him and as a loyal party member, had occasionally supported him. There were those in the black community, moreover, who felt that Williams was a bit "precious," that he thought too much of himself, and that he was more interested in furthering his own cause than the cause of his people. Williams, some contended, "had been overrated by the white people of this city," and had offended many by leaving the ministry to enter politics. "The colored people did not want so much of a champion."[19] Under such circumstances, it was not difficult to find some one willing to step out and attack Williams.

While Smith of the *Gazette* and his friend Handy sought to convey the impression that the white and black communities were opposed to the Williams candidacy, the young minister-politician had his own supporters in the press and in the community. The *Commercial* called for an end to the discussion. "He is an educated man, a soldier and orator, and if the stupid effort to crowd him off the ticket should succeed, the effect would be disastrous. . . . He is worthy of better

treatment than he has received, and if elected to the Legislature, as we
thoroughly believe he will be, he will give a good account of himself."[20]
The trustees of Union Baptist Church vehemently objected to the
rumors that Williams had been unfair in his dealings with the church
during his pastorate. They wrote to the editor of the *Commercial*, "We
take pleasure in saying that the relations existing between Mr. Williams
and the church were pleasant during the two years he was our pastor,
and they terminated pleasantly." They denied the charge that he borrowed money from members of the church, stating instead that "the
church being in debt we borrowed to pay him, but have paid every man
and every cent long ago and have the receipts in full."[21]

The *Commercial* sent a reporter out to interview certain black voters
to ascertain their attitude toward Williams. Peter Clark asserted that the
opposition to Williams had dwindled to the point that the members that
would scratch him could "be counted on the fingers." George H.
Jackson, a veteran teacher and future lawyer, took to task the "Friend of
Mr. Williams" who in an open letter had called on Williams to "leave the
ticket and give up his own selfish ambition."[22] L. D. Easton, the first
assistant at Gaines High School, said that he knew of but one man who
refused to give Williams his vote. In his travels to other cities—Dayton,
Columbus, Zanesville, Toledo, and Cleveland—Easton said that he
found no one who did not believe that Williams should remain on the
ticket. Robert G. Ball, an old citizen, declared himself "a warm supporter of Mr. Williams. . . . He is worthy and competent, . . . intelligent,
industrious, and trustworthy." According to Thomas J. Monroe, a prominent member of the Odd Fellows' Lodge, all Negroes with whom he
conversed said they would support Williams. And so the interviews
went. Of the dozen men interviewed, not one made any unfavorable
comments about Williams.[23]

Toward the end of August, criticism of Williams noticeably subsided.
Even the *Gazette* conceded that Williams was not so bad and, in the
process, praised itself for mentioning things about him that had cleared
the air and unified the black community. It also took credit for bringing
around the Democratic *Enquirer* to see some good in Williams. "Having got matters into this shape and secured the election of Williams by
an overwhelming majority, we can afford to rest on our oars . . . and now,
having discharged our duty, we advise everybody to follow the lead of
the *Commercial*, the colored people, and the *Enquirer*, and send Williams to the Legislature with a boom."[24]

With six weeks left before the election, Williams did not choose to
rest on his oars. Surreptitious opposition could still be flourishing. This
time he would not dissipate his energies, as he had done two years

earlier, by speaking for the party throughout the state. He canceled most of his appointments outside Hamilton County so that he could concentrate on the local campaign. Only Springfield, Ohio, remained on his September schedule.[25] Meanwhile, he covered Cincinnati and Hamilton County quite systematically, speaking in public halls, on fairgrounds, and on street corners.

Williams was a captivating speaker. At a late August meeting in the Fourth Ward, he made "the finest speech that the boys in the ward" had heard in a long time. On the last night of the month he made two speeches, in Cumminsville and in Green Township. He "was received in both places with the most cordial expressions of goodwill; and by his remarkable qualities as a public speaker gets up a boom for the ticket and makes friends for himself."[26] Throughout September he spoke almost daily and often twice a day. Since he seems to have made the same speech at each place, the press did little more than report the size of the crowd and whether he had been well received.

An exception was the verbatim account of Williams's speech in Springfield on September 8. A major feature was the attack on the Democratic party: "The Brigadier Confederate caucus of the present Congress has relegated the country back to that condition of affairs that threatened the National life in 1861." The Democratic party of Ohio sought to plunge the country "into the bottomless and shoreless sea of inflation," he said. It was guilty of other "crimes," including fraudulent elections, while the Republican party was "right on every vital question at issue in this canvass." Williams praised the resumption of specie payments as "timely, honorable, and helpful to all our vast concerns as a country." He warned his listeners that if they were not vigilant, the solid Democratic South would join forces with Democrats in the North and pack the Supreme Court, reexamine and even repeal the Reconstruction Amendments, and "eight hundred thousand colored Republicans will be disfranchised." He concluded with this ringing declaration:

> Let Ohio speak for human rights, for universal manhood suffrage, for fair and honest elections, for economy and purity in public affairs, for honest money and stable government. Let the old Commonwealth speak loud and distinct on the Second Tuesday in October, and the victory that shall crown this canvass will be but the broken rays of the glory that will cover the Republican party in 1880 as a mantle of light.[27]

During the week of September 15, Williams was back on the campaign trail, with speeches in various wards of the city. Saturday the 20th was a big day at the Hamilton county fairgrounds. Among the scheduled speakers was James A. Garfield, the Republican leader in the House of Representatives, who was favored by many to succeed John Sherman in the Senate. By the time General Garfield had concluded his speech, it was growing late and people were beginning to disperse. Williams was next; speaking "very earnestly and effectively," he succeeded in holding the crowd in the amphitheater for the duration of his fifteen-minute talk.[28]

In mid-September a lengthy article appeared in the Washington *Post* by its "correspondent" in Cincinnati, analyzing the dilemmas of Cincinnati voters and pointing out how the candidacy of a lone Negro Republican could change the course of politics in the state. It was reprinted in the Cincinnati *Enquirer*, much to the apparent delight of some locals and to the dismay of others. Discord among Cincinnati Republicans," claimed the writer, was caused by the nomination for the Legislature of "a darky known and hailed in these parts as the Rev. George B. [*sic*] Williams." He recalled the demand by blacks two years earlier for recognition by the Republicans, leading to Williams's first nomination. It did not matter very much in 1877, for there was not much at stake, with no senator to elect and no important legislation pending. "But this year the case is different. Not only will the next Legislature have a Senator to elect, but the duty of redistricting the State for Congressional purposes will devolve upon it. Hence, the party that succeeds . . . this fall will be placed in a position to, by a very little gerrymandering, increase its power in Congress and hold it for the next decade."

The *Post* correspondent claimed that the "weeping and wailing and gnashing of teeth" arose from the realization that the convention had "blundered into the nomination of the 'd--d nigger' who had been so badly beaten before." "Deacon" Smith of the *Gazette* had allegedly told him that the convention had no intention of honoring the "colored brother." But the huge, unwieldy body of about nine hundred delegates "couldn't very well be handled, and it 'went and done and did it before it knew itself what it was about.' " Some delegates, according to the *Post*, believed they were voting for a prominent white lawyer named Williams. Some voted for George W. Williams just to throw a "little taffy in the shape of a complimentary vote to the old African Whale."

Having realized what had happened, the *Post* reported, some made immediate efforts—led by Smith and his *Gazette*—to secure Williams's removal from the ticket. When that failed, there appeared "an able article in the Gazette, written by the Deacon's own hand, charging the Rev. George Williams with nearly all the crimes in the calendar." At this point Murat Halstead, editor of the *Commercial*, "with his banal idiocy

in political matters . . . championed Williams's candidacy and made the
Commercial the organ of the persecuted moke."

As the public rallied to Williams, the fight against him subsided. His
candidacy, nevertheless, could have a far-reaching effect on the election
results. Obviously, many voters would scratch Williams simply by
drawing a line through his name on the printed ballot. "The Republicans
claim they will elect their ticket . . . by 2,000 majority, sure, except
Williams, whom nobody with any practical sense at all expects to be
elected." That was too large, the *Post* reporter thought, and the majority
would probably not be over five hundred. If a sufficient number of
Republicans scratched Williams, it would give Democratic candidates a
chance, the number depending on how people voted who scratched
Williams. Since all the Democrats believed they could beat "that nigger," they would all get as many scratchers as they could. Under the
circumstances, it was conceivable that all Democrats running for the
legislature in Hamilton County could win. "Thus it will be seen the
negro is quite an important element in Ohio politics this year, and the
candidacy of this single one of the race may give the Democrats a United
States Senator, control of the public institutions, and power to redistrict
the State."[29]

This was an extreme, even wild-eyed view of the possibilities in
Cincinnati in the fall of 1879. Even if the very long-shot chances did not
turn out as suggested by the *Post* correspondent, his speculations
pointed up how utterly fearful some Ohio whites were of the exercise of
political power on the part of some blacks. There is no indication of what
Williams thought of the piece, with its insulting references to him.
Halstead's *Commercial* was outraged at the *Post* article's suggestion that
many Republicans would not vote for Williams because of his race. "If
there are any such Republicans," the *Commercial* stormed, "they
should be sold into slavery to the Solid South for they are already in their
hearts and bones the serfs of that section."[30]

In the last days of the campaign, no one in Hamilton County was
more active than Williams, speaking on behalf of the entire Republican
ticket as well as himself. On September 23 he received a warm welcome
at the Twenty-second Ward Club.[31] On the following evening he was
among several speakers in Hopkins Hall, crowded by Republicans. The
Enquirer grudgingly reported that the "mahogany-colored Williams led
off in a half-hour speech that was well received, as a whole, though his
labored panegyric of John Sherman fell flat on the ears of his auditors."[32]
A few days later he spoke before a large and enthusiastic gathering at
Symmes Township. He praised Republican financial policies that had
given the country the "best currency that the world ever saw." He also

referred to the dangers of "scratching," pointing out that one should vote for principles, not men. The reporter said that his speech was well received, "and his audience, many of whom were Democrats, expressed their appreciation by frequent and hearty applause."[33]

On October 3, Williams was the principal speaker at a huge rally at the Wigwam in the First Ward. Long before the meeting began, "there wasn't a seat to be had in the spacious hall, and the outside was almost as crowded as the inside." Williams was followed by Colonel A. E. Jones, who spoke "with power and warmth" for about thirty minutes, urging the people to vote for Williams. Three days before the election the *Commercial* reported that Williams was "only posted for three speeches" that day. It observed that he had made "so energetic a canvas, and shown so much ability in the discussion of the issues of the campaign, that even the Republicans who thought of scratching him on account of race or color are among his most enthusiastic supporters now."[34]

The energy with which Williams took his campaign down to the wire was matched by the determination of many whites to foil his attempt to gain a legislative seat. The *Enquirer* warned Cincinnati blacks that many white Republicans had no intention of voting for Williams. A few days later it declared that the "colored population might as well prepare their nerves for a shock" since the Republican party intended to leave Williams "high and dry. He will feel the cold winds to the measure of about 3,500 majority against his going to Columbus."[35] Even the *Gazette* was disgusted with the *Enquirer's* efforts to frighten the black community and influence the outcome of the election. With obvious reference to the Washington *Post* article, the *Gazette* claimed that letters had been fabricated in Cincinnati and sent "to Democratic papers abroad, and then have been reprinted here, all to this effect." It argued that the purpose was to anger blacks into voting against the Republicans, having become convinced that Republicans would scratch Williams. "We do not believe Republicans are of that stripe. We regret to see our esteemed but credulous and naive contemporary, the Commercial, deceived by this stratagem, and helping it along by crying . . . against Republicans who will not vote for Williams because he is colored."[36]

Despite the *Gazette's* "revelation" of the *Enquirer's* alleged motives, the latter newspaper worked right down to election day, October 14, in the effort to dissuade Republicans from voting for Williams. In a last-minute "scoop" it reported that a large number of Republican tickets with the name of Williams omitted "and none other in its stead" were being distributed through the city by the Lincoln Club. The *Enquirer* claimed that it had seen one of these tickets, printed in German, "to be used in the German wards." It then declared that the Republicans, though willing to *use* Negroes for their own purposes, did not want them to hold office. "Perhaps the colored man will yet learn how he is used by those who pretend to be his friends, but are not."[37]

The *Commercial* had its own last-minute plans to appeal to the electorate on behalf of Williams. It presented Williams as a patriotic defender of his country against whom no loyal American could vote. Fortuitously, Representative Joseph Roswell Hawley of Connecticut, a brigadier-general in the Civil War and former governor of his state, visited Cincinnati in mid-October. The *Commercial* described a very pleasant meeting between Hawley and Williams. For a time, the *Commercial* reported, Williams had been one of the captains in Hawley's brigade, "and they compared notes as to two battles in which they had been under fire together." Since Williams and Hawley were both in the Tenth Army Corps, which saw action at Petersburg and environs, they could have conversed about two battles in which they had both participated. But Williams was never a commissioned officer in the United States Army, either during or after the Civil War (see chapter 1 above), and he did not bother to correct the error. In the same issue the *Commercial* took the opportunity to underscore the sacrifices of Williams for his country. It said that he "bears upon his person the scar of a bayonet wound through the left arm, and the marks of four rifle balls. Are there Republicans here ready to scratch from their ballot the name of one of the heroes of Fort Wagner?"[38]

There was a heavy turnout of voters in Cincinnati on October 14, 1879, and it was around midnight the outcome was certain. All nine of the Republican nominees for the legislature were elected. It is not surprising that Williams trailed the other Republican candidates. Of 27,656 votes cast, he was some 2,205 votes behind Charles C. Davis, who led the ticket. He ran ahead, by 1,444, of Samuel Blair, who garnered the largest number of Democratic votes. The total returns suggest that some Republicans, perhaps two thousand or more, did not vote for Williams. He received substantial support in all wards, never running as many as a hundred votes behind front runner Davis. But Williams ran consistently behind his colleagues even in wards such as the First, Eighteenth, and Twenty-second, where he was thought to be strong. He did not lead in a single ward and was ahead of three other Republicans by one or two votes in only the North precinct of Anderson Township.[39]

It was after midnight at the Lincoln Club, the scene "a blaze of glory and enthusiasm," when the crowd of more than two thousand Republicans began to savor their victory as well as its historic significance. Amid the singing of campaign songs, the crowd demanded that the first black to be elected to the Ohio legislature acknowledge the warm greeting of his supporters. Williams, who had already sent a telegram to President Hayes telling of his victory "by two thousand,"[40] pointed out that the returns were not yet complete, but from what one could already see, he could conclude "that the people of Hamilton County and Ohio are touched by the same spirit that gave Brough the grandest majority that any gubernatorial candidate ever received in this country."[41] Williams declared that the people of Cincinnati had cast their vote for honest money, free and fair elections, free schools, and free speech, and had "elected a colored man from Hamilton County (Great applause)." He promised he would never sully the honor conferred on him by the people. "The eyes of the people of the other States of the Union are all turned to Ohio. . . . When Ohio speaks to-morrow morning she speaks for the Union, she speaks for the colored people outraged and burdened in the South, she speaks in indorsement of John Sherman's magnificent policy of resumption (Great applause)." He concluded by thanking his listeners for their support and repeated his pledge that he would "do nothing, nor say nothing, that shall ever cause any man who cast his vote for me to hang his head in shame (Cheers)."[42] What Williams did not say, of course, was that Sherman was generally conservative and that, in any case, poor people, especially blacks, had no interest in the debate on specie resumption.

If there were those who were displeased with the election of Williams, as there doubtless were, they kept their own counsel. Meanwhile, the celebrants were numerous, both in Cincinnati and elsewhere. The *Commercial* was gleeful, reminding its readers that Williams had made a "most gallant canvass," with his "effective and brilliant speeches," and that he was "the peer in ability of any of the candidates on either legislative ticket." It reproached those who did not vote for him solely because of race, but in view of the persistence of prejudice it was "a matter of congratulation rather than complaint that Captain Williams was elected at all." It expressed the belief that the good record that Williams would make in the legislature would not only gratify those who supported him but would "do much to still further relieve his race of the bias of prejudice and help them forward in their efforts to secure recognition, not as colored people, but American citizens."[43]

On the night following the election, the Negro citizens of Cincinnati were joined by a group of white Republicans in paying tribute to the "colored Representative-elect." A procession of some five hundred persons, accompanied by the uniformed Ninth Ward Hickenlooper Guards and two bands, and led by six or eight hacks occupied by Robert

Harlan, Peter Clark, and other prominent citizens, marched up to 144 Linn Street, Williams's home. Soon the French doors of the two-and-a-half-story brick dwelling opened, and there stood the victor, flanked by his wife and mother and several white personal friends. The music and the wildly cheering crowd must have warmed the young politician, especially since it contained some of his bitterest political enemies.

The very first person to speak was Harlan, whom certain elements of the city had sought to pit against Williams and who now addressed the crowd from Williams's front door:[44]

> Fellow Citizens: We have met here tonight under most peculiar circumstances, to serenade one of our fellow citizens, the first colored man ever elected to the legislature in the State of Ohio. His election puts to flight the oft repeated assertions of the Democrats of Hamilton County, that the Republicans would not vote for a negro, but they have united with us in serenading him. . . . Victory on Victory! On Tuesday last it gleamed through the great Central State of Ohio, and thundered all around the sky. The Democrats heard it and became greatly alarmed. They first called on the devil to help them . . . "What do you want with me?" said the devil. "Oh, good devil, you know that we have served you faithfully, and now that we are in great trouble we want you to protect us from this Republican storm (Cheers)." The devil's reply was, "You must fight it out among yourselves, for you have deceived me, and I will have nothing to do with you."

The witty Harlan speech set the tone for the evening's celebration. When Peter Clark arose to speak the crowd began to shout for Williams. Clark assured them that he was going to introduce Williams, whereupon some declared, "He don't need any introduction." So, after a few remarks and one anecdote, Clark introduced Williams. As he began, someone called "Come to the street so we can hear you." Williams replied, "I never made a speech in Cincinnati yet that the people did not hear me (Cheers)." Williams said that he regarded the large gathering as a compliment not to himself but to his race and to the idea he had represented "in the terrific canvass which has just closed and been crowned with such abundant success." He praised the Republican party and asserted that he was a living witness to its honesty and integrity. His election, he thought, meant the "solidification" of the colored voters of the the city and county. After speaking at some length he thanked the crowd for its "patient hearing" and said that his conduct in Columbus would be in keeping with the honesty and purity "of the grand old Republican party that I love next to the church of Jesus Christ."[45]

Elsewhere the news of the Williams victory was greeted with reactions ranging from warm enthusiasm to mild astonishment. The *People's Advocate*, a black newspaper in Huntsville, Alabama, suggested that the election of Williams proved that "a majority of Northern white Republicans will not vote for a regular candidate simply because he is colored."[46] He must also be qualified, it declared. A New Orleans newspaper expressed a similar view in stating that Williams's election meant that "the Republican party has donned its armor of warfare to enforce the prevalence of the views of which it is the exponent. It means that the rights and immunities conferred on our race by the exigencies of the war shall neither be abridged, compromised nor made a farce, but be made as practical and endearing to us as similar rights are to our white brethern."[47] The Negro paper in Topeka, Kansas, was not so optimistic. "The narrow margin of victory provided no ground for cheering," it declared. "The amount of scratching which his name received at the hands of the 'milk and water' republicans of his district, leaves us free to think that the hide-bound republicans of Hamilton Co., are rich in professing, but poor in possessing genuine republicanism."[48]

As if to demonstrate the point that he placed party above self, Williams cut short the celebration of his victory to go to New York to assist the Republican ticket there. The center of controversy in New York was Alonzo B. Cornell, state chairman of the Republican party and naval officer at the New York customs house. Shortly after Hayes was inaugurated, he issued an executive order forbidding federal office holders to engage in party management. When Cornell refused to resign either post, President Hayes suspended him from his position at the customs house. Cornell persisted in his stand, whereupon the president appointed a successor, who, over the strenuous objections of Senator Roscoe Conkling, was confirmed by the Senate. Apparently out of pique as much as anything, the state organization nominated Cornell for governor in 1879.[49]

Williams, having done much himself to gain Hayes's favor, was thus about to campaign for a candidate much out of favor with the president. In New York he was joined by two other prominent blacks, Frederick Douglass and Richard T. Greener. On Saturday, October 25, Williams spoke at a mass meeting in New York's Seventh District. Referring to the South, he said that as long as the South made bloody shirts, "so long would he wave the bloody shirt."[50] He then spoke of all the "Brigadiers" [Confederate generals] in Congress and said that if Benedict Arnold could look up from his grave and see treason rewarded in this way, "he could well remark that he had been born one hundred years too soon." Calling for the election of the entire Republican ticket, Williams warned that if the Democrats in Congress "acted next winter as they did last, menacing the liberties of the people, they would make it necessary to call on the 'man on horseback,' before whom every traitor would bow his head."[51]

Williams apparently gave about two weeks to the New York canvass, but not without some personal sacrifice as well as some personal insult. Upon his arrival he was subjected to treatment in his hotel that made it clear he was not a welcome guest. He was placed in "a little room up under the roof, and the waiter brought me the bill of fare and told me to order my breakfast, and it would be sent to my room." Williams refused to have the breakfast sent to him, saying that he preferred to go out to a restaurant. He vowed to leave the hotel immediately and find a house where he would be treated "like a gentleman." The *Enquirer* obviously enjoyed informing its Cincinnati readers of the incident, adding editorially that he would have much more to bear "when he takes his seat in the Legislature. 'Tis then that the snubbing will begin in earnest."[52]

Upon his return to Ohio, Williams went to Columbus to make arrangements for housing during the meeting of the legislature. He secured a house on Third Street and made plans to take up residence there at the end of December. During his brief visit to Columbus, Williams stopped at the city's leading hotel, the Neil House, thus permitting his detractors to have one final shot at him before the legislative session began. The *Enquirer* published a story that Williams, while at the Neil House, came down to the dining room "in a gorgeous dressing gown and slippers, and there was not a guest in the house who could stand more style to the square mile than the Hon. G.W.W. aforesaid."[53] Williams was furious and told the *Enquirer* that he did not "indulge in any such nonsense. I never had a dressing gown in my life, and as for slippers they have holes in both toes. The fact is I went to my meals there dressed just as I am now, and made no effort to put on any style."[54]

Williams patiently endured the snubs as well as the misrepresentations regarding his conduct. He did not condemn either the Columbus *Dispatch* or the Cincinnati *Enquirer*, both of which went to great lengths to embarrass the legislator-elect. He even granted an interview to a reporter from the *Enquirer*, during which "he skilfully parried questions regarding the rivalry between James A. Garfield and Judge Stanley Matthews for the seat in the United States Senate, which the legislature would decide, and the matter of reorganizing the municipal boards of Cincinnati."[55] Meanwhile, he was preparing to go to Columbus for the next session of the legislature in January.

Upon his arrival with his family in Columbus, Williams was warmly received by members of both the black and white communities. On December 29 there was a large public meeting at the Second Baptist Church, where one-third of the audience was white. Addresses of welcome were given by two venerable ministers of the city, James Poindexter and B. W. Arnett. Poindexter observed that the election of Williams "within a stone's throw of Kentucky" showed that progress had been made in overcoming prejudice on account of color beyond anything those most solicitous for the elevation of the colored people and most sanguine of ultimate success could have ventured to predict."[56] In his response, Williams reminded his audience that by their service to their country blacks had earned the right to vote and be elected to office. He promised a "clean record" in the legislature. The speeches were followed by an elaborate reception at the home of David Stanton on Court Street.[57] The welcome in Columbus had matched the send-off in Cincinnati. After such events, Williams was more than ready to join his colleagues in the legislature.

·7·
Lawmaker from Hamilton County

George Washington Williams was thirty years old when he presented his certificate of election to the Ohio House of Representatives on January 5, 1880.[1] It was a historic occasion, for no member of his race had previously sat in that body. Indeed, outside the South few blacks had been elected to state legislatures. (Black legislators during the period included George L. Ruffin, a close friend of Williams, in the Massachusetts legislature, and John W. E. Thomas in the Illinois General Assembly. Consequently, Williams's election attracted national attention.

Although Williams had not yet passed the Ohio bar, he gave his occupation as attorney-at-law. In the Hamilton County delegation of nine representatives, all Republicans, two others listed their occupation as attorney. The occupations of the others were manufacturer, retired brick mason, contractor, farmer, real estate agent, and merchant. On motions relating to the organization of the House, Williams and his colleagues from Cincinnati voted as loyal Republicans. Their candidate for speaker, Thomas A. Cowgill of Champaign County, was elected, as were the other Republican candidates.[2]

This was an important legislative session, and the major political parties as well as the state stood to gain or lose, depending on what was accomplished. Before the close of the year there would be a presidential election. If the Democrats performed creditably, they would be in a position to press the case of their party before the nation as well as recover some of the losses they sustained in the statewide elections of 1877. The Republicans had so many "available" candidates—Garfield, Sherman, Blaine, Grant—that it was a matter of the legislature's pursuing a course that would strengthen the party regardless of who the presidential candidate would be. There were, nevertheless, state and local matters of concern, such as revising the laws to accommodate the rapid growth of such cities as Cincinnati and Cleveland, and instituting reforms in line with changed functions of various government offices. These were enough to keep any fledgling legislator like Williams alert and busy.

Williams drew committee assignments in keeping with his literary and intellectual interests. In the first week of the session he received appointments to the standing committee on the State Library, of which he was chairman, and to the standing committee on universities and colleges. He also served on several select committees, including the select committee of nine, composed of the delegation from Hamilton County, which dealt with several matters of special interest to their county and their constituents. Although not present when the Hamilton County delegation organized its caucus on January 20, Williams regarded the caucus as an important legislative instrument. In subsequent meetings he was in regular attendance and sought support from the delegation for bills he planned to introduce on the floor of the House.[3]

Williams plunged unhesitatingly into the legislative process. On the second day of the session, he proposed a bill to "repeal an act entitled an act creating the office of Criminal Bailiff, and to prescribe his duties in counties of the first class having a population of 180,000 and upwards."[4] The *Enquirer* observed that this bill, like those of Williams's "Caucasian colleagues," was of the reorganizing kind. Intended for Hamilton County only, the bill "reorganizes Joe Moses [the bailiff] out of his boots and abolishes the office."[5] It went to the third reading but finally failed by a vote of 55 to 43.[6]

Williams sponsored other, more controversial measures, such as the bill for the better regulation of the police force of Cincinnati. Introduced by Williams on January 12, it proposed to vest the police powers in the mayor, who would have all the powers, rights, and duties in the matter of appointment, selection, confirmation, or removal of the police. The superintendent of police was to be appointed by the mayor, with the consent of the Common Council, and could be removed at the pleasure of the mayor. The mayor and superintendent were not only to appoint subordinates but were to "enact, modify, and publish orders, rules and regulations for the general discipline and duties of the police force." It was an exhaustive statement of the principles and practices to be instituted in the operation of Cincinnati's police department.[7]

When the bill came up for debate, Williams defended it valiantly "in the only real speech of the afternoon," said the Cincinnati *Commercial*. He said that for more than a year the people of Cincinnati had desired reform in the management of police, "and the wretched, partisan and brutal conduct of the police at the last election sealed the fate of a Commission." Each of his colleagues from Hamilton County came to the legislature with general agreement on the need for reform, although there were honest differences regarding the methods. Williams said that his bill contained the "crystallized opinion of the friends of decency and order in my city and I don't want it amended." He said that Charles Jacob, Jr., the mayor, was "competent, worthy, and has the confidence of the people. He has experience, having been president of the Police Commission appointed in 1876." He was just the man to reform the police and rid the city of "bunko thieves, cut-throats and vile shows, that are the open gates through which our young men are marching down to destruction."

At the conclusion of the speech, a member moved the previous question. Another remarked privately that he was "tired of being bull-dozed by the press . . . and we ought to go to work now and do something." When the question was put, the vote on strict party lines was 60 yeas and 39 nays. The bill then went to the Senate, where it passed without debate, the division again being along party lines.[8]

Much more inflammatory was Williams's effort to secure repeal of the law against interracial marriage. Even before Williams went to Co-lumbus he had consulted with his friend John P. Green of Cleveland about such legislation; and it is clear that he had been working on a draft in November and December 1879.[9] By the beginning of the second week of the session, the bill was ready for submission. It proposed to "repeal sections fifty-one and fifty-two of chapter eight of an act entitled an act to amend, revise, and consolidate the statutes relating to crimes and offenses and to repeal certain acts therein named, to be known as title one, crimes and offenses, part four of the act to revise and consoli-date the general statutes of Ohio."[10] The act against intermarriage had been passed in April 1861, when the Democrats sought to embarrass the Republicans by challenging them to take a position that would surely be interpreted as pro-Negro if they opposed the law. With anti-Negro sentiment in Ohio on the increase, the legislature passed the bill.[11]

One can only surmise from the reaction that the proposed bill to repeal the act against intermarriage was so far beyond the realm of possibility that overt opposition to it was unnecessary. The Columbus *Dispatch* merely announced, without comment, the introduction of the bill, as did the Cincinnati *Commercial*.[12] Only the *Enquirer* was openly critical, and more of Williams than of the bill. The "sable solon from Hamilton again made himself a target for distinction this forenoon," the reporter asserted. Williams seemed to be vying for leadership of the

House. The session was a brief one, "but in the few minutes that were allowed him he got in a bill that will create as much political discussion as anything that could have been sprung, and which will place some of the dear friends of the colored race on the record or on the ragged edge— perhaps both." The newspaper said that the bill would do away with all marriage restrictions.[13]

The bill made little progress through the legislature. In reporting on the status of bills introduced by Hamilton lawmakers, the *Commercial* observed: "Periods, semicolons, colons, commas, and other marks of punctuation sometimes perform a very important office in interpreting the meaning of a sentence." The correspondent from Columbus had listed "No. 51, by Mr. Williams—Legalizing miscegenation in the Judiciary Committee." The editor commented,

> It may be Mr. Williams has discovered a condition of things in the Judiciary Committee making such a bill necessary to protect its members from penalties of existing laws, but it is more probable the reading should have been: "By Mr. Williams—Legalizing mis-cegenation. In the Judiciary Committee."[14]

As a matter of fact, the bill died in the Judiciary Committee.

Even as he began his legislative career, Williams found time for other things. He very much enjoyed the contact and the income he earned while doing an extra job as secretary to Charles L. Fleischman. The Hungarian-born yeast manufacturer had already amassed a fortune and was one of Cincinnati's wealthiest and most influential citizens when he was elected to the state Senate, at the same time that Williams was elected to the lower house. Fleischman's business and civic interests were so numerous that he needed someone to assist him when he was away from his offices in Cincinnati. Williams, his Republican colleague and fellow legislator, got the job as private secretary. His duties, among other things, were to assist Fleischman with his correspondence and to write an occasional speech for him "when he is too busy to court the muse of oratory himself." The *Enquirer* reported that Fleischman paid Williams $50.00 a month "and everybody approves of his doing so."[15]

The *Enquirer* had its doubts about the arrangement, however. Consequently, a reporter from that newspaper sought an interview with the senator when he was in Cincinnati. An excerpt follows:

> *Reporter*—They are telling a very funny story about you. What truth is there in it?

S.F.—What is the story?

Reporter—Rev. George W. Williams, the colored member of the
House of Representatives, is your private secretary, I believe?

S.F.—He is. What of it?

Reporter—Only this. The story runs that you left him in your room
arranging some papers one night a week or so ago, and drove
to the depot expecting to find a late train to bring you to this
city. Arriving at the depot you found that there was no train
at that hour, so you returned to the hotel, where you found
that Mr. Williams had become sleepy and had retired in your
bed for the night.

S.F. (Laughing)—Oh, that story is not true. It is the invention of
some of the newspaper boys up to Columbus. They are
always up to some devilment or other.[16]

If that story was an invention, an incident involving Williams occurred almost at the same time that would provide reporters with ample
copy. During the first week of the legislative session, Williams went to
lunch at a restaurant near the statehouse. Legislators were regular
patrons, and when Williams arrived and went to an unoccupied table,
several members of the legislature were already being served. In due
course a waiter came to Williams and told him that the rules of the
establishment forbade the serving of persons of color. Williams told him
that he was a member of the legislature and he wanted to make certain
that this was the policy of the restaurant. After conferring with one of his
superiors, in the absence of the proprietor, Lawrence Beck, the waiter
returned and repeated to Williams that he could not be served. At this
point Williams left.[17]

When the House reconvened after lunch, Williams made known the
indignity he had suffered. Representative Walker, of Logan, advised
him to sue Beck under the United States Civil Rights Act of 1875.
Walker then offered a resolution declaring that "the dignity of the
House and that of the members had been insulted at a house of public
entertainment in Columbus, where the Hon. George W. Williams, of
Cincinnati, was refused entertainment in violation of the laws of the
United States." Upon passage of the resolution, the speaker appointed a
special committee of five to investigate the matter. It heard testimony
from Clement A. Vallandigham and Charles Negley, members of the
House who were in the restaurant at the time; Lawrence Beck, Joseph
Hurst, and Joseph Malone, the proprietor and two of his employees; and
Williams.

The committee concluded that Williams had indeed been "grossly and wantonly insulted." Beck's lame apology to Williams was insufficient, especially since he had in no way "condemned or disapproved" of the acts of his employees. "The fact is that a gentleman of intelligence and culture and high moral worth, and a member of this House, has been cruelly and needlessly insulted, publicly, in [Mr. Beck's] establishment, and the manager who is guilty of this offense still retained in full confidence, is conclusive evidence, in our minds, of Mr. Beck's true feeling in regard to this transaction." The committee lamented the fact that in the progressive state of Ohio, where Negroes had every reason to be treated as equals, such an incident could occur:

> Mr. Williams is a Representative on this floor of Ohio's great commercial metropolis, sent here by a constituency in intelligence, in wealth and industrial enterprise and in members not inferior to any other constituency here represented. He participates in the deliberations of this House, is intrusted with positions of honor, associates with his colleagues on this floor without dishonoring them, and legislates for the man and the establishment whose regulations humiliate him by caste distinction, and impliedly proclaims that we degrade ourselves by his association.

The committee censured the Beck establishment in the following resolution:

> Be it resolved by the House of Representatives of the Sixty-fourth General Assembly of the State of Ohio, that Lawrence Beck has without provocation grossly and indecently permitted Hon. George W. Williams, a member of this House, to be insulted in his dining-rooms, and that this House unqualifiedly condemn the act, and that we regard his actions and his treatment of Mr. Williams as an insult to the House as well as to the people of the State of Ohio.

Hopkins of Marion was the lone member of the committee who dissented and filed a minority report. He agreed that the house should condemn racial discrimination against any of its members, but he was of the opinion that the dignity of the House had been sustained by the apology. His motion failed, and the majority report was then adopted by voice vote. Williams then rose to thank the House "upon its prompt action in seeking to vindicate my right as a member of this honorable body." He then observed that Beck, though he discriminated against blacks, was willing to tolerate him because he was a member of the legislature. "I cannot allow this opportunity to pass without condemning this absurd and irrational prejudice against color," Williams declared. "I have no desire to manifest an ugly spirit. It is sufficient to know that the people of this great country do not, yes will not, tolerate an unhallowed caste prejudice. I leave Mr. Beck to his own remorse and beg him to consider whether in the Capital City of this great State, he can afford to cling to a prejudice that the people pronounce insane and unjust."[18]

The public reacted to the incident in a variety of ways. Knowing that the Civil Rights Act of 1875 was still in effect, some thought that Beck was fortunate if an apology was all that was required for his expiation.[19] The *Enquirer* wondered why Williams had accepted the discrimination in New York without a fight, but was so vocal in his condemnation in Columbus. It also made the unsubstantial claim that a servant girl, "several shades darker" than Williams, was not permitted to eat at the same table with the Williams family.[20] Williams, apparently weary of sparring with the *Enquirer*, did not bother to refute or deny the charge. The most respected black citizen of Columbus, the Reverend James Poindexter, was pleased that Beck had apologized for the "infamous proscription" which "all but the scum of society in Columbus have outgrown." If any respectable businessman in Columbus thought otherwise, "let him write in legible characters over his door, 'No accommodations for Niggers here' . . . and the presence of the sheriff will soon be indicated by a red flag over the door."[21] Perhaps Poindexter was more sanguine than experience warranted, but it was a clarion call for decency in race relations in Columbus.

Neither his work for Fleischman nor the insult in Beck's restaurant seemed to distract Williams from his legislative work. He continued to introduce bills, among them a bill to regulate the amount that could be charged by newspapers to publish legal notices.[22] It reached its third reading but was lost, although one newspaper had expressed little doubt that it would pass.[23] Williams also offered a petition of private citizens asking for the passage of a Board of Public Works bill, which was referred to the select committee of nine (the members from Hamilton County), and another petition from some seventy-five citizens of Butler County asking for the passage of a local option antiliquor law. The Butler representatives had apparently declined to submit such a petition.[24]

Early in the session it became clear that Williams was one of the most active members of the legislature, and there is no doubt that he was quite frequently the leader and spokesman for the Hamilton County delegation. He spoke at length, for example, in support of the bill proposed by his colleague Peter Stryker to establish an Infirmary Board to exercise powers previously held by the Police Board.[25] When the select committee of nine made their report on the reorganization of

these Cincinnati agencies, Williams spoke for the committee in recom-
mending its passage.[26] He seems even to have made a place for himself in
the inner councils of the House, for he occasionally performed duties
normally reserved to those familiar with the desires of the speaker or
other officials. It was on Williams's motion, for example, that the House
took a recess on March 9 and again on March 18. When he moved that a
bill to amend Section 610 of the Revised Statutes be taken from the
Judiciary Committee and referred to a select committee of one, the
speaker appointed Williams as *the* committee.[27]

Williams was the leading advocate of a bill introduced in the Senate
by Beriah Wilkins of Tuscarawas to amend the law governing the
adoption of textbooks for the public schools.[28] Under the proposed
legislation, changes in texts could only be made by vote of three-fourths
of the members of the board (the existing law required merely a majority
vote) at a regular meeting. It also barred teachers and other school
officials from serving as agents for textbook companies. Williams said
that virtually everyone favored the bill except the lobbyists for textbook
companies who wished to defeat the bill so that they could press their
own textbooks on the school boards. If this bill failed, Williams argued,
school books might be changed frequently, thus burdening parents with
needless expense in frequently purchasing new books for their children.
It was no defense of the existing bill that change was favored by a
Cincinnati publishing house that led in providing books for Ohio children. The publisher was a good one, Williams insisted, had for years
provided good, cheap books, and was the only house west of the
Allegheny Mountains that could compete successfully with the Eastern
houses. He then pointed out that in the half-century that the house had
been doing business, there was not a single blemish on its name.[29]
Williams was in for a disappointment when the House voted 65 to 37 to
postpone the bill indefinitely.[30]

Within weeks after going to Columbus Williams had become sufficiently active and influential sometimes to find himself at the center of
controversy. He did not object to this role if it gave him his moments in
the center of the stage, for he was confident that his views and actions
would prevail. But not even Williams could have anticipated the bitter
attacks on him that the Avondale cemetery bill sparked. On April 10,
1880, Williams introduced into the legislature a bill providing that
whenever the freeholders of Avondale residing within a radius of a
half-mile from the Colored American (Methodist) Cemetery petitioned
the Board of Health, claiming the cemetery to be a public nuisance, that
body, if it was convinced that the cemetery was, in fact, a nuisance,
could prohibit the cemetery trustees from making any further inter-

ments there. Williams could not have created a greater furor had he slapped the leading black citizens of Avondale in the face. Avondale was one of the better outlying areas of the city of Cincinnati to which an increasing number of blacks had been moving since the Civil War. On a hill overlooking the city, it was also a favorite residential area for well-to-do whites. Charles Fleischman was one of the wealthy indus- trialists who had built a mansion there.

The speed with which the bill began to make its way through the legislative mill contributed to the sense of outrage of many blacks. Williams, they suspected, was acting on behalf of whites in Avondale or on behalf of blacks who were Baptists and therefore not affected by the issue because the Union Baptist Church had its own cemetery.[31] These views and many others were aired at an indignation meeting at Allen Temple in Cincinnati on April 12, 1880. Many of Cincinnati's leading Negro citizens were present, including George H. Jackson, attorney, Peter Clark, educator, and Charles W. Bell, a public school teacher. Numerous speeches condemned Williams's sponsorship of the bill. William Alexander said that it pained him to observe that the very first act performed by Williams, as legislator, for the black people, was to stop them from burying their dead in Avondale cemetery. He said that he had opposed the nomination of Williams but had voted for him. Now, he was not ashamed of voting for anyone on the ticket except Williams, and he wished there was some way to dislodge him. Of Williams, Alexander said, "He is a political trickster. Hear what they have to say in Vicksburg, Baltimore and Richmond—how he acted. They say he is not fit to be trusted."

Peter Clark spoke with some reluctance, not merely because he had supported Williams for the legislature, but also because he was not certain if the meeting had been called to express indignation at Williams or to consider the consequences of the closing of the cemetery. He observed that his father and sister were buried there.

> Now then, to have that cemetery shut up today would be, in the first place, to outrage all those sentiments which are gathered around it. . . . The aristocracy of Avondale wish to drive us away from there. Where shall we go? Will they open [white] Spring Grove Cemetery to us? (Laughter). . . . The residents of Avondale have got up this bill and put it before the Legislature. As one of them said, "We looked for some one to present it, and George Williams seemed to be the man to do anything that anybody put in his hands. . . ." These white men say it was to the interest of the

colored men to close the cemetery. What do they know about our interests? (Laughter).

Clark pointed out that they would not dare close the German cemetery or the Jewish cemetery. He then praised Senator Kirby, "a true, noble gentleman" for causing the Williams bill to be laid on the table, where he hoped it would remain. Charles Bell declared that if Williams pushed the bill through to avoid discussion, then he should be condemned "now, henceforth and forever." Benjamin Graves said that he loved Williams "as a scholar, as a gentleman, as a Christian. But we cannot always tell what men will do. I am just as much down on George W. Williams tonight as any gentleman in the hall." Graves quoted Williams as having recently said, "I am the representative of the white people (understand that, not the *black*), for that reason I stop at Gibson House" (a fashionable white hotel). "In the words of the good old sister," said Graves, " 'I hope God will kill him dead politically.' If I had had the least idea that he would have proved a traitor to us, as he has, I should have fought him harder than satan ever fought a saint (Laughter and applause)." Others spoke similarly. Williams sent a message to the meeting stating that he had an explanation for what he had done and urging the group to take no action until they heard from him. No one seemed to take his plea seriously.[32]

After an almost endless round of speech making, Clark moved the appointment of a committee to draft and circulate a memorial to the legislature protesting the closing of the cemetery. The committee then submitted the following resolution:

> WHEREAS, the Hon. G.W. Williams has presented to the Legislature of this State a bill making unlawful the further use of the Colored American Cemetery of Avondale; and *Whereas*, the Legislature on his representation has adopted the bill without opposition, or without warning to parties interested; therefore *Resolved*— First, that if the bill has become a law as has been represented, that a petition for its repeal be immediately forwarded to the Legislature; if it has not become law a remonstrance against its passage be sent without delay;
> RESOLVED—Second, that we unanimously condemn the unexampled haste with which our first successful choice as Representative has lent his aid and influence to our injury, betraying a trust which has hitherto been safe in the hands of men of less influential individuals. [Sic]

The resolution, was adopted. Another, submitted by Richard Fortson, proposed that George W. Williams be requested "not to return to Hamilton County when his term of office expires." That resolution won little support from the meeting, many feeling that it was "a little too strong, savoring of a kuklux or red shirt decree." There would doubtless have been more statements of indignation and more excitement had not a motion to adjourn "nipped it in the bud."[33]

The same issue of the *Commercial* that reported the meeting at Allen Temple carried a letter from Williams explaining his actions. He said that several prominent citizens from Avondale had petitioned him to introduce a bill that would relieve them of what they believed to be a nuisance: the continuation of burials in the Colored American Cemetery.[34] Williams said that he consulted the attorney general, the chairman of the House Judiciary Committee and "about thirty other gentlemen" regarding the kind of law needed to satisfy the people of Avondale. He then drafted a law conferring on the Board of Health of Avondale "the same power with which Boards of Health of cities of the first class are clothed, so as to abate the nuisance."[35]

Williams denied having taken this action to benefit the Union Baptist Church cemetery, which would receive bodies if the Avondale cemetery were closed. "I assure you that I have no personal interest in this matter, no selfish motives, and no desire to do injustice to anyone." He then reported that he had requested Senator Kirby to have the Senate, which had passed the bill, reconsider it and lay it on the table, where it now rested and would remain "until those who opposed it can establish the fact as to whether . . . the cemetery is or is not a nuisance." Then he wished it to be disposed of accordingly. Williams closed with a final defense. "I have always been, and am now, devoted to the interests of my race in common, and would be the last person in the world to secure legislation for the benefit of one denomination to the injury of another."[36]

The following day Williams pressed his defense by answering certain allegations made against him at the meeting at Allen Temple. First, he had no personal interest in the bill. Second, it was not introduced in the interest of the Union Baptist Church. Third, the bill did not propose to abolish the cemetery but required it to be closed to further burials *if* it were found to be a nuisance. Fourth, he had never even stopped in Richmond, Baltimore, or Vicksburg as one speaker claimed in asserting that the people of those cities knew all about him. Fifth, the reason the bill was introduced and put through in such haste was, as the Board of Health affirmed, because of the approaching warm weather. Sixth, Benjamin Graves had misquoted him. Williams was in fact at the Gibson

House "because it was central, and representing all the people of the county, I wanted to be where I could be seen, and asked him to call. His statement is a deliberate lie." Seventh, no man could possibly doubt his fidelity to his fellow blacks. "I have labored long and faithfully in their interest." He concluded by saying he did not desire to injure anyone, "and now if the colored people desire to turn their back upon me, let them do as seemeth best to themselves."[37]

The *Enquirer* was gleeful over Williams's discomfort. The "off-color statesman," as it usually called him, continued to explain the graveyard bill, "but the more he explains, the less satisfactory the explanations seem to be."[38] Williams had his supporters, however. The Columbus *Dispatch* called the attacks on Williams "senseless . . . in bad taste," and "calculated to work injury to that class of the community." It pointed out that if he had made a wrong move, he could have been informed in some other manner than a series of name-calling indignation meetings. Williams was not the only member of the Ohio legislature who had made mistakes, the editor asserted, "but unlike others, he seems to have discovered the fact, and has done all in his power to correct them."[39] The editor of the *Commercial* thought that the people at Allen Temple had acted in haste in denouncing Williams. When the legislator heard of the opposition it excited, it was he who secured a reconsideration of it in the Senate. Furthermore, the editor argued, "the charge that the bill was gotten up in the interest of the Baptist Colored Cemetery was manifestly absurd, and that any intelligent person should for a moment have credited it is to show how easily the imagination, under excitement, seizes as a fact the most ridiculous stories."[40]

Williams needed no bribe or undue pressure to introduce the Avondale Cemetery Bill. He sincerely believed that he was obliged to consider the requests of white constituents as well as those of blacks. His friend and benefactor, Charles Fleischman, lived in Avondale, moreover, and a bill that would please Fleischman would be additional reason for him to introduce it. Williams was more of an integrationist than most of his black constituents, and was not inhibited by the fact that the cemetery that purportedly was a health hazard happened to be black. Many blacks disliked him because they thought him arrogant and conceited or because many whites thought him to be the brightest and the best black citizen in the town. Rarely could Williams be called naive, but he was genuinely surprised at being assailed by the Negroes of Cincinnati for introducing the cemetery bill.

When the legislature adjourned on April 17, the bill continued to lie on the table in the Senate.[41] The damage that it had done to Williams's reputation in Cininnati, however, was virtually irreparable. The explo-

sion of pent-up hostility against Williams made it obvious that he was in
deep trouble with his black constituents. "I trust that every colored man
blushes that voted for him," William Alexander had said. Peter Clark
had declared that Williams "should have stood by the interests of the
colored people while there remained a drop of blood in his veins."
Charles Bell had shouted, "I am compelled to denounce him and in
doing so I think I utter the sentiments of all our people."[42] That Williams
was defended by people such as the editor of the *Commercial* had not
the slightest effect in explaining his actions or improving his standing.

Williams was well aware of the disesteem into which he had fallen. If
his political enemies, as he called them, thought they had humiliated
him, they were mistaken. While his political fortunes were surely on the
wane, his self-esteem seemed to be as positive as ever. He later confided
to his friend John P. Green that it was time to make some important
changes in his life.[43] Meanwhile, there was much to do, completing the
legislative session, serving the party during the year of a presidential
election, preparing for the second session of the legislature, and working on his projected history of the Negro people.

As a member of the Library Committee, Williams was interested in
improving services and facilities. Already he was a regular user of the
State Library and was apparently familiar with its needs. While the
House considered appropriations for the State Library, Williams made
an unsuccessful effort to raise the allowance for magazines from $1,500
to $2,000.[44] In early March he traveled with his colleagues on the
Committee on Universities and Colleges to inspect Ohio University in
Athens to inquire into its needs for additional funds.[45] In the following
month he offered a successful resolution to erect a second balcony
around the House for the use of the ladies and to enlarge the lobby.[46] The
final days of the session, which ended April 17, were taken up with the
Avondale affair.

It had been a momentous session for him, and his presence marked it
as a historic one for the state. He had served on two standing committees
and four select committees. While only one of the six bills he introduced
was enacted into law, he made his presence felt in the debates, in
committee reports, and in his activity on the floor. The *Ohio State
Journal* described one of his speeches on the floor as "sharply pointed,"
another as having "telling effect." The Cincinnati *Commercial* often
praised Williams for his role in debates in the legislature and seemed
delighted when he "made the Democrats wince."[47] He had, moreover,
forced his colleagues to confront the ugly specter of racial discrimination
and caused them to take a stand against it. He had learned how difficult
it was to please all segments of his constituency and how close to the

surface pettiness and jealousy lurked. He would have another opportunity in the next session early in 1881, but he could use the recess to count his gains and losses and to turn his attention to other interests.

The year 1880 was a presidential election year, which gave Williams an opportunity to turn away from local problems and focus on larger matters. As in 1876, he would contribute whatever he could to a Republican victory; but the problem in the spring of 1880 was which of the prominent Republicans the party should choose as its standard bearer. This was of critical importance to Williams, especially since his future in the legislature had been jeopardized by the cemetery controversy. If he could attach himself to a winning presidential candidate, he could once again become a rising political star.

Williams had admired John Sherman for many years, as a champion of equal rights in the Senate during Reconstruction and as secretary of the treasury. He doubtless regarded him as a likely Republican nominee. During the campaign of 1879, he called Sherman "the greatest Minister of Finance since M. Rucker saved the declining fortunes of Emperor Napoleon, or since Robert Peel chalked the bobbin." In his victory speech, Williams had praised Sherman's policy of resumption.[48] Early in March, when the legislature was still in session, Williams went to Washington to see Sherman, then in the Treasury.[49] The two men may have discussed a rumor, said by some to have been instigated by Grant supporters, that during the war, as chairman of the Senate Committee on Finance, Sherman had attempted to make the bounty of black soldiers less than that given to white soldiers. In any case, a few weeks after their meeting, Sherman issued, through Williams, the following statement: "There is no foundation in the allegation that I ever sought to discriminate against the colored soldier in any way. I was one of the first to propose to enroll him in our service. John Sherman."[50]

On April 22, Williams went to Atlanta to attend the meeting of the Republican state convention of Georgia. He was there to promote the interests of Sherman, although one can discount the *Enquirer's* claim that he sat as a delegate from one of Georgia's counties.[51] The reporter of a Negro newspaper in Alabama observed that Williams was in Georgia looking after "that gold mine" (in other words, seeking his fortune), but while there he found time to attend the Republican state convention. "Remarkable coincidence that. His presence there was a good omen. Like us, he believes John Sherman is the most available candidate the Republicans can nominate."[52]

Williams arrived in Chicago several days before the Republican National Convention opened on June 2. What his role was to be is not clear, since he was not a member of the Ohio delegation. He was well acquainted with several Ohio delegates, including Amor Smith and Charles Fleischman of Cincinnati, Judson Lyons and R. R. Wright of Georgia, George F. Hoar of Massachusetts, and Blanche K. Bruce and John R. Lynch of Mississippi. Presumably he worked among them and others to garner support for Sherman, but since the secretary of the treasury could not muster support from more than thirty-four of Ohio's forty-four delegates, his chances of winning the nomination began to fade. Meanwhile, some delegates began to see in Grant's triumphal return from Europe and his continuing popularity an indication that the excesses and scandals of his administration had been forgotten.[53] Among those who took up the Grant banner was Williams, who, in turn, sought to persuade other Negro Republicans to follow him. But Grant's popularity was not sufficient to overcome the scandals of his administration or the strong tradition against a third term.

The convention was one of surprises and disappointments.[54] At the beginning, no one could have predicted that none of the three front runners—Sherman, Blaine, and Grant—would be nominated. When James A. Garfield emerged as the nominee, after the deadlock between Grant and Blaine, no one could have been more surprised than Williams. He had paid scant attention to Garfield and had flaunted his support first for Sherman and then for Grant. Now he had to adjust to an unanticipated Republican nominee. Garfield, however, was a man of considerable education (Williams College, 1856) and was a lay preacher of the Church of the Disciples of Christ. He had a distinguished record as a brigadier-general at Shiloh and Chickamauga. Later, he had served eight terms in Congress. And Williams admired men of education, religion, and military and public service.

During the summer and fall of 1880, Williams was preoccupied with two matters—working for the Republican ticket and working on his history of the Negro race. He spent much time in Ohio; in Indiana, at the invitation of John C. New, the chairman of the Republican state committee there; and in New York, at the invitation of the vice-presidential candidate, Chester A. Arthur. He spoke in Crawfordsville, Indianapolis, and Bloomington in Indiana; in Xenia, Oberlin, and Springfield in Ohio; and in New York City, Albany, and Buffalo.[55] It is not clear how effective he was. The intraparty conflicts among leaders such as Garfield, Grant, and Roscoe Conkling were so great that issues and even party preferences were sometimes obscured. In an election where the margin of the popular vote was barely more than three thousand, the Republicans could claim victory but could hardly give anyone credit for it. Under the circumstances, Williams could be pleased that he was at least on the winning side.[56]

There was speculation over what Garfield would do about appointing blacks to federal office. The *Enquirer* said that they were pressing the incoming administration for "recognition."[57] Williams was not the only one who had worked in the campaign. John Mercer Langston, who had worked for Garfield's election, was already United States minister to Haiti. James Poindexter, a party faithful and a leading citizen of Columbus, deserved consideration. Many other leading Negro Republicans were available, such as Mississippi's Blanche K. Bruce, retiring from the Senate in 1881; John C. Dancy, recorder of deeds in Edgecombe County, North Carolina; and Francis L. Cardozo of South Carolina, who had held many positions of trust in his state and in Washington. Williams might prefer "an appointment to the chances for renomination and reelection to the legislature," as one writer put it; but other things were of greater concern to him now, including vindication in the next session of the legislature.[58]

Williams answered the first roll call when the adjourned session of the legislature met on January 4, 1881.[59] He submitted fewer bills than he had in the earlier session, but in other ways he was no less active. At the first meeting of the Republican members he was elected secretary of the caucus. He continued to seek to repeal the law against racial intermarriages until the Judiciary Committee buried it permanently by securing its indefinite postponement.[60] When the question of lending Ohio's Mexican War battle flags to the Mexican War Veterans Association of Cincinnati arose, Williams thought that the matter should be referred to the Committee on Military Affairs and Soldiers' and Sailors' Orphans Home. The house disagreed, and Williams voted with the majority that the loan should be made.[61] As an active member of the Grand Army of the Republic, Williams was especially interested in securing as much recognition as possible for those who had given their lives during the Civil War. In 1868, General John A. Logan, commander-in-chief of the GAR, designated May 30 as Memorial Day and urged all states to make that day a legal holiday. By 1881, Rhode Island, Vermont, New Hampshire, among other states, had already done so. On April 1, Williams introduced a bill to make May 30 a holiday in Ohio also. On the same day it was read a second time and was referred to the Judiciary Committee, from which it never returned.[62]

As chairman of the Committee on the State Library, Williams was more successful in persuading the House to accept the committee's recommendations than he had been during the first session. On February 4, Thomas C. Snydor, representative from Stark County, offered a joint resolution calling for the Board of Library Commissioners to print the papers of Arthur St. Clair (Governor of the Northwest Territory from 1788 to 1802), which the state had purchased in 1870. The resolution was referred to the Library committee. Six days later, Williams reported that the committee recommended its passage. The joint resolution was adopted in the House by a vote of 75 to 2. After some minor amendments in the Senate, the resolution was enrolled.[63] Williams also took an interest in the welfare of library personnel and introduced a bill to increase the salaries of the state librarian and the assistant to the librarian. Sentiment was clearly favorable to an increase, but members of both houses had many different ideas regarding the amount. After the Williams bill was referred to the Committee on Fees and Salaries, where it was amended, it went to the Senate, where again it was amended. It was not until a joint conference committee worked on the matter that the salaries finally were set at $1400 and $1300 per annum respectively for the librarian and the assistant librarian. Williams had proposed $1300 and $1200 respectively.[64]

Williams took a special interest in a bill proposed by John C. Covert of Cleveland relative to taxing religious properties.[65] Directed specifically against schools and other agencies of the Roman Catholic Church, it proposed a tax on all property owned by religious societies. After it was referred to the Committee on Corporations other than Municipal, Williams felt obliged to speak against it. He was committed to the proposal "in theory, from my early education and genuine republicanism." But it was not a simple matter, he argued, largely because of the role of religious societies in American education. "The neglect of the National and State Government to educate the youth until recent years has occasioned the churches of the country to manage the vast educational interests of the land. . . . A blow at the Catholic church will fall heavily upon the schools that have grown out of and are a part of the great religious societies of the State. I speak here for God's poor, for the colored Baptists and Methodists of the State. I want the bill modified."[66] Williams had spoken his piece, but there was no need to worry. The Covert bill was never reported out of committee.[67]

Williams was more favorably disposed toward a proposal by another member from Cleveland, L. A. Palmer, who sought to release the sergeant-at-arms from liability for any loss of statutes or other books used by members of the House. This was a perfunctory resolution introduced toward the end of the session when many such sentiments were being offered. It was Williams, a regular borrower of books from the State Library, who called up the Palmer resolution. It passed without difficulty, with only fifteen nays.[68]

During this session, Williams actively sought legislation to control the use of alcoholic beverages. On one occasion he presented a petition of 6,015 citizens of Hamilton County asking for the passage of a local-option antiliquor law. Later, he presented a petition of 503 other citizens from Hamilton County seeking similar legislation. These, along with numerous petitions presented by other representatives, were referred to the Committee on Temperance.[69] Williams did not submit an antiliquor bill himself but supported the bill offered early in the session by David S. King of Clinton County. The King bill would restrict the sale of intoxicating liquors to "medicinal, pharmaceutic, and sacramental purposes," and the question of enforcement would be left to the citizens through local-option provisions. When the bill came up for a vote on February 10, it lost by one vote.[70] Although his friends who opposed the bill tried to "bulldoze him," Williams voted for the bill, saying that he thought the people of the state desired "some modified liquor measure."[71] A similar bill was introduced in the Senate by F. B. Pond of the Fourteenth District. The bill apparently had no sponsor in the House. After amendments in the Committee on Temperance and on the floor, nothing was done until Williams called for its consideration. While it was being considered, an opponent moved that it be tabled. The motion carried by two votes, with Williams voting against tabling.[72]

The session ended on April 20. Although most of the bills that became law were not his, Williams had been an active participant in the legislative process both in committee and on the floor. Except for brief leaves of absence, including several days during the cemetery controversy and two weeks when Garfield was inaugurated, he was in regular attendance. By the end of the second session, he spoke and functioned as a veteran legislator, enjoying the respect and cooperation of his colleagues.

Williams seemed to give no thought to the possibility of running for office again. Not only was he thoroughly disillusioned over the performance of many of his constituents, but he was already absorbed in a project over which he had more control and that could be even more rewarding than serving in the Ohio legislature.

Historian of the Race

The announced reason for Williams's not seeking a second term in the legislature—perhaps the real reason—was that he wished to devote his time to historical research and writing. He knew quite well that he had gone about as far as he or any other Afro-American could go in state government at that time; and surely his restlessness and his ambition would not permit him merely to tread water. He was realist enough, moreover, to know when the opposition had the upper hand, as it did in Cincinnati, and when it was time to shift his activities. He decided not to seek reelection or even to take up residence again in Cincinnati, but to use Columbus as his base in pursuing his objective of becoming the historian of his race.

Williams had long been interested in history and had made several forays into the field. His commencement oration at the Newton Theological Institution was essentially a historical survey of the work of the early Christians in North Africa. When he became pastor of the Twelfth Baptist Church in Boston in 1874, his way of gaining orientation and perspective as well as seeking greater support for the church was to write its history. There were historical pieces in the short-lived *Commoner*; and many of his columns in the Cincinnati *Commercial* were historical as well as autobiographical.

Williams's real commitment to historical studies, however, dated from his participation in the centennial of American independence. Days of prayer and thanksgiving, pageants, and expositions were among the more popular ways of observing the occasion. Many turned to the nation's history not only to relive the winning of independence but also to see how the nation had fared since that time. Historians (or publishers) seemed to know what the public wanted. The venerable George

Bancroft, who in 1834 had begun to publish his *History of the United States of America, From the Discovery of the Continent*, responded by bringing out a centenary edition of the work. The centennial year also witnessed the translation and publication of the first volume of Hermann Eduard von Holst's monumental *Constitutional and Political History of the United States*. With the major part of his career as a historian still ahead of him, Henry Adams issued *Documents Relating to New England Federalism*.[1]

Among the more modest observances were the hundreds of meetings across the country at which those who gathered would commemorate the event with patriotic songs and orations. At the centennial day observance in the Cincinnati suburb of Avondale, as we have seen, the speaker was George Washington Williams, recently arrived from the nation's capital, and whose reputation as an engaging speaker with something to say had preceded him.[2] After Williams had regaled his audience at length on the contributions of Negro Americans during the first century of independence, the speech was ordered to be printed "by unanimous vote."[3] And he was encouraged to pursue the subject at greater length.

It seems clear that even before Williams took up his legislative duties early in 1880 he had begun serious work on Negro history. In Cincinnati he used the library of the Historical and Philosophical Society, which, he said, offered "peculiar advantages to a student of American history." Even more important, perhaps, was the library of Robert Clarke, the city's leading publisher, bookseller, author, and editor. Clarke, who had published Williams's Avondale oration, owned more than eight thousand volumes of Americana and other subjects. Before Clarke sold most of his collection to former President Rutherford B. Hayes and to William A. Proctor (who gave his portion to the University of Cincinnati), Clarke's place was a favorite resort for the literary men of the city.[4] Clarke befriended Williams and placed his library at the young man's disposal; Williams took full advantage of it.

Williams also made regular use of the State Library of Ohio and the Columbus Public Library. As a member of the House of Representatives, he had access to the State Library. He later indicated that he had used 576 volumes from that library, "besides newspaper files and Congressional records." Since he expressed a debt to the "unwavering and untiring kindness and friendship" of the "accomplished and efficient Miss Mary C. Harbough," the assistant librarian, it is possible that he used many items that do not show in his tabulation.[5] In the library's "Delivery Ledger" for 1880, there is no record of Williams having

borrowed any books to take out. In the following year he borrowed four
works, all dealing with Egypt or some other part of Africa, which he kept
from two to six months.[6]

As Williams read more extensively in African and early American
history, he realized that his studies might well lead him to sources of
different kinds in various parts of the country. Other students were
reaching similar conclusions, though many had mentors who assisted
them in planning their research. In the 1870s, Harvard, Yale, and
Michigan introduced the historical seminar, where professors and students gave critical attention to specific American themes and from
which students went out in search of documents to illuminate their
inquiries. While Williams was working on his history, Cornell University appointed Moses Coit Tyler to its first chair in American history,
and James B. McMaster was preparing the first volume of his history of
the United States. It was the McMasters and the Tylers at various
universities who were doing so much to raise the professional standards
of historians through careful use of sources gathered from libraries and
archives. Although Williams had no opportunity to study at such major
centers of learning, his methods were similar to those of trained
historians.

By the summer of 1880, after the first session of the legislature,
Williams, like the seminar students and their mentors, was ready to
venture out to do research elsewhere. Armed with his experience at the
Cincinnati and Columbus libraries and with several weeks of rest and
western travel behind him, Williams went to visit the libraries in the
east. He combined his research activities with some active politicking,
whether because he appreciated the importance of the national elections of 1880 or because he saw an opportunity for extra income. The
Cincinnati *Enquirer,* no friend of Williams, reported in July that his
"literary labors" had been interrupted by invitations from John C. New
(chairman of the Indiana State Republican Committee) and Chester
Arthur to speak in Indiana and New York.[7] Arthur's nomination for
vice-president had pleased Williams immensely. Recalling that Arthur
had been involved in defending eight alleged fugitive slaves in the
celebrated Lemmon case in 1860, Williams asserted that Negroes would
support the Garfield-Arthur ticket with enthusiasm.[8]

Williams obviously gave more attention to politics than to historical
research in the summer of 1880. Presumably he made valuable contacts
for a more extensive research trip the following year. When the adjourned session of the legislature ended in April 1881, Williams filled
various engagements in Las Vegas, Indianapolis, and Akron. In mid-
June he left for New York, where he pursued historical research for nine

"Dear General O. O. Howard,

"Sir Mr. Howard—i have the Honour to inform and Enterduce my Self witch you an to let you now my Hartes Desire. an in a Brief Discorel. i will make my Self none to you as one wanting to Be useful to my fellowmen." George Washington Williams to General O. O. Howard, March 1, 1869. Courtesy, Moorland-Spingarn Research Center, Howard University, Washington, D.C.

"Early Christianity in Africa"
　　"Here Christianity flourished; here it brought forth rich fruit in the lives of its tenacious adherents." Williams's commencement speech, June 10, 1874. Courtesy, Franklin Trask Library, Andover Newton Theological School.

Williams

Williams at Newton Theological Institution
"Also George Washington Williams (Colored), res. Newcastle, Pa. – Age 22 .
. . . General Student." Faculty Record Book, September 9, 1870. Courtesy,
Moorland-Spingarn Research Center, Howard University, Washington, D.C.

Leonard Grimes

"A leader of excellent judgment, a pastor of tender sympathies, and a father who loved them with all the strength of a truly manly affection." Williams, *History of the Twelfth Baptist Church,* 1874. Courtesy, Moorland-Spingarn Research Center, Howard University, Washington, D.C.

~//~

George L. Ruffin, Clerk of the Twelfth Baptist Church

"You have touched a high point in our racial life. . . . Your elevation to a judicial position is an unmistakable evidence that the world moves." Williams speaking at dinner honoring Ruffin, November 22, 1883. Courtesy Moorland-Spingarn Research Center, Howard University, Washington, D.C.

~//~

Williams as pastor of Twelfth Baptist Church
"Now you have taken me in the freshness of young manhood, to carry forward
the work he [Leonard Grimes] loved and engaged in for so many years."
Williams, *History of the Twelfth Baptist Church*. Courtesy, Moorland-Spingarn
Research Center, Howard University, Washington, D.C.

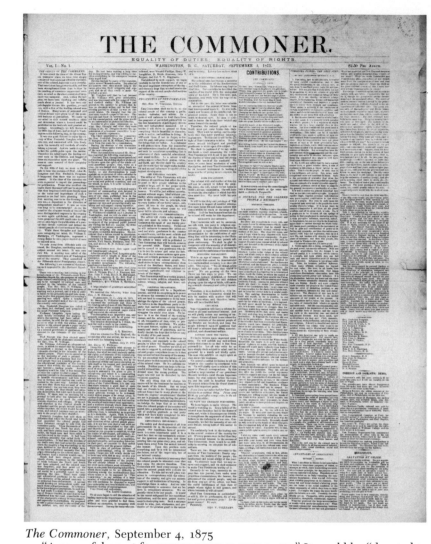

The Commoner, September 4, 1875

"A powerful agent for REORGANIZING THE RACE." It would be "devoted to the colored people, politics, arts and the events of the day." Williams in *The Commoner*, September 4, 1875. Courtesy, American Antiquarian Society.

Frederick Douglass

"I honor him for what he has done that is good, I respect him for what he is in character and personality, and trust that when he reaches the 80th winter of his discontent, he will find himself more tolerant of the talents and achievements of other men." Williams to Robert H. Terrell, October 14, 1890. Courtesy, Moorland-Spingarn Research Center, Howard University, Washington, D.C.

Alphonso Taft

The "only white man in the Cabinet of any President during the last eighteen years who had the manhood, the temerity, and humanity to exact . . . the powers of the Constitution . . . to protect the black man in the exercise of his constitutional rights." Williams, May 28, 1879. Courtesy, Ohio Historical Society.

Richard T. Greener
   "Mr. Greener, a son of Harvard College, with a keen and merciless logic, cut right through the sophistries of Mr. Douglass in the debate on whether Negroes should migrate from the South." Williams, *History of the Negro Race*. Courtesy, Moorland-Spingarn Research Center, Howard University, Washington, D.C.

Williams as judge advocate of the Ohio Encampment of the Grand Army of the Republic

"Encampments may make laws, and the Judge Advocate interpret them, but the *sine qua non* of the Grand Army . . . is, Fraternity, Charity, and Loyalty." Speech by Williams, 1881.

Senator George F. Hoar of Massachusetts

"The delicate manner in which you offered aid . . . deeply touched my heart and you have both my gratitude and reverent love." Williams to Hoar, July 3, 1889. Courtesy, American Antiquarian Society.

Chester A. Arthur, president of the
United States
"I nominate George W. Williams of
Massachusetts, to be Minister Resident
and Consul General of the United
States, to Hayti." March 2, 1885. Cour-
tesy, Library of Congress.

Williams the lecturer, 1888–89

"Major J. B. Pond takes great pleasure in announcing that he has made arrangements for a series of Lectures and Readings during the present season, by Colonel the Honorable George W. Williams, L. L. D." Courtesy, The National Archives.

Leopold II, King of the Belgians
"Your Majesty's Government has sequestered their [the Congolese] land
burned their towns, stolen their property, enslaved their women and children, and committed other crimes too
numerous to mention." Williams, *Open
Letter to . . . Leopold II,* 1890. Courtesy, The Bettmann Archives.

Collis P. Huntington
"Please accept my sincere thanks for
the generous aid you have rendered this
cause of Humanity I have championed
and suffered for." Williams to Huntington, April 25, 1891. Courtesy, Hampton
University.

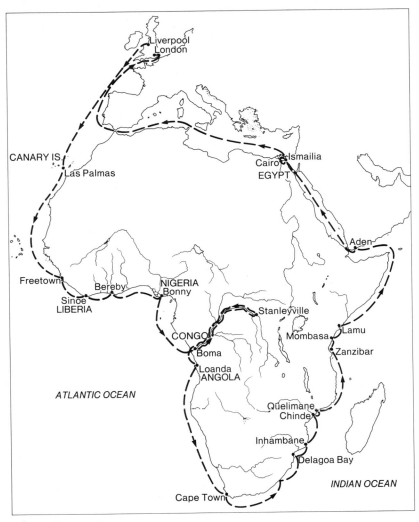

African Journey

"Sometimes, I was crossing plains which stretched days before me, as level as our own prairies; again I struggled for four days through the dense, dark and damp forest of Muyambu, where it rains every month in the year." Williams to Robert H. Terrell, October 14, 1890. Courtesy, Joe Muwonge.

Robert H. Terrell

"Well, dear Terrell, I grasp your hand across the space and pray God for your best success. Give my love to my friends; they are few but worthy. I never sought the multitude for vulgar adulation; and my real friends are those who understand me and appreciate my work for humanity and civilization." Williams to Terrell, written from Loando, Angola, October 14, 1890. Courtesy, Moorland-Spingarn Research Center, Howard University, Washington, D.C.

Williams, last photograph, June 1891
   "He [the physician in Cairo] tells me that if I can hold my own for the next two weeks I will doubtless recover, but if not I will be carried off." Williams to Huntington, February 11, 1891. Courtesy, The National Archives.

Grave of Williams, Layton Cemetery,
Blackpool
   "Over the grave of one so young, so
brilliant, and so wayward, it is safe to say
the thinking portion of the race . . . will
shed a tear." New York *Age,* August 8,
1891. Courtesy of Hannah Bowman
Watkins, 1983

weeks. John Austin Stevens, editor of the *Magazine of American History,* permitted Williams to use his office and his private library. He also worked at the Lenox and Astor libraries and at those of the New-York Historical Society and the New York Society.[9]

During his absence from Ohio, the Washington *People's Advocate* accused Williams of having departed for parts unknown, "leaving behind him numerous creditors and a sorrow stricken family." By this time Williams had gained a reputation for neglecting his wife and child but had not yet deserted them. In a subsequent issue, the paper repeated the story about Williams's "disappearance," adding, "The history of 'The Colored Race in America' may remain long unpublished, but better by far that it never go 'to press' than written by one upon whose memory there rests a dark cloud." Apparently Williams did not learn of these attacks on his character until he returned to Ohio. He immediately wrote the editor that he had been so busy with his history that he scarcely knew what was going on in the world. "I was in New York nine weeks using the libraries. I am entirely absorbed at present, but hope to get a breathing spell in the future." In the very next issue Williams gave a spirited defense of himself. He was surprised, he said, at being referred to as though he were a fugitive from justice and a disgrace to his race. Every charge against him was false, he insisted. After giving a detailed account of his summer work in New York, Williams said that the Democratic candidate for governor of Ohio, J. W. Bookwater, had spread rumors about him, recognizing in him a "formidable campaigner." The Democrats had hired a "low, vulgar fellow" to publish articles about him in papers that blacks would read. Happily, Williams said, he returned early enough to catch the plot in its early stages. He denied that he owed any money and declared that his credit was good.[10]

Williams spent much of the autumn of 1881 in Columbus working on his history. He took a study on High Street and worked there when he was not in one of the libraries, although his family was still living in Columbus. He was resourceful in securing information that was difficult to acquire. He knew that it would not be easy to render a version of history that took into account the role of the inarticulate masses and those whose records could not be found in the usual repositories. So, he placed a letter in a Negro weekly newspaper, the Huntsville (Alabama) *Gazette,* which he requested "friendly papers" to copy. He informed the readers of his ambitious project and asked for specific information on a dozen topics. He wanted to know about the process of Reconstruction in the several Southern states. He requested the "minutes of any colored church organization, statistics on Negro schools, information on so-called Negro crimes, evidence of the accumulation of capital among

Negroes, materials on social conditions among Negroes, and information on the cause or causes of the exodus of Negroes from the South." He
promised to handle all documents carefully and return them safely free
of cost.[11] It is not possible to know how much information this request
produced. When his work was published, Williams did express his
gratitude to all persons who had sent newspapers and pamphlets; some
may have done so in response to his letter to the newspapers.[12]

Williams was especially interested in providing his readers with
ample information on Negroes as soldiers throughout the history of the
country, but particularly during the Civil War. To that end he wrote
General William T. Sherman requesting answers to twelve questions.
He wanted to know if "colored men make as good soldiers as white
men," if they could stand cold as well as heat, if they were good
cavalrymen, what percentage of them deserted annually, what percentage of them was literate, what percentages were from the North and the
South, and what was the percentage of reenlistment. Sherman indicated, on his endorsement of the letter from Williams, that he had given
his personal views in answer to certain questions raised by Williams and
had referred others involving statistics to the adjutant general. The
adjutant general wrote to Williams informing him that his office was
unable to provide the information because "the heavy official demands
upon the clerical force precludes the possibility of compiling the statistics you ask for, the collation of which would consume much time and
labor."[13]

But Williams had already begun to seek the facts from other sources.
Shortly after the legislature adjourned in April 1880, he made an extensive trip to the western part of the United States. His itinerary included
military posts in Texas, New Mexico, the Indian Territory, and Kansas.
In Santa Fe he had an interesting interview with General Lew Wallace,
governor of the territory of New Mexico, about the general's conduct at
the Battle of Shiloh.[14] He also looked into the possibility of establishing a
Negro settlement in New Mexico.[15] The main purposes of the trip,
however, were to improve his health, which had not been robust since
he sustained the gunshot wounds at Fort Arbuckle in 1868, and to talk
with Negro veterans of the Civil War. He interviewed many black
enlisted men and noncommissioned officers, as well as white officers in
command.[16] Thus he gathered valuable firsthand information not only
for his general history but also for his history of the Negro troops, which
he published subsequently. These interviews surely mark Williams as
one of the pioneer investigators in the field of oral history.

Williams was also a pioneer in the use of newspapers. In history
seminars at the universities, little stress was laid on newspapers; so the

monographs written by the first generation of scientific historians reveal no extensive use of this critical source. John Bach McMaster, who was teaching civil engineering at the University of Pennsylvania and working on the first volume of his *History of the People of the United States*, was one of the few researchers committed to their use. He got his first opportunity to teach history at Pennsylvania *after* the first volume appeared, and thereafter he urged his students to use newspapers. Before that time, however, Williams was already deeply involved in research in press archives in Ohio, New York, and Washington in order to broaden and deepen the base of his findings.

Since Williams was not formally trained in the canons of historical research, we do not know whether he actually saw all of the newspapers that he cited, though he referred specifically to his use of newspapers in the State Library of Ohio and the Library of Congress. In the nineteenth century, newspapers frequently copied from one another, sometimes giving attribution and sometimes not. Authors may well have engaged in similar practices. In any case, Williams cited some seventeen newspapers in the second volume of the *History*.[17] He may have used others that he did not cite.

Aware of his limitations, Williams sought the advice and support of a hand-picked mentor, George Bancroft, who, like him, had no formal training in the historical seminar. Now in his eighty-second year, Bancroft was still active, and his works were still widely read. Many regarded him as the dean of American historians. Williams first made contact with Bancroft in June 1881, when Bancroft was in Newport, Rhode Island, and Williams was doing research in New York. Williams told Bancroft he had always admired him and had read his works "with profit and delight." He asked whether Bancroft might suggest "any obscure materials of value," which could help make Williams's work more thorough "and entirely trustworthy." Williams also indicated that he would like to visit Newport if it was convenient to Bancroft, so that he could tell him of the book and its plan.[18] In his cordial reply, Bancroft said he regarded the work in which Williams was engaged as being "of the utmost importance." He had no doubt that Williams would follow "the good rule of applying the severe laws of historical criticism in the use of his materials." If so, he would be doing the public and science a great service. He indicated that he was busy seeing a book through the press, but if Williams should chance to come to Newport, he would hope to see him. He was almost always at home in the evening.[19]

Although they did not meet that summer, Williams kept in touch with Bancroft and continued to seek his advice. After he returned from his research trip to the East, he wrote to the older historian, enclosing copies of the centennial oration he had delivered at Avondale, and his speech on the education of freedmen. Again, he asked Bancroft for any material that would aid him in a "more thorough prosecution" of his labors. By this time he was confident enough to tell Bancroft that on the subject of hereditary slavery in Massachusetts, the Negro's militia status during the War for Independence, "and several other points," he had reached conclusions different from those of his correspondent. He hastened to add that in a work of such magnitude as Bancroft's *History,* "one with which you have honored all men who speak the English tongue throughout the world . . . you could not be a specialist."[20]

When the first volume of his work was already in press, Williams was still seeking Bancroft's assistance. He had cited Bancroft as authority on "very many questions," he wrote the venerable historian. Referring to Bancroft's assertion that the roll of the army at Cambridge bore the names of men of color and that General Artemas Ward had a return made of the "complexion" of the soldiers, Williams wished to know Bancroft's sources on these matters.[21] Bancroft replied that he put in his own history all that he knew on those subjects. "I have never been able to find a copy of the whole original return." He said that he was looking forward "with great interest" to the appearance of Williams's history and wished him much success.[22]

Williams doubtless had the advice and assistance of other historians as well. John Austin Stevens gave him more than the office facilities of the *Magazine of American History*. He did "everything in his power" to aid him in his investigations, help that Williams gratefully acknowledged. George H. Moore and S. Austin Allibone of the Lenox Library had also shown him "many kind favors."[23] When the first volume of the Williams history appeared, Justin Winsor, then working on his *Narrative and Critical History of America,* took note of the expression of thanks that Williams wrote to Moore in the preface. "I have looked into it enough to see he has had a helper in you," Winsor wrote Moore. "Good for you and good for him."[24]

Although Williams sought and received assistance from many historians, librarians, bibliophiles, and others, he remained fiercely independent. The organization and interpretation of his materials were his very own; and he was neither taken in nor awed even by the most important and influential authorities. He acknowledged that George H. Moore's "refined sarcasm, unanswerable logic, and critical accuracy give him undisputed place amongst the ablest writers of our times." Yet on the very next page he noted: "Dr. Moore says Josselyn's Voyages were printed in 1664. This is an error. They were not published until ten years later, in 1674."[25] In another work he said, "I have found it necessary, in the interest of history and science, to prick some bubbles of alleged history, and to correct the record."[26]

Williams regarded his sources with the healthy skepticism of a careful scholar. He was constantly checking one source against another and, where necessary, pointing out contradictions or irreconcilable differences. For example, he worked as hard on the question of abolition as he did on any other single topic. He was anxious to give the abolitionists due credit for their part in the struggle against slavery. But he would not accept every word they uttered as evidence of their uncompromising opposition to slavery on humanitarian grounds. After examining the writings of Horace Greeley, Williams concluded that Greeley "wished the slave free, not because he loved him, but because of the deep concern he had for the welfare of the free, white working-men of America."[27] After examining the writings of the antislavery leaders and the work of their societies, Williams concluded that it was the writings of black abolitionists such as Jermain Loguen, David Walker, Samuel Ringgold Ward, Austin Stewart, and Frederick Douglass that "exposed the true character of slavery, informed the public mind, stimulated healthy thought, and touched the heart of two continents with a sympathy almost divine."[28]

Thus, as historian of his race, Williams was essentially a revisionist. In his centennial oration he had lamented the neglect by many historians of the role played by Negroes in the American Revolution. "To take the negro out of the history of the Revolution is to rob it of one of its most attractive and indispensable elements; it is to impoverish it by the withdrawal of some of its most wealthy and enduring facts. In short, the negro is an integral part of revolutionary history."[29] This statement anticipated the general position that characterized his larger work. For example, in looking at the prohibition of slavery in Georgia when the colony was founded, Williams corrected those who had argued that the exclusion was based on humanitarian grounds. If slavery was "'against the gospel, as well as the fundamental law of England,'" as Georgia's founder, James Oglethorpe claimed, then why did Oglethorpe himself own slaves and a plantation in South Carolina, Williams asked. He pointed out that, even in official Georgia documents, slavery was prohibited on "political and prudential" grounds, considerations which were themselves brushed aside in less than twenty years.[30] His extensive comments in Chapter 6 of his *History* on the role of black leaders in the antislavery movement were another example of his revisionism.

Nor did Williams shrink from the unpleasant task of correcting black writers who were guilty of misinterpretations in the history of their own people. Of Benjamin Banneker, the black astronomer, Williams asserted that "William Wells Brown, William C. Nell, and all the Colored men whose efforts I have seen, have made a number of serious mistakes respecting Banneker's parentage, age, accomplishments, etc." To set the record straight he then cited his own sources—the Banneker memoirs prepared by J.H.B. Latrobe and J. Saurin Norris and "other valuable material" in the Maryland Historical Society.[31] William Still, the black abolitionist, was not only a participant in the activities of the Underground Railroad but, from the time that his book on the subject appeared in 1872, was regarded as a leading authority. This regard did not place Still beyond the reach of Williams's criticism, however. "It is to be regretted," Williams wrote, "that William Still, the author of the U.G.R.R. [*The Underground Railroad*], failed to give any account of its origin, organization, workings, or the number of persons helped to freedom. It is an interesting narrative of many cases, but is shorn of that minuteness of detail so indispensable to authentic historical memorials."[32]

Objectivity is an ideal to which most historians aspire, but few attain it, even under the most favorable, but rare circumstances. It is even more difficult to attain if one's function is largely revisionist, for such a historian takes essentially an adversary position with regard to the historians he is seeking to revise. In his vigorous attempt to make his case, the danger of overstating it and thereby yielding to an unremitting subjectivity is ever present. Well aware of this danger, Williams was constantly striving to avoid it. "My whole aim," he said in the preface to the *History of the Negro Race*, "has been to write a thoroughly trustworthy history; and what I have written, if it have no other merit, is reliable."[33] He was seriously committed to the scientific approach; and he later told the president of the American Antiquarian Society that he wished to use the materials of the Society to "promote science and history."[34] Even so, he was forced to admit in the preface to the second volume that "many pages . . . have been blistered with my tears." This was hardly the most desirable state of mind for the writing of scientific history.

Even though Williams knew what the highest canons of historical research and writing required, it was not easy to abide by them when the very atmosphere in which he wrote was charged with racial antipathies and filled with assumptions of Negro inferiority. The zeal to "revise" could lead, at times, to excesses, and he could be as guilty of excesses as others. In the antebellum north, he said, the only thing to which a young Negro could aspire was "the position of a waiter, the avocation of a barber, the place of a houseservant or groom, and teach or preach to their own people with little or no qualification."[35] But he wished also to tell what Northern blacks could achieve by overcoming their disadvantages. So he described in detail how they had made remarkable strides in antebellum Boston in education, the ministry, business, law, and letters.[36] Perhaps these were exceptions to prove the rule, but Williams's generalization had been so sweeping as to permit few, if any, exceptions.

The completion of the *History of the Negro Race from 1619 to 1880: Negroes as Slaves, Soldiers, and as Citizens* was a major achievement. Williams had done an enormous amount of research, employing new as well as traditional methods. He said that he had consulted "over twelve thousand volumes—about one thousand of which are referred to in the footnotes—and thousands of pamphlets."[37] The work was comprehensive, extending in the first volume from a discussion of biblical ethnology and African civilizations through the colonial and revolutionary periods. The second volume dealt with the antebellum years, the Civil War, and Reconstruction. While Williams did not subscribe to the view that slavery was ordained by the scriptures, he felt justified in discussing the problem because "the defenders of slavery and the traducers of the Negro built their proslavery arguments upon Biblical ethnology and the curse of Canaan." Williams assumed that "God gave all the races of mankind civilization to start with," thus reflecting his own general views regarding the divine role in man's conduct and activities.[38] In order to provide the proper background out of which Afro-Americans came, Williams discussed the African kingdoms of Benin, Dahomey, Yoruba, and Ashanti. Then, after giving attention to African languages and writings, he turned to the colony of Sierra Leone and the Republic of Liberia as examples of modern development in Africa.

Williams was greatly interested in slavery in the colonies, and he took to task one historian after another for having erred in asserting that slavery was established in 1620 in Virginia, "the mother of slavery as well as the 'mother of Presidents.'" He insisted that the historians who gave the date as 1619 were also in error, "that the ship 'Treasurer' was the first to bring them to this country, in 1618." His discussion of the problem reveals an extensive mastery of the literature on early Virginia history. In the final analysis, Williams observes, the fact is that the Colony of Virginia purchased the first Negroes, "and thus opened up the nefarious traffic in human flesh."[39] This preceded by a generation the revisionist findings of later historians that those first Africans in Virginia were not slaves at all but indentured free Negroes.[40]

Although Williams devoted at least a chapter to each of the colonies, he reserved for Massachusetts his most extensive treatment as well as his most severe strictures. "The poor Negro of Massachusetts found no place in the sympathy or history of the Puritan—Christians whose deeds and memory have been embalmed in song and story." Williams scoffed at those historians and laymen of Massachusetts who claimed that while slavery did creep into the colony, it was "not probably by force of law, for none such is found or known to exist." Meanwhile, he argued, from the time that slavery was introduced in Massachusetts, "her white citizens were forging legal chains for the Negro." Worse still, no historian can dispose of the *"historical reality of hereditary slavery in Massachusetts,* down to the adoption of the Constitution of 1780. "[41] Perhaps it was the excessive claims that Massachusetts made of her role in the fight for freedom that prompted Williams to attempt to bring those claims closer to the truth. Perhaps it was something in his own experience in the state from 1870 to 1875 that caused him to withhold any undeserved praise for Massachusetts. Whatever the reason, Massachusetts did not fare very well at the hands of the historian of the race.

Williams had a special interest in military history not only because of his own service in the Civil War but also because he was anxious to emphasize the patriotic role of blacks in the nation's wars. It was in the crucible of war, he believed, that a people showed whether or not they deserved the favors and protection of the government under which they lived. In this nation's civil conflict Williams was certain that his people had won the right to full citizenship. In the Revolution, "the Negro soldier fought his way to undimmed glory, and made for himself a magnificent record in the annals of American history." In the War of 1812 the commissioners who concluded the terms of peace were "armed with ample and authentic evidence of the Negro's valorous services." No history of the Civil War "has ever been written, no history of the war can ever be written, without mentioning the patience, endurance, fortitude, and heroism of the Negro soldiers who prayed, wept, fought, bled, and died for the preservation of the Union of the United States of America!"[42]

Williams anticipated his subsequent full-scale treatment of the subject, *A History of the Negro Troops in the War of the Rebellion 1861–1865,* by devoting no less than seventeen chapters—148 pages—in the *History of the Negro Race* to various aspects of the Civil War. He gave considerable attention to the equivocation of the federal government in the early years of the war on such matters as the use of Negro troops and the status of slaves behind Confederate lines. The war took on a new and different character after Lincoln issued the Emancipation Proclamation. Although originally not a humanitarian but a war measure, emancipation was nevertheless destroying slavery, the cornerstone of the Confederacy, "and the ponderous fabric was doomed to a speedy and complete destruction." To the slave "it was like music at night, mellowed by the distance, that rouses slumbering hopes, gives wings to fancy, peoples the brain with blissful thoughts."[43]

Williams wrote bitterly—perhaps from personal experience—of the treatment of Negro soldiers, including the "persecuting hate of white Northern troops. . . . Hooted at, jeered, and stoned in the streets of Northern cities as they marched to the front to fight for the Union . . . there was little of a consoling nature in the experience of Northern soldiers." Even so, no one could dispute the Negro soldiers' fighting qualities. In pointing this out, Williams relied on neither his opinion nor his memory. Rather, he used the testimony of others. Of the First South Carolina Volunteers, commanded by Thomas Wentworth Higginson, he referred to a piece in the New York *Times*: "The bravery and good conduct of the regiment more than equalled the high anticipations of its commander." He quoted from the report of General Nathaniel P. Banks regarding the First Regiment of Louisiana Engineers, "composed exclusively of colored men, excepting the officers. . . . Their conduct was heroic. No troops could be more determined or more daring."Of the assault on Fort Wagner by the Fifty-Fourth Regiment of Massachusetts Volunteers under Colonel Robert Gould Shaw, Williams quoted the celebrated letter from Edward L. Pierce to Governor John A. Andrew: "The Fifty-fourth did well and nobly, only the fall of Colonel Shaw prevented them from entering the Fort. They moved up as gallantly as any troops could, and with their enthusiasm they deserve a better fate. . . . Could anyone from the North see these brave fellows as they lie here, his prejudice against them if he had any, would all pass away."[44]

There is no extensive treatment of the Reconstruction years in *A History of the Negro Race*. Williams offered the explanation that he was preparing "a History of the Reconstruction of the late Confederate States," in two volumes.[45] There are other possible explanations, however. Reconstruction was barely concluded when Williams was writing, and there had been insufficient time to provide any perspective on the matter. It was a massive topic whose sources were scattered throughout the South, where he could well have experienced problems in the early eighties trying to consult documents. He was anxious, moreover, to complete the history whose significance he fully recognized, and from which he understandably wished to escape after a period of such concentrated effort. The book on Reconstruction could wait. Unhappily it never was written.[46]

Instead of dealing with Reconstruction as a major political, economic, and social problem of the postwar years, Williams gave attention to the growth of black institutions—primarily schools, colleges, and churches—and the emergence of a cadre of black leaders, whom he called "Representative Colored Men." Six of them were women, including Frances Ellen Watkins Harper, the poet; Fanny Jackson Coppin, the educator; and Edmonia Lewis, the sculptress. It is not without significance that of the six men whom Williams treated at some length, only one —Blanche K. Bruce—was a Reconstruction officeholder. The others, J. Milton Turner, David Ruggles, Frederick Douglass, Richard T. Greener, and John P. Green represented a variety of public and private pursuits. Although his evaluation of Douglass was, on the whole, favorable, Williams earned Douglass's eternal wrath by criticizing his view that the Constitution was an antislavery document and by insisting that Greener got the better of Douglass in the debate over whether Negroes should leave the South and settle in the North.[47] Greener declared that they should, while Douglass insisted they should not. The issue is still subject to debate.

There is no question but that *A History of the Negro Race* was hastily written. In less than two years, part of which time Williams was serving in the legislature, he put together a work of some 1092 pages including appendixes and index. He said in his preface that it had been seven years since he began "this wonderful task." He was counting from the time he wrote his centennial oration in 1876, but there is no evidence that he began to work seriously on the history before 1880. It was characteristic of him to work at breakneck speed; and although he was as diligent and as earnest as it was possible to be, he could not have properly assimilated and interpreted all the data he had collected. The wonder is that he managed to produce a work so ambitious in scope and so comprehensive in treatment. One problem Williams never solved satisfactorily was what to do with supporting documents. He placed some in the appendixes but most in the text itself. This gave the work the appearance, in some places, of a documentary history, but it also suggested improperly digested material.

Although he insisted that he was objective and scientific, Williams's history reflects his personality, experiences, and values. In his zeal to identify with the upper classes, he not only separated himself from most of the freedmen but misunderstood and misinterpreted their position as well. In the parlance of the day he called the Reconstruction governments of the South "Negro governments," although Negroes did not control any of them. He showed the extent to which he had yielded to the current anti-Negro propaganda when he declared, "An ignorant majority, without competent leaders, could not rule an intelligent Caucasian minority." It is a statement worthy of his Southern white contemporaries, Philip A. Bruce and Thomas Dixon, Jr. He was strong in his advocacy of industrial education and, by implication, tended to minimize training for the professions. He said, "We would rather see a Negro boy build an engine than take the highest prize in Yale or Harvard."[48] It is a statement worthy of Booker T. Washington fifteen years later, but it seems not to recognize that the best place to learn to build an engine was in the best engineering schools in the land.

Williams's *History* also reflects his optimism, which was based on faith in a divine power that preordained events and enlisted adherents to assist in evangelizing the rest of the world's peoples. When black Hiram R. Revels took the seat in the United States Senate occupied by the former president of the confederacy, Jefferson Davis, Williams declared that it was "God's work, and marvellous in the eyes of the world." In his discussion of the early life of D. W. Anderson, pastor of Washington's Nineteenth Street Baptist Church, Williams said that "God was training this man for the great mission which he afterward so faithfully performed."[49] He was particularly interested in extending education and Christianity to Africa. He said that it was his "hope and prayer" that the friends of missions in all places "where God in his providence may send this history will give the subject of the civilization and Christianization of Africa prayerful consideration." In closing his work he expressed the hope that after Negro Americans achieved a high level of education, they would then turn their attention to the civilization of Africa. He hoped that the United States would establish a steamship line "between this country and the Dark Continent." In this way the ship would carry "missionaries, Bibles, papers, improved machinery, instead of rum and chains." Africa, in turn, would send useful commodities for American consumption, instead of slaves. "Tribes will be converted to Christianity; cities will rise . . . geography and science will enrich and enlarge their discoveries. . . . In the interpretation of *History* the plans of God must be discerned, 'For a thousand years in Thy sight are but as yesterday when it is passed, and as a watch in the night.'"[50]

As early as June 1880, during the first summer that Williams gave most of his attention to his *History*, the press announced that Harper and Brothers had engaged him to write a history of the Negro race in America. Since the Cincinnati *Commercial*, to which Williams had contributed a column, was among the papers making the announcement, one can assume that Williams had no objection to it.[51] Before the end of the summer, however, in reply to a Cincinnati citizen with "an inquiring turn of mind," the house of Harper stated that it had made no arrangement with Williams "for a work of the kind referred to."[52] Unfortunately, it cannot be ascertained whether there was ever any serious negotiation between Harper and Williams.[53] Nor is it clear when G.P. Putnam's Sons entered the picture. In August 1882, Williams stated that he had signed a contract with Putnam and that he would be in New York for some time "directing the work of publication."[54]

Doubtless, Williams hoped for substantial financial gain from the publication of his *History*. During the final stages of production he took off little time to earn a living, and even after the work appeared, he was, for a time, virtually destitute. It was at this point that he sought assistance from a Beacon Hill matron, Mary Trail Lowell Putnam, the sister of James Russell Lowell. Mrs. Putnam's late husband had been a well-to-do Boston merchant, apparently unrelated to the publishers. We do not know when and under what circumstances Williams met Mary Putnam, but in the winter of 1883 he called on her and they discussed many matters. Shortly thereafter he wrote to the seventy-three-year-old widow that since his visit to her home, he had been thinking of her "with intensity." He praised her for having given so much to humanity, including a husband and son in the war as well as her own numerous literary works. This rendered his own efforts insignificant by comparison. He thanked her for the "generous aid" she had given to save his library, which was still in danger if he did not secure additional aid soon. He also thanked her for her "Sacrifices and noble labors" in behalf of his race.[55]

In June 1883, Williams wrote to Mrs. Putnam again, this time on a more personal matter. His wife, whose father had just died, was ill, and he had moved her and their son to Plymouth, Massacusetts, for the summer. Since he could not draw any money on his forthcoming publication until August and was in very great need, he requested Mrs. Putnam to advance him $35 or $50 until that time. When he had not heard from her within a week's time, he sent her a brief note indicating that he was working at the Massacusetts Historical Society, "and should you grant me the privilege of calling, I shall be glad to receive the answer there."[56] There is no record of Mrs. Putnam's having replied to any of Williams's letters.

In the summer of 1883, when not at Young's Hotel in Boston (from which he wrote Mrs. Putnam) or at Plymouth with his family, Williams was in New York, seeing the *History* through the press.[57] He wrote the preface in November 1882 while in New York, and apparently remained there until bound copies were ready. The appearance of the new work was recognized by the Boston *Transcript* in February 1883, by which time it was for sale in Boston, New York, Washington, and elsewhere.[58] Williams had done his part. He needed only to wait and see if his efforts would be received with the acclaim that a "scientific" historian's work deserved.

The *History of the Negro Race in America* was a handsome work, first published as a two-volume set and subsequently appearing in a "Popular Edition—Two Volumes in One." Its cloth binding was dark green with the author, title, and publisher in gold lettering on the spine. On the face were two gold stripes near the top and two near the bottom, between which were the words "History of the Negro Race" in black letters. The title page conformed to the current practice of providing a long, descriptive title and an extensive statement on the author's career. The frontispiece was an autographed steel engraving of the author.

The work was dedicated to the Reverend Justin Dewey Fulton, a well-known Baptist clergyman in Brooklyn, and the Honorable Charles Foster, former member of Congress and governor of Ohio from 1880 to 1884. Of the "Illustrious Representative of the Church of Christ," Williams said that Fulton had stood as the "intrepid champion of divine truth" for a quarter of a century and had pleaded the cause of the "Bondmen of the Land" during the dark days of slavery. He praised Foster, the "Distinguished Statesman," for "Sacrificing Personal Interest to Public Welfare" and for being the "first northern governor to appoint a colored man to a position of public trust."

George Washington Williams, at thirty-three years of age and with no formal training in the field of history, had achieved what no other Afro-American had achieved and indeed what no other person had ever achieved. He had provided a sustained, coherent account of the experiences of the Negro people. And, anxious to be judged by the most exacting critics, he was quite ready to see what others would say about his work. He did not need to wait long.

·9·

The Historian and his Public

The first reaction to *History of the Negro Race* was one of amazement that a member of that race had produced a work so extensive and at the same time written with authority and felicity. Reviews began to appear in December 1882, shortly after the first volume was published, and continued with the publication of the second volume in the spring of 1883. The Cincinnati *Commercial* declared that it was a work that will "without doubt be placed at the head of books prepared by a colored man." The New York *Independent* called it "an epoch-making book," written by an "educated colored man" who had "devoted the best years of his life to the sad history of his race in bondage, not for controversy or revenge, but to 'give the world more correct ideas of the colored people,' and to incite the latter to greater effort in the struggle of citizenship and manhood. If this does not mark a new epoch in the history of the negro race and in the historical literature of America, what event since the abolition of slavery does mark a new epoch?" The New York *Times* said that thirty or forty years earlier "it would have been very generally doubted if one of that race could be the author of a work requiring so much native ability, as well as the acquired habits of the student."[1] Recent events as well as the appearance of the work by Williams had surely dispelled such doubts.

Williams must have been pleased that many regarded the very appearance of his work as epoch-making, but he was much more interested in critical appraisals of the content of his *History*. In due course they too came, running the gamut from fulsome praise to merciless criticism. The Cincinnati newspaper to which he had contributed a column for several years stated that Williams had faults as a writer, but they were not "the vital ones of lack of diligence and accuracy in collecting and handling his facts, nor an ability to make his history coherent, fair, even-tempered, and comprehensive. . . . His style is at times stilted and rhetorical." Yet Williams had dug out the solid truth "from a thousand scattered places," and made a book that would always hold a prominent place in American chronicles. It would be welcomed by every student of the history of Negroes in the New World.[2]

The New York *Times*, which clearly appreciated the significance of the work's appearance and was enthusiastic about its contribution, was more restrained in its appraisal. The reviewer felt that Williams should have omitted the earlier chapters dealing with the unity of mankind, African ethnology, and the history of Negroes in Africa. While Williams seemed not to know that Liberia was founded originally by slaveholders, "to get rid of the free blacks of the South," his history of slavery in the United States was, for the most part, as accurate and valuable as it was full, and showed habits of careful and patient research and of power of analysis. The reviewer concluded that on the whole there was much more in the work to praise than to find fault with, "and for obvious reasons one is much more inclined to be considerate than critical."[3]

In the early spring of 1883, shortly after the second volume appeared, Boston's leading newspaper, the *Evening Transcript*, published its review. It was "a remarkable work in more than one way," the *Transcript* declared. "Its style is clear and forcible, and its statements are supported by a large army of authorities, which show that the author gave much time to his task, and that his researches were conducted with singular judgment and thoroughness." The reviewer did not even take exception to Williams's strictures about New England's early commitment to slavery. "Humiliating as some of his statements are to the fair fame of the early New England colonists, it is nevertheless right that the facts should be told, and that responsibility for the evils of the past be placed where it properly belongs."[4]

By the spring of 1883 the magazine press had begun to review the *History*. There was as yet no *American Historical Review*, the first issue of which would not appear until 1895. But the *Magazine of American History*, the only periodical in the country devoted to American history, was already in business. Its founder-editor, the well-known financier, John Austin Stevens, who had extended many courtesies to Williams when he was doing research in New York, gave up the editorial direction in 1881. His successor, the Reverend Benjamin Franklin DeCosta, reviewed the *History of the Negro Race*. The work showed "much labored research," DeCosta observed, "and if there are those who, in some respects, could have performed the task better, few could have worked more enthusiastically or produced more acceptable general results." DeCosta thought, nonetheless, that the author's style was "not

sufficiently restrained." Unfortunately neither the origin nor the abolition of American slavery was treated with the precision and care that was
desirable. It would have been well, DeCosta continued, if Williams had
provided the details of emancipation, so that the critical reader could
have a better view of the subject. The editor was not inclined to cavil,
however, because "the author has achieved a large degree of success and
has endeavored to tell the story of the black man in an impartial spirit,
which will secure the sympathy and respect of all intelligent readers."[5]

One of the most favorable evaluations of the Williams opus appeared
in a rather unlikely place, the *Kansas City Review of Science and
Industry*. Its reviewer commended the volumes to anyone who doubted
"the ability of the colored man to accomplish excellent literary work."
Williams had produced what was easily the best account of the Negro
race that had yet been written. "Historical work is by no means easily
managed so as to convey the facts in an attractive manner." Williams had
succeeded admirably in maintaining the interest from beginning to end,
while keeping all the important points before the reader. There were a
few minor inaccuracies and some inelegances of expression, the reviewer said, but the book would long remain "a monument to the author's
laborious study and marked ability as a writer, while to future students it
will be a text-book, full, reliable and accurate."[6]

Williams was fortunate that the review in the *Atlantic Monthly*,
Boston's leading magazine, was, on the whole, favorable. The reviewer
found the general plan and arrangement of the work "excellent" and
"methodically worked out. . . . It is, in short, in all externals, a most
creditable and presentable book." He was less impressed when he
examined some of the chapters on early Africa and found them both thin
and lacking in substantial research. He hastened to add that the book
grew better as it went on. This was especially true when the author dealt
with various aspects of the African sojourn in the New World. He found
Williams's handling of slavery in Massachusetts flawed by a series of
unfortunate misstatements and petty hostility. "But with whatever
defects of omission and commission, the author has produced a work of
great value; one that will be a treasury of facts for future students, and
greatly facilitate their work, although it will inevitably be superseded in
time by a history prepared with yet fuller research, more careful literary
training, and a more judicial spirit."[7]

Perhaps the most unfavorable review appeared in the *Nation*. Expressing reluctance to disparage the work, the reviewer had a duty to
perform as critic. "He would be glad to say it was readable, but he has
not found it so; or a valuable book of reference, but it is not that; or
intellectually remarkable, but, by the only standard of comparison

which Mr. Williams would exact, it must be judged the crude performance of a mind in no way exceptionally endowed." There was no method
in the arrangement or classification. We may note, however, that the
reviewer was himself capable of some disorderly thinking as the following non sequitur will indicate: The reviewer was shocked to find Williams, educated in Massachusetts, arraigning the state as "conspicu-
ously sinful in her colonial slaveholding and heaping upon her epithets
which no one of her sister colonies provokes. . . . To conclude, we
cannot commend this work for originality, ability or accuracy."[8]

The one thing on which the reviewers were in agreement was that the
appearance of a work of such scope and magnitude and written by a black
man was itself an event worth noting. There was little agreement as to
the merits of the work. If one said it was poorly organized, another found
its general plan excellent. If one was distressed by its literary infelicities,
another was pleased with its clear and forcible style. If one found that
the work had little to commend it substantively, another declared that
Williams had done marvelously well as a historian. Williams was doubtless pleased that his work excited so much interest, even if some was
stimulated by reviewers skeptical of its value. Perhaps a Massachusetts
education should have made Williams look more kindly on colonial
slaveholding there.

By 1883, G. P. Putnam's Sons was a respected publishing house not
only in New York but also in London, where it had maintained a branch
for many years.[9] When the *History of the Negro Race* was published, it
was immediately available in London and received considerable attention in the literary press there. Most British reviewers—even those who
gave extensive attention to the work—insisted, with obvious conde-
scension, that it contained little that was new and found it bulky,
repetitive, and more declamatory than literary. The *Spectator* said that
in the strict sense of the word it was not a history at all, "but a mass of raw
material which, though it may be of inestimable service to the historian
of the future, will leave little but weariness and vexation of spirit with
the reader of the present." The *Athenaeum* complained that it was very
hard to wade through Mr. Williams's slough of facts, which added up to
no more than a "magnified Fourth of July oration." The *Academy* said
that the work showed "less judgment and critical experience than
industry," while the *Westminster Review* conceded that it contained "no
needless or offensive vituperation."[10] It is quite likely that the attention
the *History* received in the British press had something to do with
Williams's subsequent interest in visiting the British Isles (see chapter
12 below).

The Afro-American press was not well established at the time the

History came out. Among those publications that appeared regularly were the New York *Globe,* the Washington *Bee,* the Huntsville (Alabama) *Gazette,* and the *People's Advocate,* published in Washington, D.C., or Alexandria, Virginia. (There were others, but their appearance was at best irregular. Boston, Philadelphia, and Chicago were without Negro newspapers, although they would repair that deficiency within the next decade.)[11] Under the circumstances, it is not surprising that at the outset few blacks knew of the existence of the work by Williams. In its first issue in 1883, the Huntsville *Gazette* reprinted a very favorable review of the work that had appeared in the New York *Independent.* It may be assumed that if the editor of the *Gazette* had read the work, he shared the opinion of the *Independent's* reviewer.[12]

The Washington *Bee,* edited by William Calvin Chase, did not review the first volume but, by its remarks on the editorial page, left no doubt in the reader's mind what it thought of the volume. "The history of the Colored Race so-called, has been written by Rev. Geo. W. Williams, the editor of the late defunct *Commoner.* The history is unreliable and contains some gigantic lies that are familiar to the people of this day and time." Chase was especially offended by "one of the most gigantic lies" that asserted that Frederick Douglass and Richard T. Greener met in debate in 1879 before the Social Sciences Congress in Saratoga.[13] The editor was correct in arguing that the two men never met in debate in Saratoga. They did, however, prepare statements for the Congress on the question of the exodus of blacks from the South, with Greener favoring the exodus and Douglass opposing it. Undoubtedly, it was Williams's judgment of Douglass's performance that infuriated Chase. Williams had said that Greener, "with a keen and merciless logic, cut right through the sophistries of Mr. Douglass." Perhaps another criticism of Douglass that offended Chase was Williams's assertion that Douglass was wrong in viewing the Constitution as an antislavery instrument that contained "no guarantees in favor of slavery." In this view Douglass differed with the abolitionist leader William Lloyd Garrison, who believed that in order to secure the overthrow of slavery one had to work outside the Constitution.[14] Small wonder that Chase, whose admiration for Douglass was without bounds, said of the *History,* "Had we time we could pick out at least two hours of errors and lies in this so-called history of the colored race."[15]

Despite his occasional criticism of the most important black man in the United States, Williams too was a great admirer of Douglass. In the *History,* Williams devoted several pages to the career of Douglass, calling him "the first man of his race in North America," and declaring that "his memory and character, like the granite shaft, will have an enduring and undying place in the gratitude of humanity throughout the world."[16] At the large Washington banquet honoring Douglass on January 1, 1883, Williams was one of the featured speakers. His subject was "The Author." In describing the event, the editor of the *Bee* referred to him as the author of "a work which will be widely read." Chase, perhaps not yet familiar with the work, praised Williams for his "brilliant piece of word painting. . . . His glowing words, so full of hope and sentiment, carried his audience by storm, and he had scarcely taken his seat ere he was surrounded by men eager to grasp him by the hand and congratulate him."[17]

It is not clear when Chase began to turn against Williams. By the end of February 1883, Williams had joined the august company of the editor of the New York *Globe*, T. Thomas Fortune, and Philadelphia's leading Negro citizen, Dr. C.B. Purvis, both of whom had been called liars and cowards by Chase.[18] The editor's relentless attack on Williams attracted the attention of other editors and critics. The editor of the *Palmetto Press* of Charleston, for example, wondered what the *Bee* saw in the Williams volume that compelled it to pronounce the work a fraud. He felt certain that the *Bee* had not given the matter much consideration. Chase countered that he had given the matter "careful and most profound consideration"; he said that within a few weeks he would give the public "a true exposé of this book of fraud."[19]

T. Thomas Fortune's New York *Globe* was one of Williams's staunchest defenders. Its reviewer, J.B. Peterson, regarded by Fortune as "one of the brightest young men in New York," found few flaws in the work. He said that it should be carefully read by every member of the race "as it embraces a fund of valuable information which is accessible in no other form, and which is calculated to make every colored man feel that his race has something to be proud of, in the many obstacles to progress met and overcome."[20] In the week following its own review, the *Globe* opened fire on Williams's detractors. It was with "unmeasured indignation," the *Globe* declared, that it even mentioned the "few ruthless, ignorant attacks which have been made upon the subject matter of the 'History of the Negro Race in America.'" No other work from the pen of a colored author "bears upon its face greater industry, greater love of race, greater learning. . . . That there was one colored man, one colored newspaper, which would assail this work as a history of 'lies' fills us with amazement." The writer—undoubtedly editor T. Thomas Fortune—pointed out that the New York *Times, Sun, World,* and *Independent* had declared that Williams had made a valuable contribution to literature. It was unfortunate that one of his own had claimed otherwise.[21]

Chase kept his promise to review the *History* and give his "exposé." When the piece appeared in early May, it was little more than another tirade. Chase defended himself against the charges that his attacks had been urged by someone else. "The only inspirator which prompted us to do things, is our duty." He said that Negro papers throughout the country had, to a great extent, endorsed the book because the majority did not know of the "fraudulent historical representation made by Mr. Williams." Again he assailed Williams for his account of the so-called Douglass-Greener debate, charging that Williams had given inaccurate reasons for Douglass's parting with Garrison. He called the work a mutual admiration book in which Williams "tickled the fancy of his admirers and has thus brought himself down to shame and disgrace as a historian and philosopher." In another place in the same issue Chase said that he hoped that "the colored historian will be benefitted by our friendly criticism."[22]

Chase was so pleased with what he had said about the *History* that he printed an attack on himself by the editor of the Boston *Leader*. "We dare the *Bee* to show the fraud in the work of Mr. Williams," the *Leader* had railed, "and we will answer every charge made. . . . We defend the book because it deserves it, but the contents of the book is its best defense against the attack of narrow minded and jealous journalists. Bro. Chase, come to the front or shut up." Chase was apparently satisfied that his review more than met the *Leader's* challenge. Indeed, he thought it was the *Leader's* turn to reply to *his* points. He warned, "If you fail in your attempt to acquit Mr. Williams of his historical fraudulent publications, we shall consider you a liar and a narrow-minded journalist."[23]

Chase's sense of the correctness of his position, however intemperately he may have expressed it, was greatly strengthened by the open letter to Williams written by Frederick Douglass and carried in the same issue in which the review appeared. Douglass complimented Williams for having written a "very valuable work." He said that he had bought the book and would not be without it. The work showed industry, perseverance, and literary ability. Nevertheless, Douglass said, he felt Williams had been unfair to him. Williams placed him in the wrong light in asserting that it was the dissolution of the Union that abolished slavery when, as a matter of fact, "it was the salvation of the Union that secured the abolition of slavery." Williams was also unfair to Douglass on the question of the exodus. Douglass denied he had ever debated Greener on the matter. "I do not know how you can expect to win a reputation for honesty and veracity while you allow your pen to write deliberate falsehoods. I admire your talents, and am proud of your attainments, but I warn you that all success obtained by smartness uncoupled with truth will be transient."[24]

T. Thomas Fortune was impatient, even disgusted, with William Calvin Chase. In commenting on the *Bee*'s review of the *History*, Fortune referred to the *Bee* as the mouthpiece of Frederick Douglass "and frequently a very filthy spokesman." He said that the sole ground for the wholesale denunciation of Williams's "laborious and meritorious work" was that on one or two points he drew a wrong conclusion from incidents and utterances made by Douglass. This was certainly an unsufficient basis for rejecting the work altogether. Fortune could only lament the "very odious spirit" in which the *Bee* presented its objections, and he pronounced the review a "baseless conglomeration of incoherent platitudes." He conceded that Williams invited criticism in undertaking to write about living persons; and it would have been better if sketches of all such persons had been omitted. Even so, the *Bee* should not think that the history of the race begins and ends with any colored man, living or dead.[25]

Williams took the opportunity provided by the *Globe*'s reply to the *Bee* to direct some remarks of his own to the *Bee* and to Douglass. In a lengthy letter which Fortune published he thanked him for the "manly tone" of his editorial in the *Globe*, a paper that was conducted "upon the highest journalistic principles." He then requested space to reply to Douglass's letter "and the abuse of his organ." Although more than three hundred magazines and newspapers had thought the *History of the Negro Race* worthy of review, the *Bee* had not seen fit to review the first volume. "Mr. Douglass, if friendly to the writer, could have had the *Bee* review the volume, but he did not." Williams said that the attempt by the *Bee* to review the second volume was too feeble to notice. "The writer cannot get high enough to reach the level of my contempt. I proffer him the mercy of my silence."[26]

Williams insisted that Douglass was in error in claiming that slavery could have been abolished without a war. Even after Lincoln's election, his plea to the South went unheeded, and only *after* the dissolution of the Union was there a chance to abolish slavery. In reply to Douglass's charge that he had given only one side of the exodus question, Williams said he was not obliged to give all fifteen reasons why Douglass urged Negroes to remain in the South. He further criticized Douglass for advising the former slaves to remain in a section where Douglass himself was obviously unwilling to live.

Williams refuted the claim by Douglass that the debate on the question of the exodus between him and Richard T. Greener never took place. The two men were scheduled to debate in Saratoga before the American Social Science Association. Greener arrived, and Douglass was expected up to the day on which the discussion was to take place.[27] When Douglass failed to appear, his paper was read by Francis Wayland, dean of the Yale Law School and president of the association. Greener replied to it, and "according to the audience and the press of the country Mr. Douglass was vanquished. If Mr. Greener did not reply to Mr. Douglass in person, he did reply to his ideas, carefully and elaborately prepared, on the exodus. So much then for 'the truth of history.'" The exodus went on despite the "factious opposition" by Douglass, "and the debate proceeded at Saratoga, although he was absent. History made up her mind on the position Mr. Douglass took against his persecuted brethren. He should accept the result without repining."[28]

As the weeks passed, the *Bee* continued its attack on Williams and his history. Although it announced it would not waste its space "upon a man who will persist in lying,"[29] it reprinted criticisms of Williams that had appeared elsewhere. The *National People* told its readers that Williams could never be compared to "Gibbon, Motely [sic], or Bancroft, as far as accuracy of statement is concerned." The *Bee* reprinted the review in full.[30] The Boston *Leader* attacked Williams for coming into Boston and campaigning for the election of Congressman George Dexter Robinson who was attempting to unseat Governor Benjamin Butler. The paper quoted Williams as saying that Butler was not and never had been a friend of the Negro. It then quoted a passage from the Williams history in which Butler was praised for declaring runaway slaves to be contraband of war. The *Leader* did not quote that part of the history where Williams told of Butler's wishing to use his contrabands "for mere fatigue duty and . . . not as soldiers."[31] Believing that the position of Williams in Massachusetts confirmed its own low esteem of the historian, the *Bee* published the *Leader* pieces in full as well as the letter from H. L. Smith, editor of the *Leader,* to the editor of the Boston *Globe* containing a similar attack on Williams.[32]

If Williams was at all worried about the adverse criticism, he gave no indication of it. Whereas the level of criticism in the black press was much lower than that in the white press, hostility was much greater. Jealousy was probably one factor. Another could have been Williams's sharp verbal assault on Douglass, whom many regarded as beyond criticism. There may also have been the fear that Williams's achievement would give him an advantage over competitors for other opportunities and positions. If his name was not yet a household word, it was becoming widely known in the United States and even in Europe.

Williams appreciated more than most people that the history of Negro Americans was neither widely known nor seriously studied even among his own people. As a remedy, he suggested in 1883 the establishment of an American Negro Historical Society. Already there were numerous historical societies in the United States, in Ohio, New York, Massachusetts, and in other places where Williams had lived or visited. The Huguenot Historical Society and the American Historical Association were in the process of being organized.[33] Williams's suggestion was thus in keeping with a general increase in interest in historical activities in the United States.

He wrote the editor of the New York *Globe*, "If I have the floor I move that an 'American Negro Historical Society' be created, with a president, vice-presidents, secretary, recording and corresponding, and a librarian." He proposed an annual meeting at which time participants would read historical papers. He hoped that there would be an ongoing program of collecting and preserving manuscripts, books, and newspapers that constituted the "record of the race." He invited readers to signify their endorsement, after which he could set a time and place for an organizational meeting.[34] In the following week, Henry McNeal Turner, a former member of the Georgia legislature and a bishop in the African Methodist Episcopal Church, called the proposal "a grand conception." He hoped that Williams would press the idea to a complete fruition. He was especially anxious to encourage the preservation of the "Records and doings of our race. . . . Our posterity and the civilized world will need them."[35] Another reader "seconded the motion" for the historical society and nominated T. Thomas Fortune as president. Fortune declined "in favor of Col. Williams."[36]

Some Negro newspapers heartily approved the proposed American Negro Historical Society. The Charleston *New Era* called it a "capital idea" and expressed a willingness to aid the cause in any way possible. It suggested that local debating clubs collect and bind their essays on historical subjects and send them to the historical society. "It is time that the Negro had a literature," the writer concluded.[37] Even the Washington *Bee* conceded that the proposal had merit. With all due respect to Negro writers, biographers, "and even historians, the colored American soldier has not yet been placed in history, as he should be. This defect might be partially remedied through a national association." It therefore offered its "humble service to the colored or Negro historical society."[38] Unfortunately, there were not sufficient offers of any kind to bring the proposed society into existence. Nothing more was heard of it after the summer of 1883.

Regarding the promotion of his *History*, Williams was fortunate in the willingness of the press to expose it to the general public. The New York *Globe* offered it to its readers at $3.50 per volume and provided two addresses where it could be purchased. In Boston the agent for the *Globe* was also selling it.[39] Apparently Fortune's newspaper office was a principal source in New York for books by and about blacks. In June and July 1884, the *Globe* advertised the "Best and Latest Books on the Race," Tourgee's novels and Douglass's *Life and Times* among them. The largest portion of the advertisement, however, was devoted to Williams's *History*, giving the table of contents of both volumes.[40]

When the one-volume edition appeared in March 1885, it was advertised immediately in the New York press. One advertisement by G. P. Putnam's Sons carried words of praise from the New York *World*, the Indianapolis *Journal*, and the Boston *Zion Herald*. The new edition was priced at $4.00 and agents were invited to participate in the selling. Later, a writer in the New York *Freeman* called the work "admirable" and "the most extensive and comprehensive history of the race in this country."[41] In Boston the *Advocate* was giving copies of the *History* to any person who would send in the names of twenty-five paid yearly subscriptions. Some years later the New York *Freeman* offered the *History* to anyone who sent in four one-year subscriptions to the paper.[42]

Since there are no sales records, it is reasonable to infer from the issuance of an inexpensive edition and the accelerated advertisement by the publisher that the sales had not been as brisk in the first year as the publisher and Williams had wished. One may wonder how reliable was the statement by Williams in January 1885 that the work continued to have a good sale which brought him "the handsome royalty of $2,500.00 per annum." T. Thomas Fortune, who had done so much to promote the work, was not happy with what he called the "limited purchases." Calling the *History* "the most pretentious and most widely advertised work from the pen of a colored author," Fortune complained that "it has not indemnified one-hundredth part the industrious author for the years of investigation, compilation, and actual cash expended in preparing it for the press, to say nothing of the cost of production to the publishers of it."[43]

Few writers earn enough from their books to sustain them, and it is difficult to believe that Williams was one of those few. He may well have benefited from having become better known after the appearance of the *History*. He went on the lecture circuit and seemed to do well (see chapter 10 below). He was also in demand as an orator on patriotic holidays and other special occasions; and he continued to contribute articles to newspapers. He had been admitted to the practice of law in Ohio and Massachusetts (see chapter 10 below). This doubtless provided some opportunities to build his income. Writing history continued to be his greatest interest, however.

Williams was much more successful in his *History of the Negro Troops in the War of the Rebellion, 1861–1865*. Although the Civil War had ended more than two decades earlier, the role of the black soldier had received scant attention from the many white historians who had been writing about the conflict. It was as though 180,000 black soldiers had not participated at all.[44] "Even the appearance of the Negro soldier in hundreds of histories of the war has always been incidental," Williams declared. "These brave men have had no champion, no one to chronicle their record, teeming with interest" and many evidences of their patriotism.[45] By the mid-eighties the time was ripe for someone to give attention to the Negro troops in the Civil War. Williams had been interested in the subject for many years. In 1874, during his final month as a student at the Newton Theological Institution, he delivered a Memorial sermon, "The Advent of the Colored Soldier," before the Robert Bell Post of the Grand Army of the Republic in Boston.[46] His 180-page treatment of that conflict in his *History of the Negro Race* was informed by his own experience as a veteran.[47] Once the *History* was completed, he moved naturally and easily into the subject of Negro soldiers. Already he had accumulated a large body of sources from which to draw. Other sources were becoming available, moreover, as the War Department, especially the adjutant-general's office, organized and opened their papers, and as major sources were published, such as the *Official Records of the War of the Rebellion* (1880–1900).

Williams was a much more experienced student of history by this time. He traveled widely to collect his sources, working in the State House in Boston, the Departments of State and War, and the Library of Congress. He even went abroad—to Mexico "to examine the fields on which Negroes fought," and to England, France, and Germany to hear stories of their "matchless courage." The official sources that he used were most impressive. In addition to the *Official Records*, of which he must have been one of the early users, he examined manuscripts provided by the secretary of war, the state adjutants-general, war offices of foreign governments "through their ambassadors in Washington," and orderly books of general officers who commanded Negro troops. He also used the *Congressional Record and Globe*, the *Journal of the Confederate Congress*, and newspapers such as the New York *Times, Herald, World, Tribune*, and the Boston *Journal*. As he had done for his *History of the Negro Race*, he interviewed a variety of persons and sought the advice of knowledgeable participants in the war itself.[48]

Williams said that as an active member of the Grand Army of the

Republic he had heard many accounts of the heroism of Negro soldiers, but he would not permit those accounts to lead him from the record. He was also keenly aware that his view of events might be colored by his personal reminiscences. "I participated in many of the battles herein described," he wrote, "including some of the most severe conflicts of Negro troops with the enemy in Virginia. But I have relied very little on personal knowledge, preferring always to follow the official record." This, he was certain, would help him "avoid partisan feeling and maintain a spirit of judicial candor."[49]

Williams did not achieve objectivity merely by stating his goal; and there were instances in which he fell short of it. At least he was not always able to conceal his feelings. He described white troops who did not care to serve with blacks as persons upon whose "pedigree it would not be pleasant to dwell." Regarding the Fort Pillow affair in 1864, in which numerous black soldiers were allegedly "massacred," Williams declared that the incident demanded "great fortitude in the historian who would truthfully give a narrative of such bloody, sickening detail." Yet he managed to call the Confederate participants "barbarous," "fiends," "human hyenas," and their actions a foul deed "blacker than hell itself."[50] Many more people than Williams were outraged by these incidents. His judgment of them in subjective terms merely indicates how difficult it was even for Williams to remain dispassionate.

No earlier work had dealt extensively with Negro soldiers in ancient and modern times. Williams deemed it proper, therefore, to bring together in one work certain salient facts so that his contemporaries would understand the military capacity of black soldiers throughout history. He gave attention to the employment of Negroes in the armies of France, Britain, Brazil, and Peru to illustrate how widespread and important they were. He also treated the services of blacks in the War for Independence and the War of 1812 as well as their role in Haiti's struggle for independence from France.

Williams had an intimate knowledge of conditions in the South during slavery and of the critical problems attending the disruption of the Union after Lincoln's election. Knowing of the debates in the army and in the government preceding the employment of Negro troops in 1863, he covered the ways in which blacks were used by both the Union and Confederate forces while the debates were in process and before any blacks were armed. He also discussed the political and military implications of using Negroes as soldiers. In his book one can follow the process, "both logical and inevitable,"[51] that led to the policy of employing Negroes as soldiers.

Williams was obviously pleased to have been a part of the "largest force of civilized Negroes ever armed and marshalled for the field," with a total of 178,975 men. Devoting a chapter to each of the major areas in which Negroes were involved in the fighting, he followed them in the Departments of the South and the Mississippi and in the Armies of the Potomac, the Cumberland, and the James. There was a chapter on the Fort Pillow incident, where, Williams charged, Confederate generals Nathan B. Forrest and James R. Chalmers "violated the laws of civilized warfare" in not honoring the flag of truce offered by black troops. In a chapter on prisoners of war, he insisted that the men who murdered Union prisoners "disgraced their uniform" and committed a "crime against the profession of arms."[52]

The final chapter, "The Cloud of Witnesses," contained testimony of the "martial valor of the Negro Soldier . . . from the lips of friend and foe alike." Among those who had praised the Negro soldiers was Edwin M. Stanton, secretary of war, who remarked that in the battle of Petersburg "the hardest fighting was done by black troops." The adjutant-general of the army, Lorenzo Thomas, said that "their fighting qualities have . . . been fully tested a number of times, and I am yet to hear of the first case where they did not fully stand up to their work." Praise also came from Major-Generals James G. Blunt, S. A. Hurlbut, Alfred H. Terry, and W. F. Smith. Williams also quoted officers at other levels who complimented the Negro troops on their performance. There was praise, moreover, for blacks serving as laborers—perhaps as many as 150,000—and those on fatigue duty in many parts of the Union.[53]

One of the great results of the war, as Williams put it, was that the United States government "was taken from the shifting sands of the delusion of State Rights and built upon the adamantine foundation of National Unity." This was not all. The "disinthralment of 4,500,000 bondmen" was the brightest star that shone at the close of the war. "To wash out the foul stain of human slavery by the blood of patriots, to elevate the slave to the dignity of a soldier, and invite him into the arena of civil war . . . was an achievement hardly ever vouchsafed to a government before." Williams was distressed that nowhere in the country was there a monument to the "brave Negro soldiers," 36,847 of whom died in the war. To remedy this defect he suggested that the government erect a monument to them in the park in the front of Howard University.[54] In the months ahead he expended a great deal of energy in the effort to bring this about (see chapter 12 below).

Harper and Brothers did full justice to the *History of the Negro Troops* when they brought it out in 1887. The upper left-hand corner of the tan cloth cover bore the impression of a Negro sergeant, dressed in the uniform of the Union Army and shouldering a rifle. In the center was depicted a scroll of the Emanciption Proclamation that had been hurled against the chains of slavery, breaking them into a splash of gold. The frontispiece was a steel engraving of Williams dressed in full militia uniform and wearing a medal. The book was dedicated to his comrades in arms, "The Negro Soldiers who Heroically Served Their Country in the War of the Rebellion."

The appearance of the new work had been widely heralded. Fortune's paper, the New York *Freeman*, reported already in September 1886 that Williams was in the city arranging for the publication of the work.[55] Similar announcements appeared in Boston, Cleveland, and Washington.[56] When the book came out, it was praised even in the news articles. The Indianapolis *World* said that it would be a valuable addition to Negro literature.[57] Even the Washington *Bee*, so hostile to Williams's earlier work, called the *History of the Negro Troops* "a credit to the author and an honor to the dead heroes."[58]

An early review in the New York *Sun*, which must have delighted Williams, called the work "a striking and trustworthy account." The materials that resulted from Williams's research had been "verified and sifted with an amount of care and candor that reflect high credit on the author. . . .No honest reader of this volume will deny that Col. Williams has demonstrated at one stroke that the negro race possesses not only the gifts of a soldier, but those of a judicial expounder of events and of an accomplished man of letters." The lengthy review in the Boston *Transcript* was more restrained but conceded that Williams "simply substantiates his statements of fact everywhere by abundant references to official documents and State papers."[59] The reviewer for the Boston *Post*, on the other hand, was annoyed by Williams's failure to give a more detailed account of the organization of the United States Colored Troops. What he gave was "so shiftless and incomplete . . . that the reader has no clear idea of the progress nor of the military significance of this great enrolment." There was similar dissatisfaction with the treatment of some of the military engagements. "Port Hudson and Fort Pillow and Millikin's Bend and Nashville are here—but what mention is there of the rest of the 125 actions in which black troops were engaged during the last two years of the War?"[60] The reviewer failed to mention James Island, Port Hudson, Poison Springs, and Petersburg, among other battles Williams did discuss. And to have described all 125 actions in which black troops were engaged would have burdened the reader.[61]

In early 1888 the magazine press began to carry reviews of *History of the Negro Troops*. The *New Englander and Yale Review* said that

Williams had told the story "with wondrous effect." The *Literary World* declared that the author deserved commendation "for the intelligence, discretion, and excellent workmanship with which he has prepared the book." The reviewer said that the work was a credit to Williams, his race, and their part in the war. It was also well written "considering our common impressions of the racial source of it." The reviewer in *The Dial* called the work "a valuable contribution to our literature of the civil war . . . full of absorbing interest, and . . . told in a graphic and finished style." He was particularly pleased with the manner in which the author analyzed and described the slow progress of the military status of Negroes from contraband to fighting men. He detected a certain understandable impatience on the part of Williams with the dilatory steps toward freedom and enfranchisement at a time when the president was of necessity preoccupied with whipping the South back into the Union.[62]

By remarkable coincidence, just a few months after Williams's book was published another history of Negro troops appeared: *The Black Phalanx: A History of the Negro Soldiers of the United States in the Wars of 1775–1812, 1861–65*, by Joseph T. Wilson of the Second Regiment of the Louisiana Native Guard Volunteers and of the 54th Massachusetts Volunteers. Wilson, a son of Massachusetts and a graduate of the New Bedford schools, had had a variety of experiences ranging from steersman on a whaling vessel to the mercantile business before he became a journalist in Virginia in the era of Reconstruction.[63] At the suggestion of his comrades in the Grand Army of the Republic, he decided in 1882 to write a history of Negro troops in the Civil War. It was inevitable that when the *Black Phalanx* came out in 1888, it would be compared with Williams's work. The two books were frequently advertised together by editors who operated bookstores in the editorial offices, and they shared some joint reviews.

One such review appeared in the *Nation*. The reviewer was as condescending and ungracious to both authors as he had been to Williams five years earlier. He began his review with the statement, "The history of the American colored regiments is yet to be written." That was unfortunate, the reviewer felt, for their achievement was one of the most picturesque and most essentially interesting features of the war. "Both of these books show honest intentions and a certain amount of praiseworthy diligence . . . but both show a want of method and an inability to command their own materials, so that they leave the reader with a renewed interest in the subject, but with a very imperfect sense of clear comprehension." In a curious way the works complemented each other, the reviewer felt, for each gave some facts and documents which the other omitted. He did concede that Williams's book was better arranged, "although it leaves in this respect much to be desired."[64]

Neither book received the attention that had been accorded the *History of the Negro Race*. There is little doubt that Williams's popularity had slipped since the appearance of his first work largely because of various controversies in which he had been involved.[65] By this time, T. Thomas Fortune had become disenchanted with him; Fortune's New York *Age* did not even review *A History of Negro Troops*. Meanwhile, Fortune not only reviewed *Black Phalanx*, calling it a "valuable compilation" but offered it at a premium to anyone who sent in six subscriptions to the *Age*.[66] Wilson, moreover, enjoyed considerable popularity on his own. His comrades in the Grand Army of the Republic had urged him to write the history of Negro soldiers, and many of them doubtless purchased it. There is no proof, however, for a contemporary claim that the sales of the Wilson book "surpasses that of any other work written by an Afro-American."[67]

Although Williams talked of completing other major historical works that he had under way, we have no evidence that he published any of them.[68] In the winter of 1885 he was in Washington working on a history of Reconstruction and a biography of Benjamin Lundy.[69] Nothing more was heard of the Lundy biography, but reports persisted that the Reconstruction book was forthcoming. In June 1885, a Boston paper said that Williams had completed the second volume of his Reconstruction work.[70] That obviously was not so, for almost three years later Williams was still collecting material. In January 1888 he requested assistance from Senator George F. Hoar of Massachusetts. For the chapter he was writing on affairs on the Texas border, he wanted the senator to secure for him seven volumes of *Diplomatic Correspondence on Mexican Affairs, 1861–67* and some five House Executive Documents of the Thirty-Seventh Congress.[71] The following month he wrote historian George Bancroft that he was composing chapters for his Reconstruction history, "consisting of four parts in a two-volume work."[72]

In the summer of 1888 an Indiana paper reported that Williams had just completed a "critical non-partisan history of reconstruction" in two volumes. Williams would be in Europe for several months, the paper continued, where he would be attending a conference in London and collecting material on the Continent for a life of Toussaint L'Ouverture.[73] The Reconstruction history was *not* completed, however. The previous year, Williams had told the librarian of the Massachusetts Historical Society that he expected to have the manuscript in the publisher's hands "by the first week in June."[74] Now, a year later, he was still fretting with it, even as he was turning away from historical studies altogether.

By the end of his career as historian, Williams enjoyed wide esteem. His works continued to be advertised, sold, and discussed. In Indianapolis, for example, the Reading Circle discussed "at considerable length" the career and writings of Williams. An autographed letter from Williams was read, after which the historian was tendered a vote of thanks and made an honorary member of the Circle.[75] At about the same time T. Thomas Fortune placed Williams "at the head of the bookmaking class among us," although he regretted that his *History of the Negro Race* was "a bit too discursive and voluminous to become a standard work."[76] In 1888, W. E. B. DuBois, then a graduating senior at Fisk University and editor of the *Fisk Herald*, rejoiced that "at last we have a historian, not merely a *Negro* historian, but a man who judged by his merits alone has written a splendid narrative."[77] Later, DuBois would call Williams "the greatest historian of the race."[78] Another editor, more extravagantly, dubbed Williams "the Herodotus and Pericles of the Negro race, the author of its civil and military history!"[79]

A Touch of Distinction

As Williams completed his *History of the Negro Race*, he was making rather elaborate plans to change his life. First, he decided to leave Ohio. It is not clear how much this decision was due to increasing opposition to him during his term in the legislature. There is no question that by 1883 his feelings toward his fellow Ohioans had cooled considerably. From New York he wrote his friend in Cleveland, John P. Green, that he was "done with Ohio, and the 'Grand Old Republican Party' within its limits. I shall never make any more sacrifices for Race or Party at the expense of myself and family. In the future we will look after number *one.*"[1] Second, Williams decided to continue his writing, having in mind some historical volumes as well as several works of drama and fiction. He was persuaded by the large number of favorable reviews of his *History* that many people would purchase his books, the income from which would support future literary efforts. In March 1883 he reported that he had signed a contract for a literary position "at a salary of $150.00 per month" and would move his family to New York.

Even as Williams wrote about moving to New York, he seemed to be focusing more attention on Boston. While in New York in January 1883, waiting for the second volume of his *History of the Negro Race* to appear, he visited friends in Portland, Maine, and stopped over in Boston for a few days. Some weeks later he was back in Boston to deliver an address at the annual convention of the Massachusetts Department of the Grand Army of the Republic. The following month he was again in Boston, this time to speak at a "large and fashionable literary and musical gathering . . . at the residence of J. A. Lewis."[2] Indeed, he seems to have been a regular commuter between New York and Boston in the spring of 1883. In April he made "fine speeches at several of

Boston's leading white clubs." He continued to be a guest at Young's hotel when in Boston;[3] his family apparently remained in Ohio.

After his departure from Ohio, Williams enjoyed immense popularity as a public speaker. Wherever he went, he was referred to as the distinguished historian of the Negro race. On April 9, 1883, almost coincidental with the appearance of the second volume of his *History of the Negro Race*, Williams delivered an important address in New York City. It was for the benefit of the Widows and Orphans Fund of Mount Olive Lodge of the Free and Accepted Masons. A major auditorium, Chickering Hall, had been engaged; and advance ticket sales were brisk, sufficient tickets having been sold a week before the event to meet expenses.[4] The lecture was a success in every way. There was a large and appreciative audience, and the platform was filled with distinguished personages, including E. W. Blyden, the President of Monrovia University, John F. Quarles, New York civic leader, and a number of prominent local clergy.

Choosing as his subject "The Future of the Negro Race in America," Williams briefly sketched the history of blacks in North America. Since Africans were brought in to do the work, he said, it took white Americans two hundred years to learn that every man must live by the sweat of his own brow. He took issue with the president of Brown University, E. G. Robinson, who believed that Negroes could never become Americanized, must always be subservient, and must ultimately return to Africa. "Well, we came here against our will," Williams said, "but now we're here we'll stay."[5] He also took Professor E. W. Gilliam to task for urging the colonization of Negroes outside the United States. Williams contended that the future of the Negro would rest in his own hands if he had education, ample economic opportunity, and freedom of religion.[6] Among favorable reactions to the lecture was an article in a white magazine in Memphis, *Meriwether's Weekly*. For the future of Negro Americans, the writer pointed out, it was urgent that the Southern white people give them the best of education. "We must remember that all Negroes are not destined to be coachmen, barbers, and waiters forever. The number like the historian, Williams, is increasing every day, and they will be considered valuable and honorable men."[7]

By the late spring of 1883, Williams had taken up residence in Plymouth, Massachusetts, where he and his family had previously spent several summers. In May, the Shaw Guard Association tendered a banquet in honor of Williams and Major Martin R. Delany, the physician and colonizationist. For Williams it was something of a homecoming as many of his old Massachusetts friends were present. It was rumored that he had purchased an interest in the Boston *Leader* and was a contributor or correspondent. He quickly protested that the use of his name in connection with the paper was without his knowledge or authority.[8] Even the rumor, however, confirms the view that Williams was by this time regarded as a resident of Massachusetts.

Once in the Bay State, Williams, in characteristic fashion, became active in politics. In the early fall of 1883 the lines had been clearly drawn and candidates had been nominated for the annual state elections. Benjamin F. Butler, elected governor the previous year, was renominated by the Democrats. To oppose him the Republicans nominated George D. Robinson, a member of Congress from Chicopee. Williams had been ambivalent about Butler, praising him for his support of passage of the Civil Rights Bill in 1875, but criticizing him for aspects of his conduct during the war. He had no difficulty, however, in throwing his support to the Republicans. In September he was on the official list of campaign speakers offered by the Republican State Committee.[9] Williams seemed to relish being back in Boston among friends and taking to the hustings with old cronies such as James H. Wolff and George L. Ruffin. Although the press sometimes referred to him as "George W. Williams of Ohio," the campaign gave him an opportunity to make the claim of being a Massachusetts man.

Williams spent the early fall stumping the state. In early October he spoke at New Bedford and Lynn. Later he was in Marblehead with gubernatorial candidate Robinson and made "an exposure and denunciation of some of Governor Butler's acts and methods." At a huge rally at the Twelfth Baptist Church, with George L. Ruffin presiding, Williams delivered a "masterly speech" for forty-five minutes "severely criticizing Butler's war record and denouncing Independentism." Indeed, he spoke right down to the end of the campaign, visiting rallies in Boston's south end, Chelsea, Cambridge, and other places.[10] With Robinson's election by 10,000 votes on November 6, 1883, Williams could rejoice that in his tireless efforts he had contributed to the Republican victory.[11]

A curious and unexpected turn of events gave Williams an opportunity to reintroduce himself to the Boston community in a most gracious manner. During the campaign there had been some discussion of the possible appointment of a Negro to a judgeship. Many seemed to think that the greater chance for such to happen would be under a Republican governor. Rumor had it that Governor Butler was seriously considering making such an appointment. His black supporters—among them James Monroe Trotter and George T. Downing—hoped but would not permit themselves to believe that the general would do what the Republicans had not done for twenty years. After his defeat, Butler surprised his supporters as well as his enemies by nominating George L. Ruffin, who had campaigned so arduously against him, to be judge in Charlestown.

The appointment of a Negro American to a judgeship in Massachusetts was a historic event. Indeed, there would not be another such occasion in Massachusetts until 1948. Williams fully appreciated the importance of the appointment, and began to make plans to celebrate it as soon as Ruffin was confirmed by the Commonwealth Council in mid-November. Working in the Commonwealth Archives, Williams was at hand when the council met. He testified in Ruffin's behalf and kept Ruffin informed of developments.[13] "I beg to tender you a Complimentary Dinner," he wrote his old friend Ruffin immediately following the confirmation, "in celebration of this event that clearly marks an epoch in the history of the Negro Race, and as a slight expression of my personal regard, my affection for your person, my admiration for your character." Williams suggested that the dinner be held on November 22, at 7 P.M., at Young's Hotel; the new judge apparently agreed.[14] Williams then invited fourteen leading Negro Bostonians, six of whom had been members of the Massachusetts legislature. Among them were veteran abolitionist Lewis Hayden; lawyer, editor, and civil rights leader Archibald H. Grimke; merchant tailor J. H. Lewis; and realtor J. C. Chappelle.

The dinner was an elaborate affair, complete with a printed program and menu. Presenting the honoree, Williams reviewed the history of Negroes in Massachusetts—in the "Massacre" at Bunker Hill, the Civil War, and Reconstruction. To Judge Ruffin he said, "You have touched a high point in our racial life . . . . Your elevation to a judicial position is an unmistakable evidence that the world moves." Williams then reviewed his long friendship with Ruffin, when he was a student at Newton, as a Sunday School teacher when Ruffin was superintendent, as Ruffin's pastor at the Twelfth Baptist Church, and as his companion at the Louisville convention earlier that year. "When I thought of going South or West, you were the only man whose advice I sought. And for the first time during our acquaintance we differed. I disobeyed your orders, sir; I went West, became editor, legislator, lawyer, and historian." The romance of modern history was revealed in the commonwealth of Massachusetts, Williams said, "where slaves were once hunted and from under whose world-famed institutions Anthony Burns was dragged back into the hell of slavery," but where a Negro judge "now clothes his decisions with the majesty of 'The Commonwealth of Massachusetts.' Indeed, truth is stranger than fiction." The *Transcript* observed that his remarks would compare favorably with after-dinner efforts of the most notable orators of Massachusetts. "Colonel Williams may worthily stand by the side of Frederick Douglass, and for stirring, graphic, eloquent speech, the twain need not be afraid to challenge the generality of white speakers to discuss public questions with them."[15]

Meanwhile, Williams had to make a living. The income from his writings and lectures was, at best, irregular. He had never really practiced law in Ohio, but now he wished to try his luck at it in Massachusetts. Immediately following the 1883 fall campaign, he requested the Supreme Judicial Court of Massachusetts to admit him to the bar. In his petition Williams informed the court that he had studied law with Judge Alphonso Taft and at the Cincinnati Law School, and was admitted to the Ohio bar in the fall of 1879. Actually Williams had failed the Ohio bar both in 1879 and in the following year; he was finally admitted in June 1881.[16] He also presented evidence of good moral character and professional qualifications. The petition was contained in a letter from George L. Ruffin, assuring the court that Williams was a man "of good character and in every way qualified to be admitted so to practice." Two days after Williams presented his petition, the Board of Examiners of Suffolk County admitted him as an attorney at law.[17] On December 5 he was sworn in before Judge Holmes of the Supreme Judicial Court; and fifty leading lawyers of the city were there to congratulate him.[18]

Williams was engaged as counsel for the Cape Cod Canal Company shortly after he opened his office on School Street in downtown Boston. At that time one reporter asserted that he was doing "an excellent business."[19] For a while, at least, the Canal Company business must have absorbed him. In late March 1884, he was in Washington making a legal argument before the Committee on Rivers and Harbors of the House of Representatives.[20] Since 1870 the Congress had been considering building a canal across Cape Cod as a part of various acts proposed by the committee.[21] In May, Williams was among those at Sandwich for the inspection of the "great dredger in the Cape Cod Ship Canal." Others present were E. C. Corrigan of the company's counsel; Samuel Fessenden, treasurer of the corporation; and members of the legislature—E. J. Thomas of the Senate and Edwin R. Bosworth of the House. It is not clear what role Williams played. Doubtless he had been in Washington to assist in convincing members of Congress that they should provide funds for the use of the company to construct the canal. The inspectors at Sandwich found the work of the dredger "most satisfactory," and the contractor and the company were "highly congratulated for success of the work shown."[22] But the company was no more successful than its predecessors had been. The canal would not be completed until July 1914.

The practice of law by no means occupied all of Williams's time. He was busy in Boston and elsewhere with his writing and lecturing, fraternal and military organizations, traveling, and politics. Like many Negro Americans, Williams had been greatly troubled by an article by Professor E. W. Gilliam of Charleston that appeared in the *Popular Science Monthly* in February 1883. Gilliam argued that the black population was growing faster than the white and would, in time, overtake it. Since blacks were not as intelligent as whites and could not expect to govern well when they came to power, the best course of action would be to colonize them in Central America, the West Indies, Africa, or anywhere, "while a peaceful adjustment is yet practicable." Recalling the views of a pioneer colonizationist, Henry Clay, Gilliam said, "happy would it have been for the country if his views had prevailed.[23]

Williams took the time to answer Gilliam, and in a lengthy piece published in the Boston *Evening Transcript* in January 1884 he refuted the professor point by point. After reviewing the fluctuation of census figures from decade to decade, he insisted that Negroes were "not gaining on the whites" because (1) the census of 1870 (the basis for Gilliam's alarm) was not at all accurate; (2) whites have two sources of increase: immigration and births, while Negroes only have births; and (3) the mental, moral, religious, and social development of Negroes would diminish their fecundity as it had that of whites. There was no evidence to support Gilliam's argument that blacks would always "cast a solid ballot" against whites. Blacks, Williams insisted, have shown "patience under great wrongs, and have taught the civilized world the gospel of forgiveness." Recalling that many whites, shortly after the Civil War, had predicted that blacks would die out because they no longer had masters to provide for them, Williams said, "We are confronted now by a new state of things." Instead of lamenting the untimely end of Negroes as citizens, "the class of Americans Professor Gilliam represents . . . sound a new alarm at the unprecedented increase of negroes."

Williams belittled the Gilliam argument that the "increase" and "improvement" of blacks would constitute "a menace to the whites." Such an idea, he said, was "un-American, undemocratic, and a slander upon the men and women, dead and living, who did so much to raise up the negro to the position of manhood and intelligent citizenship." On colonization, Williams said, "As well try to colonize the stars of the heavens, or shovel up the sands of the seashore, as to transport the negroes of America to the shores of Africa. . . . When asked to quit these shores the negro will reply, 'Intreat me not to leave thee, or to return from following after thee, for whither thou goest I will go. . . . Where thou diest I will die, and there will I be buried.'" The *Transcript* called the Williams article "remarkable." It ventured the opinion that "fair-minded readers will come to the conclusion that our colored townsman more than holds his own—in fact, that he shows the proposition of the Southern professor to be merely the old Southern prejudices wrapped in a quasi-scientific bag."[24]

Williams continued to be in great demand as a public speaker, for his reputation had spread far and wide. One reporter who had heard him at the Louisville convention said of him, "No man of our race with whom we are acquainted possesses his peculiar power in public speaking."[25] He was especially popular among fraternal and military groups. When the Lewis Hayden commandery of the Knights Templar of Boston held its fifth anniversary banquet in April, it was one of their own, "Sir George W. Williams," who was the principal speaker. In tracing the history of the organization, Williams claimed that the noble order of Knighthood "taught Europe and the civilized world the alphabet of human kindness, and exemplified the character of the Divine Master in deeds and humanity and acts of kindness." Some 175 couples applauded him, after which they dined and danced through most of the night.[26] An even bigger occasion was the centennial celebration in September of the receipt of a charter by the African Lodge of the Free and Accepted Order of Masons. As the orator of the day at the huge meeting in Tremont Temple, Williams provided his audience with vivid vignettes of Afro-American history over the past century.[27]

A major event in the nation's capital was the anniversary of the emancipation of slaves in the District of Columbia which had occurred in April 1862. For the 1884 celebration, Williams was selected as orator. The demonstration on April 16 was "the grandest" that one reporter had ever witnessed. "Thousands of people of all colors, classes, and descriptions turned out in full to behold the scene."[28] Williams came down from Boston and took rooms at the Ebbitt. It was from there that he sent tickets to his friend, Senator George F. Hoar of Massachusetts, and his wife to hear his oration at the Asbury Church that evening.[29] The church was packed when Williams's old nemesis, W. Calvin Chase of the Washington *Bee*, rose and introduced "in glowing terms" the former Ohio legislator.[30] Williams was in good form and in a good mood. Speaking of slavery in Washington, he said that emancipation transformed the nation's capital from a prison into a castle. That made it possible for educated and talented Negroes to come to Washington to live. Then he made a generous gesture to the man with whom he had been in sharp disagreement less than a year earlier: "The District of Columbia is the home of Frederick Douglass, and he will always remain the great historic negro." In closing, Williams called for new leaders of the race. "We want, we demand leaders . . . who are not ashamed of the race; who are possessed of brains, character, courage, zeal, and tact . . . . Men they must be of noble instincts and generous impulses; who have a genius for hard, self-sacrificing labor to build up the race . . . . God grant that such men may be forthcoming.[31]

Shortly after he returned to Boston from his triumph in Washington, Williams was into another activity out of which he could have made a new career. On April 25, the members of Company L of the Sixth Regiment of the Massachusetts Volunteer Militia elected him as their captain.[32] Since his days as a private in the Civil War, Williams had maintained a lively interest in military affairs. He spoke before many military groups and was, for several years, judge advocate of the Grand Army of the Republic in Ohio (see below, chapter 12). Consequently he experienced no difficulty in passing "a creditable examination" before the Military Board of Examiners the following month. Williams entered into his new responsibilities with characteristic energy and enthusiasm. Within a few days after his election, he met the company, known as the Shaw Guard (in memory of Robert Gould Shaw), and gave the members some information about his plans for it. In June the company went on a training mission at the State Camp Ground at Framingham. Upon its return, reports regarding the training and conduct of the men were generally favorable, "owing mainly to the strict discipline of the new commander." Williams had, meanwhile, created such a favorable impression among the officers of the Sixth Regiment to which the company was attached "that the Adjutancy of one of the battalions" had already been offered him. "The majority of the members speak in glowing terms of their new commander, and it is evident that he can do more, far more, for its elevation than any of its predecessors."[33]

Williams did not, however, become an adjutant in the militia; nor did he even remain as commander of his company. In November he resigned or was discharged. Even worse, his first lieutenant was arrested on a charge of stealing funds of the command,[34] though there was never any suggestion that Williams was implicated.

In the summer of 1884, Williams had little time for the discharge of his military duties. In late June he wrote his wife Sarah that he was called to London to sign a contract before the middle of July and was compelled to sail on the first available ship. We do not know the nature of Williams's business in Europe. It may have been connected with the promotion of his *History* or with the Cape Cod Canal Company. He also wrote Sarah (or "Sallie," as he called her), "I will be able to get through my business early, and except my company desires me to go to Egypt, will return home in about three weeks."[35] If Williams thought that his company might wish him to inspect the Suez Canal, it did not work out. But Williams did not return in three weeks, either. Instead, he visited France, Germany, Switzerland, Belgium, and Holland. From Heidelberg he wrote Sarah that he was having a marvelous time, had dined with a duke, and had abstained from alcoholic beverages throughout his trip.[36]

When Williams finally returned to the United States near the end of September, he remained in New York for a day of rest at the Hoffman House. Then he proceeded immediately to Boston to speak at the Masonic Centennial. Already the presidential campaign was heating up, but Williams could summon little enthusiasm for the Republican ticket of James G. Blaine and John A. Logan. The *Transcript* commented that most of the Negro Masons assembled in Boston were probably Republicans, "not only because they ought to be, but also because they always have been and always will be." Blaine, the newspaper said, was no believer in Negro suffrage. Then it quoted from Williams's *History of the Negro Race* to support its argument: Blaine "has never seen fit to explain his opposition (in caucus of the Republicans of the House) to the force bill which was intended to strengthen the hand of the President in his efforts to protect the negro vote of the South."[37]

Williams had included other critical comments on Blaine in his *History*. Blaine, he said, "never allowed an opportunity to pass in which he did not throw every obstacle in the way of the success of the Grant administration." He had a presidential ambition to serve, "and esteemed his own promotion of greater moment than the protection of the Colored voters of the South."[38]

It would thus be difficult for Williams to support Blaine; and others knew it. Even before he returned from Europe, Williams's critics began to harass him. "We wonder how George W. Williams will feel when he hears that Blaine is elected," the editor of the Washington *Bee* mused in mid-September. In October the Cleveland *Gazette*, noting that Williams was visiting friends in Cincinnati, indicated that he was opposed to Blaine. That was a bad sign, the *Gazette* stated, for Grant had been elected in 1872 despite opposition from Williams. If Grant had pulled through "contrary to the wishes of G. W., we suppose the Hon. James G. Blaine can do the same." It seems clear that Williams was ambivalent about the Republican ticket. Although the New York *Globe* announced in October that Williams would stump for Blaine and Logan, his activity was very limited if he did anything at all. T. Thomas Fortune, editor of the *Globe,* later said that the nomination of Blaine was supremely distasteful to Williams. It was also distasteful to many other Republicans, who associated his name with corruption in the early eighties. Williams "took no active part in the campaign, although one of the most effective campaign speakers in the country." Indeed, he was indisposed for much of the final weeks of the campaign and was convalescing in New York for several weeks.[39] For once, he seemed not to care about politics.

Whenever Williams was at a loss for something to occupy his attention or gratify his ego or make him a few dollars, he took to the platform. During the 1880s he delivered hundreds of speeches in many parts of the country, mainly the Midwest and Northeast. He received more than his share of invitations to deliver commemorative orations, especially to observe Emancipation Day, Memorial Day, or the anniversary of the organization extending the invitation. In 1886 the Philomathian Literary Society of Washington invited him to deliver the oration celebrating Cuban emancipation. The group was complimented in its choice by the Washington *Bee,* which said that "no man is more competent for that honor than Mr. Williams, who is the recognized literary man among the colored people in this country. He is an honor to the rising young men and a credit to the colored race." It would be a "masterpiece of composition," the newspaper predicted. Williams reminded the huge crowd at Lincoln Temple on November 10, 1886, that the emancipation of blacks in the United States did not effect much change. Everyone knew that blacks in the South continued to be trodden under the "remorseless iron heel of bourbon despotism." He hoped the same would not happen to the Cuban freedmen, whom he saluted for their achievement. The *Bee* called it "the greatest oration of the age" and said its reception was "evidence of [Williams's] popularity and his recognized ability as a scholar and a historian."[40]

When Williams returned to Washington the following year to deliver the oration commemorating Emancipation Day, changed circumstances in his own life affected the content of his remarks. He had failed to hold on to his appointment to be United States minister to Haiti, and he was obviously smarting under this misfortune (see chapter 11 below). He praised the patriotism of the freedmen and described how the race had improved itself. He then launched into an attack on President Cleveland for failing to protest the outrages against blacks in the South. He branded blacks who accepted appointments from Cleveland as Judas Iscariots, and said that if they had the courage they would go out and hang themselves. T. Thomas Fortune was appalled. Williams had "disgraced the proprieties of the occasion and placed himself on a level of a partisan demagogue in the heat of an election," Fortune said in his New York *Freeman*.[41] Several newspapers recalled that Williams had been quite willing to hold office under Cleveland if he had been able to secure it, and contended that his bitterness on this occasion was deeply personal.[42] None went as far as Fortune, however, who by this time had his own problems with the Republicans and was advocating an independent course for blacks.[43]

Williams did not always yield to the temptation to offend his listeners as he did in the Emancipation Day address in Washington. After all, his appearances on such occasions were an important source of income, on which he came to rely. If the orations in the early days were services for which he may or may not have received remuneration, this was not true of the later years. When the Knights of the American Eagle of Worcester announced that Williams would give a lecture under its auspices, Williams said that the announcement had been made without his knowledge or consent. He said that he had told the group's leader that he made it a practice to lecture free for charitable purposes only, and as an admission fee was to be charged, "I should expect pay for my services and named my price." The leader said that they could not pay the fee and would have to get along without him. On learning that the group continued to advertise his speech, Williams disavowed the announcement.[44]

Such experiences no doubt prompted Williams to seek the protection of a manager, whereby he could expect a steady flow of engagements and, hopefully, a steady income as well. In 1888 he engaged New Yorker James B. Pond, the most famous and most successful lecture manager in the country, who had been in business for more than a decade. Among the personages Pond handled during his quarter of a century of lecture management were Henry W. Beecher, Arthur Conan Doyle, Henry M. Stanley, and Mark Twain.[45]

For the 1888–89 season Pond produced an elaborate brochure announcing the availability of Williams, illustrated by an engraving of the likeness of "Hon. Geo. W. Williams, L.L.D., Historian and Orator." The brochure began, "Major J. B. Pond takes great pleasure in announcing that he has made arrangements for a series of Lectures and Readings during the present season, by COLONEL THE HONORABLE GEORGE W. WILLIAMS, L.L.D." Pond said that Williams would give readings from the battle scenes of his *History of the Negro Troops* and recite " 'The Black Regiment' and other beautiful, heroic and descriptive poems." Among his lecture themes were "Toussaint L'Ouverture,"

"The Rise and Fall of the Maximilian Empire," "The Congo Free States," "The First Quarter of a Century of Freedom," and "Books and Reading: What to Read, How to Read, When to Read." Pond also provided press comments on the *History of the Negro Troops* from such papers as the New York *Tribune*, the Boston *Globe*, the Springfield *Republican*, and the *Living Church*. Individual comments were from Senator George F. Hoar, who called his speeches "a high order of eloquence," and Henry Cabot Lodge, who said that he was "an eloquent and interesting speaker."[46] But it would take more than the efforts of impresario J. B. Pond to put on a successful lecture tour for Williams. He was so distracted by other developments and by serious health problems that he gave fewer lectures during the 1888–89 season than during earlier years. He was in Europe, moreover, in 1888 and again in 1889.

Several of Williams's more successful speeches were printed and made available to a wider public. His very first published work was a memorial sermon, "The Advent of the Colored Soldier," which he delivered in May 1874, before the Robert Bell Post of the Grand Army of the Republic in Boston.[47] The celebrated Avondale, Ohio, Centennial speech had been ordered printed "by unanimous vote, at the conclusion of its delivery."[48] Since his widely discussed Emancipation Day oration in Washington in 1884 was printed in Boston, one may assume that its readers extended at least that far.[49] The only oration known to have been printed during the season that Williams was managed by Pond was one he delivered on Memorial Day 1889.[50] The 1889 lecture on the Congo Free State, which Williams delivered in Worcester, though itself un-printed, doubtless inspired several pieces on Africa that did appear in print.[51]

Williams was as busy with his writing as he was with his speaking. Since becoming fully literate only at the age of twenty, he had written prolifically. At his very first post he wrote a history of the church he was serving as pastor. The following year found him establishing and editing a newspaper, for which he wrote almost all the copy. As "Aristides" on the Cincinnati *Commercial* he was perhaps the first Negro American columnist to contribute regularly to a daily newspaper. Later he con-tributed occasional pieces to the Boston *Evening Transcript*, the Worcester *Gazette*, and other newspapers. Williams seemed always to have numerous writing projects underway. In 1887 he was engaged by the *Encyclopaedia Britannica* to write an article on the Negro race for its supplement. The *Bee* called the invitation "a tribute to an industrious scholar of whom the race is proud."[52] Early in 1889 he sent in a piece to the *Magazine of American History*. The magazine regretted that it could not purchase his "excellent article" since it already had sufficient material for several issues.[53]

Williams experimented with various literary forms, including drama and fiction. His play, "Panda," was said to be "remarkable for the originality of its design." Some of the scenes take place in Africa, where a royal party of an African court are seized by six American slavers and brought to the United States. In this way Williams was able to present the horrors of slavery and the slave trade as it existed earlier in the century.[54] The hero, Panda, was said to be a "second Othello in character and appearance."[55] There is no record of the play's having ever been produced, and no copy is known to have survived.

Williams had more success as a writer of fiction. In 1885 he began work on a novel, "The Autocracy of Love," completing it the following year.[56] He sent it to a publishing company that had asked to see it, presumably for possible use in the magazine that it produced. When the publisher asked Williams to make certain emendations, he withdrew it. He then sent it to Lee and Shepard in Boston because, he told them, he knew of no publisher outside New England "brave enough" to deal with an interracial romance in print. The novel, he told Lee and Shepard, was based on fact; and the couple featured in the work were in Germany, which Williams had left "not many months ago."[57] Six weeks after Williams had submitted it to Lee and Shepard, he requested its return, having concluded "not to request you to pass it to other hands." Two days later, they returned it to him.[58]

No doubt, Williams thought, it was the interracial theme in his novel and his unwillingness to change it that created the difficulty in getting it accepted by a publisher. As a last resort he turned to the black press. Most of them carried some fiction for fillers as well as entertainment. Since the Washington *Bee*, the New York *Freeman,* and the Cleveland *Gazette* were not on friendly terms with Williams, he had to turn to a paper of somewhat lower standing. Consequently, he sent the manuscript to the Indianapolis *World*, which welcomed the prospect of running *The Autocracy of Love* serially, beginning with the paper's first issue in January 1888. The newspaper said that its agents everywhere "should see that subscribers have an opportunity to renew their subscriptions so as to begin with the first chapter of George W. Williams's great romance."[59]

In order to whet its reader's appetite, the *World* printed a brief summary of the novel, together with a biographical sketch of the author, in its issue of December 24, 1887. The summary was long enough to introduce the hero and heroine and give some notion of the problems they would encounter. Captain Percival Winslow, West Point graduate and scion of a well-to-do Boston family, is the first-person narrator of the story. While visiting in Washington, he meets and falls in love with Ethel Maitland, "a white lady with an invisible admixture of Negro blood in her veins." When he expresses his feelings to her, she reciprocates, thus establishing a relationship that was a serious breach of custom throughout the United States and a violation of the law in some states. Even before she gave him any encouragement, Winslow had decided not to consult his family, which would surely disapprove, and to live abroad, where interracial marriages were more acceptable.[60]

Between January and June 1888, the *World* published eight chapters of *The Autocracy of Love,* carrying the story in detail through the experiences sketched in the first installment. In some issues the Williams novel was on the front page, while in other issues it was on an inside page. On June 9, 1888, the last installment appeared. It was not the end of the novel, no problems raised had been resolved, and no explanation was given for terminating its publication. The next reference to *The Autocracy of Love* was in the New York *Freeman,* which claimed in September 1888 that the prayer meeting scene in the work by Williams was "taken almost bodily from Bulwer's 'Ernest Maltravers.' "[61] (There is, in fact, no prayer meeting scene in Edward George Bulwer-Lytton's *Ernest Maltravers.*)[62]

Thus, in the years following his service in the Ohio legislature and the publication of his *History,* Williams enjoyed considerable public recognition. He was driven to achieve more, however. Real distinction for him involved doing something to improve the lot of his fellows.

A Diplomatic Appointment

Black Americans, for the most part, feared that the 1884 election of the Democratic ticket headed by Grover Cleveland and Thomas Hendricks spelled doom for them. In his reorganized and refinanced paper, now called the *Freeman*, T. Thomas Fortune wrote a long, gloomy letter arguing that blacks had few friends and must work for their own salvation. "Black men, Wake up! You must fight your own battles."[1] Meanwhile, some blacks wondered what specifically would happen in the South where whites might take the election of a Democratic president, even one from New York, as a signal to them to oppress blacks as much as they pleased. Others had narrower concerns: for example, whether blacks—or which blacks—would hold on to the few posts that were their patronage plums, such as the Liberian and Haitian legations, the Registry of Deeds in the District of Columbia, and the Fourth Auditorship of the Treasury.

These matters seemed of little interest to Williams as he prepared to go to the capital to do research and writing on the Reconstruction era and other subjects. By mid-January 1885 he had settled in Washington, "engrossed in literary pursuits." He was also available for lectures and had agreed to participate in the lecture series at the Fifteenth Street Presbyterian Church by giving a talk on the Congo, scheduled for March 2.[2] He became active in the Bethel Literary Society, where he had a public argument with Frederick Douglass at the conclusion of the Douglass lecture on the female suffrage movement. The following week Williams was scheduled to talk on technical education.[3] He was getting into Washington social life, moreover. In February he was one of the dinner guests in the home of Civil War Captain and Mrs. O. S. B. Wall. Others present were Susan B. Anthony, Mr. and Mrs. John R. Lynch,

Mr. and Mrs. Frederick Douglass, William E. Matthews, and two ladies from Ohio. It appeared that Williams would have a profitable and pleasant period of work and study in Washington.

Then suddenly, on March 2, 1885, within hours before leaving office, President Arthur sent the following message to the Senate: "I nominate George W. Williams of Massachusetts, to be Minister Resident and Consul General of the United States, to Hayti, vice John M. Langston, resigned."[4] On the evening of March 2, in executive session, the Senate confirmed the nomination.[5] The following morning, the president presented Williams with his commission, and on March 4 at 10 A.M. he was sworn in at the Department of State by John Chew.[6] It was curious, of course, that the outgoing Republican president should choose to fill a foreign post immediately before stepping down, for an appointee holds office at the pleasure of the president. But Arthur had the right to make the appointment, even if the exercise of that right was, in this case, mischievous or even cynical.

When the news broke, Williams had already been confirmed by the Senate. Early reaction was generally one of surprise—even amazement. Later, people in Washington and in other parts of the country began to express their views on Williams's fitness for office. The Boston *Evening Transcript*, informing its readers of the appointment, described Williams as "one of the colored orators of the Republican stump."[7] T. Thomas Fortune described him as "a very shrewd colored man" who had undoubtedly placed President Arthur in his debt. "The appointment . . . was a genuine surprise, as no one knew he was an applicant for the post." Among those who did think they knew was W. Calvin Chase of the Washington *Bee*: "It was reported that Mr. Williams was writing a book on Reconstruction, but we have always said Mr. Williams was here after an office . . . and our assertion has been verified."[8] Williams vigorously denied it. "I have no inclination or aspiration for public place," he wrote Senator George F. Hoar. "I was nominated without seeking the place."[9]

Meanwhile, the guard had changed not only in the White House but in the Department of State as well. Thomas F. Bayard had taken over the department two hours after Williams's commission was signed. Frederick T. Frelinghuysen, who signed the commission, had become a private citizen. Some observers began to speculate on whether President Cleveland could recall Williams "before he proceeds to Hayti, or after he arrives there, without cause, within the time for which he is appointed."[10] There could have been no doubt in Bayard's mind, however, for he well knew that a United States minister had no stated term of service and could, in fact, be "recalled" whenever the president wished to do so. The new secretary of state may also have known what Williams reportedly thought of him, for Williams's views had not only made the rounds in Washington but were in the print media as far away as Cleveland. An editor there said, "Colonel George Williams, ex-member of the Ohio legislature, now Minister to Hayti, tells me that Bayard does not scruple to show his contempt for the Negro." Williams had allegedly told him how Bayard, while in the House of Representatives, made it clear that he did not want the House post office to distribute his speeches to any Negro members. Williams further stated, the reporter said, that when Bayard was in the Senate he "studiously avoided meeting and bowing to Blanche K. Bruce, the sole black member.[11] Whether or not these were accurate reports of what Williams said about Bayard, they were not calculated to make it easier for the new secretary to send the new minister to his post.

For one reason or another, Williams did not proceed to Port-au-Prince promptly. He had not executed the bond that he would be required to give as consul general, but no one had given him the form. He had not received any instructions regarding his new assignment, but no one had offered any. Soon there began to emerge in some quarters the view that there would be some difficulty about the appointment. In a letter to Bayard ten days after his appointment, Williams seemed to share that feeling. "Having been sworn, commissioned, etc., I will await your orders, rather than in Boston, here; and will use the Congressional Library." There he would examine the trade statistics between Haiti and the United States and several histories and encyclopedia articles that he found informative.[12]

When the department persisted in declining to order Williams to his post, Williams called on the secretary of state to ask the cause of the delay. The secretary replied that it was embarrassing to report that some charges had been prepared against him. Declining to inform Williams of the nature of the charges, Bayard told him that they would be investigated.[13] Williams then called on President Cleveland and informed him of his appointment. Upon learning that the president was pleased, he declined his "avowed purpose" of tendering his resignation. Vice-President Thomas Hendricks, however, subsequently told Williams that he expected him to resign because he had another man for the position. Williams then returned to the president and told him he would resign if the president wished to appoint one of his own choosing. The president assured him, Williams said, that he had no candidate for that post.[14]

With this assurance from President Cleveland, Williams returned to the Department of State and requested his salary for his first month as United States Minister to Haiti. According to Williams, the clerk said he had been directed by the secretary to inform Williams that he could have his salary immediately, provided he resign his post.[15] Bayard denied this in an interview with a reporter. "I treated Mr. Williams with the same consideration that I do everybody, and his statements are disgracefully false. He came to me and said that he needed money, having been sick, and I felt commiseration for the man and tried to arrange for an advance." When the reporter asked Bayard if the money was not due, Bayard replied "Yes, but he had not executed a bond, as required, and was, therefore, not really entitled to a salary." He said that Williams took the bond away with him and never returned it. He reiterated that there were some charges against Williams and they would be investigated. "His assertion that I, through my chief clerk, attempted to bribe him, is an infamous lie," Bayard declared, as he closed the interview.[16]

Williams had indeed been ill during much of March. He told Senator Hoar in mid-March that he had suffered all winter "with a bronchial trouble" and hoped that the climate of Haiti would improve his health."[17] A week later he had moved from Ebbitt House to a house on M Street NW. From his bed, he wrote his wife: "It seems as if my head would explode from a severe pain," he told her. "But I am willing to endure it since Dr. C. B. Purvis tells me I am better.[18] My right lunge was closed up, and I could only breathe through my left lunge. I can breathe through both lungs now; and although weak am much better." In reference to his "fight" to win the Haitian post he reminded her that he had "the nerve to meet my enemies; and feel that if God is for me those opposed can do but little. I am calmly awaiting the decision. I trust in God only." He promised to send her a telegram as soon as he learned the outcome.[19]

Williams wrote his friend Senator Hoar that he had been passing through "a rather unpleasant ordeal."[20] He could not have known, however, how anxious many people were to assist the Department of State in preventing him from taking up the Haitian post. The department had put together a memorandum summarizing the Williams case in the form of questions and answers. It pointed out that he had been appointed and confirmed. In answer to the bond question, the memorandum asserted that although a blank form had been given to Williams, he had not yet, on April 15, filed his bond. Then the memorandum indicated that Williams had been sworn in and that "the only paper

connected with his appointment which has been given to him is the
blank bond." His commission remained with the Department. Other
statements were added as follows:

> The 3rd of July, 1884 Mr. Williams received a letter of introduction
> [from the Secretary of State] to the Diplomatic and consular officers
> in Europe, whither he went. The letter was given, it is understood
> at the instance of the Register of the Treasury, Mr. Blanche K.
> Bruce.[21] Williams while abroad appears to have succeeded pretty
> well in obtaining the "friendly consideration" which his letter
> asked.[22]

To the memorandum's brief account of Williams's borrowing money
from Europeans as well as American officials, numerous documents
were attached supporting its assertions. One, for example, was a note
from Williams to Lyell Adams, the Consul at Geneva, promising to
repay him within ten days the fifty francs he had borrowed from Adams.
Two weeks later he wrote Adams that, due to some confusion about his
mail, which he had not received, he would not be able to pay him until
he reached London late that week. There was no further communication
between Adams and Williams.

Other documentation showed that Williams had borrowed sixty
marks from Ferdinand Gehrung, a German-American living in Stuttgart, in order to go to Brussels to see Leopold, King of the Belgians.
Upon arrival in Brussels, he sent Gehrung a telegram requesting six
dollars, which was sent, so that Williams could follow the king from
Brussels to Ostend. From London, Williams wrote Gehrung that he had
lost the card containing the number of marks he owed him. He promised
to repay Gehrung as soon as he knew the exact amount. "God bless
you," Williams said, "and if you ever come to Boston you must hunt me
up." When Gehrung had not heard from Williams by September 15, he
wrote George Catlin, United States consul at Stuttgart, reminding him
that it was Catlin who introduced Williams to him. Otherwise, he said,
he would not have given him one penny. Gehrung asked Catlin to help
him recover his money. The following day Catlin gave Gehrung the
ninety marks that Williams owed. Meanwhile, Lyell Adams wrote the
secretary of state from Geneva about his "unfortunate" experience with
Williams, adding that it seemed important that the secretary should
know about it. Catlin, similarly, wrote the department about Gehrung's
experience. Addressing the chief of the Consular Service, Catlin complained about the department's giving out letters of introduction which

placed people in the foreign service in a difficult position. Catlin did not think he should have to sustain the loss of lending money to a person who had been commended to him by the secretary. He hoped he would be reimbursed, and he also hoped that "no more colonels will happen along."[23] An official in the department with an illegible signature wrote on the letter of introduction that had been issued Williams that he was inclined to have the president issue an order forbidding departments to issue any letter of introduction unless the holder was going abroad in a public capacity. "Better stop them altogether than have even one scandal like this."[24]

The real scandal was that the Department of State, with the information about Williams that it had in its possession, had concurred in the president's appointment of Williams to be the nation's highest representative to another country. As early as October 1884, the department had the complete story on Williams's conduct abroad. If it had some question about the story, it had ample time to raise it before the appointment was made. United States diplomats in Switzerland and Germany had complained that Williams had been an embarrassment to the country, and officials in Washington declared that his conduct was a scandal. Why, then, did the president appoint him as United States Minister to Haiti? When John Mercer Langston resigned from his post in Haiti, it was no more than was expected of him since it was the end of a presidential term. The president was not expected to appoint a chief of mission two days before he left office, and the Williams appointment is the only one of this nature that he made. To have appointed Williams with full knowledge of what he had done in Europe displayed a cynical disregard for the consequences of the appointment either to Williams, to Haiti, or to the United States. Arthur may have been indicating his resentment of the fact that, when he was seeking reelection, some of the loudest voices in the Negro press were promoting others for the Republican nomination; Williams was in the minority in supporting Arthur.[25]

Williams's appointment to Haiti offended a considerable segment of the black community; active opposition began almost as soon as the announcement was made. Black Americans had no knowledge of the damaging information in the Williams file in the Department of State, but they had their own objections. "Mr. Arthur made a grave mistake," the Washington *Bee* railed, "by appointing such a bombastic furore as George W. Williams to so high and responsible a position as United States Minister to a foreign court. He is devoid of every qualification to fill acceptably the position. His impudence is unparalled [sic] and is only equalled by egotism. . . . His self-esteem is matchless, and if taken at his own valuation, would command an amount sufficient to pay off the public debt. . . . In the name of the colored people we ask the recall of Mr. Williams."[26]

The *Bee* continued its attack and in succeeding weeks was joined by two other leading Negro newspapers. The Boston *Advocate* expressed the hope that the position would be given to a man "fit in point of character and educational ability to represent the race creditably. . . . The citizens of Boston are not at all pleased with the appointment, and many of our leading politicians are inclined to think ex-President Arthur did a very unwise act, as well as throwing a bad reflection on the integrity of the race, by appointing him." The *Advocate* even asserted that "a wish has been expressed by some of the residents of Hayti, that [Williams's] commission not be issued." The Cleveland *Gazette* not only reprinted the *Advocate*'s hostile editorial but pleaded, "Will somebody show George W. Williams the way to 'Bosting' or any other place except one in Ohio, so as to get him out of Washington?"[27]

Peter Clark of Ohio, who moved from Republican to Socialist and then to Democrat, was not a disinterested opponent. When visiting Washington in early March, he was asked what he thought of Williams's going to Haiti as United States minister. His answer was evasive: "Mr. Williams was nominated by a Republican President and confirmed by a Republican Senate. It is therefore a question to be asked and answered in Republican circles."[28] Clark himself had been mentioned as a possible candidate, and rumor had it that he had come to Washington in quest of the position. Sarah Williams heard it in Boston and wrote her husband about it. He wanted to know more, and asked her anxiously, "What paper did you see that said Peter A. Clark was to have the Haytian mission? What date and from what point?"[29]

Clark was outraged by the Williams appointment and, at President Cleveland's suggestion, communicated his views to the new secretary of state. He wrote Bayard that in his audience with the president he had "protested as a friend, solicitous about the honor of his administration, and as a colored man, solicitous about the honor of my race, against the sending of George Williams as minister to the republic of Hayti." Williams was "a notoriously untruthful man," neglected his family shamefully, and was utterly unreliable in word and deed. Clark attached a list of persons, "almost all" of whom would testify against Williams. Among those on the list of twenty-four were Frederick Douglass, John W. Cromwell, George Ruffin, Dr. J. L. Brotherton, Robert Purvis, James Poindexter, and Monroe Trotter. Brotherton, who lived in Philadelphia, had turned over to Williams some materials on Benjamin Lundy with the understanding that Williams would write a magazine article on the life of the abolitionist. Brotherton had written to Clark and Thomas Bayard, complaining that Williams had neither written the piece nor returned the materials. Robert Purvis, on the other hand, who had been mentioned by both Clark and Brotherton as one who "knew" Williams, told the State Department, "I have no personal knowledge, upon which to base an opinion, of the 'personal qualifications' of Mr. George W. Williams." If the department made inquiry of others on Clark's list, no replies have survived.[30]

One of the more interesting protests came from a Negro Republican, S. R. Scottron, secretary to two national societies of Negro men. His work took him all over the country, and he had spent much time in places where Williams had lived, such as Boston, Cincinnati, and Columbus. "I have it on every hand," he wrote President Cleveland, "that Williams is an unfit man for any public trust, where the honor of our Government is at stake." He called Williams "an unscrupulous politician of the lowest order, without honor or a just sense of his obligations to his fellowman." Scottron had a curious view of the responsibility of a Democratic president to Negro Republicans. He advised Cleveland that in order to encourage the present tendency of blacks to divide up between Republicans and Democrats, he should appoint a black man with *known* Republican views and antecedents to the post in Haiti. He suggested Richard T. Greener of Washington, Charles L. Reason of New York, or John P. Green of Cleveland. Scottron advised Cleveland to stay away from Democrats such as Peter Clark of Cincinnati or George T. Downing of Providence.[31] Cleveland's nonpartisanship obviously did not go as far as Scottron would have liked.

Some whites were as vehement as blacks in their opposition to the Williams appointment. Most whites who protested the appointment were Democrats, however, and presumably had a partisan interest in the outcome. William Means, a former Democratic mayor of Cincinnati, sent a telegram to Senator George H. Pendleton of Ohio, calling Williams a "deadbeat" and unfit to serve. Pendleton transmitted the telegram to the secretary of state, requesting that he investigate the case. Former Brevet Major General William Birney, who had organized the United States Colored Troops during the Civil War, called Williams "notorious" and had committed "numerous offences against the rules of morality in money matters." A Democrat who served in the legislature with Williams told the secretary of state that Williams had accepted a bribe to introduce a measure to close a Negro cemetery in Cincinnati. "I do not think him a proper person to represent us even in Hayti," he declared. He concluded by extending "best wishes for the success of this democratic administration." A lawyer in Indianapolis claimed that the appointment of Williams was part of a "deep layed scheme to defeat the prospects of well deserving Democrats." Williams's great offense was that he had worked "like a Turk" at Chicago for Arthur, and after his defeat "he worked and voted for Blaine." Meanwhile, he had done everything he could to defeat the Democratic ticket.[32]

Surely one of the most elaborate indictments of Williams appeared in a newspaper in Middletown, New York, which Williams had visited in 1880 and 1882. As a result of the influence of his sponsors, he was "coddled and feted, until his vanity overflowed the confines of his shallow soul." The paper stated that Williams "swaggered and strutted through the streets, the personification of under-bred self-importance." It mercifully spared its readers "the disgraceful narrative of the social courtesies extended him, of the tea parties given in his honor, of the croquet parties of which he was the central figure, of drives and walks taken by the white young ladies with the saffron hued and jewelry bedizened author of the History of the Colored Race." Williams left Middletown after his creditors began to hint at the payment due of the large bills he had run up. Even so, the scene at the Erie depot was "pathetic" as his retinue of admirers expressed sorrow over his departure. Only the "oft repeated assurances that the parting was not for long, assauged [sic] their grief. . . . The gorgeous, jewel bedecked Croesus-like Colonel was not all that he had presented himself to be. He was instead an errant humbug, a purposeless prevaricator, a conscienceless liar, an impecunious adventurer, a bare-faced fraud."[33] With his ravings, the Middleton editor joined a long list of Williams-haters whose disinterestedness is open to serious question.

Few individuals or organizations rushed to support Williams. There were no delegations arguing in his behalf and no blacks in Cincinnati, Columbus, or Boston writing letters endorsing his appointment. In its support of Williams the New York *Tribune* seemed a lone voice. Despite its vigorous Republicanism, it scored some important points in discussing the case. It criticized Bayard for claiming that there were charges against Williams while failing to bring "those so-called charges to the knowledge of Minister Williams." If Bayard refused to give Williams the information, yet allowed it to influence his mind, "as he asserts," he was guilty of a breach of official propriety, the *Tribune* argued. It also accused Bayard of acting in an ungentlemanly manner in informing the press that Williams, in need, had asked for an advance on his salary, which Bayard had in fact tried to arrange. If Williams had not filed a bond and was therefore not entitled to a salary, as Bayard claimed, why did he agree to the advance unless it was to tempt

Williams to resign? This was the tone of several articles and editorials in the *Tribune*, which added up to support for Williams and no confidence in Thomas F. Bayard and the Department of State.[34]

As the opposition to Williams built up, the chances of his ever taking up his post in Haiti correspondingly diminished. With each postponement of the departure date, rumors would resurface that Williams had been forced out. Despite his disappointment and his persistent illness, Williams continued to give the impression that he would be successful. After waiting forty-nine days following his confirmation, he again wrote to President Cleveland asking that the charges against him be aired so that he could answer them or that he be given orders to proceed to his post of duty. He told Cleveland that while he had not been permitted to see the charges, they had been given out to a few favorite journals. "I should be summoned before yourself and the Secretary of State," he argued, "I should be called upon to meet the charges. If I shall fail then I could expect nothing less than a request to resign." Williams never received a reply from the president.[35]

Among the "favorite journals" that had received from the Department of State information about the charges against Williams was the Democratic Boston *Post*. In its issue of April 13, 1885, it alleged that when Williams was in Europe "two years ago or so" he had a letter of introduction from Secretary of State Frelinghuysen and "borrowed money right and left and started back to this country without recollecting to pay it."

At last Williams could reply, if only through the press. He was not in Europe "two years ago or so," he said, and had never been to Europe until the previous summer in 1884. He borrowed money only on one occasion, he insisted. "While I was in Geneva Consul Adams recommended to me to change the route I had marked out through Switzerland," he recounted. He had little money, and his letter of credit was in London, so he told Adams that he could not make the change. It was only $10, and Adams offered to lend the money until he got to London. "When I reached London I was seriously ill and a friend took me down to Liverpool and saw me aboard the steamer. I was ill when I arrived in New York." After he delivered a few speeches that were on his schedule, he had a relapse and was confined to his bed for weeks. When he finally was able to write Adams and promise an early remittance, Adams replied that Assistant Secretary Davis had paid it. "I paid the $10 to Assistant Secretary Davis and, so far as I know, he and Mr. Freylinghuysen were both satisfied with my explanation of the circumstances and delays." If Freylinghuysen thought he had acted dishonorably, he would have offered some objection to his appointment. "On the contrary he signed my commission as minister," Williams asserted, "and congratulated me upon my appointment."[36]

The final move that Williams made in his effort to hold on to his appointment came on April 26. During the morning he went to the Bureau of Diplomatic Instructions and, once again, asked for a blank bond. "I was referred to the Chief Clerk, and he instructed me to apply for the bond in writing. I hasten to comply with his instructions," he wrote the secretary of state. Williams then said that he had heard there was a printed circular of instructions that was given to newly appointed consular and diplomatic officers. He had never been honored with one, he admitted, "and this fact must be my apology for any ignorance I may have exhibited, or blunders I may have been guilty of. An early reply is solicited, as I am anxious to comply with the letter as well as the Spirit of the Law."[37]

The letter to the secretary was a futile gesture, and Williams must have known it. Already there were remors that Bayard had asked for his resignation.[38] The Cleveland *Gazette* reveled, "That is right, he should never have been appointed. Such political acrobats should be relegated to the rear."[39] Williams continued to insist that he had qualified for the office, that no charges had been prepared against him, and that the president had not indicated to him that he should step aside. As late as December, long after his successor had been named, he was making essentially the same argument to the chairman of the Senate Committee on Foreign Relations.[40] By that time he was also trying to make a case against the government of the United States.

Yet Williams could no longer pretend that he was the United States minister to Haiti or that the president had no objection to his holding that office. On May 7, two months after Williams had been confirmed by the Senate, President Cleveland appointed and commissioned John Edward West Thompson for the post.[41] A thirty-year-old New York physician, Thompson was an honor graduate of the Yale Medical School with eighteen months of postgraduate study in Paris. His appointment met with almost universal approval but not a little surprise. The Boston *Evening Transcript* was delighted not only that Thompson was a "colored man and a gentleman of high standing and liberal education," but that in appointing him Cleveland had done exactly what it was said he would never dare to do. The New York *Freeman*, which had been generally friendly to the Williams appointment, approved of Thompson and was delighted that the Republican press, in predicting that the post would go to a white man, now found itself "in a nice pickle." Fortune, the editor, declared that he was "ashamed of those colored editors who made indecent haste to arraign Secretary Bayard and the President in the Williams matter—what have they to say now?" The Washington *Bee*, the first to oppose Williams, was among the first to praise the Thompson appointment as excellent.[42] Indeed, most people—aside from Williams himself—were pleased to see the matter closed.

After Thompson's appointment and confirmation as United States Minister to Haiti, Williams at last reconciled himself to the unhappy fact that he must now regard himself as merely the former minister who had not been compensated. Even here there was no agreement. He insisted that he *had* been in office and was entitled to compensation. The government said that he had *not* been in office and was not entitled to compensation. The only place to settle the dispute was in the United States Court of Claims.

In April 1886, Williams, through his attorney George A. King, brought suit against the United States for a year's salary of $7,500.00. King argued that Williams had fully qualified for the office by virtue of having been appointed by the president, confirmed by the Senate, and taken the oath of office. A manual delivery of the commission had been made to Williams but even this was not necessary in order for the plaintiff to enjoy the full investiture of office. "It would seem clear then," King insisted, "that his salary began to run from the date of his commission, and in fact this court has held, with express reference to consular officers, that compensation begins to run from the date of commission." Heretofore, King stated, the giving of bonds had not been considered anything more than directory statutes. They had never been regarded as preventing the complete investiture of the office "upon the signing of the commission and the taking of the oath." In a brief statement, the government's attorney, Heber J. May, said that Williams never gave the bond required by law as a condition precedent to investiture of the office in him. The excuses he offered were not legal excuses and could not affect the merits of the case.

On January 3, 1888, the Chief Judge of the Court of Claims, William Adams Richardson, delivered the opinion of the court. Quoting the Revised Statutes of the United States—"Every consul-general, consul, and commercial agent, before he receives his commission or enters upon the duties of his office, shall give a bond to the United States, with such sureties . . . as the Secretary of State shall approve"—the judge ruled that, since Williams never gave a bond, he neither received his commission nor entered upon the duties of his office. "Until the bond is given or tendered it can not be known that the appointee ever will accept the office, and the office can not be forced upon him without his consent." The judge gave no consideration to the fact that the taking of the oath of office was itself one indication of the claimant's willingness to accept the office. In conclusion, the judge dashed all hopes that Williams had of at least receiving some compensation. He said, "In our opinion the claimant was never fully invested with the office of minister resident and consul-general to Hayti. To use a familiar expression, he failed to 'qualify' for the office . . . and is, therefore, not entitled to the salary."[43] There is no record of William's reaction to the verdict.

Williams made one more effort to secure the Haitian appointment after the inauguration in 1889 of President Benjamin Harrison, whose election Williams had supported.[44] Doubtless he hoped that the appointment would vindicate him before all those who witnessed with pleasure or pain the fiasco of four years earlier. Fortunately Williams had several influential supporters. Among them was Senator George F. Hoar, who interceded on behalf of Williams with the new secretary of state, James G. Blaine. On March 23, 1889, in a long, confidential conversation, Blaine spoke "very highly" of Williams. He thought there might be a place of honorable service for him, though maybe not Haiti. It seemed that the new administration was under strong pressure to depart from the custom of sending Negroes to Haiti and to appoint a white man instead. Blaine told Hoar that the Haitians themselves paid more respect to the white representatives of European countries than they did to U. S. ministers, who were men of their own race.[45]

Hoping to make his new quest for office very quietly, Williams maintained a low profile in Worcester, where he was living, and worked through Hoar rather than in Washington. Soon, however, his ambitions were the subject of street talk and newspaper columns. "Col. George W. Williams of Worcester, Cincinnati, Washington, and Boston (you pays your money and you takes your choice), preacher, lawyer, soldier, legislator and historian is a candidate for the Haytian mission," wrote T. Thomas Fortune of the New York *Age*.[46] Fortune and his newspaper had supported Williams when the Washington *Bee* and Frederick Douglass attacked him in 1883. His patience was severely tried in 1885 when Williams accused the press of being responsible for his losing the post in Haiti.[47] Now, he was clearly anti-Williams, mocking and chiding him.[48]

Williams had no time to quarrel with Fortune. He was more disposed to use his flagging energies in securing the Haitian appointment. In early April 1889 he wrote President Harrison that he had learned from Hoar that the administration was considering sending a white man to Haiti. He was aware, he told the president, that Senator Hoar had recommended his appointment. He hoped that this fact would not detract from his observation regarding the "unwisdom" of the proposed change of policy. To make such a change would "discourage the Negro in the United States and humiliate the race in Haiti."[49]

Williams did not pass up the opportunity to press his own case. For the president to appoint a capable and energetic man who was identified with the Haitians "by ties of blood" would be a blessing to both countries. "I think I am well informed about Haiti, as any man who has not lived there, and it would be a noble task to be commissioned to restore to that lovely island peace and prosperity," he asserted. He was willing to serve in the diplomatic corps in any land, he hastened to add, but he "naturally desired" to be where he could render "signal service to the cause of liberty and human progress." The following day he wrote the secretary of state in a similar vein. He told Blaine he was confident he could carry out in the letter and spirit "any instructions you might give me; and protect and promote the interests of America and Americans."[50]

Blaine assured Williams that either Hoar or Williams had misunderstood him. No new policy had been adopted. What had been suggested was that a white man of diplomatic experience might be sent to "untangle the Diplomatic and Commercial troubles now existing in Hayti." The request for such a person had been made by men of New York and New England with commercial interests in Haiti. Blaine indicated that if Williams could furnish the name of a Negro "better fitted or equally fitted" for the task, he would receive the most serious consideration by the Department. Williams replied that he had not misunderstood Hoar. He then quoted from Hoar's letter that the department and the president were under strong pressure "to depart from the policy which has previously existed of sending colored men to Haiti." Since he was quoting a confidential letter, he also took the opportunity to cite that part in which Hoar quoted the secretary as saying he knew Williams well and thought "some place of honorable public service might be found" for him. Williams reviewed his own career for Blaine, reminding him of his legal training as well as his intensive study of Haiti and its problems. A senator of "wide influence and stainless integrity" had discussed the Haitian problem with him and had told him that the Postmaster General, John Wanamaker, with great business and financial interests in Haiti, preferred to have a white man represent the United States in Haiti. The senator had conferred with Williams because he knew Williams was a student of the history of Haiti and "because I was your friend and admirer and had worked with him to promote your interests in the past."[51]

Meanwhile, Senator Hoar had followed up his interview with Blaine with a letter to President Harrison urging the appointment of Williams.

He called Williams "a colored gentleman of very great ability. . . . If any better person than Col. Williams, in the estimation of yourself or of the Secretary of State, can be found for the service, neither he nor I would desire that his name should be pressed," he said. Among others pressing Williams's name were Senators John Sherman, William B. Allison, and Henry W. Blair. "I need pay no tribute to the abilities and political services of Col. Williams," Blair wrote the president, "for they are too generally known and especially to yourself, but I hope that the opportunity now afforded to set right a serious wrong done him by a former administration may be performed as an act of simple justice to him and to his race."[52]

With prominently placed and influential members of Congress supporting him and with the president and secretary of state having a high opinion of him, there was every reason for Williams to be optimistic about an appointment in the summer of 1889. Yet month after month passed and no appointment was made. Two items should have caused some uneasiness. One was the fact that the Harrison administration was very slow in appointing any black Americans to office.[53] The other was the persistent rumor that the president would send a white man to Haiti, not as a special agent but as the United States minister.

Nothing seemed to go well for Williams. His health was deteriorating; already the malady that proved to be fatal seemed to be approaching the chronic stage (see chapter 15 below). During the previous months, illness had confined him in New York, Boston, and Washington. He was unable to fill lecture engagements, his law practice was inconsequential, and his expenses were mounting. He longed for a stable position with a regular income. As early as December 1888 he had applied for the position of librarian of Clark University. He had taken up residence in Worcester and found it much to his liking. His life, he told Senator Hoar, had been a "stormy and eventful one" and he longed for a quiet position in harmony with his tastes. He would rather have the job of librarian at Clark "than any Foreign Position now in the gift of the Government." Williams was also applying "for the work of making a catalogue for the Library of the University." Since the president of the university, G. Stanley Hall, was in Europe, and no appointments would be made until he returned, Williams was quite willing to leave his future opportunity "to God and my friends."[54]

In the summer of 1889, when all hope of a diplomatic post was vanishing, Williams's weakened physical condition exacerbated his depression. Developments in Washington made matters even worse. The president did not send a white man to Haiti, but the appointment he did make was especially galling to Williams. On June 26, 1889, Harrison gave a recess appointment to Frederick Douglass as minister to Haiti. When the Senate met in December, Douglass was promptly confirmed.[55] Williams, ever the good sport, sent a congratulatory message: "I have no doubt but that the weight of your honored name, your zeal for the Negro race, your experience in the public service will give you great facilities for aiding the unfortunate people of Haiti to the restoration of peace and prosperity."[56]

Williams's dejection was relieved only by Senator Hoar's expression of sympathetic understanding and his offer of further assistance. "The delicate manner in which you offered aid yesterday deeply touched my heart and you have both my gratitude and reverent love," he wrote the senator. Williams only wished to be "useful and good and have my bread and pay my honest debts." He owed about $1,200, he said, and if he could just secure regular employment, he was confident that he could get through without serious trouble. He would like to work in Worcester in the revenue service "at twelve or fifteen hundred dollars a year." "Please think of me as needy and distressed," he begged Hoar, "and get me a temporary place at least until we know that there is no hope of a diplomatic position."[57]

There really was no hope. Despite their kind words, the president and the secretary of state knew that Williams had no constituency and was therefore not a political asset. Blaine may well have known, moreover, of Williams's hostility to him in earlier campaigns. The few appointments of blacks were "safe" appointments, in spite of some grumbling from the black community.[58] Williams could not be regarded as "safe" and was therefore expendable. Fortunately for him, he would have other options.

Advancing His People

Many of the activities that engaged Williams for varying periods of time gave him an opportunity to advance his people as well as himself in a general way. Among them was the prospect of blacks' moving out of the South to escape the numerous difficulties they experienced there. Williams favored migration and had praised Richard Greener's advocacy of it in Greener's celebrated "debate" with Frderick Douglass (see chapter 9 above). Later, while a legislator, Williams seized on what seemed to be an opportunity to assist blacks in leaving the South. In 1880 a company of New York businessmen, the New York Land League, purchased a tract of land in New Mexico upon which they proposed to establish a colony of blacks who had migrated from the South. They asked Williams to visit them to learn more of the project.

After doing so at their New York headquarters, Williams visited General James A. Garfield and told him of the scheme to settle Southern Negroes on 700,000 acres of land in New Mexico. Garfield pointedly asked whether the company had acquired the land from the railroads or the federal government. The question, which Williams could not answer, was enough to increase his curiosity. Williams then wrote General T. W. Conway, the first company official to have approached him, with numerous questions, expressing his willingness to go to New Mexico at the company's expense. He would have to return to Ohio, however, before the opening of the legislature in January. Receiving no reply, he decided to go at his own expense, and so informed them. Only then did they ask him to "make no movements on our account." Williams, nevertheless, proceeded to the Southwest.[1]

In New Mexico, Williams talked with several people, including the governor of the territory, General Lew Wallace; the surveyor, Atkinson;

a Santa Fe newspaper editor, Manderfield; and the son of one of the men
he had seen in New York, Fleming. He soon discovered that the acreage
was not 700,000 as the New Yorkers had claimed, or 1,000,000 as
Fleming had stated, but 51,000 as declared by the land surveyor. He
found that the land was "the poorest in all New Mexico; that nothing
could be had there upon which to subsist, and that if a colony were sent
there, nothing but great suffering and death would await it."[2] Chief
Justice L. Bradford Prince congratulated Williams for the initiative he
had taken to investigate the matter, thus saving innocent settlers from
undertaking the impossible task of trying to survive in the area where
the New Yorkers proposed to settle them. He assured Williams that
there was some rich, arable land in the Rio Grande Valley to which
anyone of good character would be welcome.[3] Under the circumstances,
Williams indicated, he could not recommend that blacks join the
scheme of the New York Land League either by settling in New Mexico
or purchasing land there. One editor asserted that Williams "deserves
the thanks of his race for the action" he took.[4] Hereafter Williams would
be more cautious before embracing colonization schemes of any sort.

Like many black leaders of his generation, Williams looked for ways
to eliminate the oppressive treatment of blacks by whites. Sharecropping and the crop lien system—which approached involuntary servitude—caused some to flee the South, but most blacks would remain
there for several more decades. Political repression had led to their
disfranchisement virtually everywhere in the South. Education for
blacks was all but scorned by whites, who refused to consider providing
anything resembling equality for black children.

The churches had made some efforts to improve conditions in the
community, but achieved little more than provide places for social and
political gatherings and produce a few important leaders. Although the
press was active, all too often the editors themselves not only were bitter
rivals but used their powerful media for narrow personal and political
ends. Negro conventions had long been a vehicle for airing grievances.
The first convention had met in Philadelphia in 1830, with delegates
from New York, Pennsylvania, Maryland, Delaware, and Virginia "to
devise ways and means of bettering our condition." In the years following, conventions were held quite regularly; and in the decade before the
Civil War they met in Rochester, Cleveland, New York, Philadelphia,
and other cities. During the Reconstruction era—even in the summer of
1865—the freedmen used conventions to air their grievances, protest
their inhuman treatment, and call on the federal government for
protection.[5]

In the decade of the 1880s, the problems of black Americans seemed to multiply. Reconstruction had ended, and what little political influence blacks had wielded during that era had all but disappeared. Intimidation and violence were increasing, and at the same time opportunities were declining for blacks to seek out jobs or withstand the rigors of the emerging sharecropping system. The Civil Rights Act that went on the federal statute books in 1875 was not being enforced; indeed, its very constitutionality was being considered by the Supreme Court. If anything, blacks were being segregated, discriminated against, and insulted as never before.

In May 1883, a group of men issued a call for a National Convention of Colored Men to meet in September. The political condition of a vast number of Negroes was such as to demand attention and careful consideration as to its improvement. Among the signers were Frederick Douglass, John F. Cook, William C. Chase, and a George W. Williams.[6] Williams, however, denied that he had either seen or signed the call. "The 'George W. Williams' who may have signed, and who lives in Washington, keeps a saloon," Williams wrote from his vacation home in Plymouth, Massachusetts. "I am not that man. I am opposed to a convention in Washington. I am opposed to Negroes asking or demanding anything as Negroes. . . . A convention not of the people can do no good and may do much harm."[7]

What Williams doubtless meant was that he was opposed to a convention dominated by Douglass, Chase, and others he regarded as unfriendly to him. Chase, the editor of the *Bee,* suspected as much and chided Williams for making an invidious distinction between himself and the George W. Williams of Washington. Williams of Washington is "the senior proprietor of the well regulated and popular hotel on the Avenue, the Philadelphia House," Chase declared. "He has a large, influential surrounding of friends, admirers and backers, and in all things tending to the welfare of the race, he is foremost among our advanced people." Chase presumed that the Washingtonian had decided to sign the call after talking with people from all parts of the country who make Philadelphia House their headquarters when visiting the nation's capital.[8]

The site of the convention was changed from Washington to Louisville, to the delight of some Southerners, and by midsummer there was considerable discussion of the prospective agenda as well as possible leaders. The Huntsville *Gazette* took the position that since the great majority of Negroes lived in the South, "the South must control and shape the plans and policies of the Convention." It also insisted that the

South decide on the chairman, even if it opted for the "venerable and distinguished leader" Frederick Douglass. The *Gazette*, therefore, urged Southerners to elect their full complement of competent delegates in order to be able to do their duty in Louisville.[9] The Charleston *Mercury* urged delegates to refrain from endorsing any political party. "The colored people are too widely scattered, too numerous, too diverse in their interests, to have a single and common political interest," the paper counseled. What would the *Mercury* have thought if, by some miracle, the convention had endorsed a Democrat for president? It strenuously discouraged "silly and inane" resolutions such as one that asserted Negro "should be spelt with a big N." The delegates should also recognize the fact that the large mass of Negroes were largely dependent on whites, who were the best and most powerful friends that Negroes had.[10] When the convention met, it did not heed the *Mercury's* advice.

Meanwhile, Boston blacks were preparing for the Louisville meeting. A convention of voters met on September 17 to consider the best method of attaining their civil and political rights and to effect an organization. They elected officers, including J. H. Wolff as president and a permanent executive committee of twenty-one, and adopted an address to the "colored men of Massachusetts and the Country." The address was an eloquent, sometimes passionate statement of grievances and an expression of concern about the plight of Negroes in the South. In its manifestation of fidelity to Christianity and to the Republican party and in its general approach, the address could well have been written by Williams, who was present and active. At the conclusion, the group elected Williams, George L. Ruffin, and Emmanuel Sullavon as its delegates to the convention in Louisville.[11]

Ruffin and Williams travelled to Louisville together and were present for the opening of the convention on September 24. Nearly three hundred delegates from twenty-seven states answered the roll, and there were many black and white spectators. A number of Williams's acquaintances were present. Among participants were B. W. Arnett, W. Calvin Chase, James E. O'Hara, D. Augustus Straker, John W. Cromwell, James M. Gregory, and J. C. Napier. The nominees for permanent chairman were Frederick Douglass and D. A. Straker of South Carolina. Straker's nomination was seconded by Williams "in one of his masterly speeches." He argued that Straker, "by his scholarly talent, his sufferings in the South, his prominence there and his complete acquaintance with the vexed difficulties of the Negro question," was best fitted to be the permanent chairman. He added that this was in no way to be construed as disrespect to Douglass "whom he revered, but as a matter of right and fair play." The debate lasted four hours, ending in Douglass's election by a vote of 190 to 74.[12]

After the balloting, Douglass was escorted into the hall "amid the wildest enthusiasm of his friends." Because of the late hour he did not deliver his speech until the following morning. A large crowd, including former Attorney-General James Speed and General James A. Eakin, listened to the two-hour speech by the "really fine-looking old colored apostle of his race." Douglass said many things the delegates wanted to hear: "Now that we are free, we must . . . take the reins in our hands and compel the world to receive us as their equals. . . . We have been given numerous platforms, but we are still in the same condition. What we want is not words, idle epithets in our praise, but action." He then described discrimination against Negroes in the labor market, in educational institutions, and even in the churches. "Follow no party blindly," he advised. "I never was a politician. I began my career as a pleader for the aggrandizement of my race, and I am not afraid to tell what I think about all kinds of equality. This stamping out of the black Republicans of the South has been done in the face of the Republican party. This convention should implore Congress for a restoration of justice, and for the abolition of this most detestable state of affairs."[13]

At the conclusion of the address, a Louisiana delegate moved that it be adopted as *the* address of the convention and sent to Congress. This motion was opposed by several delegates—including Williams, who spoke at length—who accused Douglass of leading a covert attack on the Republican party. The resolution was defeated. A resolution endorsing the Republican party was referred to committee. Another, endorsing President Arthur, was tabled "with hisses."[14] The convention did agree, after a long and stormy session marked by acrimonious debate, on an "Address" to present the delegates' views to the country. The address complained of the numerous injustices to which black people were subjected. It wanted no more class legislation because many of the laws intended to secure the rights of blacks were nothing more than dead letters. Jobs, education, and sound moral training were of top priority. The "unjust and ungrateful" distinctions made between white and black troops in the United States Army were condemned and an end to the convict lease system was called for. An indication of the broadth and perspective of the delegates was their expression of sympathy for the Irish, who were also fighting to gain their rights. With the adoption of the address the convention adjourned.[15]

Williams should have been pleased with his role at the convention. As the historian of his race, he was highly regarded. He had unsuccessfully fought for the election of a Southerner as chairman, and in doing so had won the admiration and gratitude of people such as the editor of the Huntsville *Gazette*. He worked successfully to prevent the adoption of the Douglass address as the address of the convention, and was as impressive as ever in debate.

> Honorable George W. Williams is a man of giant intellect. He has a brain of the German type that never seems to tire. His mind, as it were, is like a mill, capable of receiving facts, information of every description, and of grinding and turning them out in logical and forcible arguments. . . . It may be properly said of him what the celebrated Longinus said of the greatest of the Grecian orators: "Demosthenes, from the force, the fire, the mighty vehemence with which he bears down all before him, may be compared to a tempest or a thunderbolt.[16]

Even before beginning his work on his *History of the Negro Troops*, Williams devoted much attention to veterans' affairs. In 1874, when he delivered the memorial sermon before the Robert A. Bell Post of the Grand Army of the Republic in Boston, he was already a member of that leading veterans' organization. As a candidate for the legislature in 1879, he asked for the veterans' support; and during the campaign he spoke to the Colored Veteran Soldiers of Cincinnati, who received him enthusiastically.[17] At the time he was affiliated with Cincinnati's George H. Thomas Post, which boasted 150 members, including Joseph B. Foraker, a future United States senator, and General Andrew Hickenlooper, who became the state's lieutenant governor in 1880.[18] When the Encampment of the Department of Ohio met in Cleveland in January 1880, Williams left his legislative duties to serve as one of three delegates from his post. As secretary of the Committee on Resolutions, Williams read a report which he admitted he had written himself. It asserted that the Grand Army of the Republic should receive into its ranks "only true and loyal men who served their country faithfully and were honorably discharged." General James B. Steadman, the commander, objected to the resolution on the ground that it could be interpreted as a rebuke to members of the Democratic party. Williams, however, declared that he had not intended to suggest anything political. On the other hand, it was worth stating that "a rebel could obtain admission to almost any body in the country but the G.A.R." When Steadman persisted, Williams finally withdrew the resolution, affirming meanwhile that the resolution "expressed his sentiments exactly."[19]

In the spring of 1880, Williams was the principal guest at a camp fire given by Veterans Post No. 5 at the National Soldiers' Home in Dayton. His address on the Union soldier was "one of his happiest efforts and highly appreciated."[20] In June, as a delegate to the national encampment of the Grand Army of the Republic, also in Dayton (he had been elected at the Ohio encampment in January), he was a member of the committee on the commander-in-chief's address and thus had an opportunity to emphasize the passages he found especially attractive. He and his colleagues on the committee—Theodore Lang of Maryland and E. W. Chamberlain of Illinois—commended William Earnshaw, their leader, for his excellent address. They took particular note of the growth of the organization and Earnshaw's promoting the Sons of the Veterans. At a later session, Williams, who by this time must have regarded himself as a part of the establishment, nominated Earnshaw for another term as commander-in-chief, but Earnshaw declined.[21]

It was at the 1881 Ohio encampment, meeting in Columbus, that Williams achieved even greater prominence as a member of the Grand Army of the Republic. At the opening session he was among the "distinguished personages" on the platform. The commander being busy with other duties, Williams was asked to respond to the mayor's welcome. For the veterans, Williams thanked the mayor and the entire city for the very cordial reception accorded them. He eulogized the great men of Ohio as well as the brave men on the battlefield. He spoke "most impressively on the objects accomplished by the war, and of the gratitude due the soldiers and their families." The high point for him came when the newly elected commander appointed him judge advocate with the rank of colonel.[22]

As judge advocate for the year 1881–82, Williams had the responsibility of interpreting the rules and regulations of the GAR, of making recommendations for clarification of the rules, and of reviewing courts-martial of members of the organization. In his report at the end of the year, Williams called for the establishment of a committee to codify the laws of the GAR since the existing rules bore the marks of "hasty and unconsidered preparation." He was gratified that there had been small occasion for discipline and few courts-martial in the posts. Of the two that he reviewed, he affirmed one and reversed the other. He hoped that a greater effort would be made to preserve the history of the GAR. "Our history,—the history of these annual Encampments,—is not for the present only.—It is to be the immemorial and immutable heritage of the muse of history, and the imperishable *souvenir* of loyal Americans through all coming time. Encampments may make laws, and the Judge Advocate interpret them, but the *sine qua non* of the Grand Army and of the Nation is, Fraternity, Charity, and Loyalty."[23] At the end of his one-year term as judge advocate, Williams remained active in the GAR, although he never held office again.

The task of securing the erection of a monument to black Civil War soldiers was a much more tangible if also more difficult objective than anything Williams could hope to accomplish in the GAR. By the time he completed his *History of the Negro Troops*, he had become a strong advocate of such a monument. In the final chapter of the work, he made a specific proposal:

> A government of a proud, patriotic, prosperous and free people would make a magnificent investment by erecting at the capital a monument dedicated to its brave black soldiers. The large and beautiful Government Park, immediately in front of Howard University [which Williams proposed to rename the Robert Gould Shaw Park] would be an admirable place for a monument to the Negro soldiers who fell in their country's cause.

Williams then described the proposed monument in considerable detail. It would be carved from Southern granite. At the top there would be a private soldier, fully equipped, "fixed bayonet, gun at parade rest, looking south towards the Capitol." At the four corners, four figures would represent the three arms of the field service and the navy. There would be appropriate inscriptions on all sides. One, for example, would read:

A GRATEFUL NATION CONSECRATES THIS MONUMENT TO THE 36,847 NEGRO SOLDIERS WHO DIED IN THE SERVICE OF THEIR COUNTRY. "THE COLORED TROOPS FOUGHT NOBLY."[24]

The campaign that Williams launched for the erection of the monument was to coincide with the publication of his *History of the Negro Troops*. As early as August 1886, the press began to print proposals for the monument that were clearly advance sheets of the book that was about to be published. Williams's good and faithful friend, George F. Hoar, agreed to introduce a bill in the Senate, and the two of them worked together on its drafting. Williams sent Hoar some "newspaper excerpts"—advance sheets, no doubt—which would give Hoar some idea of the plan of the monument "as well as the scope of my work." He also hoped the senator would support the proposal to name the park for Robert Gould Shaw, the white leader of the black 54th Massachusetts Regiment. Perhaps the Massachusetts legislature would erect a monument to Colonel Shaw to be placed in front of the monument to the

Negro soldiers. If things could be orchestrated properly, Williams was convinced that Congress would pass the proposed bill.[25]

By December, 1886, Williams had prepared a draft of the bill that Hoar was to introduce. "I send the bill I promised on the Monument for Negro Troops," he wrote Hoar. "I leave it to your judgement to determine the amount of money needed for such a worthy enterprise."[26] On the following day Senator Hoar introduced Senate Bill 2928 "for the erection of a monument to the negro soldiers and sailors who gave their lives for the preservation of the government."[27] No more certain than Williams of the cost of the monument, Hoar left the amount blank in the original bill, quoting a figure of $100,000 only when he amended the bill in January 1887.[28] Meanwhile, in December, Representative Thomas Ryan of Kansas, a Civil War veteran himself, had introduced a similar bill in the House, also quoting $100,000.[29] In each house the bill was read twice and referred to the Committee on the Library. Williams warmly thanked Senator Hoar for sponsoring the monument bill and offered to provide any data required "in urging a favorable consideration of the measure." He was certain that Harper and Brothers would be willing to permit the use of such extracts from the *History of the Negro Troops* as might be helpful to the monument plan. He believed the adjutant general would also provide valuable information. Williams hoped that the senator would be able to meet with him, at which time they could plan strategy for the bill's enactment.[30]

Some members of Congress were not familiar with the area in which Howard University was located and where the monument was to be erected. This could well have included Senator Hoar, for Williams sent him a detailed description of the land in question. He emphasized that the monument would increase the attractiveness of that section of the city, which already had the government reservoir, the soldiers' home, Scheutzen Park, and Howard University, the "Harvard of the Negro Race." It would be very fitting, Williams said, to have the proposed monument near Howard, "where the young men of the race, gathered from every state in the South, into a great institution of learning, could have before their eyes a monument commemorating the valor of their kinsfolk who helped save the nation, and whose sacrifices for freedom made possible the educational privileges of their posterity." If there was any objection to a separate monument, it should not be held against blacks. After all, the government "made the *distinction* in pay, rank, organization of Negro troops, and even in our National Cemeteries they are proscribed in death."[31]

In January 1887, the Senate Library Committee held hearings on the proposed monument; Williams testified in support of Senator Hoar's bill.[32] While his testimony has not been preserved, one surmises that he put forth many of the arguments he had used in his letters to the senator.[33] The committee reported the bill favorably.[34] When the session adjourned with neither house acting on the bill, however, Williams became very anxious about the ultimate fate of the proposed monument. That summer he told Senator Hoar that he wished to review the entire matter with him to plan future strategy.[35] He also attempted to bring public pressure on Congress to pass the bill. In October he went to Providence, where he spoke before the Soldiers and Sailors Historical Society of Rhode Island. The president of the society said that Williams presented "in graphic and eloquent words a picture of the gallant and faithful service rendered by our Colored Soldiers."[36] The society was so impressed that it elected Williams a corresponding member and passed the following resolution:

> That this Society cordially approve of the suggestion of Col. George W. Williams, looking to the erection at Washington of a monument to commemorate the valor and patriotism of Negro Troops in the War of the Rebellion.[37]

When the Fiftieth Congress met in December 1887, Senator Hoar and Representative Ryan again introduced identical bills on the Negro Soldiers and Sailors monument in their respective houses. Again the bills were referred to the Library committees. This time when the Senate committee reported the bill favorably, Senator Hoar brought the bill to the floor. Senator George Vest of Missouri suggested, "Let the bill go over," but Hoar was adamant and insisted it be brought to a vote. Vest finally agreed, announcing that he would vote nay. The bill passed 31 to 19, with 26 voting absent.[38] Williams was delighted with the results and grateful to Hoar for his role.

The next hurdle was the House of Representatives, where the bill was still in committee. "Have you conferred with any members of the Massachusetts delegation in Congress in reference to it?" Williams asked Hoar. As for his own efforts, Williams reported that he had talked with three members of the Massachusetts delegation, former Governor John Long, General William Cogswell, and Henry Cabot Lodge. He urged them to speak out in support of the bill because Negro soldiers from Massachusetts had particularly distinguished themselves and because it was proposed to name the monument park for Robert Gould Shaw. Williams wished to know what else he could do.[39] Alas, the bill was never reported out of the House committee to which it had been referred on the day it was introduced.[40] Thus, many months of strenuous effort had come to naught.

Deeply interested in the elevation of his race, Williams was willing, even anxious, to enlist the aid of any whites who showed an interest. He had no intention of confining his activities or relationships to Negro groups. This determination is reflected in his brief but important contact with the distinguished Southern writer, George Washington Cable.[41] The former Confederate cavalryman and author of *Old Creole Days, The Grandissimes,* and other literary successes had long since moved to Northampton, Massachusetts, from New Orleans when Williams made contact with him. Cable was an uncompromising advocate of civil rights for blacks. Even before he published *The Negro Question* in 1888, white Southerners lashed out at him, and Northern magazines began to reject his essays. In order to continue a constructive discussion of the problems of the New South, especially the race problem, he established the Open Letter Club. Charles W. Chesnutt, another Southern writer who had moved north, to Cleveland, was the only Negro member of the group. From time to time, Cable sought and received information from other blacks, including Booker T. Washington and Bishop Daniel A. Payne.

It was James B. Pond, the lecture agent used by both Williams and Cable, who suggested to Williams that the two men should meet. Williams, living in Worcester, took the initiative. He wrote Cable that he was the best conscience of the South, "the John the Baptist of a new dispensation of good works and good will between the races and Sections of our common country so long estranged."[42] The two men got together on January 7, 1889, and apparently they were immensely pleased with each other. Cable called Williams "a Christian, a scholar, a man of affairs, polished, graceful, laborious in life, author by profession and actually making his way in white society."[43] To a friend, Cable said that Williams was "a man of strong sense and a perfect gentleman, at ease, at home and entertaining even among ladies of unusual accomplishments." He was certain that Williams would be an excellent addition to the Open Letter Club. "He joins the Club with ardor," he exulted.[44]

Williams was obviously ready to work for the Open Letter Club. In June he sent Cable a copy of a Memorial Day oration that he had recently delivered at Milbury, Massachusetts. Entitled "The Constitutional Results of the War of the Rebellion," the lengthy address covered the history of Negroes in the United States from the beginning down to the end of the Civil War. After dealing with the Reconstruction Amendments, Williams complained that the Fifteenth Amendment was violated with impunity. Toward the end of the discourse he talked about Cable's Open Letter Club and Cable, who believed that the "still small voice of conscience, reason and love will in time secure to the freedman his rights of every kind, sustained by a healthy public sentiment."[45] Williams hoped Cable would read it carefully, and offered to send extra copies at cost, "which is a mere trifle."[46] Cable did not reply, nor did Mrs. Cable reply when Williams sent her an inquiry about her husband.[47] By the end of the summer of 1889, Williams was absorbed with plans for another trip to Europe. Although Cable would maintain an intense interest in the "Negro question," the Open Letter Club ceased to be a vehicle for his views, and expired in 1890. Cable, like Williams, had many other preoccupations.[48]

From the time of his military service, Williams was afflicted with a wanderlust from which he seemed never to recover. As a student in Massachusetts, he traveled to the nation's capital and the Midwest. While editing *The Commoner* he went as far south as New Orleans and as far north as New Hampshire. When in the Ohio legislature he visited New Mexico to investigate the availability of land for blacks, and Georgia to attend the state Republican convention. As a serious student of history he went wherever the clues to the facts led him—to the military posts of the Southwest as well as to the great libraries of the Northeast. At times he traveled for his health and for relaxation, spending holidays at Plymouth Rock, on Mount Wachusett, in western Pennsylvania, in the area of his boyhood, and in Deming, New Mexico.[49]

In the summer of 1884, Williams spent several weeks in Europe, traveling in Switzerland, Germany, France, and Great Britain. He spoke of gazing upon the "dungeon floor where the virtuous Toussaint died from the studied neglect of Napoleon." Later, he stood at the tomb of the young Prince Napoleon, who, he recalled, had been killed by the Zulus in Africa. "I felt a sort of savage satisfaction that I was compelled to restrain," he admitted.[50] He remained until he was short of money, which would be a source of considerable embarrassment in subsequent months (see chapter 11 above).

Williams's constant movements were not conducive to a stable and happy family life. The early years of his marriage to Sarah S. Sterrett seemed blissful. Whenever he moved, even temporarily, she went with him. After their son George was born in 1875, Williams was most attentive. For their fifth ("wooden") wedding anniversary in Cincinnati, they gave a large reception, sending invitations of "electrified wood" to more than a hundred people. Among those attending were Judge

Alphonso Taft, General Andrew Hickenlooper, and Colonel Robert Harlan. The supper was "elegant," and the gifts were "numerous and costly."[51] After he began to travel extensively, he expressed considerable affection for his family in the few letters that survive. He told his "Sallie" that he prayed "day and night" for their son "Georgie" and wished him a "happy and useful life." He usually requested her to kiss Georgie for him. To his wife he was either "Faithfully yours" or "As ever."[52]

From the time he was in the legislature his absences became more frequent; in the recess periods he would usually be away from home, traveling or doing research. When he took up residence in Massachusetts in 1883, he took his family to Boston with him. He did not take them to Europe in 1884. Instead, he sent Sarah to Louisville to visit relatives and friends. From Heidelberg he advised her to "visit until I come home and then we will settle in Salem." Upon his return they lived together for a short time until Williams left for Washington, where he remained for an extended period. He kept Sarah informed about the protracted controversy over the Haitian appointment.[53] After it became clear that Williams would not go to Port-au-Prince, the couple did not live together again. Sarah stayed in Louisville.

It came as a surprise to Sarah Williams but perhaps not to the general public when her husband sued for divorce in July 1886.[54] The ground was desertion, which Sarah, through her lawyer, vigorously denied. She alleged that she had received no support from her husband since he went to Europe in the summer of 1884 and that meanwhile she had lived with friends in Boston and Louisville. The Washington *Bee* immediately editorialized that Williams would have a difficult time trying to prove that his "amiable and inoffensive wife deserted him." In the following week, however, the *Bee* concluded that it should give Williams's side of the affair. It conceded that it had criticized Williams from time to time and had no reason to regret it. Regarding the divorce, however, the paper said, "We have investigated carefully the circumstances in the case of Mr. Williams's divorce suit and instead of condemning him he should be applauded. As a husband he has not been found wanting. . . ."[55] No specific reasons were given for the *Bee*'s unexpected turnabout in supporting Williams. Whatever the reasons, others began to share the *Bee*'s view that there were at least two sides to the case. A Cleveland newspaper advised the *Bee* "to let George W. Williams, his treatment of his wife, etc. alone."[56] Much more suggestive was a set of assertions in a Boston paper under the column called "They say": "That Mrs. Col. George W. Williams is in Washington; That she is the friend of Hon. Fred Douglass and his family; That she is the guest of Mr.

Douglass' son."[57] The divorce suit was apparently dropped because Williams was unable to establish desertion by his wife.[58]

At the State University at Louisville in 1887, Williams delivered two lectures, one on the history of Negroes in America and another on books and reading. While he was there, the university conferred on him the honorary degree of Doctor of Laws.[59] Although others, such as Rufus L. Perry and James Poindexter, were also honored, Williams was easily the main attraction. One of his lectures was described as an "extraordinary production of thought and genius."[60] Presumably it was on this occasion that the president of the university, William J.Simmons, interviewed Williams for the biographical sketch that appeared in his forthcoming *Men of Mark, Eminent, Progressive and Rising*.[61]

With the *History of the Negro Troops* published and the proposed monument bill disposed of, Williams was able once again to engage in foreign travel. In June 1888, he was off to London to attend the Centenary Conference of Protestant Missions. Appointed as a delegate-at-large by the New York committee for the conference, Williams was one of several prominent black Americans in attendance. Others were Fanny M. J. Coppin, lecturer and educator, and the Reverend J. A. Taylor of the Baptist Foreign Missionary Convention of the United States. Taylor and Coppin each spoke once, Williams twice. During the discussion on the opium traffic he spoke at considerable length. To those who said nothing could be done, Williams pointed out that the same lame excuse had been offered by the apologists for slavery in the United States. Consequently, slavery was written in the Constitution, and it took eighty years and a bloody civil war to wipe it out. He argued that "the question of putting down the liquor traffic in the Congo, the question of expelling opium from China, is a question of legislation, is a question of statesmanship, and it rests upon the Christians of this great British Empire to display the sentiments that will force your Parliament to legislate against it."[62]

Toward the end of the conference, Williams chaired a session on "the missionary in relation to literature." In his opening remarks he declared that the most important literary accomplishment in man's history was the Bible. It had done more "to enlighten men, to give them an extended intellectual horizon than anything else in the world." He said that the great products of literature owed their influence to the Christian religion. Missionaries and others should "preach Christ to the people through . . . literature . . . and hold up the Bible as the sum total of all Christian effort as the rule of practice of our Christian conduct."[63] It was a rather powerful keynote for the several papers that were to follow.

Williams returned to Europe later in 1888 to engage in research on a subject that had periodically claimed his attention, a biography of Toussaint L'Ouverture. He visited archives and libraries in England, France, and Spain and went home in December with ten large volumes of source material. His lack of enthusiasm for the Republican presidential and vice-presidential candidates, Benjamin Harrison and Levi P. Morton, could have had something to do with his remaining out of the country during most of the fall campaign.

The year 1889 was a difficult one for Williams. He saw his last chance to secure a foreign post vanish when Frederick Douglass was appointed minister to Haiti. He was unsuccessful in gaining employment in other areas of the federal or state government, and his quest for the position of librarian of Clark University came to naught. Worst of all, his health was failing, and his physician strongly advised him to take a trip to a warm climate.[64] He might have gone to the Caribbean or even to southern Europe had not the antislavery leaders of the world been planning a conference in Brussels later in the year. For some time Williams had set his heart on attending the conference, hopefully as a delegate from the United States. In July 1889 he published an article describing the persistence of the African slave trade and calling on the people of the United States to fight the "gigantic evil." He suggested placing an economic boycott on those countries engaged in the trade. He also urged the United States to have proper representation at the forthcoming conference.[65] He even sent the secretary of state a copy of his article, stating that the great powers must do something "to make the crusade against the Slave-trade effectual."[66] He would go to Brussels, delegate or not, and hope that his health would improve in the not-so-warm climate of Leopold's capital.

On September 28, 1889, Williams sailed for Europe. The moment he arrived in London, reporters sent dispatches to the United States telling of his romance aboard ship. One account said that he had met an English girl traveling with her brother and sister. Williams and the girl, his table companion, "fell in love with each other, and with the consent of the family, they have become engaged to be married."[67] In a lengthy piece in the Worcester *Telegram* a few days after the original announcement, a reporter said that Williams had shifted from the Baptist to the Methodist ministry after he tired of politics. He also said that Williams passed as a bachelor in Worcester, although he had a wife who supported "herself and her 14-year-old son as a hairdresser, in Washington, D.C." He accused Williams of "skipping out" on his bill at the Hotel Adams and sending a friend to pack up his personal effects. To some, Williams claimed to be divorced, the reporter declared; to others, he claimed that his wife and son were dead. The reporter finally made the preposterous assertion that Williams was one of the wealthiest Negroes in the United States and that his parents "are living in Europe and are well to do."[68]

It was difficult for Williams to control his anger when he learned of this "investigative reporting." In a stinging rebuke, which he sent to the *Telegram* from Brussels, he denied even knowing the name of the young lady who had sat next to him in the dining salon, or in what part of England she resided. "My deportment toward her and every other lady was that of a gentleman and not of a lover," he insisted. He was never a Methodist clergyman, as the reporter claimed, but had been a member of the Baptist denomination for twenty-one years, in which he hoped to "live and die." He denied that there was anything mysterious about his past, which was, indeed, "an open book." He had never attempted to avoid any honest obligations; and, upon learning in September 1889 that his health required him to set sail immediately, he had a friend pack his things. Meanwhile, he had paid his bill at the Hotel Adams. He called the story of the desertion of his wife a "falsehood," but would not discuss the relationship because he was "too gallant and magnaminous a man to strike a helpless and defenseless woman." Even so, his enemies— purveyors of social scandal—might one day force him to strike in his own vindication, Williams concluded, but that time had not yet come.[69]

It was typical of Williams to become the center of a heated discussion of desertion, nonsupport, interracial trysts or marriages, or affluence. He had no well-to-do parents living in Europe, nor was he one of the wealthiest Negroes in the United States.[70] His finances were so tangled that no one with the possible exception of Williams himself, could have understood them. What his relationship was with his wife by 1889 is not clear. One supposes that they were still estranged and that she was adamant in refusing a divorce. In the absence of denials based on incontrovertible evidence, Williams was compelled to endure the strictures and censure of his black brethren who could scarcely tolerate his being in the family. Meanwhile, he could resolutely turn his attention to the Old World, the land of his fathers, knowing that in the New World he no longer had a place as his brother's keeper.

·13·

African Journey

If the American press tried, almost desperately, to make something of the alleged shipboard romance of Williams and a young Englishwoman, Williams's own conduct suggested that he was much more interested in other matters. Immediately upon landing in England, he proceeded to the Continent, where he vigorously pursued his African interests. Having failed to secure an appointment as a delegate to the antislavery conference, he was determined to have some impact on its deliberations. Perhaps as an observer and a lobbyist he could present to the conference, through some of its delegates, his ideas about controlling the slave trade.

Williams was also to serve as a journalist-reporter for the conference. Two days before he sailed, he had obtained a commission from S. S. McClure to write articles on Europe and Africa for the Associated Literary Press. "Any information given or facilities afforded him for the acquisition of information pertaining to his mission will be greatly appreciated by me," McClure wrote in his commission to Williams.[1] McClure, who had begun to issue syndicated articles in 1884 from his modest New York apartment, had a thriving business by 1889 and had been forced to rent offices in the Tribune building, from which he served more than a hundred newspapers. Among his correspondents at one time or another were Robert Louis Stevenson, Rudyard Kipling, Arthur Conan Doyle, Mark Twain, Henry James, and Randolph Churchill.[2] Williams was proud of the McClure connection, for it gave him some standing in Brussels as well as some remuneration. He referred to himself as a "special representative of the Associated Literary Press of the U.S.A."

The first and surely one of the most exciting assignments that Williams undertook was an interview with Leopold II, King of the Belgians.

As early as the summer of 1884 he had tried to see the king, following him, it will be recalled, from Brussels to Ostend, apparently without success. Even then Williams had been interested in the Congo and knew that the king was a key figure in the destiny of Central Africa. This time he would not be denied. He may have succeeded because of the personal intercession of the Belgian minister to the United States, Alfred Le Ghait, with whom Williams was acquainted. The fact, moreover, that Williams proposed to write a syndicated piece on the king that would be read by thousands in the United States must have made some impression. The king had sent word that on this occasion he would forego the tradition of having the resident minister present a citizen of his country and would simply receive Williams, thus establishing a certain informality for the royal audience.

Williams was enormously impressed with the regal bearing of Leopold II, his more than six feet towering over the modest-sized American. The warmth of his greeting and his urbanity put Williams completely at ease, as we can gather from his description of the king:

> While a large man, Leopold II has all that distinguishes the student, carrying no superflous flesh; and proved himself a good listener as well as a pleasant and entertaining conversationalist. His hair and full beard were carefully trimmed and liberally sprinkled with gray. His features were strong and clear cut and keen; and his eyes, bright and quick, flashed with intelligent interest from behind a pair of eyeglasses. His head was broad and capacious; ears set well back of a brain that towered far above them. His mouth showed both strength and generosity, and his chin was indicative of decision and courage. His voice was clear and soft, with minor tones that had held close fellowship with sorrow.

The king spoke freely about a number of matters, but those that Williams took the liberty of mentioning had to do with the Congo State, "a subject in which he is deeply interested, and to which he has devoted his splendid talents and vast wealth for some years." Williams knew, of course, that the Congo State was not a Belgian possession but a personal fiefdom of the king. Leopold said that his people had two motives in developing the Congo. "One is trade and commerce, which is selfish . . . and the other is to bring the means and blessings of Christian civilization to Africa, which is noble." To the question as to what he expected in return for the great outlay he had made in the Congo, the king replied, "What I do there is done as a Christian duty to the poor African; and I do not wish to have one franc back of all the money I have expended." His reward came, he said, in the gratitude of the people of the Congo for lawful government and the administration of justice. Williams concluded that Leopold was "one of the noblest sovereigns in the world; an emperor whose highest ambition is to serve the cause of Christian civilization, and to promote the best interests of his subjects, ruling in wisdom, mercy, and justice."[3]

Williams was scheduled to have another audience with Leopold on October 31, but he made no mention of it in later dispatches. Meanwhile, he was meeting other people and writing other articles for the Associated Literary Press. One person he wished to see was Henry S. Sanford, a long-time resident of Brussels and former United States minister to Belgium. For years Sanford had been advocating the idea that Negro Americans should emigrate to the Congo, where they would find unexampled opportunities to assist in the development of the state while at the same time contributing to the solution of the race problem in the United States.[4] Williams had met Sanford some years earlier, when President Arthur introduced the two men at the White House. He sought to renew the acquaintance by interviewing Sanford for an article which would reveal not only Sanford's views but those of Collis P. Huntington, Francis William Fox, and others on the best methods for suppressing the slave trade. Sanford declined to be interviewed.[5]

Williams early made an impression on observers in Brussels, and the press took notice of him. "The antislavery conference has already brought one of the most interesting figures to Brussels," *L'Indépendance Belge* reported. "Colonel Williams, with whom we have had the pleasure of speaking, has some well formulated ideas about the kind of action which should be taken to suppress permanently the horrible traffic in human flesh and even domestic slavery. It is also likely that his propositions will be communicated to the antislavery congress by the United States Minister, Mr. Terrell, or the latter will at least draw inspiration from them." The newspaper also referred to Williams's plan to visit the Congo "and, perhaps, to spread antislavery propaganda among the Arabs."[6]

In September, President Harrison appointed Edwin H. Terrell, the United States Minister to Belgium, as his principal delegate to the conference on the slave trade. In December he appointed Henry S. Sanford as delegate with the same rank and limitations accorded Terrell.[7] Williams, meanwhile, had met other notables, including Collis P. Huntington, the American railroad magnate, who had expressed a lively interest in the proposed railroad through the Congo as well as a desire to bring the slave trade to a close.[8] Williams told Huntington of his own interests in the Congo, which coincided with Huntington's at two points: to end the slave trade and to encourage development of the Congo, perhaps by having cadres of young black Americans go there and help in various ways. He would remain in Brussels for the conference; then he would travel to Africa so that he could write about conditions firsthand.[9]

Apparently Williams requested Huntington's assistance on the African leg of his journey, a request that was not cordially received. "I regret that you should have left the United States for such an extensive journey as you propose to make in Africa without making any provision at all for the money which you must have known that you would need," Huntington wrote when they were both in London. He added that he might assist Williams and wished for him every success, "but you must pardon me for feeling misgivings about it considering the manner in which you have set about it, which seems to be somewhat incomprehensible, I must confess, in a man who appears to have the common sense and at the same time determination to do a long and probably expensive work that you have." Huntington was obviously softened by a flattering request by Williams for his photograph, which he promised to send if he should have any taken. Shortly before leaving London for New York, he told Williams that he might send him some money when he arrived in the States. Meanwhile, he extended "good wishes for yourself and your work."[10] By this time Huntington was clearly involved in Williams's projects both in Brussels and in Africa.

The collaboration between the two men in Brussels took the form of monitoring the position of the United States Department of State on questions that came before the antislavery conference. Delegates from seventeen nations met in Brussels on November 18, 1889, to look into the question of the slave trade and to establish adequate mechanisms to prevent it. The Berlin conference of 1885 had given virtually no attention either to the slave trade or to a problem closely associated with it, the liquor traffic. Britain was among the powers that had urged the Brussels conference and, once it had convened, led in insisting on strict control of the liquor traffic. Germany was not anxious to interfere with the profitable sale of liquors, while Holland was opposed to any effective interference. Holland, moreover, hoped to capitalize in the Congo on the experience and skills of its commercial houses and was therefore vigorously opposed to the imposition of any import duties on companies trading in the Congo. It hoped the matter would be taken up and resolved at the Brussels conference. France was sensitive to the exercise of the right of search by other than nationals of ships suspected of being engaged in the slave trade.[11] Meanwhile, the representative of the United States, E. H. Terrell, said that while his government took great interest in the conference, it had not given him full powers to sign but had instructed him to take any proposal "ad referendum."[12]

Before the proceedings began, Williams had sent Huntington a copy of the articles that the Department of State proposed to place before the conference. Huntington promised to give the matter his immediate attention. The following day he wrote Williams at great length, observing in passing that he understood that the draft Williams had sent him had been read "and provisionally approved by the King of Belgium." He thought most of the provisions dealing with the slave trade and the liquor traffic "salutary." He suggested some modification, however, of a proposed article dealing with fugitive slaves and the indemnification of alleged owners who surrendered all claims to ownership and servitude. He also wished to see inspectors of wholesale and retail importations into the Congo authorized to seize and destroy all adulterated spirituous liquors or beverages.[13]

The extent of Williams's contact with the United States delegation to the conference is not clear. He did not know Terrell well, and Sanford did not become the second United States plenipotentiary until after Williams had returned to the United States. In any case, Sanford apparently did not care for Williams and had refused to grant him an interview. To be sure, the American influence at the conference was minimal anyway, all the more so since the delegates had no authority to commit the United States to anything. In the late spring of 1890, when the weary delegates were plodding toward the conclusion, Sanford was insisting on an amendment that not even his colleague Terrell wanted. Sanford was attempting to reinforce the Dutch effort to prevent the imposition of import duties in the Congo. The British delegate assured his government that the proposed amendment would be "decently buried in a protocol."[14] By the time the conference was over, it had hammered out the first international agreement on the abolition of the slave trade. It was a personal triumph for Leopold II, who, by directing attention to the slave trade in the Congo, had succeeded in securing the imposition of import duties and persuading financiers to invest more capital there.[15] Meanwhile, Williams was about to direct attention to the Congo in quite another way.

There is no doubt that when he left the United States in September 1889, Williams had plans to visit the Congo in the near future; and he wished to further his notion that American blacks should help improve conditions there. The press had indicated as much, and he had revealed his plans to Collis P. Huntington.[16] He not only had discussed his plans with King Leopold but had involved him in them. If Williams initiated the idea that Negro Americans should personally assist in Africa's development, Henry S. Sanford found himself in agreement but probably for different reasons. They would be the kind of "civilizing influence" that whites could never be," he said.[17] "What an opening for our people of African descent, awaiting another Moses to show them the way to this new land of promise, their fatherland," Sanford wrote in 1886.[18] In the autumn of 1889, Williams proposed to be that "Moses." He had long been an advocate of programs that would employ Negro Americans as ordinary laborers as well as office workers in the Congo. The king became interested, as did Captain Albert Thys, chief administrative officer of the Belgian Commercial Companies operating in the Congo Free State.

Williams proposed that the Belgian Commercial Companies recruit educated Americans of African descent to work in their offices. Their presence and example would have a "good effect on the natives." The companies adopted the proposition and commissioned Williams to engage twelve clerks and twelve engineers and skilled mechanics.[19] Under the circumstances it was not difficult for him to tear himself away from the conference. He sailed for New York on the *Aurania*, arriving there December 9, 1889. He hoped to bring the men back with him within a few weeks.

On the morning of his arrival in New York, Williams sent a note to Huntington: "I would like to confer with you at the earliest moment convenient to you in reference to my mission and will await your reply to this by this messenger."[20] Huntington was a member of the Board of Trustees of Hampton Institute and one of its principal benefactors. He believed that if Williams were to talk personally with General Samuel C. Armstrong, the founder, and with faculty and students, he should be able to recruit most if not all of his workers right there.

In interceding with Armstrong for Williams, Huntington revealed to the head of Hampton Institute something of his own connection with Williams as well as his tentative appraisal of him:

> He is a mulatto who first came under my notice through a letter received from him when I was in London. From what he wrote I learned that he was a Massachusetts man who has been a correspondent for Worcester journals on the subject of the slave trade in Africa and the enterprises on the Congo. He announced that he was on his way over to the Conference at Brussels, as a representative of the United States or delegate, rather, and sometime later he called upon me at my hotel and explained that he was going down to the Congo to write letters for a number of American newspapers and periodicals, being commissioned by them to do so.

> Mr. Williams is a bright man, as you will see by talking with him
> if you should have the opportunity of doing so. . . . I know very little
> of him personally, but what I do know is, I am glad to say, favorable
> in its nature.[21]

Within less than a week—on Friday, January 10—Williams was at
Hampton, making the rounds among the various groups and delivering
an address before the student body. It was a disappointing experience,
however. Interest among the students in going to the Congo was not as
great as he had hoped. Nor were his answers to their questions about
Africa as cogent as he would have liked. General Armstrong explained to
Huntington that the students at Hampton were not "developed enough
to stand the test in Africa." Only a few were fit to go, he said, and they
were not easily moved. Since Armstrong had no firsthand knowledge of
Africa, he was reluctant to advise the students one way or another. Still,
Armstrong would not characterize Williams's visit a failure, "for he has
sown much good seed." The experience at Hampton convinced Wil-
liams that he should visit the Congo himself to gain firsthand knowledge. He returned to New York and made arrangements to sail for
Europe early in January. In that conenction, of course, he asked to see
Huntington at his convenience.[22]

Meanwhile, Williams continued to make preparations for the future
recruitment of Negro Americans for Africa. In December he had several
conversations with Michael E. Strieby, corresponding secretary of the
American Missionary Association, about recruiting among some of the
association's schools in the South. Williams was interested in securing
clerks, carpenters, blacksmiths, and engineers "with stipulations as to
salary and support for three years." He referred Strieby to Huntington
for additional material and information on the venture. Strieby told
Huntington that he had no doubt that properly qualified men could be
obtained for service, but he was unwilling to advise them to prepare
themselves for such a venture "without adequate assurances that the
terms and stipulations will be fulfilled." He conceded that Williams was
a "brilliant writer and enterprising man" and was no doubt reliable, but
since the matter was so important he wished "further guarantees and
assurances" that those recruited would enjoy the security that additional
documentation would provide.[23] There is no evidence that Huntington
provided such guarantees. In any case, Williams did not recruit students at American Missionary Association schools.

On December 23, Williams went to the White House and told
President Harrison of his plans to go to the Congo. The president was
interested, particularly with regard to the question of whether or not the

United States should ratify the Berlin Act, which had facilitated Leopold's acquisition of the Congo Free State. It is clear from Williams's account of the interview that the president had serious reservations about pursuing such a policy. There was "danger of annulling the traditions of a century; of violations [of] the Monroe Doctrine, and of approaching the stormy circle of European politics." Williams promised to prepare for the president a memorandum on "the International Law and sentimental reasons" why the United States should ratify the act. From the White House, Williams went to see John Sherman, an old friend from the Ohio days, now chairman of the Senate Committee on Foreign Relations. Sherman shared the president's hesitation to ratify the Berlin Act. He promised, Williams reported, to suspend action on the matter until Williams had completed his investigations. On Christmas Day 1889, after only three weeks in the United States, Williams sailed once again for Europe.[24]

The Belgian Commercial Companies had agreed to pay Williams $150 a month to recruit forty American Negroes and escort them to the Congo. Upon returning to Brussels he told Captain Thys he did not think it could be done. Thys agreed with Williams's assessment, discharged him, and gave him two months pay. Huntington expressed disappointment when he learned that Williams was no longer on the Brussels payroll. (At his urging, Williams had sought employment, but the king had told him that he must reserve all posts for Belgians only.)[25]

By his own account, Williams received rather cool treatment when he called at the royal palace. Various officers of the king's household sought to dissuade him from making the trip. The climate was "deadly" during the rainy season, one of them argued, and the expenses of the voyage and of traveling by caravan would be very heavy. To all of the arguments Williams replied simply that he was going. Then King Leopold sent for him and received him cordially. The king told him that Stanley believed the Congo "would not be worth a shilling" without a railway. Travel was difficult, and it was virtually impossible to obtain wholesome food "for white men." His Majesty, therefore, hoped that Williams would postpone his trip for at least five years, by which time, according to Stanley, the railway would be completed. When Williams said that he was going to the Congo immediately, the king replied sternly, "Then you cannot go on the State-Steamers, and must rely upon the Mission-Steamers." Williams made no reply to that royal declaration, and after a few harmless exchanges he left the palace.

A young Belgian nobleman with whom Williams had been on friendly terms and who knew all of the court gossip volunteered an explanation for the rather sudden change in attitude toward the black American. He told Williams that Henry Sanford was suspicious of his mission to the Congo. Sanford thought Williams was going either as the representative of an American company to open up trade there or as an agent of Sanford's enemies in the United States who wished to prove the falsity of his statements regarding the fertility of the country and the volume of trade.[26] Sanford, though he had an interest in blacks' migrating to the Congo, may have been wary of the kind of intelligent leadership that Williams might offer. He would have preferred to have a hand in the selection of black Americans to work in the Congo. He had opposed the abolitionists in the years prior to the Civil War, and thought blacks, whether in the United States or in the Congo, should remain subordinate to whites.[27]

Even without a commission from King Leopold and the Belgian Commercial Companies, Williams had sufficient assignments to make a visit to the Congo worthwhile. He would visit as much of the country as possible in order to give President Harrison a detailed report on the state of affairs there, as he had promised. He would write a series of letters to the Associated Literary Press to be distributed to its subscribing newspapers, pursuant to his commission from S. S. McClure. He would also look at the route of the proposed Congo Railway and make a report, presumably to Collis P. Huntington, regarding its feasibility.

Huntington was already involved in two railway projects in Africa. One, the projected road from the East African coast to the interior as far as Victoria Nyanza (Lake Victoria), was to be built by the British East Africa Company, in which Huntington had invested $75,000. The other, in which he had put $50,000, was the road to be built by the Belgians along the Congo River from Matadi to Stanley Pool. Huntington insisted that even if the investments were wholly lost, as he expected, he would obtain much satisfaction in "aiding the opening of the country and thereby promoting civilization."[28]

During his final weeks in Belgium, when he was discussing his future with members of the royal household, Williams cabled Huntington that he was about to leave for Africa and required money. Huntington replied by cable that he was sending a letter. Enclosed in the letter was a check for £100 drawn on the London and Westminster Bank. "I hope all will go well with you in your new field of work," he wrote, "and shall await with interest your first letter giving impressions of the Congo country. I think you are well qualified to enlighten Americans upon this subject—particularly as to the actual condition and extent of civilization of the native population, concerning which I believe much misapprehension exists."[29]

Now without a royal supporter, Williams apparently had an American benefactor on whom he could depend. Collis P. Huntington would become the principal source of support for Williams in the months ahead. As soon as he received Huntington's letter, Williams spent a week in London purchasing supplies and tropical clothing.[30] From Liverpool, on January 30, 1890, he sailed for Africa on the *Gaboon*, owned by the British and African Steam Navigation Company.

Just before leaving Brussels for the last time, Williams received some disturbing news from an undisclosed source. The Belgian minister to the United States informed the king that Williams was going to the Congo as Huntington's representative. Huntington was "vastly rich," so the news went, and Williams was "very shrewd." He was to purchase large tracts of rubber lands as a way of getting Huntington's head into the Congo. Like the proverbial camel he would then get his whole body in. For that reason the government of the Congo State and the Belgian companies should do everything in their power to defeat Williams's mission.[31]

Williams made the most of his trip of fifty-three days from Liverpool to Boma, in the Congo Free State. Happily for him, the ship made frequent stops once it reached Las Palmas, Canary Islands. He visited Sierra Leone; Sinoe, Liberia; Bereby, on the Ivory Coast; and various towns along the Gold Coast (Ghana) and Slave Coast (Benin and Nigeria). At Bonny, Nigeria, he attended Sunday services at a "native" as well as a European church. He took every opportunity to visit missions and schools. When time permitted, he visited local people, observing their customs and inquiring of their relations with Europeans. He was distressed that Europeans had no qualms about selling cannon for use in the "childish and destructive hands of the natives, so that with an unrestricted trade in firearms and rum it will not be long ere the African will perish by his own hands."

Williams never relented in his quest for information on the treatment of Africans by Europeans. Even on the *Gaboon* he questioned British government officials, who were among his fellow voyagers.[32] Each time the ship called at a port, Williams was observing, asking questions, and taking notes. After only a few days in the Congo, he began to understand why the Belgians had not wanted him to go. The miserable conditions provided a "dozen excellent reasons why my coming is, in the Providence of God, the best thing that could happen for the poor native and the misguided Belgian."[33]

Williams had been on the verge of making an adverse judgment of the situation in the Congo from the time King Leopold urged him to cancel his trip. It was not merely that the king opposed his going. Williams thought the opposition more widespread, even conspiratorial. Henry Sanford must be one of the conspirators. From the *Gaboon*, Williams wrote Sanford that a gentleman of position, character, and ability had intimated that Sanford had been "the instigator of all the opposition with which my mission to the Congo was beset." He said he had told his friends in the United States, particularly President Harrison and Senator Sherman, of the opposition and that he expected protection "as an American citizen in visiting a country that had been opened to a great international commerce and free trade." He was determined to discharge the mission, he told Sanford, and "if anything should happen to me, you will be held responsible."[34]

While still en route, Williams was virtually overcome by the fear that something would happen to him. From the Canary Islands he wrote Huntington that the Belgian companies operating in the Congo were so strenuously opposed to his going there that he feared the worst. "I have reason to believe that I may be assassinated or poisoned," he wrote. "However, I shall take every precaution to preserve my life, and shall do my duty to history and humanity with unflagging zeal and dauntless courage."[35] After his arrival in Boma, Williams was certain that he was being watched and followed wherever he went. He could not trust the Belgians with his mail, he complained to Senator Hoar, and "in order to get this letter out I must make a trip of 90 miles in a small boat." He told the senator to reply by sending his letter through the Dutch House in Holland, and it would be sent to him in Boma. He made another, bolder request:

> Will you call upon the President and request him to send a man of war here and enquire for me of the Governor General of the Congo State and of the Dutch House. I ought to be able to cover the 6,000 miles [to the headwaters of the Congo River and return] . . . by the month of August or September; but the man of war ought to come as soon as possible, its presence here may save me from embarrassment and from assassination . . . . Will you also request the President to ask the King of the Belgians to give me safe conduct through the State of Congo. . . . If this is done and the man of war arrives and makes inquiries about me, my mission will prove a great success. The Man of war should remain until I return, or until my death is assured beyond a doubt. In such a case my Diaries will be found with the Dutch House, and with my personal effects should be taken to the United States and delivered to yourself. An order to this effect will be found at the Dutch House at Banana, mouth of the Congo River.

Please show or read this letter to the President and urge the above action.[36]

Williams's request for assistance and a "show of force" was not as unusual as it might have appeared. The United States engaged in such practices in the late nineteenth century, no doubt in its effort to notify the Europeans that the rising power in the west could not be ignored. As early as 1879 the United States had sent a warship, the S.S. *Ticonderoga,* to the Congo to warn King Kala, King Pala Bala, and others that the United States expected them to accord ships and persons under the American flag protection and assistance when necessary. In 1885 the United States sent another warship, the S.S. *Kearsarge,* to the Congo to assist the U.S. agent W. P. Tisdel in his insistence that the interest of the United States in the Congo be taken seriously. Williams received no response to his request, causing him further apprehension.[37]

His first impressions of the Congo were, predictably, highly unfavorable. Three weeks after his arrival he wrote Huntington that "this seems to be the Siberia of the African Continent, a penal settlement." He was certain that King Leopold had acquired the land by the "most brutal frauds." He said he was studying the labor and wage systems, the currency, the liquor question, the importation of firearms, the system of punishment, "the relation of which would make you shudder," the courts, the ethics of trade, and the military system. He had already looked into health conditions enough to pronounce them extremely poor. The hospitals were unfit even for healthy people. The dirt floors were "turned into mud by the rain which pours through the roofs. There is not one blanket in these hospitals—not one! The mortality is something marvelous. There is no Chaplain to console the dying or bury the dead, who are cast into an open field where their emaciated remains are devoured by snakes and wild animals."[38] Comments such as these filled the letters from Williams to his three principal correspondents—Huntington, Hoar, and the black lawyer in Washington, Robert H. Terrell. Copies of the letters, harshly critical in virtually every respect, would provide important sources for Williams's subsequent writings on the Congo.

His early comments on the proposed Congo Railway were equally adverse. Before the middle of May, Williams had passed over "every foot of the surveyed route of the proposed Congo Railway to the mouth of the Mpozo River where the advanced Engineer's Camp is located." He was unhappy with the time, four years, or the capital outlay, $10 million, that the Belgian company had estimated for completion of the railway. If each figure were doubled, it would be more realistic, he wrote Huntington. "I have investigated the labor system, the transit method, the food and quarters of the men, and when I return from the interior . . . will make a complete report on every thing, impartial, judicial, and honest."[39]

For a man of Williams's limited experience, delicate health, and uncertain financial support, a venture far into the African interior in 1890 was no mean undertaking. Yet on May 15 of that year, with a caravan of eighty-five men, this forty-year-old American set out to see all that he could by water as well as by land. Williams already knew a good deal about Henry M. Stanley, the intrepid explorer-journalist who had "found" Dr. David Livingstone in 1871. It was clear that Williams was attempting to second-guess Stanley regarding the railway; and he seemed to be vying with him in matters of exploration.[40] Others also were taking a hard look at the Congo in 1890. If Williams did not meet them, he doubtless heard of them, and the mutual interests of these investigators gave his own mission added significance. Roger Casement, the British Foreign Service officer whose celebrated *Report* on the Congo more than a decade later would profoundly affect attitudes toward the Congo, was already an observer in 1890. Joseph Conrad, who would steadfastly resist numerous efforts to involve him in Congo reform, based his *Heart of Darkness* on his own experiences there in 1890. Even as he began his own journeys of exploration, Williams knew there was a major book to be written on what he found in the Congo.

Where possible, Williams used the Congo River mission and commercial steamers. The *Holland* seems to have been the one most frequently used. Since there were five Dutch Trading Company stations between Stanley Pool and Stanley Falls (Kisangani), and Williams depended on the Dutch for his mail as well as supplies, those houses proved to be good bases. The regular route of travel seemed to be the river, with regular excursions into the countryside. It was during such forays that Williams experienced the greatest difficulties. For two weeks, he wrote, "I had traveled through a country absolutely desititute of food. The courage of my men began to abate and it looked on several occasions, as if I would be compelled to execute one or two subordinate fellows who were endeavoring to bring on a mutiny. But with firmness and heroic suffering without a murmur I triumphed."

Williams's descriptions of the countryside were equally dramatic. "Sometimes I was crossing plains, which stretched days before me, as level as our own prairies, again I struggled for four days through the dense, dark and damp forest of Muyambu, where it rains every month of the year." He was fortunate when he encountered friendly people who

offered him food and shelter if he "would honor them by remaining over
night with them." Others, however, were hostile, denying him food and
warning him to move on. "But I never consented to go," he wrote. "I
knew too well the virtue of my modern fire-arms; and I usually gave
them to understand that I wanted food for my people and would pay for
it, and if it were not forthcoming within one hour I would come and take
it. Hungry men are usually heroes for the hour, and I always got food
when there was any to be had. Brass-rods, three kinds of goods, knives
and powder were the articles with which I bought food. . . . I am glad to
say that I did not lose one of my 85 men, although several were sick. I
think two may have died since we reached the coast, but after leaving
my service."[41]

At no time during his African journey did Williams have an ample
supply of money and other resources. In his very first letter to Huntington following his arrival in the Congo, he was requesting assistance. "I
am in need of funds to push this work to gather material for my book," he
wrote. "Any thing you may be moved to send me should be sent direct to
Rotterdam, Holland, and the Dutch House there will understand and
send it to me in their private mail bags." The following month he told
Huntington, "If you will aid me further place it to my credit with the
Dutch House in Rotterdam, Holland." By the time that he reached
Stanley Falls, he was pleased to report that he had made "a little money"
by trading some items he had purchased on credit. Even so, he was
disappointed not to have received any communication from Huntington. "I need aid at this time," he pleaded, "and if you will grant it, I feel
sure it will assist a good cause." Huntington could send it to Zanzibar, in
care of the British consul-general. In early September, he asked Huntington to send him two or three hundred dollars, assuring him that he
would find it a good investment. "I will show some results later of which
you do not dream." This doubtless had reference to Williams's impending report on the proposed Congo Railway.[42]

An important source of assistance and hospitality during the journey
was the missions, which Williams visited regularly. There he secured
not only important data regarding the treatment of the Africans by the
Europeans but the kind of food and shelter that were quite rare on the
Congo River and in the interior. One such mission was maintained at
Bolobo by the Baptist Missionary Society of London, under the leadership of the Reverend George Grenfell. In June, Williams visited the
mission and talked at length with Grenfell. Of the various reasons for
Williams's being in the Congo, Grenfell thought an unannounced one
the most important: "to hunt up reasons against the expatriation (or

repatriotism is it?) of Negroes from the United States."[43] Apparently
Grenfell thought no more of the idea than Williams, although to combat
it was by no means Williams's major purpose in visiting Africa.

By the time Williams reached Bolobo, his largely negative impressions of the Congo were already formed. He did not hesitate to tell the
missionaries there what he thought. "Lots of talk," Grenfell wrote in his
diary. "Pessimistic mainly as regards the Congo." "I fancy he is not at all
favorably disposed towards the [Congo] State, and may possibly paint
things pretty black," he wrote his colleagues in London. For obvious
reasons, Grenfell was hesitant about speaking out against the king of the
Belgians. To London, however, he could comment on those dismaying
things that Williams had an opportunity to see. "I wonder what he
would say if he saw, as we did, nine slaves chained neck to neck in the
State Station at Upoto and waiting for a steamer to carry them down to
Bangala. . . . Or what would the Colonel say if he met, as we did, a big
canoe with a State employee on board and were told they were out
trying to buy slaves. . . . The evolving of a great free people out of the
present chaos I fear will be a bitter process under the present administration, but even the best of governments and the wisest of administra-
tions would need strong hands, and would often have to hit very hard.[44]

It was from Williams that Grenfell learned of the possibility of
concessionnaire companies coming into existence in the Congo, where
they would enjoy extensive privileges "in the development of the
State."[45] Not all these companies would be Belgian; some might be
German or from other countries. Williams was convinced that Henry
Sanford had placed the idea of *concessionnaire* companies before the
king as early as 1888. Grenfell was greatly disturbed by this information,
not only because such companies were, he thought, in clear violation of
the Act of Berlin proclaiming the Congo Free State, but also because
they would subvert the independence of the State. Surely, he said, the
Free State "has a firmer foundation than all this would seem to suggest."
In any case, Grenfell confessed sadly, his circumstances were such that
he did not "feel called upon to publicly question the action of the
State."[46] News such as Williams brought would always make him a
welcome guest at Bolobo.

Two months after Williams began his trip into the interior, he
reached Stanley Falls. His observations along the way had to do with the
climate, soil, topography, flora and fauna, and the people. From Stanley
Pool to the mouth of the Kasai River, a distance of some one hundred
miles, the banks were steep and of white clay, and the channel was
narrow. From that point, the steep banks gave way to lowlands, "fertile,
open, green, wide and beautiful." This was the equatorial area, in which

nearly every vegetable known in Europe could be grown. The country continued "fairly good" beyond the great bend of the river until the Lomani River. From there to the headwaters at Stanley Falls, a distance of about eighty-five miles, the land was poor. It was in this region that Williams found the climate most severe. At Stanley Falls he recorded a change of thirty degrees in a period of sixteen hours. It was, he concluded, much "too severe" for northern people. He encountered many human types in his journey to Stanley Falls, ranging from the industrious and prosperous tribes near Stanley Pool to those "in a deep state of degradation" from Iringi to Upoto. There were also great variations in size and appearance, from the "perfect types of the North-American Indian" among his carriers, to the water gypsies near the Lomani River, to the tall, dark, agile types around Bangala and the Equator.[47] Although not always pleased with what he saw, he felt he had seen enough to have a fairly clear notion of Africa.

Williams was of the opinion that the population of the Congo Free State was relatively sparse. Stanley had estimated it at somewhere between forty-nine and fifty million. This was a gross exaggeration, thought Williams, who judged it no more than fifteen million. "I have travelled over the same route Mr. STANLEY took, and stopped at the same towns. I had the same or as good facilities for finding out the population, and with his book in my hand I endeavoured to test his figures. First of all, it must be understood that the towns are numerous but thinly populated; and where he found ten thousand . . . I found only 4,000 people, and so on in proportion."[48] This was just one of the many areas in which Williams would disagree with Stanley's findings.

Despite the unfavorable climate, Williams remained at Stanley Falls for several days to rest, ruminate, and write. It was there that he wrote *An Open Letter to His Serene Majesty Leopold II* and *A Report on the Proposed Congo Railway* (reprinted below as Appendixes 1 and 2). He also wrote Huntington, breaking the news to him that he had been disappointed with the "deceit, obtusiveness, ignorance and cruelty of the State of the Congo."[49]

The day he completed the railway report, he began the return journey. At Bolobo he disembarked from the *Holland* for another visit with Grenfell.[50] Proceeding to Stanley Pool from Bolobo, Williams took a new route to the sea through the French Congo. This gave him an opportunity to visit such towns as Bouenza and Loudina before arriving at the port city of Loango. There Williams received a cordial welcome from the French, Portuguese, Dutch, Americans, and English. He must have been tempted to compare his own emergence from the interior with that of Stanley's, as one group after another acclaimed his feat. "A series of dinners were given in my honor," he wrote Terrell, "the American House starting first, as they claimed that honor. Even the Bishop of the French Congo called upon me and invited me to dine with him." During his days of rest, he visited the countryside, crossing Lake Cayo, "one of the most beautiful bodies of water in Western Africa," and spending some time at a "prosperous and promising plantation" which abounded in coffee, cocoa, and rubber trees. He returned to the Congo Free State long enough to ship from Banana "five large boxes of curiosities, such as arrows and bows, spears, swords, knives, paddles, grass mats, shields, etc."[51] Then he took the Dutch ship *Andrea* for Loanda, Angola, arriving there September 17, 1890.

By the time Williams arrived at Loanda, his original study proposal had expanded into a much more ambitious plan to examine conditions in other parts of Africa as well. From Loanda he wrote Huntington that he would "investigate the Penal Servitude and Labor Systems here, and then start for Cape of Good Hope, Natal, and Zanzibar." With Huntington's interests ever in mind, he reported that he had examined the St. Paul de Loanda and Ambecca Railroad, "passing over it in the private car of the Director General whose guest I was."[52] He found Loanda most impressive, with two seventeenth-century churches, which he visited, a cable railway, a meteorological station, a public garden, and a hospital. He was pleased that he was "a social favorite" in Angola. He was "a white man" there as elsewhere in Africa and in Europe, he wrote his friend Terrell. He was impressed with the "beautiful white ladies and handsom [*sic*] mulatto ladies, and a Small coterie of choice Spirits [black ladies] not to be slighted."[53]

The labor and social situation in Angola was unique, Williams thought. The life of the black slave was not "sweet and comfortable," he discovered, but once he acquires his freedom he leaves the old life behind. "The change is instantaneous. He simply steps across the line, on one side of which he was a 'nigger,' but on the other side he becomes Signor Lopes. There is more genuine, heartfelt democracy here than in your boasted America," Williams exclaimed. "Every black man in Loanda has a vote at the municipal elections. There are mixed schools. There are no separate churches—a great thing for the Catholic religion—Wherever you find a black man here with education and means, a man who displays ability of the most ordinary kind, he is appreciated and treated with consideration."[54] Williams did not comment on how easy or difficult it might be for an ordinary black man to acquire an education as well as substantial means.

On October 14, after a month's sojourn in Angola, Williams

embarked on a leisurely six-week journey to Zanzibar. He stopped at
various ports and often made excursions inland to pursue his "studies
and investigations." He seemed thrilled to see "those splendid savages,
the Zulus and Kaffirs," and to visit the leading men of those groups for
information on various local affairs. He touched places in the Cape
Colony, Natal, and the Orange Free State. He investigated the Delagoa
Bay railroad, "which runs up to the Transvaal and from the border there
runs the Netherland Railway through the South African Republic." He
met the vice-president of the Transvaal, N. J. Smit, and several other
prominent men, and "of course gathered much valuable information."[55]

In Southwest Africa, Williams had shown an intense interest in the
Portuguese colony of Angola; and in Southeast Africa he showed a
similar interest in the Portuguese colony of Mozambique. He was very
impressed with the city of Laurenco Marques in Delagoa Bay, with a
population of three thousand Europeans and an excellent harbor. Some
three million dollars' worth of goods passed annually through the harbor
into the interior. "It is a promising place," Williams reported. "The only
drawback is that it is Portuguese territory." From Delagoa, Williams
went to other towns along the coast, including Inhambane, Chindé, and
Quelimane—all valuable entrepôts for interior commerce. Quelimane
was an old town "containing some imposing structures" and several
trading houses: two German, two French, one English, one Dutch, and
one Portuguese. It was the transport station for the Zambezi River and
Lakes Nyasa and Tanganyika. The importance of Quelimane and, indeed, of the other coastal towns depended in large measure on the
effectiveness of the transport system into the interior.[56]

Williams was gathering such information in order to assist Huntington in making decisions on investments in Africa. He was unequivocal
about what he had to offer.

> If you wish to build one of the African roads, and I have seen
> several in operation, have studied their statistics etc., I can give you
> all the data necessary for a first draft and judgement. I mean a road
> from Quelimane to the navigable Zambesi, a distance of about 80 or
> 85 miles, across an almost level country presenting no serious
> engineering difficulties. Such a road would divert to itself all the
> commerce of Lakes Tanganyika and Nyassa, and that of the rivers
> Zambesi, Chindé, and Shiré. It would do all the transport service
> for the English and Portuguese governments, the missions and
> trading houses. . . . Both the Portuguese and the English would
> welcome any American who would build the road, but are jealous of
> any attempt made by the one or the other of these naval Powers.

Should Huntington want to consider the matter, Williams was pre-pared to submit a first draft "adequate for forming a judgment to apply to the Portuguese government for the concession." Williams would also provide copies of the charters of the other Portuguese companies, "submit figures as to cost per mile, post you as to the kind of machinery required, the number of blacksmiths, track-layers, laborers, food, trans-portation, terminal facilities, character of rolling stock, stations, fuel, water, etc."[57] Huntington, however, had already become involved with Sir William Mackinnon in various East African transport schemes.

Williams reached Zanzibar on November 25, 1890. He had looked forward to this stop with pleasure, and he was not disappointed. He was cordially received by Sir Charles Euan Smith, the British consul gen-eral, and E. D. Ropes, the United States consul. Sir Charles, he told Huntington, was doing everything possible to aid in his investigations of slavery and the slave trade. Several Europeans there, including the officers of a British man of war, received Williams warmly, regarding his travels as "worthy of all praise."[58]

The two things that may have pleased Williams the most were his honorary membership in the English Club and his private audience with Sayyid Ali, the sultan of Zanzibar, who gave him "many valuable and beautiful presents."[59] He saw much of the sultan who, according to Williams, became much attached to him.[60] This association enabled Williams to learn more about the operation of the emancipation edict issued by Sultan Sayyid Ali the previous August.[61]

Another valuable contact that Williams made in Zanzibar was with Charles Alan Smythies, bishop of Zanzibar and missionary bishop of East Africa.[62] A courageous opponent of slavery, Smythies had long advocated a more humane policy toward Africans on the part of Euro-peans. After the sultan's edict, Smythies was in an excellent position to assist in the eradication of slavery in Zanzibar. Williams was familiar with the bishop's work and looked forward to meeting him. On Sunday, November 30, he met the bishop at the cathedral and heard him preach. He was greatly impressed and concluded that Smythies would render him "very great assistance." Williams also had plans to see the commander of the German forces in East Africa, Baron Major Weissmann. He was anxious to get some clarification from the major regarding German East African policy and especially whether Germany would press for the eradication of slavery and the slave trade in Tangany-ika and her other possessions in the area.[63] He did not report the results of that consultation but did claim to have learned much about Zanzibar, including "imports and exports, the prison system, hospitals and social condition of the population, . . . the transfer of the Germans to the mainland, the English Protectorate, the various missionary schemes, etc."[64]

Williams then made his way back to the mainland, visiting Mombasa and Lamu, principal ports of the Imperial British East Africa Company. He dutifully reported to Huntington that he had carefully gone into the "history, present condition, and future outlook" of the company. In view of the growing distrust of Williams by Mackinnon, the head of the company, and of the close collaboration between Huntington and Mackinnon, such proclaimed scrutiny was perhaps more valorous than prudent (see chapter 14 below). After sailing around the Horn of Africa, his ship laid anchor at Aden, where, for the first time, Williams touched Asian soil. He was already suspicious of the Arabs as key figures in the slave trade. Egypt, however, was beckoning, and he proceeded through the Red Sea to Suez. From that point he entered the Canal, going as far as Ismailia, where he took a train "through the garden spot and over the battle fields" to Cairo, arriving January 21, 1891.[65]

Williams was not in Cairo many days when he decided that living there was much too expensive for him to remain longer than three or four weeks. He had received nothing from the Associated Literary Press, and although, according to him, he had managed his money carefully, he had only £14 left. Happily, he was so cordially received that he was certain his investigations would be expedited by men of position and influence. The British minister, Sir Evelyn Baring, the acting American consul general, and several officials of the Egyptian government assured Williams they would cooperate with him in his investigations. He doubtless developed other valuable sources of information and assistance through his private audience with the khedive and through his address before the Khedivial Geographical Society.[66]

Williams was convinced that the slave trade in the Sudan had flourished as a result of the death of General Charles George Gordon and the collapse of the Equatorial Province under Emin Pasha. Gordon as governor-general of the Sudan had been effective in suppressing the slave trade between the Sudan and Egypt at least until the dissensions in 1884 that led to his murder the following January. Emin Pasha (Eduard Schnitzer), the German naturalist and traveler who became governor of the Equatorial province in 1878 and who attempted to increase Germany's influence in East Africa, was for a time in a position to restrain the slave trade. After the abandonment of the Sudan by the Egyptian government in 1884, Emin Pasha's influence declined significantly.[67]

The greatest evil, Williams thought, was the slave trade between Arabia and Egypt. He learned much at Aden about how slaves were obtained in Arabia and sold in Egypt and how the whole arrangement was the most degrading of all human experiences. Williams had "uncontestable proof" of all this, he told Huntington, and he would write about it in the work he was preparing for publication. The only bright spot was the "growing sentiment in favor of free labor, the condition of women," and the pronounced antislavery views of the khedive himself.[68]

A serious illness interrupted Williams's work in Cairo. Shortly after addressing the Khedivial Geographical Society on January 30, he collapsed, suffering from a cold and lung congestion. Sir Evelyn Baring sent an excellent physician to attend him, who said that the next two weeks would determine whether or not Williams would survive. He was "trying hard" to get well, he wrote Huntington, and the care and kindness of the Egyptians were doing much to help him. By February 11, the physician said he had improved enough to take solid food. He asked Huntington to send money to pay the physician. If he died, his very expensive watch would pay his funeral expenses and hotel bill. He willed to Huntington his six boxes of African curios—a veritable museum containing "at least $1,000 worth of ivory"—to reimburse him for what he had advanced Williams.[69]

Even if he did not have the strength to pursue certain questions in Egypt, Williams expressed satisfaction with his work: "I thank God it is done." He had written three reports on the Congo and had "six journals full of valuable information, being the daily record of my marches and studies for the last year." In the event of his death, the journals and "other valuable data and documents" were to be sent to Huntington. Williams hoped that Huntington would have them published "for the enlightenment of the world." The income would easily reimburse Huntington for the cost of publication as well as for his loans to Williams. It would be very good if Huntington would write an introduction, "terse and pointed, like the circular you issued on Africa last year and make a plea for justice and humane treatment of the natives." Williams vowed that, if he recovered, he would do much for the poor Africans by arousing public sentiment on their behalf. "I shall have a hearing on the public platform, in the pulpit, in the press and in the magazines."[70]

Williams received a brief reprieve from the dread disease from which he was suffering. "Through the mercy of God and the kindness of strangers" he had made sufficient progress to be able to leave Egypt at the end of April.[71] He would go to England and write a full-scale work not only on conditions in the Congo but on the impact of Europe on various other parts of Africa where he had traveled and made investigations. By the time he reached Europe, the reports he had already written had drawn considerable attention to himself as a pioneer critic and keen observer of the African scene.

·14·

Observer and Critic

The fears Williams harbored regarding the mistreatment to which the Belgians might subject him had predisposed him to have an unfavorable impression of their conduct in the Congo. The manner in which railway workers were recruited in the ports where his ship called merely added to his doubts about the humanitarianism of King Leopold's rule in the Congo. At Cape Palmas a vessel approached the *Gaboon,* and the captain informed the officers that he had 140 Kroomen, whom he had recruited for the Congo Railway Company.

> It was after 4 o'clock, and the work of transferring these people was begun by use of the ship's surf boats, and I witnessed a sight I shall never forget. Each boat brought thirty-five or forty Kroomen packed as closely as chocolates in a box, and the anxious and inquiring glances they cast at the white men who watched their transfer made a deep impression upon me. . . . By the time the sun had set the transfer had been consummated, and 140 Kroomen stood upon the deck of the steamship Gaboon of 1,860 tons burden. . . . The next day was devoted to recruiting Kroomen along the Kroo coast; and by the time we had passed Lagos we had precisely 470 Kroomen and Haoussahs! Here was a scene, then, equal to anything in the slave trade, with but one element unsupplied, these victims of the avarice of Europeans—who at home pose as philanthropists—had no chains about their necks! In every other respect they were treated as slaves.[1]

By the time that Williams had arrived in the Congo State and visited the Baptist mission at Bolobo, he was convinced that there was more venality in King Leopold's Congo policies than most people believed. George Grenfell wrote his superiors in London that Williams had

expressed doubt about "the King's disinterestedness in his Congo enterprises, and [had] hinted that among future possibilities was that of the
sale of the royal interest to a big Belgian Company."² With every mile
that Williams covered in his extensive travels through the Congo, the
unfavorable impression increased. When he reached Stanley Falls, at
the headwaters of the Congo River, he was convinced not only that the
entire Congo project was grossly inhuman but that he must share his
findings with the world. Then and there, in mid-July, 1890, he shaped
his convictions into *An Open Letter to His Serene Majesty Leopold II,*
King of the Belgians and Sovereign of the Independent State of Congo
(reprinted as Appendix 1 below).

The *Letter* of sixteen printed pages was a systematic, wide-ranging,
rather calm indictment of the king's rule in the Congo. Beginning with
a cordial salutation, "Good and Great Friend," Williams said that he
wished to submit for the king's consideration "some reflections" on the
Congo, "based upon a careful study and inspection of the country and
character of the personal Government you have established upon the
African Continent."³ Williams rested his own claim for disinterestedness in his affection and friendship for the king, "of which you have had
ample practical proofs," extending over a period of nearly six years.
Williams had looked upon Leopold's enterprises in the Congo as "the
rising star of hope for the Dark Continent." All the praise he had heaped
on the Congo State "was inspired by the firm belief that your Government was built upon the enduring foundation of *Truth, Liberty,*
Humanity, and *Justice.*"

Williams said his visit to the Congo had left him thoroughly disenchanted. Every charge he was making had been investigated and sub-
stantiated. Documents supporting his charges would be deposited with
the British minister for foreign affairs "until such time as an International Commission can be created with power to send for persons and
papers, to administer oaths, and attest the truth or falsity of these
charges." Williams then raised a serious question about Leopold's legal
claim to the Congo, insisting that his title was "badly clouded." The
treaties made with local chiefs by the International Association of the
Congo, of which Leopold was director and banker, were "tainted by
frauds of the grossest character." By the use of "dirty tricks," Henry M.
Stanley and his men—representing the king—were able to dupe the
tribal chiefs and persuade them to cede their lands to the king's men.
Among the tricks was the lens act, in which the white man lighted his
cigar with a glass through which the equatorial sun shone. The white
man then explained his intimate relation to the sun, and declared that if
he were to request the sun to burn up his black brother's village, it

would do so. By this and other means "too silly and disgusting to mention, and a few boxes of gin, whole villages have been signed away to your Majesty."

It had been claimed by some that Leopold's reign in the Congo had been characterized by his "fostering care, benevolent enterprise, and an honest and practical effort" to increase the knowledge of the Congolese and to secure their welfare. Williams declared that he found little or no evidence to support such a characterization. There was no hospital, even for Europeans, from the mouth of the Congo River to its headwaters. There were only three sheds for sick African employees of the state, "not fit to be occupied by a horse." As for "fostering care," the Congolese everywhere insisted that the government was cruel and arbitrary and declared that they "neither love nor respect" the government and its flag. "Your Majesty's Government has sequestered their land, burned their towns, stolen their property, enslaved their women and children, and committed other crimes too numerous to mention in detail." Williams was particularly distressed that Leopold's government in the Congo had never spent "one franc for educational purposes, nor instituted any practical system of industrialism."

Under such circumstances the labor situation was degrading. Most laborers and soldiers were imported from Zanzibar, Accra, Lagos, Sierra Leone, and Liberia. (Not one Congolese was employed by the government in Boma, the capital.) The conditions surrounding the recruitment and transportation of the laborers caused many to die en route. Laborers were promised one shilling a day, and soldiers sixteen shillings a month, in English money. Williams found that both groups were usually paid "in cheap handkerchiefs and poisonous gin." Their cruel treatment frequently broke their spirits and caused them to distrust and despise Leopold's government. Of the sixty or seventy officers of the Belgian army in the service of the Congo State, only about thirty were in the Congo. The rest were in Belgium, on furlough, and all of them drew double pay as soldiers and civilians. Many were quite young and lacked experience, patience, and a sense of justice in dealing with a people of whom they knew little. "They have estranged the natives from your Majesty's Government, have sown the seed of discord between tribes and villages, and some of them have stained the uniform of the Belgian officer with murder, arson and robbery."

Williams then made twelve specific charges against Leopold's government in the Congo. First, it was deficient in the moral, military, and financial strength to govern a territory of 1,500,000 square miles, 7,250 miles of navigable waters, and 31,600 square miles of lake surface. In some vast areas such as that between Leopoldville and N'Gombe, a

distance of some 300 miles, there was not a single soldier or civilian in
the service of the state. Consequently, Leopold was unable to maintain
any order or to deal with the rampant slave trade or extensive cannibalism. Second, Leopold's government had established nearly fifty posts,
manned by mercenary soldiers from Zanzibar, who had to raid the
countryside and rob local tribes to secure provisions, "and whenever the
natives refuse to feed these vampires, they report to the main station
and white officers come with an expeditionary force and burn away the
homes of the natives." This practice was the greatest curse from which
the country suffered. Third, the government was guilty of violating its
contracts with its soldiers, mechanics, and workmen, many of whom
were from other lands and whose letters never reached home.

The fourth charge was that the courts of Leopold's Congo State were
"abortive, unjust, partial and delinquent." Williams had personally
witnessed "their clumsy operations." Laws printed and circulated in
Europe for the protection of the blacks in the Congo were "a dead letter
and a fraud." He had heard a Belgian officer plead for the exoneration of
another white man accused of beating and stabbing a black man, "urging
race distinctions and prejudices as good and sufficient reasons why his
client should be adjudged innocent." Numerous instances of the miscar-
riage of justice could be witnessed, he stated. The fifth charge was that
the government was excessively cruel to its prisoners, "condemning
them for the slightest offences, to the chain gang, the like of which
cannot be seen in any other government in the civilised or uncivilised
world." The chains "eat into the necks of the prisoners," producing sores
attracting swarms of flies for further annoyance. They were frequently
beaten with a dried piece of hippopotamus skin, called "chicote," that
drew blood with every stroke.

Especially offensive to Williams was the sixth charge—that women
were imported into the Congo for immoral purposes. Black men who
went to the Portuguese coast to engage women as mistresses of white
men were paid a monthly sum for doing so. Others captured women
from local villages, charging them with some imaginary crime. When
convicted and unable to pay the fine, they were sold to the highest
bidder, "the officers having the first choice and then the men." Children
born of such unions were regarded as property of the state, since the
mother belonged to the state. Thus, white men brought "their own flesh
and blood under the lash of a most cruel master, the State of Congo."
The seventh charge was that Leopold's government was engaged in
trade and commerce, competing with trading companies of other countries that suffered the disadvantage of having to pay taxes from which
Leopold's companies were exempt. Eighth, Leopold's government had

violated the General Act of the Conference of Berlin by firing upon native canoes, confiscating the property of natives, intimidating native traders, and in not following the prescribed course of conduct regarding trading in the Congo.

The ninth charge was that Leopold's government "has been, and is now, guilty of waging unjust and cruel war against natives, with the hope of securing slaves and women to minister to the behests of the officers of your Government." Williams had no words to describe the raids on villages and the brutal acts of Leopold's soldiers in connection with those raids. Closely related to this was the tenth charge: that Leopold's government was engaged in the slave trade, wholesale and retail. Williams stated categorically that Leopold's Congo State paid £3 a head for able-bodied slaves for military service. Middlemen received twenty to twenty-five francs a head. Shortly before writing the *Letter*, Williams had learned that some three hundred slaves had been sent down the river. The labor force at the government stations in the Upper River was composed of slaves of both sexes and all ages. Recaptured runaways were dealt with severely. For example, one such slave was given 100 "chicotes" each day until he died.

Eleventh, Leopold's government in the Congo had concluded a contract with the Arab government at Stanley Falls for the establishment of a line of military posts from the Seventh Cataract to Lake Tanganyika, "territory to which your majesty has no more legal claim, than I have to be Commander-in-Chief of the Belgian army." The Arab governor was to receive, in return, "500 stands of arms, 5000 kegs of powder, and £20,000 sterling." As to the significance of this move, "Europe and America can judge without any comment from me, especially England." The twelfth and final charge was that the agents of Leopold's government had misrepresented the Congo Country and railway. Stanley, for example, grossly misrepresented the character of the country. "Instead of it being fertile and productive it is sterile and unproductive. The natives can scarcely subsist upon the vegetable life produced in some parts of the country. Nor will this condition of affairs change until the native shall have been taught by the European the dignity, utility and blessing of labour." Europeans up to this point had not done much to bridge the gap betwen themselves and Africans. Stanley's name, for example, "produces a shudder among this simple folk, when mentioned; they remember his broken promises, his copious profanity, his hot temper, his heavy blows, his severe and rigorous measures, by which they were mulcted of their lands."

Williams concluded his *Open Letter* by observing that, against the "deceit, fraud, robberies, arson, murder, slave-raiding, and general policy of cruelty" of Leopold's government to the natives, stood the natives' record of "unexampled patience, long-suffering and forgiving spirit, which put the boasted civilisation and professed religion of Your Majesty's Government to blush. . . . All the crimes perpetrated in the Congo have been done in *your* name, and *you* must answer at the bar of Public Sentiment for the misgovernment of a people, whose lives and fortunes were entrusted to you by the august Conference of Berlin, 1884–1885." Williams then called on the member states of the Berlin Conference to create an international commission to investigate the charges herein preferred "in the name of Humanity, Commerce, Constitutional Government and Christian Civilisation." He also appealed to the Belgian people and to their constitutional government, "so proud of its traditions, replete with the song and story of its champions of human liberty, and so jealous of its present position in the sisterhood of European States,—to cleanse itself from the imputation of crimes with which your Majesty's personal State of Congo is polluted." He also appealed to antislavery societies, philanthropists, Christians, statesmen, and the great mass of people everywhere to call on the governments of Europe to hasten the close of the tragedy that Leopold's government was enacting in the Congo. Finally, he appealed to "our Heavenly Father, whose service is perfect love, in witness to the purity of my motives and the integrity of my aims; and to history and mankind I appeal for the demonstration and vindication of the truthfulness of the charge I have herein briefly outlined."

In addition to the *Open Letter*, Williams also wrote *A Report on the Proposed Congo Railway* (reprinted as Appendix 2 below) while at Stanley Falls.[4] In part it was a refutation of the claims that Stanley had made regarding the cost of the railway and the time it would take to construct it. In part, it was to inform King Leopold of the realities of the problems of construction so that he would not base his assumptions regarding immigration and commerce on Stanley's miscalculations. It was also intended to provide Huntington with a body of information if he decided to invest more heavily in the railway project than he had already done. Henry M. Stanley had proposed such a project at the Conference of Berlin, but it had received no more support there than it had in England. In Belgium, however, the king and some Belgian financiers "fell under the spell of Mr. Stanley's figures, so fearfully and wonderfully made," and the railway scheme for the Congo took definite shape.

In March 1887, the Independent State of Congo issued a ninety-nine-year charter to the Congo Company for Commerce and Industry to survey and build a railway of 230 miles from Matadi to Stanley Pool. The government was to grant the company about 375,000 acres of land, to be selected by the company within one hundred days after submitting the survey. The road was to be completed within four years at a cost of $5 million. After three and a half years, "not one mile of the road-bed has been made, and only twenty miles of the survey completed." There were real difficulties, including the rocky terrain and the controversy regarding the navigability of the Congo River along certain points where the surveyors assumed it to be navigable.

Williams asserted that the surveyors and the railway company had made numerous miscalculations. They estimated that there would be nine bridges, while Williams insisted that there would be "twenty-six others of importance." The company believed it could secure a labor force in the area of construction. Williams said that would not be possible, for "the harsh policy of the State towards the natives has produced in them a dread and suspicion of the white man, and they would be loathe to work for the company."[5] The company, following the estimates of Henry M. Stanley, looked forward to opening the railway in 1891 or, at the latest, in 1892 and to paying $5,000,000. "The Congo Railway ought to be built," Williams asserted, "and from the bottom of my heart I hope it will be. But capitalists and philanthropists must remember what I have declared, that it cannot be built for less than 40,000,000 francs [$8,000,000], nor in less than eight years. By skillful and practical management, and with all the machinery employed in the construction of European and American railroads, the time could perhaps be reduced by two or three years. Meanwhile Africa needs the blessing of a practical labor system which, while it addresses itself to the soul, will not ignore the body, its earthly temple; and while inculcating spiritual truths will not fail to teach the native the primal lesson of human history: *For in the sweat of thy face shalt thou eat thy bread.*"[6]

By July 18, 1890, Williams had finished writing the *Open Letter* and the *Report on the Proposed Congo Railway*. The reports were printed by some gentlemen in Europe whom Williams did not know, he told Huntington, "because they believed them valuable." Obviously, Williams was not telling Huntington all that he knew. If he did not know the men, he must have had correspondents in Europe who passed the reports on to them. A few weeks later, Williams wrote Huntington that he had corrected the printed copies (presumably proofs) of his three reports on the Congo.[7] Still later, when Stanley charged that the circulation of the proofs of the reports was a blackmailing scheme to force the king to let Huntington control the Congo Railway, Williams insisted that the letters were printed in Europe without his knowledge or consent. When he learned they were already in circulation, he ordered them reprinted after revision.[8] In any case, the reports seemed to be generally accessible both in Europe and the United States by the autumn of 1890.

An early reaction to the Williams reports came from Sir William Mackinnon, head of the British East Africa Company and an intimate acquaintance of both King Leopold and Collis P. Huntington. "It is much to be regretted if Mr. Williams has adopted as bitter a tone in the letter he has sent to the King of the Belgians as in that he has written you. . . . It can do no good and cannot fail to harm. . . . The King is the last man in the world to permit or sanction any inhumanity on the part of his officers or servants."[9] A month earlier, in a letter to Mackinnon asking him to convey £50 to Williams at Zanzibar, Huntington himself had said, "I do not like the way in which Mr. Williams speaks of King Leopold and his ministers in the Congo State, as I feel quite sure that the King, at least, is solicitous of the best welfare of the natives of that country and would not, if he knew it, tolerate any departure from the rules of honest and kind administration that I know he laid down for the guidance and government of those he sent to the Congo country."[10] It bode ill for Williams's future that two men in a position to assist him in many ways should be so critical of his strictures against the king.

In mid-April 1891, the New York *Herald* ran a news article telling of the *Open Letter* and asserting that Williams had made the "gravest charges of the cruelties and deceptions by the government of the Free State." After identifying Williams as a man of some prominence, the *Herald* appeared to accept the factual content of the *Open Letter*, saying that Williams was spoken of "as a man whose word is as good as his bond." Since Henry M. Stanley, then in New York, came in for much of the criticism by Williams, a *Herald* reporter called on him at the Plaza Hotel to get his reactions. "I need not read the letter," he began, for Sir William Mackinnon had handed it to him the previous October, just before Stanley sailed for the United States. Williams, he said, had told Sir William that he proposed to make a similar investigation of the East African territory controlled by Sir William's company. Stanley continued:

> I then told Sir William, and I say the same now, that I regarded the letter or pamphlet as a deliberate attempt at blackmail, and I advised him, as a friend of the King of Belgium to have nothing whatever to do with this Williams. I told him that I had met the man, who was a negro, as far back as 1884, when he had applied to me for a place under the government of the Congo State. I went so far as to recommend Williams to King Leopold, dwelling particularly on his good record and education.

The King, however, was not particularly smitten with Williams, and the negotiations fell through. This was the last I saw of him and positively all I know about him. I will say, however, that the statement that Williams had charge of the surveys of the Congo railroad are absolutely false.

Stanley observed that Huntington had helped finance Williams's African journey and that both Huntington and Sir William had invested considerable sums in the development of the country. He said that he put it to Sir William whether he could reconcile it with his friendship and close relations with King Leopold to do anything "to further the blackmailing schemes of a man like Williams."[11] Williams, of course, did not have charge of the official surveys for the Congo Railway, but he *did* survey, on his own—or for Huntington—the route of the proposed railway. The charge of blackmail would recur frequently and would become a weapon of defense for the king and his men, in Belgium and the Congo.

When Alfred LeGhait, the Belgian minister to the United States, read the piece in the *Herald*, he immediately dispatched a letter to the editor protesting the publication of the article without the reprobation and commentaries that should have accompanied it. He pointed out that the civilizing work of King Leopold was too honorable and too universally appreciated to require defense against the low, false accusations that Williams made. LeGhait associated himself entirely with what the "illustrious" American explorer, Henry M. Stanley, had said of Williams's character. LeGhait claimed to have good reasons to support the view that Williams was a blackmailer. He then sent a copy of his letter to his superior in Brussels, Baron Lambermont, minister of state, observing that in Europe everyone was familiar with Williams's criticisms of the king, but only in the United States could he attempt to rectify them. He could not allow them to be published without a protest reinforcing Stanley's clear statements about Williams.[12]

A member of the British legation in Brussels wrote the British foreign secretary, Lord Salisbury, that the *Open Letter* had been circulated in Paris and Brussels as well as in the United States and had created "some considerable stir in the Radical Press, always prone to regard with an evil eye anything connected with the administration of the Independent State." This writer, too, implied that the early, private circulation of the *Open Letter* might have been intended to blackmail the king.[13]

King Leopold shared that point of view. Indeed, the British minister to Brussels, Lord Vivian, reported to the foreign secretary that the king had asked him "to warn your Lordship that he has received notice of a certain Colonel Williams, a mulatto and citizen of the United States to send the Foreign Office a pamphlet which he has lately written descriptive of his visit to the Congo State, containing scandalous and utterly unfounded charges against the administration of the Congo State." Vivian said it appeared that, before leaving for the Congo, Williams had unsuccessfully sought employment in the service of that state and, "though his request was refused, gave out that he was employed on a special mission." The king told Lord Vivian that Williams "has since asked him to purchase his book on the Congo State, which request he had also been refused, and he was then seeking to levy blackmail by publishing his violent attack against the administration of the State." King Leopold told Vivian that any inquiry respecting Colonel Williams would show that he was "utterly unworthy of credit" and that the United States minister would confirm this.[14]

Williams had talked and written so widely and so candidly about his views of the administration of the Congo State that it seems unlikely that he had in mind a scheme to blackmail King Leopold II. He had expressed his views to the Baptist missionaries, who, in turn, had reported them to their superiors in London. He had told both the secretary of state, James G. Blaine, and his friend Senator George F. Hoar what he was experiencing in the Congo. He had told Sir William Mackinnon and Collis P. Huntington, both friends of the king, precisely what he thought of the king and his Congo State. He had vowed to write a book on the subject and to deposit the documentation for his findings in the British Foreign Office. Many months before the king was expressing his concern over the *Open Letter*, it was making the rounds in Britain. On November 4, 1890, R. Cobden Phillips of the Manchester Chamber of Commerce read portions of the letter to an open meeting in London.[15] A work already so widely known as the *Open Letter* would hardly seem of any value as an instrument of blackmail. Indeed, the *Open Letter* had all of the earmarks of a one-man crusade, however impractical. Lord Vivian was not altogether taken in by King Leopold's sounding the alarm against Williams. In an endorsement of his letter to Lord Salisbury he added, "Colonel Williams may be all the King says he is, but I suspect there is a good deal of disagreeable truth in his pamphlets."[16]

The king and his men were not content merely to discount the *Open Letter* as the evil prattle of a would-be blackmailer. Too much was at stake in terms both of the Congo State as a commercial enterprise and of the credibility and integrity of the king. In June, an article entitled "Un Colonel noir," appeared in *Mouvement Géographique*, a semiofficial organ of the Congo State, enumerating and answering seriatim the accusations leveled by Williams against Leopold and the Congo State.

After relating the failure of Williams to recruit students at Hampton and accusing him of misrepresenting his accomplishments, the article undertook to refute the charges that Williams had brought.[17] To the first charge—that the government of the Congo was deficient in the moral, military, and financial strength necessary to govern the territory—the author insisted that with thirty posts already established and others to follow, it would be strong enough to prevent cannibalism, guerrilla raids, and numberless atrocities that were committed every day all over Central Africa, in areas of English, German, French, and Portuguese influence as well as in the Congo State. In response to the fourth charge, that justice was partial and poorly administered, and that the laws for the protection of the natives were a dead letter, the writer declared that the judges were specialists, "docteurs" in Belgian law. Had there been errors or questionable arrests? One could not know. If so, the same had happened in Europe, where the guilty sometimes went free and the innocent were condemned, and in the United States, where the Sioux and the Apache Indians did not always receive reasonable treatment. "Ultimately, as the Colonel can testify, justice does function in the Congo."[18]

"Un Colonel noir" was merely the opening argument in the debate over Leopold and the conduct of his men in the Congo. Before the middle of June 1891, virtually every newspaper in Brussels and several in Paris had plunged into the melee, some defending the administration of affairs in the Congo State, some condemning it, and some uncertain what to do. *La Réforme*, one of the more liberal newspapers of Brussels, led off by observing that the Williams reports seemed quite serious, especially since he made statements regarding conditions "which have been kept quiet by the people of the Congo." The paper asserted that Williams's accusations were having "considerable impact. . . . Now is the time for the State to speak."[19]

The nearest thing to an official spokesman for Leopold and the Congo State was the *Journal de Bruxelles*, which captioned its first article on the subject, "The Congo and its Slanderers." Here followed an extensive discussion, not of the Congo but of George Washington Williams, beginning with a highly imaginative biographical sketch:

> First of all, who is Mr. Williams? This man is not a United States colonel. His name does not appear in the U.S. Army Register, and a prominent American political figure passing through Brussels told us this morning that he did not know whether Mr. Williams had even been a private in the United States army. In any case he has never held even the lowest rank in the United States army. From

1865 to 1867 he enlisted in Juarez's army in Mexico, and he was totally illiterate at the time.

He drilled as a recruit after the death of the emperor Maximilian and completed his term in 1874. He was a minister in 1875, that is, he was paid so much per day by an American sect to address edifying speeches to the passers-by on street corners and in public squares. In 1876, he joined a newspaper, then in 1877 he took a graduate examination in Cincinnati and for two years he was a clerk in a lawyer's office. In 1879, he was a member of the Ohio State Legislature; by 1881 he was no longer a legislator. In 1885, he succeeded in having himself appointed minister to Haiti by Arthur's administration. In 1886 he resigned from this post. At the time of the antislavery conference in Brussels, the Negro gentleman, flexible and diverse as usual, asked his government to make him a part, in some way, of the United States delegation at this conference, but his efforts failed. He arrived, therefore, in Brussels where he persistently offered his services to the king of the Free State, who declined them.

If it did nothing else, the sketch provided the *Journal de Bruxelles* with the justification it obviously wanted to refer to Williams subsequently as "the so-called 'Colonel,'" "the pseudo colonel," "the former soldier of Juarez," "Juarez's somber disciple," "an unbalanced negro," and "Mr. Williams, who is not a colonel." Having impugned his character and credibility, it then chastised other Belgian papers and their reading public for paying any attention to Williams. Williams obviously regarded certain gullible newspaper editors "as fools and takes advantage of their hostility [to the Congo State] to get them to accept his falsehoods for truth."[20] The *Journal de Bruxelles* then undertook to refute Williams's claims that the Congo State had made no contribution to science and geography, was involved in the slave trade, had no real commercial resources, administered justice unfairly, and mistreated its workers. The Congo's contributions to the advancement of science and geography "speak for themselves," the paper declared. Of course, the State buys slaves "and so do the missionaries, the merchants, and even the whites . . . who have a heart and a few goods to trade." This was the best way to protect certain hapless victims of unscrupulous traders. The justice of the State "administered by Belgian doctors of law, is above the reproach of a 'Colonel' Williams, even if he is a law clerk, 'minister,' journalist, legislator, diplomat, and anti-alcoholist."[21]

The *Journal of Bruxelles* made much of the fact that certain Belgian editors received copies of the Williams reports but none came to it through the same channels. It was able, finally, to obtain copies, and pronounced the *Open Letter to Leopold* as "a web of insults and atrocious slanders" against the king and his work. The salutation "Good and Great Friend" was repugnant. It was "insolent and insulting" for Williams to refer continuously "to our sovereign in a personal manner." Leopold was a "promoter of civilization" and thus could hardly have "sequestered land belonging to the natives, burned and stolen their property, and reduced their women and children to slaves. . . . The republicans whose goal it is to overturn the dynasty and to abolish the throne are free to spread the numerous absurdities and foolishness brought forth by Colonel Williams. However, we will take care not to follow in their footsteps."[22]

La Réforme persisted in its demand that the Congo State speak out and report on affairs there. It pointed out that it was by no means alone in its wish that the state answer the charges made by Williams. The *Courrier de Bruxelles*, for example, insisted that "if Colonel Williams, an unknown foreigner, can be looked upon with distrust, we are not inclined to accept as gospel truth everything the Congolese administration wishes to offer in its own defense." *La Réforme*, like the *Courrier*, thought the great concern of Williams's critics with his career was not germane to a critical examination of the grave charges made against an administration that had never seen fit to inform the public about conditions in the Congo:

> The Congo State, which has had contacts and negotiations with Colonel Williams, does a poor job of attacking him when it reports that the colonel was a soldier under Juarez, an illiterate for a short time, a protestant minister and that he has practiced various professions.
>
> For an American, especially, it is better to have defended Mexico's independence under Juarez than the usurpation of power in Mexico by Austria's Maximilian. If Williams was an illiterate, his present writings prove that he has ceased to be one and that he is now in a position to meet with Congolese writers. Moreover, the fact that he has practiced many professions is not dishonorable, since this is a common occurrence in America. This would only prove that he is a self-made man, something that is very worthy of praise.[23]

As *La Réforme* and the *Journal de Bruxelles* carried on their battle, each picked up support along the way. *La Nation* repeated the charges against Williams that had been aired by the *Journal* and added some of its own. Recalling that Williams had been denied passage on the State steamers in the Congo and had traveled on Dutch vessels, *La Nation* was certain that the Dutch, who frowned on Leopold's commercial policies in the Congo, had a role in shaping Williams's negative view of the king's domain.[24] On the other hand, the strictures against Leopold by *Le Jour* were as harsh as those of *La Réforme*. "We were aware that the head of the Congo Free State saw in the conquest of part of the African continent a good commercial venture which would increase his patrimony and civil list, but we did not think that his involvement in trade would cause him to neglect the interest of civilization. It seems we were mistaken. . . . The slave practices for which the Arab slave traders were reproached are faithfully followed by the Belgians."[25] Meanwhile, *Flandre Libérale* seemed content to request that the Free State speak out and make its position known before the "American indictment" could have any unfortunate influence.[26] A similar view was voiced by *Le Temps* (Paris), which declared that the Williams indictment was "probably exaggerated," but its publication demanded an official reply.[27]

The clamor by the press for a reply to Williams was at long last answered when the Belgian parliament met on June 18, 1891. The session, *Le Patriote* declared, was a demonstration against the American slanders.[28] The matter was brought up by Deputy Carlier, who condemned Williams, his libel, and the Belgian newspapers "without which Williams's libel would have gone almost unnoticed." He said that the assertions in the *Open Letter* were an insult to the army, the lawyers, the medical corps, and the major administrative officers, all of whom had served in Africa with devotion and sacrifice and beyond the call of duty. Carlier then called on the government to make public the information in its possession and the plans for the Congo in the next budget that would clearly show the direction in which the Congo State was moving.

Prime Minister Beernaert, who was also minister of finance, then took the floor. He thanked Deputy Carlier for referring to the accusations against the Congo State in language so true, so profoundly patriotic that he had spoken for the entire chamber. He reported to the chamber on the progress that had been made in the Congo State, much of it due to the fact that in 1890 alone the king had placed in the treasury of the Congo, from his own private funds, 1,900,509 francs. "Violà la spéculation! (Très bien! Très bien!)" The prime minister said that the administrators of the Congo—gallant men, known to the members of the chamber—were working on a report to the king that would summarize the "remarkable results that have been achieved in Africa."

Deputy Northomb closed the discussion by observing that the prime minister's report would clarify the picture. It would not, however, quiet the rumors, the accusations, and the defamations, which he thought resulted from the intense rivalries in Africa. Trade was the only means of creating a peaceful civilization in Africa. Surely it should be preferred to the cannon or the sword. In concluding, Northomb said, "Bravo M. Carlier! You have earned the approval of us all! The incident is closed."[29]

What was remarkable about the incident was the furor raised by a relatively brief statement by a relatively obscure black American about the conduct of one of the most important and most powerful men in the world. The king and his men were deeply embarrassed, to say the least. They knew that in the end they had to win. The Congo was a possible source of enormous wealth and was of unquestioned strategic importance. Consequently, even at the risk of dignifying Williams's attack, it had to be answered.

The report of the administrators-general of the Congo State was available a few weeks after the discussion of the matter in the parliament. There is every reason to believe, on the basis of their comments about it, that the prime minister and the other deputies were aware of its contents when they spoke. Even a cursory comparison of the report with the charges made by Williams in his *Open Letter* indicate that it was drawn up for the specific purpose, as a British official declared, of "refuting the accusations brought by Colonel Williams and others."[30] A work of some forty-five printed pages and signed by the administrators-general, E. Van Eetvelde and C. Janssen, it dealt with five main topics: The exploration and occupation of the State's territory, the public services rendered there, the financial prospects, the export and import trade and related activities, and the moral and religious development of the Congo State, including the government's effort to combat the slave trade.

Whereas Williams had charged that 2,300 soldiers were insufficient to govern the vast territory, the administrators reported that there were 3,127 men at the beginning of 1891 (six months after Williams wrote his *Open Letter*) and efforts were under way to recruit a thousand more in the country itself. Williams had contended that the government lacked the financial strength to manage the affairs of the Congo. The report, conceding that the financial condition of the young state was not satisfactory, claimed that the situation would be eased by the Belgian government's willingness to advance about $400,000, almost one-half of the financial needs of the Congo State. Williams had excoriated the government for its abysmal health facilities. The report admitted there had been only two physicians in the Congo in 1885 but affirmed that there were eight by 1891—one each at Banana, Boma, Leopoldville, New

Antwerp, Bosoko, and Lousambo and two at Quelle. Medical services were free to whites and black employees of the state and to natives in the vicinity.

Williams was relentless in his insistence not only that the slave trade existed in the Congo but that the government was involved in it. The report categorically countered that slavery had disappeared from the regions of the Lower Congo. Since the importation of firearms had been forbidden on the Upper Congo, the situation should improve there. Steps had been taken, moreover, to check the trade in alcoholic liquors and to put an end to slave hunting by establishing fortified posts in areas where the offense was greatest. There persisted the problem of the Arabs, whose slave trading habits had not yet been checked by the Christian missionary groups that had worked so diligently in the Congo State. The report ended on a note of general optimism regarding future progress. Slowly but surely, the native would be transformed, his intellectual horizons enlarged, and his sensibilities refined.[31]

The report did not respond to several of the charges Williams had made. It was silent on the use of women for immoral purposes. Nor did it address the matter of the partiality in the government's treatment of its employees. Williams, for example, had said he saw a white servant of Governor-General Camille Janssen—incidentally, one of the authors of the government's report—detected in stealing a bottle of wine from a hotel table. A few hours later the procurer-general searched his room and found "many more stolen bottles of wine and other things, not the property of servants." Since no one in the Congo State could be prosecuted without an order of the governor-general, who, in this case, refused to give the order, the white servant went unpunished. The mere knowledge of the infraction, however, pleased the black hotel servants who had often been "accused and beaten for these thefts, and now they were glad to be vindicated."[32] It was too embarrassing, one may presume, for Governor Janssen to do anything in the report about the conduct of his own servant, except to ignore it.

A distinguished British foreign service officer, Roger Casement, was in the Congo at the same time Williams was there. With his experienced eye, he doubtless saw many of the things that Williams saw. Years later, in 1902, he wrote,

> I remember seeing in 1890 a letter written by an officer, directing one of the most important administrative districts of the Congo State, to a subordinate officer engaged in one of these . . . man-catching raids. The object at that time was not military service. The Government needed porters for the transport of the many loads of

equipment it was seeking to send to Stanley Pool, and being unwilling to pay the established rate fixed by Europeans collectively (missions and traders) as remuneration to the native porters the Congo Government compelled the carriage of its loads by force, giving an inferior wage to that paid by everyone else.[33]

Casement was all too familiar with the Congo State and its problems. In 1886–88 he had worked on various jobs in Henry Sanford's efforts to build up the transport system there. This involved one stint at Matadi and another at Equator on the upper Congo. Before leaving, he also worked at a mission station as a lay helper for the Reverend W. Holman Bently.[34] When he returned in 1890 to serve as manager for the company that was to construct the railway from Matadi to Stanley Pool, he was doubtless familiar with some of the more unsavory features of Congolese policies. More than a dozen years later, as the British Foreign Office was preparing to "go public" in its criticisms of the Congo State, it turned to Casement, who had been there many times and who, in 1903, was his government's consul at Boma.

The reports Casement began to send from Boma to the Foreign Office in London indicate the nature and extent of the injustice that he saw in the administration of the Congo State. A Congolese could not sell the ivory he had carefully hoarded. His lands were not his own. He could not dispose of his produce in the open market. Indeed, the work of his own hands were not his.

> The very children he has begotten are born less to love their father and mother than to fear with that perfect fear, which casteth out all love, a distant being whom their 1,400 white oppressors term his sovereign. . . . All these things are not his, they belong to a 'Sovereign' he never saw, who rules him through an Administration of aliens—strangers in speech, thought, habit and home—who in turn make their will terribly felt by an armed and drilled force of 20,000 men—swift to anger and of great wrath.

In language similar to that used by Williams in the *Open Letter,* Casement expressed grave doubts regarding the validity of the titles by which Leopold claimed the lands of the Congo. The chiefs could not grant what they did not possess, and since they were merely the trustees of the tribal families, their public rights were "well defined and strictly limited by popular control." Consequently, Leopold's title to lands "granted" by the chiefs was, at best, cloudy.[35]

After a final, two-month inspection of the Upper Congo, Casement returned to London to write his report. Though outraged by what he had seen, he was moderate in his utterances, thus adding force to what he said. The railway was efficient and convenient. The work force at Leopoldville was truly national, since the employees of the government there were drawn from nearly every part of the country. A hospital for Europeans "and an establishment designed as a native hospital are in charge of a European doctor. The open selling of slaves and the canoe convoys, which once navigated the Upper Congo, have everywhere disappeared."

Casement could make few other favorable statements about the Congo State. Many of his comments were similar to those that Williams had made thirteen years earlier. One wonders whether Casement had seen the *Open Letter* that had been discussed in England, Belgium, and France in 1891. The native hospital at Leopoldville was "an unseemly place" of three mud huts with the patients poorly attended. People in the riverside towns were forced to keep the government telegraph lines clear of undergrowth, for which they had received no payment for more than a year. When soldiers needed food or other supplies, they could require it of the local people, whose failure to comply would earn them a beating or imprisonment. The government could call upon a village, with no prior notice, to supply canoe paddlers, day laborers (male and female), timber gatherers, and woodcutters. Congolese were still subjected to terrible floggings with the "chicote," even for complaints about injustices they sought to make. It was the beatings, mutilations, and killings that distressed Casement the most. The cutting off of hands by government soldiers was a common form of mutilation. One young man's hands had been beaten off against a tree with the butt ends of rifles.[36]

As he had done in the case of Williams, King Leopold sought to discredit Casement even before the report was released. The two men had met in October 1900; the king told Casement, as he had told Williams in 1889, that his chief desire, then as always, was "the well-being and good government of the natives."[37] Three years later, on learning of the impending revelations in the Casement report, Leopold asked whether Casement was not the same British consul who had written the governor-general of the Free State in July 1901. In that letter, the king recalled, Casement had said, "Pray believe me, when I express now, not only for myself, but for my fellow-countrymen, in this part of Africa, our very sincere appreciation of your efforts to promote goodwill among all and to bring together the various elements in our local life." Leopold did not bother to place Casement's words in their proper context; Casement in fact was referring only to certain developments in the community of Boma and not to any general policy set forth by the king or his men.[38]

Although Casement had made no mention of Williams in his report, they had seen very much the same things and both were deeply moved by their experiences. If Casement was more restrained, it was perhaps because diplomatic experience had taught him the virtue of understatement. Edmund D. Morel, who in 1904 was to found the Congo Reform Association at Casement's urging, saw in Casement and Williams similar sources of strength in a real reordering of conditions in the Congo. R. C. Phillips read portions of the *Open Letter* to a gathering in London in November 1890; and Morel said in 1902 that it "might have been written a few weeks, instead of eleven years ago. The state of affairs pictured by Colonel Williams has worsened instead of bettered. The evil is more widespread and the means of perpetuating it more extensive and more powerful."[39] Morel met Casement, before *The Report* was published. "From the moment our hands gripped and our eyes met," Morel wrote, "mutual trust and confidence were bred and the feeling of isolation slipped from me like a mantle. Here was a man indeed."[40]

Another person who plied the Congo in the summer of 1890, when Williams and Casement were there, was Joseph Conrad. Not yet the celebrated writer that he would become early in the next century, Conrad, an experienced seaman, had gone to the Congo in June 1890 to command the *Roi des Belges* for the up-river voyage. While some of his experiences are recorded in his novella, *Heart of Darkness*, the voyage affected most of his subsequent writings and, indeed, much of the remainder of his life. Although Williams and Conrad were on the river at the same time, they apparently did not meet. Conrad and Casement did, however. "Made the acquaintance of Mr. Roger Casement, which I should consider as a great pleasure under any circumstances and now it becomes a positive piece of luck," Conrad wrote in his diary. "Thinks, speaks well, most intelligent and very sympathetic."[41]

Conrad was almost mesmerized by the Congo country and especially the river, as indeed were many other sojourners there. "Going up that river," he wrote, "was like travelling back to the earliest beginnings of the world, when vegetation rioted on the earth and the big trees were Kings."[42] Conrad also had to confront the reality of the present. There was the disgusting spectacle of the inefficiency of Leopold's Congo. Marlow, in *Heart of Darkness*, was revolted by wrecked vessels on the river, "a railway truck lying on its back, a stack of rusty nails, and other pieces of decaying machinery."[43] He was also revolted by the exploitation of the Congolese by the king and his men. It was not necessary that Conrad admire the Congolese or greatly respect them—and it is to be doubted that he did—in order to be outraged by some practices he saw in 1890.[44] He wrote Casement that he thought it "an extraordinary thing that the conscience of Europe, which seventy years ago had put down the slave trade on humanitarian grounds, tolerates the Congo State today. It is as if the moral clock had been put back many hours. . . . In the old days England had in her keeping the conscience of Europe. . . . But I suppose we are busy with other things—too much involved in great affairs to take up the cudgels for humanity, decency and justice." Conrad declined to join the fight to reform the Congo. After all, he pleaded, he was "only a wretched novelist" and surely not the man Casement needed.[45]

Thus, of all the 1890 observers and critics of Leopold's rule in the Congo—Grenfell the missionary, Casement the diplomat, Conrad the novelist, Williams the reporter, and doubtless others—only Williams saw fit to make his unfavorable views widely known immediately. The others had their own reasons for remaining silent at the time; and in due course they would all express their disapproval with varying degrees of fervor. When they did speak out, not one mentioned Williams's *Open Letter* or his other reports. The Williams file at the British Foreign Office was thick, thanks to the detailed dispatches from Brussels by Lord Vivian and Martin Gosselins. Casement could have used it to advantage, but he gives no credit to Williams. Grenfell knew more about misrule in the Congo than Williams would ever know; and he indicated as much after his first meeting with Williams in 1890. Nevertheless, he remained quiet for another dozen years. He even accepted appointment by Leopold to serve on a commission of missionaries to watch over and protect native interests, though he conceded that the commission was a farce.[46] In 1903, Casement sharply criticized Grenfell's acquiescence in the king's rule, pointing out that Grenfell's own "garrison district is the severest condemnation of state rule."[47] By that time, Grenfell was having rather stormy sessions with the governor-general of the Congo, who upbraided him for the mildly worded protests he had begun to utter.[48]

It took courage for Williams to write the *Open Letter* in 1890. As an extremely ambitious man, he must have counted the costs of such a disclosure. Collis P. Huntington, his benefactor, would obviously be distressed to read in the *Open Letter* the indictments against the man with whom he hoped to have a number of intimate business arrangements in the Congo. Yet Williams seemed never to falter in his determination to expose the king. The man of "flexible values" of a decade earlier was, by 1890, a person of considerable moral strength.

After the Congo Reform Association was organized in 1904, a veritable crusade against conditions in the Congo was conducted by people such as E. D. Morel and Sir Harry Johnston in Britain and Lyman Abbott and G. Stanley Hall in the United States.[49] Except for the reading of the *Open Letter* at a London meeting in 1890, one searches in vain for any mention of Williams. Williams's eloquent indictment had certainly been taken seriously in Brussels. If later critics, as William K. Parmenter claims,[50] did not know of it, they were ignorant of an important chapter in the history of the Congo State.

·15·

The Final Phase

Williams desperately needed financial aid; yet he alienated what support he had by speaking out against Leopold. Huntington, though displeased, continued to send him money for a time because, as he said, he was confident that Williams had no evil intentions.[1] Mackinnon was not so sure and sought to restrain Huntington's benefaction. "It was my intention to have added something to the donation you are so kindly sending him," Mackinnon wrote when acknowledging receipt of the money for transfer through his company, "but his remarks about the Congo and his abrupt attack on Stanley warn me that I must hold my hand. I give my help to those I consider more worthy of it."[2] Mackinnon then sent a "report" to Sir Charles Euan Smith, the British Consul in Zanzibar, on Williams's conduct in the Congo.[3]

Huntington, no doubt, had already come to perceive the conduct of Williams as inimical to his own interests. He wrote Mackinnon:

> I have received several letters, too, from George H. [sic] Williams, but have not answered them ["yet" is excised], as they criticize severely and I believe, from all I know, unjustly the administration of the King of Belgium in the Congo State, and I feel somewhat indignant at it; for I have never seen any reason to say anything of the King's work there except in praise of it and his broad-minded spirit. . . . I was expecting to send Williams a little more money; but I am not disposed to send him anymore. I would send you his letters if I had them here, as they are quite interesting, and you could destroy them after reading.[4]

Williams suspected that Huntington's long silence was a rebuke for his criticisms of the king. He was not going to apologize for his stand, however. From Cairo, he wrote Huntington:

I expected . . . after doing my duty in Africa and breaking down
my health that if you did not care to render further financial aid you
would have at least written me a kind letter. And now I take it you
mean by your silence that you are anxious that our relations shall
cease. Very well.

However, I wish to bear testimony to your philanthropy and to
say that you never in any way indicated a desire to control the
Congo road; that you always told me that your contribution to the
Railway fund was a gift, and you have always spoken of the King of
the Belgians as a friend of humanity. I wish I could say as much of
him. But I shall tell the whole truth!

Williams branded as "absolutely false" Stanley's claim that the printing and circulation of his report in galley proofs was a blackmailing
scheme to force the king to give Huntington his way with the Congo
Railway. "I am going to bring an action against Stanley for slander," he
warned, "and will unearth his cruelties, falsehoods, and double-
dealings." He would also write Sir William Mackinnon denying the
charges (see chapter 14 above). Yet Williams seemed to harbor no ill
feelings for Huntington:

Please accept my sincere thanks for the generous aid you have
rendered this cause of Humanity I have championed and suffered
for. . . . Through all these trials God brought me safely; and I trust I
may do much to improve the condition of the natives and advance
the cause of civilization. I have no fear of Kings or men before me.
One only I fear, God; and by His aid I shall cry aloud and spare not
until the wrongs of the African are righted, unswayed by
friendships and undeterred by enemies. I shall do my duty as God
gives me to understand it.[5]

As he closed this final letter, Williams told Huntington that, while in
London completing his book on Africa, he would be staying at Morley's
Hotel in Trafalgar Square. Did he hope to hear from Huntington once
more?

It is strange that Mackinnon, who had been so hostile to Williams,
should be among the last to extend him financial assistance. He continued to complain about the manner in which Williams conducted
himself. "He wrote me a most intemperate letter from Cairo denouncing in unmeasured terms everything that Stanley has done and everything the King of the Belgians has attempted to do. . . . He may be
animated by very high motives and principles but I do not think he goes
to work quite in the spirit that becomes his professions of high Christian

principle." Then Mackinnon had to confess to Huntington that he was doing what Huntington had said that he would no longer do. "I sent him £20 to Egypt and gave him free passage from Egypt to London." Then, he again became firm. "Before leaving Egypt he telegraphed me to send him £50 more, as he was sick and had no means of paying his bill. I took no notice of this telegram but continued my orders to let him have a free passage. He seems to have got somebody else to give him what he required to leave Egypt, and he is now in London."[6]

It was in late April 1891 that Williams informed Huntington of his plans to go to London. Since Mackinnon had given him passage on one of the ships of his British India Steam Navigation Company, he went first to Ismailia, where he boarded the SS. *Golconda* for Britain. He was in London in early June and took up lodgings at Morley's Hotel,[7] intending to work on what he regarded as his final statement on Leopold's rule in Africa.

During an earlier stay in London, in 1888, Williams had worked frequently at the Public Record Office. From July to October in that year he had incurred debts amounting to £195.8.9 to four employees there for searching, copying, and translating. In the following year Williams made repeated promises to pay, but no money arrived. The creditors took up the matter with B.F. Stevens, United States Dispatch Agent in London, who, in turn, sought the advice of Henry S. Sanford regarding possible ways of collecting the debt. Sanford offered no advice and must have been pleased to have yet another piece of information to confirm his low opinion of Williams. Senator Hoar, learning of Williams's difficulties with the Public Record Office, asked the Department of State to send him its file on the subject. Nothing ensued from this inquiry, and there is no record of any reimbursement of the staff at the Public Record Office.[8] At all events, it is unlikely that Williams worked there in 1891.

The London weeks were filled with a quite pleasant distraction. On the ship returning to Britain, Williams had met a young Englishwoman named Alice Fryer, a governess with a British family in India, who was returning to her home in Southsea, near Portsmouth. The two passengers immediately became good friends. By the time they arrived in London, they were engaged to be married.[9]

A greater distraction from Williams's work was his health. Back in November and December 1888 he had suffered "a long and painful illness." He had lost the entire lecture season of 1888–89 and was unable to write a "single paragraph" on his proposed "history of Santo Domingo, 1789–1804."[10] The African journey must have further weakened his physical condition, as his serious illness in Cairo indicated. In the ensuing weeks his health declined steadily. When Francis William Fox saw him in London at the end of June 1891, he wrote Huntington that Williams was "very ill," suffering from congestion of the lungs. Williams told Fox that the physician did not expect him to live "for more than two months."[11]

His rapidly deteriorating condition greatly disturbed Alice Fryer, who, with her mother, accompanied him to Blackpool. There, on Britain's west coast, they hoped that the air from the Irish Sea and the curative powers of a hydropathic establishment would restore his health. On July 7, 1891, they arrived at Blackpool and took three rooms at the Palatine Hotel.[12] Williams spent the next few weeks taking walks along the ocean front, alone or in the company of Alice Fryer. He also spent some time with James Howarth, a resident and real estate broker in Blackpool, whom he had met by a chance encounter. In three weeks Howarth had become "warmly attached" to Williams.[13] He met others, including the Reverend Samuel Pelling, pastor of Blackpool's only Baptist church, the Union Baptist. Williams also had with him his unfinished manuscript on Leopold.

Most of the time in good spirits, Williams appears to have been enjoying a slight improvement in his health. Then, he caught a "violent chill" and by Friday, July 31, had become very ill indeed. The following evening Miss Fryer and her mother summoned a physician, George C. Kingsbury. Williams also asked for the Reverend Pelling, who offered prayers and provided "spiritual consolation" in those final hours. Williams experienced great difficulty in breathing; Dr. Kingsbury told Pelling that "his lungs were completely done." Williams died at 4:45 Sunday morning, August 2, 1891, at forty-one years of age, in the presence of Alice Fryer and her mother, Kingsbury and Pelling.[14]

The death certificate, duly filed in St. Catherine's House in London, listed the cause of death as "phthisis 1 year" and "pleurisy 4 days." The right lung, the report concluded, "had been wounded in the Egyptian war." Williams had in fact been in Egypt less than two weeks; and the only battle that he was fighting was for his health, which was rapidly deteriorating as he lay in a Cairo hotel.

When James Howarth learned of his new friend's death, he insisted that Williams's body should lie in state in his home. The Reverend Pelling conducted funeral services on the following Wednesday, August 5, at his church. Howarth also paid all burial expenses. After a brief ceremony Williams was interred in Blackpool's Layton Cemetery.[15]

Alice Fryer, prostrate with grief, "would not believe he was dead for a day or two after the event."[16] She had been much more optimistic about Williams's future than had his physician. Apparently not knowing he was already married, she had looked forward to early nuptials. Shortly after the burial, she returned with her mother to their home at Southsea. She was in constant touch with United States officials, who, in the absence of any family, went from Liverpool to Blackpool to manage Williams's affairs. Miss Fryer wondered why there had been no notice of his death in the London *Times* before August 7. The deputy consul explained that the Department of State wished to notify the next of kin first, in order to forestall their learning the news in the press.[17] Later, Miss Fryer was anxious to retrieve some two dozen photographs of herself and Williams that had been taken in London. There was a problem, Consul Thomas H. Sherman informed her, for the London photographer who took the pictures had not been paid his charges of £3.13.6. The consul would release the photographs if the photographer were paid. A few days later, the consul sent the photographs to Miss Fryer, retaining one, with her "kind permission," for the purpose of identification. One can assume that Miss Fryer had paid the bill.[18]

Miss Fryer also requested, immediately after Williams's death, to have returned to her the letters she had written Williams. Consul Sherman told her that, as in the case of the photographs, he could not disturb the deceased man's personal papers until he received clear instructions from his superiors in Washington. When Williams's widow, Sarah, was appointed administratrix of the estate, she gave the consul permission to "sell such of the effects" as he could, for the best possible advantage to the estate. Since those letters could be "of no possible use to the estate or to the administratrix personally," he told Thomas D. Crawford of Belfast, Ireland, he would "correspond with Miss Fryer respecting them if she were within reasonable distance." He then added that if Crawford planned to be in Liverpool within the next week or two, he would be pleased to have him call at the consulate.[19]

Thomas Crawford's interest in the matter is not clear. He paid the better portion of the hotel bill incurred by Williams and the Fryers. The consul went out of his way to assure Crawford that Miss Fryer's conduct had been above reproach. It was too bad that "respectable and honest women" could be deceived by "such adventurers," he volunteered. "I do not hesitate to say that Miss Fryer and her friends should consider themselves very fortunate in that her relations with Colonel Williams went no farther. And I may be permitted to add that at no time since my knowledge of the unpleasant affair began has one word reached me from any source in any respect detrimental to Miss Fryer."[20] A sentiment such as that would doubtless favor Miss Fryer's rescuing from posterity her letters to Williams.

Outside of the group at the Palatine Hotel and a few Blackpool residents, the first to learn of the death of Williams were the United States officials in Britain. On August 4, a justice of the peace in Darwen, Lancashire, sent a telegram with the news to Robert Todd Lincoln, the United States minister to London. *"No one* that I know of to look after his affairs. Wire instructions at *once,"* the justice urged. Lincoln immediately informed John C. New, the U.S. consul general in London, who, in turn, sent instructions to Thomas H. Sherman in Liverpool, to "take such action in the matter as required in the Consular Regulations."[21]

Sherman had already learned of the death, having received a telegram on August 3 from the manager of the Palatine Hotel in Blackpool, asking, "Do you know anything of him. He has been lately in Africa." Sherman then sent Martin, one of his clerks, to Blackpool "to see that the remains were properly interred, to take charge of the effects and bring them to the Consulate, and to learn what he could respecting Colonel Williams's illness; and the whereabouts of his relatives and friends." Martin was diligent in carrying out his responsibilities. He supervised the funeral and interment and made an inventory of Williams's personal effects. Some had been left at Morley's Hotel in London; but since Williams had left no debt there, the consul had no difficulty in persuading the hotel proprietor to release them so that they could be collected in one place for appraisal and disposition.[22]

The consulate in Liverpool also sought information regarding relatives of the deceased. To that end, it placed the following advertisement in the London *Times* for August 10, 1891:

> GEORGE WASHINGTON WILLIAMS:—Wanted by the United States Consul at Liverpool, the address of the relatives of George Washington Williams, a citizen of the United States, who died at the Palatine Hotel, Blackpool, on the 2nd instant, who lately returned from Africa, and who is understood to have been in communication with several persons in this country.

News of Williams's death had reached the United States before the notice in the *Times*. Through the efforts of the consulate as well as the initiative of relatives and friends in the United States, Consul Sherman soon had as much information as (perhaps more than) he needed. Alice Fryer had told the consul that Williams had an aunt in Worcester, Massachusetts, Mrs. Lois A. Staples. A deputy consul immediately wrote to Mrs. Staples to inquire about any family that Williams may have had in the United States. In her reply, Mrs. Staples provided no information about the family but expressed a strong desire to have him send to her anything found among Williams's effects that had her name on it. The consul informed her that he had no authority to dispose of any portion of the effects. He also told her he had learned that Williams left a widow, and he could not resist adding, "I notice that you make no reference to a widow."[23]

The consul rightly suspected that Mrs. Staples was no aunt of Williams. Mrs. Staples was apparently a "passing acquaintance" whom Williams had met during his brief sojourn in Worcester. After hearing from the consulate, she wrote to Samuel Pelling, who had conducted the funeral services. She wanted to know more about Williams's illness and death. Pelling replied, "So far as I can ascertain nearly all his friends are in the same position as yourself. They have known him for a short time comparatively and have learned to esteem him highly, but they are not acquainted with the real facts of his life." "Aunt" Lois Staples, twenty-one years older than Williams, apparently decided not to pursue the matter at that time.[24]

Among others who wrote from the United States to inquire about Williams's death were a brother, Harry, eleven years younger than George and living in Dunsmuir, California, and a still younger sister, Lola, living in Sacramento. The consul gave them essentially the same information: that Williams's personal effects were of little value and that they would doubtless be claimed by his widow, Sarah Williams of Washington. A Mrs. C. M. Hubbard of Plymouth, Massachusetts, where Williams had spent summer vacations in the early 1880s, also wrote. The consul was less reticent with her, telling her of Williams's intended wife, Alice Fryer, of the manner in which he made friends wherever he went, and that all Williams's personal effects were being held in Liverpool for disposition by his legal representatives.[25]

We do not know when Sarah Williams received word of her estranged husband's death. In any event, by the end of August she had written to United States authorities in Britain indicating that she was Williams's wife and that he left one son, and inquiring about his illness and effects. Three weeks later, Consul Sherman advised her that she could secure the desired information from the assistant secretary of state.[26] Sherman had sent the Department of State a detailed inventory of the personal effects, which consisted of two tin boxes and several bundles of African curios that had been stored at Morley's Hotel in London, and all items Williams had with him at the time of his death. Among the African curios were twenty-four swords and spear points, four knives, four tusks, thirty-nine spears, two bows, three quivers of arrows, and an assortment of straw mats, bamboo canes, oars, rawhide thongs, and basket shields. Other items included a Prince Albert coat, full dress coat and vest, an opera hat, coats, trousers, shirts, neckties, a silk hat, dressing gown, scarf pins, gold watch, Masonic watch charm, and twenty-four photos of Williams and Alice Fryer.[27]

By early November, Sarah Williams had qualified as administratrix of her late husband's estate and was ready to negotiate directly with the consular officials in Liverpool. The consulate informed her that it awaited her instructions regarding the sale of items in the estate and the debts charged against the estate.[28] The debts were considerable, if the bills submitted by creditors were to believed. The proprietors of Morley's Hotel in London claimed that Williams owed £5.5.4, although they had earlier informed the consul general that he owed nothing.[29] The proprietor of the Palatine Hotel in Blackpool submitted a bill for £30 for board, lodging, wine, and other items. He also stated that he was responsible for the undertaker's bill, amounting to £20.11.0, and the cost of the grave, about £3. The consul challenged him on the amount, reminding him that Thomas Crawford had paid the hotel bill and that a friend, James Howarth, had paid the burial expenses. The proprietor then admitted that the bill for board and lodging had been paid up to the last few days. There were, however, some additional costs of wine and "other extras" as well as the expenses of redecorating and refurnishing the room in which Williams died. The consul refused to pay more than £10. He informed the other creditors, such as the pharmacist and the physician, that there were no estate funds to pay more than a fraction of their claims.[30]

An exaggerated estimate of the Williams estate had probably been stimulated by the notion that his African curios and his manuscripts would bring high prices. Shortly after Williams's death, the consul began to receive inquiries about these items. R. C. Phillips of Manchester, who had early praised Williams's blast against King Leopold, was anxious to acquire the manuscripts. On the consul's advice, he wrote to Mrs. Williams offering her £5 for the diaries and other documents among the effects "with the exception of such as I and the Consul agree to destroy."[31] She did not take Phillips up on his offer.[32] Williams had doubtless encouraged the belief that he had collected a small fortune in African curios. He had written about his collection long before he left Africa (see chapter 13 above). It was surely no secret in and around Morley's Hotel, where it was stored. If its sale were to bring a good price, Williams's creditors would make certain that they got their rightful share—or more.

In consultation with Sarah Williams, the consul at Liverpool decided

to offer the effects for sale at auction with the hope that they would bring
enough to settle the debts against the estate arising from Williams's
illness and death. There was no hope that they would be sufficient to pay
his bills at the British Museum.[33] The consul distributed large posters
advertising the items:

> To Be Sold by Auction—
>
> By Authority of the American Consul—Interesting collection of
> genuine African weapons and curios, by Messrs. Branch and Lette,
> on next Friday, the 22nd of January, 1892, at one o'clock in the
> Hanover Gallery, Hanover Street, Liverpool.
>
> A unique and valuable collection of African curios, comprising
> copper knives, quaint daggers and swords, carved spears,
> ornamental paddles, shields, bows and arrows, ivory tusks, trum-
> pets, brass rings for neck, ankles, and wrists, fishing spears, and
> other interesting objects, obtained from the natives during an
> extended tour of exploration by Col. Geo. W. Williams, an Amer-
> ican citizen, lately deceased at Blackpool.

The poster concluded by pointing out that many items were suitable for
the decoration of billiard rooms, halls, or museums. They would be on
view the preceding day as well as the morning of the sale.[34]

The net return from the sale of the African collection was a disappointing $248.95. Williams had said in late June that the curios should
bring about $1000, "sufficient to pay all his expenses until he died."[35]
The only other assets available to the consul were uncashed checks for
£10.19.0, which he could transmit solely to the widow. He offered to
settle with the creditors at 50 percent of their bills. All but the proprietor of the Palatine Hotel in Blackpool accepted the offer. The hotel
manager insisted on payment in full for what the consul claimed was a
"most unreasonable" demand. When the consul refused to accede, the
manager claimed all the effects, with the exception of manuscripts,
which were in Williams's possession in the hotel at the time of his death.
These included a watch and chain that the consul had hoped to send to
Sarah Williams for her son.[36]

On March 29, 1892, seven months after Williams's death, Consul
Sherman made his final report to Mrs. Williams, showing how he had
tried to close matters to the best advantage of the family. By shrewd
maneuvering and some duplicity he was able to send her a check for
$149.68. He had become quite protective of the woman he regarded as
living in destitute circumstances, forced to support herself and her
fifteen-year-old son. He also sent her two tin trunks, containing "all the

books and manuscripts and several small items as shown by the inventory."[37]

The news of Williams's death had appeared in the American press on Wednesday, August 5, 1891—the day of his interment. The New York *Tribune* had very few of the facts, except that he died in Blackpool. The paper alleged that he went to the Congo "under the auspices of the Belgian Government," that he was alone at the time of his death, and that he had no friends in Blackpool. Since there was no basis for any of these assertions, one can assume that the *Tribune* merely speculated in order to provide answers to its own questions. On the following day the *Telegram* in Worcester, Williams's last place of residence in the United States, reported that he had died of consumption. As a friend of Worcester's most distinguished resident, Senator Hoar, and as a frequent user of the library of the American Antiquarian Society, Williams had been a regular visitor to Worcester long before he took up residence there in 1887. The newspaper expressed certainty that his many friends and acquaintances there would be surprised and saddened to learn of his passing.[38]

The Afro-American press, all weekly newspapers, carried the news the following Saturday. Beginning August 8 and in the following several weeks, the press editorialized on Williams's career. The New York *Age* captioned its editorial "The Historian is Dead." In part, it said,

> Over the grave of one so young, so brilliant, and so wayward, it is safe to say the thinking portion of the race in the United States will shed a tear. He was a man of remarkable talents and erudition and of tireless industry, and had he possessed an even moral character and scorned to abuse the confidence of the great men of many nations who admired and trusted him, he could early have ranked as one of the famous men of his times. . . . He died in England, a stranger in a strange land, estranged from the wife who loved him and the friends who had remained true to him long after he had ceased to be true to himself. Peace to his ashes.[39]

On its front page, the Indianapolis *Freeman* carried a large drawing of Williams under which were the words, "Hon. George W Williams (deceased), Legislator, Historian and Traveler." Its editorial was headlined "The Silent Messenger":

> The silent messenger of death touches his chilling fingers upon buoyant youth and the enfeebled; the touch is forever lasting. The

imprint is ineffaceable, unalterable. . . . George Washington Williams is dead. The first and only true recorder of his people's
history. Far from their presence, among an alien people, his life's
work closed. 'He was a man, take him for all and all,' but his faults
fled with his breath and his goodness perishes only with his name.'
George W. Williams, the soldier, the minister, legislator, historian, and traveler has ended his earthly, mortal career. 'He lived,
loved, wrote; and died but to be known.'[40]

"Larph," whose column appeared in several Afro-American newspapers, was not so kind. In a piece that appeared in Cleveland and in
Huntsville, Alabama, he lamented the death of the Honorable George
W. Williams "at Blackpool, Congo Free State, Africa" (*sic*). He said that
in the death of Williams "the race lost one of the most, if not the most
brilliant men." He compared Williams with Benedict Arnold and Aaron
Burr. "Like Arnold there was a dash, a brilliancy about George Williams
that challenged the admiration of his enemies. Like Burr, there was a
crafty cunning in his composition that awoke distrust in his most intimate friend, and like Burr, there was a disregard for woman's honor and
virtue in his makeup that disgusted." "Larph" argued that it was his
entry into politics that caused Williams to have deteriorated as "an
ornament to society as well as a source of happiness to his family. . . . He
plunged into the political sea and was swallowed by its treacherous
malestrom [*sic*]. His rise *and* his fall could be dated from his election to
the General Assembly of Ohio," he said.

In the legislature, Williams's eloquence "held the members and
audience spell-bound," "Larph" admitted. "His logic was indisputable,
his erudition unsurpassed. . . . He plunged into politics with an abandonment of all ideas of morals, principles or religion. . . . For a few
dollars he attempted to play traitor to the interests of his race. Mark the
Arnold here. To appease an animal passion he sacrificed virtue and
despoiled a home. Mark the Burr here." "Larph" said he knew Williams
well, had sat in his home, "marked the bliss, the devotion and love, that
found an abiding place there, and almost envied the happiness of such a
home. . . . George Williams had a wife beloved by everyone, as true a
little woman as ever plighted a vow with man. . . . He abandoned this
true wife and her and his child. For what? To follow the bend of a
depraved mind." "Larph" observed that Williams passed the bar but
added, incorrectly, that he never practiced law. He praised him for his
writings in the field of history, referring to his principal work as "a
remarkable work emanating from a remarkable brain." He said that
when Williams began his history he borrowed $1,000 from Governor

Charles Foster, but never repaid the debt, "save in the dedication of a book to his name."

"Larph" was as reckless with the truth as were other detractors of Williams. Like some others, he claimed—quite erroneously—that Williams had been in the Congo for the past two years, "in the service of the Belgian government." He reported that Williams's wife was living in Chicago with her son and mother, when, as a matter of fact, she was living on 15th Street NW in Washington, D.C. He begrudgingly conceded that Williams's history of the race was "without doubt the richest legacy ever bequeathed to the race by one of its members, beyond that he will sleep in a forgotten grave. His death, thousands of miles from home and country, in the dark continent . . . seems a striking reward. . . . Thus ended the life of a man, talented and unscrupulous, brilliant and unfaithful. . . . To get the best view of George Williams, we must look at him through that magnificent work, his history, and veil all else from view."[41]

There were white writers in the daily press whose opinion of Williams was not much higher than that of "Larph." The Boston *Herald* said that "he never made any money, so far as his acquaintances could see, yet, he always had plenty of it. . . . A gentleman once said to him, 'Colonel, I marvel at your good clothes, full face, plenty of money, and no work. As a cheeky character, you seem to be a success.' " The Springfield *Republican,* after remarking that the history showed much ability, added that "unfortunately, Mr. Williams did not bear a good reputation. The best men of his own race of late years have refused to endorse him, and he has been under a cloud." It then added in a gesture of generosity, "He was an intellectual man, of fine manners, and social tact, and made his way easily."[42]

It was left to Sarah Williams to make a final summary of her husband's life and character. Their long estrangement provided her a perspective that was cool, detached, and with a trace of bitterness. In reply to a letter of condolence from their old friend, John P. Green of Cleveland, who in 1881 had followed Williams in the Ohio legislature,[43] she wrote:

> I well knew your feelings toward Mr. Williams and I think in his heart of hearts he care [sic] for you to the fullest extent his nature would allow him to care for anyone. It is a sad thing indeed to feel relieved at the death of one you have love [sic] as your life but such is my feelings, it would be untrue were I to write otherwise. His death is not the saddest thing that could have happened to me, for has he not been worse than dead to me for years? He had hoped to be in this country this fall, let us hope that he would have made

amends for the past. I have always thought of him in pity and
sadness that he should be so unkind to himself and friends.[44]

Other evaluations of Williams pertained to his public and professional life rather than to his personal and family life. In 1890, when he
was in Africa, the Indianapolis *Freeman* conducted a poll among its
8,000 readers to ascertain their views on the ten greatest Negroes who
ever lived. The results placed the following men (no women) in that
select group: Blanche K. Bruce, Peter H. Clark, Edward E. Cooper,
Frederick Douglass, T. Thomas Fortune, Daniel A. Payne, Toussaint
L'Ouverture, J. C. Price, J. Milton Turner, and George W. Williams.
"Surely it is," the editor said of Williams, "that the nearest and fullest
report of the Negro in historic form came from his facile pen. He is not
only a prolific writer, but an elegant and captivating speaker. He is the
soul of untiring industry, and if spared will yet add much to the literature of the world."[45] The results of the *Freeman's* poll was compromised
by the fact that the paper's editor, Edward E. Cooper, was among the
ten persons chosen. This did not escape notice. One newspaper
observed that "a judge of a contest who will decide himself a great man,
or allow himself to be so decided, is a fit subject for a dime museum."[46] It
conceded that Williams, Bishop Payne, Douglass, and some of the
others were able men but insisted that the only great man on the list was
Toussaint L'Ouverture.[47]

Posterity has treated Williams little better than his contemporaries
did—perhaps for some understandable reasons. Although Negro Americans had been important contributors to the making of America, historians and other scholars working on the nineteenth century have taken
little notice, until quite recently, of that contribution. They have been
dismissed as docile slaves or corrupt politicians of the era of Reconstruction. There was the widely held assumption, moreover, that they lacked
the intellectual and social qualities that would make them worthy of
consideration. They were invariably regarded as outside the main-
stream of American life and history—as exotics at best or, at worst, as
unassimilable creatures with a dark past and an even more dismal
future. Williams and many other nineteenth-century blacks were victims of this disesteem and consequently were largely ignored by those
who kept the records. Senator George Hoar is a case in point. The two
men were in regular touch, and the Hoar papers contain scores of letters
from Williams to Hoar on matters ranging from problems of the Congo
to a proposed monument to black soldiers in the Civil War. Yet Hoar
makes no mention of Williams in his two-volume autobiography.[48]

Historians of American history have generally ignored Williams, although he was the first historian to write a serious, widely reviewed history of the Negro race. Michael Kraus, author of the first comprehensive history of United States historians, does not mention Williams when he discusses the historians of the people. Williams fares no better in the work by Harvey Wish, who deals with abolitionists and revisionists writing in the 1880s and with the rise of social history during the same period. Under the circumstances one can hardly be surprised that the British historian, Hale Bellot, makes no mention of Williams in his survey of the writing of American history.[49]

Some of Williams's more articulate black contemporaries completely ignored him when they wrote about the period in which he lived. Frederick Douglass did not mention Williams in the editions of his autobiography that he published in the later years of his life; and John Mercer Langston, one of the sponsors of Williams's newspaper, *The Commoner*, ignored Williams in his autobiography. Their silence may have reflected their disapproval of political or other positions taken by Williams. Although John P. Green and Williams had been friends and political allies in Ohio for years, Green makes no mention of Williams in his 1920 autobiography either, though the passage of time could have blurred his memory.[50]

There were other Afro-Americans, however, both lay and professional, who were loyal to Williams's memory and continued to praise his work. In reviewing the *History of the Negro Race* before the Georgia State Teachers Convention in 1898, John Hope—later president of Morehouse College and Atlanta University—said that Williams "is no partisan pamphleteer [but] writes like a man who desires his work to be lasting, like one who has sufficient confidence in his subject and in his own ability to believe that his history will be read by posterity." Hope asserted that "Mr. Williams' method has been to present indisputable facts and to let them tell their story." Future historians of Afro-Americans, Hope thought, would have greater difficulty than Williams had.

> He has treated us when we were in bondage and when we had but tasted of the sweets of freedom. The task of the historians will grow increasingly arduous as our civilization advances and becomes more complex. The links that bind cause to effect will be less easily perceived. . . . Nevertheless, the fact remains that Williams ploughed his furrows through fallow ground and removed many obstacles. . . . He has left landmarks; and, heavy and tedious as may be the journey of future historians, he has reduced the hardships.

. . . He has boldly leaped into the trenches and called on other
colored men to follow him in the effort to vindicate and ennoble our
race in history.[51]

Hope was correct in indicating that later historians would be indebted to Williams. Booker T. Washington, in his two-volume *Story of
the Negro* (1909), borrowed extensively from Williams, especially in his
treatment of the 1741 slave conspiracy in New York and the service of
black soldiers in the War for Independence and in the Civil War. "He
was a writer and newspaper man of some note," Washington asserted,
"and is the author of a 'History of the Negro Race in America' to which I
have frequently had occasion to refer, in the preparation of this book."[52]
While an undergraduate at Fisk, W. E. B. Du Bois spoke with pride of
Williams as "historian of the race,"and as late as 1924, he referred to him
as "the greatest historian of the race." In *The Gift of Black Folk*, Du Bois
used information provided by Williams on such matters as the quest for
freedom by the slaves, the arming of blacks, and their service in the
Civil War.[53]

Carter G. Woodson's *The Negro in Our History* (1945) makes only a
passing reference to Williams, along with Booker T. Washington and
John W. Cromwell, as having written in the field of history.[54] Among
Woodson's papers, however, is a five-page sketch of Williams in which
Woodson offered some opinions of the man and his work. "He never
stuck to any position very long," Woodson said, "and seemed all but to
roam from one part of the country to the other, but wherever he went he
always maintained his interest in literary matters and original research."
He called the *History of the Negro Race* "unique and valuable." Of the
History of the Negro Troops in the War of the Rebellion Woodson wrote
that "no one has yet written a work in this field to measure up to it."[55]
Woodson strongly believed that Williams deserved a full-length biography, and it was in the *Journal of Negro History*, of which he was then
editor, that the first article on Williams ever to appear in a learned
journal was published.[56]

Vernon Loggins, in 1931, gave considerable attention to Williams in
his examination of Negro writers. Much may be said against Williams's
task, he contended, but little against his industry in research. "Although
the *History of the Negro Race in America* appeared almost a half century
ago, it is still perhaps the most comprehensive general history of the
American Negro."[57] When Benjamin Brawley undertook to write a
comprehensive history of Negro Americans in 1921, he conceded that
Williams's study of the legal aspects of that history was "not likely soon

to be superseded." He justified his own undertaking on the ground that he sought to go beyond what Williams had attempted and was seeking to study the "actual life of the Negro people in itself and in connection with that of the nation."[58]

When the historian Rayford Logan, in 1954, looked at the period in which Williams lived and worked, he observed that Williams's history had been used "by all subsequent historians of the Negro. Not always scientific or restrained," Logan warned, "it was well documented and filled with evidence that Negroes had not always been hewers of wood and drawers of water."[59] In 1958, Earl E. Thorpe reviewed the works of Negro historians in general. Inevitably, Williams received considerable attention. Since he was untrained in the field, Thorpe observed, "it is only natural that Williams violated many of the canons of good historical scholarship and writing." His documentation was faulty, Thorpe claimed, and he did not always cite the proper authority. Nevertheless, Thorpe believed that "no historian has yet brought out a general history of the race in America of comparable scope and based on such broad research."[60]

American writers—historians and others—who have written about Williams have concentrated on his achievements as a historian. There has appeared to be little interest in his many other activities; following his death, no one took notice of his landmark writings about the Congo. Not until 1966 did François Bontinck, a Belgian historian living in Zaire and teaching at the university in Kinshasa, write of Williams's activities in Africa. In his *Aux Origines de l'Etat Indépendant du Congo,* Bontinck became the first historian outside the United States to give some attention to Williams's career. In the appendix to his collection of documents, Bontinck briefly traces Williams's early career, then treats his attendance at the antislavery conference in Brussels in 1889, his failure to secure appointment, and his unsuccessful effort to interview Henry Sanford, one of the United States delegates. Bontinck also gives a brief account of Williams's journey through the Congo, his *Open Letter* attacking the king's rule there, and his other writings on the Congo.[61]

In 1968, during the all-out drive to achieve civil rights for blacks in the United States, Williams's *History of the Negro Race* was reprinted.[62] Although there was no great flurry of excitement marking its reissue, at least it became available again to libraries and the general reading public. In 1971, along with Ira Aldridge and Frederick Douglass, Williams was inducted into the Hall of Fame of the Black Academy of Arts and Letters at its second annual awards banquet.[63] At its first meeting the previous year the Academy had inducted W. E. B. Du Bois, Henry

O. Tanner (the painter), and Carter G. Woodson.[64] Williams's presence among the first six members of the Hall of Fame was reminiscent of his selection in 1890 as one of the ten greatest Negroes.

If the recognition of Williams by the Black Academy of Arts and Letters did not transform him into a popular hero, it did bring him once again before the general public at a time when there was a growing interest in the Afro-American past. In subsequent years, Williams was the subject of brief biographical sketches in the weekly Afro-American press. In 1974, Continental Features in its regular series "Things you should know," included a piece about George W. Williams. Under the pen and ink drawing of Williams he was referred to as a "celebrated lawyer and historian." It mentioned his two major historical works. "One fact he helped unearth," the feature pointed out, "is the Battle of Milliken's Bend on the Mississippi River, June 6, 1863, in which a Negro soldier took his former master prisoner."[65] Seven years later, in Morrie Turner's widely distributed Sunday feature, "Soul Corner," Williams was the subject of discussion between two youngsters, one white and one black. The young black was instructing the white child on the many-sided career of Williams. After learning of his service in the United States and Mexican armies and of his work as a clergyman, publisher and historian, the white child asked, "Did he ever find steady employment?"[66]

Meanwhile, there was a gradual increase of interest in Williams's writings on the Congo. This arose not out of the civil rights revolution but from the marked improvement in the scholarship dealing with various aspects of African life and history. In 1952, William K. Parmenter completed a doctoral dissertation at Harvard dealing with critics of the Congo. He recognized Williams as a major one. His three reports, Parmenter observed, "drew up an indictment nearly as damning as anything the Congo reformers published fifteen years later." "Along with the astoundingly accurate prophecy that the railway would take at least eight years to complete, Williams recited a series of charges" against the state and its personnel. "But Williams's pamphlets had no effect, and later critics do not seem to be aware of their existence."[67] A few years later, Paul McStallworth affirmed Parmenter's findings and credited Williams with the revival of interest in the Congo. The participation of the United States in the Brussels antislavery conference and the personal involvement of President Benjamin Harrison in the effort to improve relations with the Congo were evidence of that revival. Williams's role was manifested in his promotion of the conference and his gentle prodding of President Harrison.[68]

In her 1962 study of Leopold's policies in the Congo, Ruth Slade cited Williams as one of the first to show that the Congo State violated the Berlin Act by taxing other traders and exempting itself, also a trader, from all financial burdens.[69] In 1968, S. J. S. Cookey referred to Williams's "startling denunciations of the Congo system," citing him as "one of the earliest to launch an open attack" on the "callous and inhumane methods of the administration" in the Congo in the plunder and destruction of villages there. "His death in August 1891 coupled with the fact that the King-sovereign took care to discredit him in advance, saved the Congo government from what might have been an embarrassingly formidable opponent."[70]

For all his efforts in military service, religion, journalism, lawmaking, the practice of law, historical writing, and African studies, Williams made it hard for posterity to appreciate him. To be sure, he had defied every reasonable expectation in making the leap from a crude, barely literate soldier to a polished clergyman in five years. With his superior oratorical and literary talents he captivated a large reading and listening public that gave credence to virtually every word he uttered. With his relentless drive he challenged nature as he ignored his own physical ailments for the sake of accomplishing the goals he had set for himself. He was the object of both admiration and envy. The average person would have been more than content to have succeeded in any one of the several fields in which Williams did so much.

As one looks back on the career of George Washington Williams, however, one can be certain that he was not merely unhappy with what he had done but actually felt unfulfilled as he went from one career to another. With all his knowledge and talents, he seemed utterly ignorant of how to show posterity his best side. Sarah Williams correctly described him as "unkind to himself" as well as to friends. He was careless with the facts, even when the truth was not especially damaging—for example, permitting people to believe that he had attended Harvard instead of Howard or that he was a colonel in the United States Army instead of the Grand Army of the Republic. No one expected him to be a man of great wealth, but he relished giving that impression, even if it later cost him untold embarrassment. In an age when convention demanded fidelity to the family, he flaunted his sexual freedom. He was never more unkind to himself than when, with a lung weakened from a gunshot wound and a generally frail constitution, he drove himself for fifteen years in the United States and Europe and for fifteen months in the inhospitable climes of many parts of Africa.

Nevertheless, Williams achieved a great deal in his brief life. In his

Massachusetts years he had a great impact on the Twelfth Baptist Church and political and social life in Boston and Worcester. In his Ohio years, becoming a columnist for a major newspaper and getting himself elected to the Ohio legislature were landmarks, as were his major role in the state's leading veterans organization and his authorship of the first serious history of the Negro race. In the years that he was involved in foreign affairs, particularly as the pioneer antagonist to King Leopold's policies in the Congo, he pointed the way for all those who were interested in ending European and American domination in Africa.

The accomplishments of Williams were far outdistanced by his boundless energy and indomitable will. His political activities, even when he did yeoman service for the party of Abraham Lincoln, were hardly appreciated. In the legislature his white constituents were more interested in his conduct while seeking to be served in a Columbus restaurant than in his committee work. His black constituents were more interested in his alleged sellout in seeking the closure of an all-black cemetery than in his role as secretary of the Republican legislative caucus. The cynical manner in which the Republicans threw him to the Democrats in their last-minute nomination of him as minister to Haiti indicated how expendable Afro-American Republicans were. His historical writings, even when criticized, were regarded as remarkable "for a man of his race." His vigorous efforts to stimulate support for a free and independent Congo reflected his naive views of the real interest of white Americans in the underdeveloped areas of the world. It was too much to hope that the United States—whose view of the white man's burden was already more selfish than altruistic—would take the lead in building a healthy future for black Africans.

Despite the disinclination of white America to concede that George Washington Williams was a true American, he had achieved the full stature of a real nineteenth century American by the time of his death. He had exemplified those qualities that had come to be associated with Americans and that had been described by Crèvecœur in 1782: a boundless, restless energy; an insatiable appetite to achieve; the grasping of any and every opportunity to venture into new areas of endeavor; an independence of mind and spirit; and a fierce devotion to the idea that success depended on the use of one's own talents and abilities. He possessed yet another trait about which Crèvecœur said little and to which too few Americans of Williams's time were committed: a deep compassion for the dignity as well as the rights of darker peoples everywhere.

By any standards, the career of George Washington Williams was remarkable. In forty-one years he had fought in two wars and had become pastor of two major churches, editor, columnist, legislator, historian (the first serious one of his race), appointee to a diplomatic post, world traveler, and the first public critic of King Leopold's policies in the Congo. Along the way he had been erratic, restless, controversial, overambitious, faithless, and capable of misrepresentation if not downright falsehood. As such he was human. It can be debated whether he was one of the ten greatest Negroes who ever lived, as determined by a poll in 1890. That he was possessed of great gifts cannot be debated. Williams was one of the small heroes of this world; but it is well that one should not try to make more of him than what he was—a flawed but brilliant human being.

Appendix 1

An Open Letter to
His Serene Majesty Leopold II,
King of the Belgians and Sovereign
of the Independent State of Congo,
by Colonel the Honorable
Geo. W. Williams,
of the United States of America.

Good and Great Friend,

I have the honour to submit for your Majesty's consideration some reflections respecting the Independant State of Congo, based upon a careful study and inspection of the country and character of the personal Government you have established upon the African Continent.

In order that you may know the truth, the whole truth, and nothing but the truth, I implore your most gracious permission to address you without restraint, and with the frankness of a man who feels that he has a duty to perform to *History, Humanity, Civilization* and to the *Supreme Being,* who is himself the "King of Kings."

Your Majesty will testify to my affection for your person and friendship for your African State, of which you have had ample practical proofs for nearly six years. My friendship and service for the State of Congo were inspired by and based upon your publicly declared motives and aims, and your personal statement to your humble subscriber:— humane sentiments and work of Christian civilization for Africa. Thus I was led to regard your enterprise as the rising of the Star of Hope for the Dark Continent, so long the habitation of cruelties; and I journeyed in its light and laboured in its hope. All the praisefull things I have spoken and written of the Congo country, State and Sovereign, was inspired by the firm belief that your Government was built upon the enduring foundation of *Truth, Liberty, Humanity* and *Justice.*

It afforded me great pleasure to avail myself of the opportunity afforded me last year, of visiting your State in Africa; and how thoroughly I have been disenchanted, disappointed and disheartened, it is now my painfull duty to make known to your Majesty in plain but respectful language. Every charge which I am about to bring against your Majesty's personal Government in the Congo has been carefully investigated; a list of competent and veracious witnesses, documents, letters, official records and data has been faithfully prepared, which will be deposited with Her Brittannic Majesty's Secretary of State for Foreign Affairs, until such time as an International Commission can be created with power to send for persons and papers, to administer oaths, and attest the truth or falsity of these charges.

I crave your Majesty's indulgence while I make a few preliminary remarks before entering upon the specifications and charges.

Your Majesty's title to the territory of the State of Congo is badly clouded, while many of the treaties made with the natives by the "Association Internationale du Congo," of which you were Director and Banker, were tainted by frauds of the grossest character. The world may not be surprised to learn that your flag floats over territory to which your Majesty has no legal or just claim, since other European Powers have doubtful claims to the territory which they occupy upon the African Continent; but all honest people will be shocked to known by what grovelling means this fraud was consummated.

There were instances in which MR. HENRY M. STANLEY sent one white man, with four or five Zanzibar soldiers, to make treaties with native chiefs. The staple argument was that the white man's heart had grown sick of the wars and rumours of war between one chief and another, between one village and another; that the white man was at peace with his black brother, and desired to "confederate all African tribes" for the general defense and public welfare. All the sleight-of-hand tricks had been carefully rehearsed, and he was now ready for his work. A number of electric batteries had been purchased in London, and when attached to the arm under the coat, communicated with a band of ribbon which passed over the palm of the white brother's hand, and when he gave the black brother a cordial grasp of the hand the black brother was greatly surprised to find his white brother so strong, that he nearly knocked him off his feet in giving him the hand of fellowship. When the native inquired about the disparity of strength between himself and his white brother, he was told that the white man could pull up trees and perform the most prodigious feats of strength. Next came the lens act. The white brother took from his pocket a cigar, carelessly bit off the end, held up his glass to the sun and complaisantly smoked his cigar to the great amazement and terror of his black brother. The white man explained his intimate relation to the sun, and declared that if he were to request him to burn up his black brother's village it would be done. The third act was the gun trick. The white man took a percussion cap gun, tore the end of the paper which held the powder to the bullet, and poured the powder and paper into the gun, at the same time slipping the bullet into the sleeve of the left arm. A cap was placed upon the nipple of the gun, and the black brother was implored to step off ten yards and shoot at his white brother to demonstrate his statement that he was a spirit, and, therefore, could not be killed. After much begging the black brother aims the gun at his white brother, pulls the trigger, the gun is discharged, the white man stoops. . . . and takes the bullet from his shoe!

By such means as these, too silly and disgusting to mention, and a few boxes of gin, whole villages have been signed away to your Majesty.

In your personal letter to the President of the Republic of the United States of America, bearing date of August 1st, 1885, you said that the possessions of the International Association of the Congo will hereafter form the Independent State of the Congo. "I have at the same time the honour to inform you and the Government of the Republic of the United States of America that, authorised by the Belgian Legislative Chambers to become the Chief of the new State, I have taken, in accord with the Association, the title of Sovereign of the Independent State of Congo." Thus you assumed the headship of the State of Congo, and at once organised a personal Government. You have named its officers, created its laws, furnished its finances, and every act of the Government has been clothed with the majesty of your authority.

On the 25th of February 1884, a gentleman, who has sustained an intimate relation to your Majesty for many years, and who then wrote as expressing your sentiments, addressed a letter to the United States in which the following language occurs: — "It may be safely asserted that no barbarous people have ever so readily adopted the fostering care of benevolent enterprise, as have the tribes of the Congo, and never was there a more honest and practical effort made to increase their knowledge and secure their welfare." The letter, from which the above is an excerpt, was written for the purpose of securing the friendly action of the Committee on Foreign Relations, which had under consideration a Senate Resolution in which the United States recognised the flag of the "Association Internationale du Congo" as the flag of a friendly Government. The letter was influential, because it was supposed to contain the truth respecting the natives, and the programme, not only of the Association, but of the new State, its legitimate successor, and of your Majesty.

When I arrived in the Congo, I naturally sought for the results of the brilliant programme:—*"fostering care," "benevolent enterprise,"* an *"honest and practical* effort" to increase the knowledge of the natives *"and secure their welfare."* I had never been able to conceive of Europeans, establishing a government in a tropical country, without building a hospital; and yet from the mouth of the Congo River to its head-waters, here at the seventh cataract, a distance of 1,448 miles, there is not a solitary hospital for Europeans, and only three sheds for sick Africans in the service of the State, not fit to be occupied by a horse. Sick sailors frequently die on board their vessels at Banana Point; and if it were not for the humanity of the Dutch Trading Company at that place — who have often opened their private hospital to the sick of other countries — many more might die. There is not a single chaplain in the employ of your Majesty's Government to console the sick or bury the dead. Your white men sicken and die in their quarters or on the caravan road, and seldom have christian burial. With few exceptions, the surgeons of your Majesty's government have been gentlemen of professional ability, devoted to duty, but usually left with few medical stores and no quarters in which to treat their patients. The African soldiers and labourers of your Majesty's Government fare worse than the whites, because they have poorer quarters, quite as bad as those of the natives; and in the sheds, called hospitals, they languish upon a bed of bamboo poles without blankets, pillows or any food different from that served to them when well, rice and fish.

I was anxious to see to what extent the natives had *"adopted the fostering care"* of your Majesty's "benevolent enterprise" (?), and I was doomed to bitter disappointment. Instead of the natives of the Congo "adopting the fostering care" of your Majesty's Government, they everywhere complain that their land has been taken from them by force; that the Government is cruel and arbitrary, and declare that they neither love nor respect t[h]e Government and its flag. Your Majesty's Government has sequestered their land, burned their towns, stolen their property, enslaved their women and children, and committed other crimes too numerous to mention in detail. It is natural that they everywhere shrink from *"the fostering care"* your Majesty's Government so eagerly proffers them.

There has been, to my absolute knowledge, no *"honest and practical effort made to increase their knowledge and secure their welfare."* Your Majesty's Government has never spent one franc for educational purposes, nor institu[t]ed any practical system of industrialism. Indeed the most unpractical measures have been adopted *against* the natives in nearly every respect; and in the capital of your Majesty's Government at Boma there is not a native employed. The labour system is radically unpractical; the soldiers and labourers of your Majesty's Government are very largely imported from Zanzibar at a cost of £10 *per capita,* and from Sierre Leone, Liberia, Accra and Lagos at from £1 to £1/10.- *per capita*. These recruits are transported under circumstances more cruel than cattle in European countries. They eat their rice twice a day by the use of their fingers; they often thirst for water when the season is dry; they are exposed to the heat and rain, and sleep upon the damp and filthy decks of the vessels often so closely crowded as to lie in human ordure. And, of course, many die.

Upon the arrival of the survivors in the Congo they are set to work as labourers at one shilling a day; as soldiers they are promised sixteen shillings per month, in English money, but are usually paid off in cheap handkerchiefs and poisonous gin. The cruel and unjust treatment to which these people are subjected breaks the spirits of many of them, makes them distrust and despise your Majesty's Government. They are enemies, not patriots.

There are from sixty to seventy officers of the Belgian army in the service of your Majesty's Government in the Congo of whom only about thirty are at their post; the other half are in Belgium on furlough. These officers draw double pay, — as soldiers and as civilians. It is not my duty to criticise the unlawful and unconstitutional use of these officers coming into the service of this African State. Such criticism will come with more grace from some Belgian statesman, who may remember that there is no constitutional or organic relation subsisting between his Government and the purely personal and absolute monarchy your Majesty has established in Africa. But I take the liberty to say that many of these officers are too young and inexperienced to be entrusted with the difficult work of dealing with native races. They are ignorant of native character, lack wisdom, justice, fortitude and patience. They have estranged the natives from your Majesty's Government, have sown the seed of discord between tribes and villages, and some of them have stained the uniform of the Belgian officer with murder, arson and robbery. Other officers have served the State faithfully, and deserve well of their Royal Master.

Of the unwise, complicated and stupid dual Government of the State of Congo I cannot say much in this letter, reserving space for a careful examination of it in another place. I may say that the usefullness of many a Congo official is neutralised by having to keep a useless set of books. For example: an officer is in command of a station and he wishes to buy two eggs. He makes this entry in a ruled and printed book: "For nourishment bought two eggs for two Ntaka." In another book he must make this entry: "Two Ntaka gone out of the store." And in another book he must enter this purchase *seven times!* Comment upon such supreme folly is unnecessary. We need only feel compassion for the mental condition of the man in Brussels who invented this system, and deep sympathy with its victims in the Congo.

From these general observations I wish now to pass to specific charges against your Majesty's Government.

FIRST.—Your Majesty's Government is deficient in the moral, military and financial strength, necessary to govern a territory of 1,508,000 square miles, 7,251 miles of navigation, and 31,694 square miles of lake surface. In the Lower Congo River there is but one post, in the cataract region one. From Leopoldville to N'Gombe, a distance of more than 300 miles, there is not a single soldier or civilian. Not one out of every twenty State-officials know the language of the natives, although they are constantly issuing laws, difficult even for Europeans, and expect the natives to comprehend and obey them. Cruelties of the most astounding character are practised by the natives, such as burying slaves alive in the grave of a dead chief, cutting off the heads of captured warriors in native combats, and no effort is put forth by your Majesty's Government to prevent them. Between 800 and 1,000 slaves are sold to be eaten by the natives of the Congo State annually; and slave raids, accomplished by the most cruel and murderous agencies, are carried on within the territorial limits of your Majesty's Government which is impotent. There are only 2,300 soldiers in the Congo.

SECOND.—Your Majesty's Government has established nearly fifty posts, consisting of from two to eight mercenary slave-soldiers from the East Coast. There is no white commissioned officer at these posts; they are in charge of the black Zanzibar soldiers, and the State expects them not only to sustain themselves, but to raid enough to feed the garrisons where the white men are stationed. These piratical, buccaneering posts compel the natives to furnish them with fish, goats, fowls, and vegetables at the mouths of their muskets; and whenever the natives refuse to feed these vampires, they report to the main station and white officers come with an expeditionary force and burn away the homes of the natives. These black soldiers, many of whome are slaves, exercise the power of life and death. They are ignorant and cruel, *because* they do not comprehend the natives; they are imposed upon them by the State. They make no report as to the number of robberies they commit, or the number of lives they take; they are only required to subsist upon the natives and thus relieve your Majesty's Government of the cost of feeding them. They are the greatest curse the country suffers now.

THIRD.—Your Majesty's Government is guilty of violating its contracts made with its soldiers, mechanics and workmen, many of whom are subjects of other Governments. Their letters never reach home.

FOURTH.—The Courts of your Majesty's Government are abortive, unjust, partial and delinquent. I have personally witnessed and examined their clumsy operations. The laws printed and circulated in Europe "for the protection of the blacks" in the Congo, are a dead letter and a fraud. I have heard an officer of the Belgian Army pleading the cause of a white man of low degree who had been guilty of beating and stabbing a black man, and urging race distinctions and prejudices as good and sufficient reasons why his client should be adjudged innocent. I know of prisoners remaining in custody for six and ten months because they were not judged. I saw the white servant of the Governor-General, CAMILLE JANSSEN, detected in stealing a bottle of wine from a hotel table. A few hours later the Procurer-General searched his room and found many more stolen bottles of wine and other things, not the property of servants. No one can be prosecuted in the State of Congo without an order of the Governor-General, and as he refused to allow his servant to be arrested, nothing could be done. The black servants in the hotel, where the wine had been stolen, had been often accused and beaten for these thefts, and now they were glad to be vindicated. But to the surprise of every honest man, the thief was sheltered by the Governor-General of your Majesty's Government.

FIFTH.—Your Majesty's Government is excessively cruel to its prisoners, condemning them, for the slightest offences, to the chain gang, the like of which cannot be seen in any other Government in the civilised or uncivilised world. Often these ox-chains eat into the necks of the prisoners and produce sores about which the flies circle, aggravating the running wound; so the prisoner is constantly worried. These poor creatures are frequently beaten with a dried piece of hippopotamus skin, called a "chicote," and usually the blood flows at every stroke when well laid on. But the cruelties visited upon soldiers and workmen are not to be compared with the sufferings of the poor natives who, upon the slightest pretext, are thrust into the wretched prisons here in the Upper River. I cannot deal with the dimensions of these prisons in this letter, but will do so in my report to my Government.

SIXTH.—Women are imported into your Majesty's Government for immoral purposes. They are introduced by two methods, viz, black men are dispatched to the Portuguese coast where they engage these women as mistresses of white men, who pay to the procurer a monthly sum. The other method is by capturing native women and condemning them to seven years' servitude for some imaginary crime against the State with which the villages of these women are charged. The State then hires these women out to the highest bidder, the officers having the first choice and then the men. Whenever children are born of such relations, the State maintains that the woman being its property the child belongs to it also. Not long ago a Belgian trader had a child by a slave-woman of the State, and he tried to secure possession of it that he might educate it, but the Chief of the Station where he resided, refused to be moved by his entreaties. At length he appealed to the Governor-General, and he gave him the woman and thus the trader obtained the child also. This was, however, an unusual case of generosity and clemency; and there is only one post that I know of where there is not to be found children of the civil and military officers of your Majesty's Government abandoned to degradation; white men bringing their own flesh and blood under the lash of a most cruel master, the State of Congo.

SEVENTH.—Your Majesty's Government is engaged in trade and commerce, competing with the organised trade companies of Belgium, England, France, Portugal and Holland. It taxes all trading companies and exempts its own goods from export-duty, and makes many of its officers ivory-traders, with the promise of a liberal commission upon all they can buy or get for the State. State soldiers patrol many villages forbidding the natives to trade with any person but a State official, and when the natives refuse to accept the price of the State, their goods are seized by the Government that promised them "protection." When natives have persisted in trading with the trade-companies the State has punished their independence by burning the villages in the vicinity of the trading houses and driving the natives away.

EIGHTH.—Your Majesty's Gouvernement has violated the General Act of the Conference of Berlin by firing upon native canoes; by confiscating the property of natives; by intimidating native traders, and preventing them from trading with white trading companies; by quartering troops in native villages when there is no war; by causing vessels bound from "Stanley-Pool" to "Stanley-Falls," to break their journey and leave the Congo, ascend the Aruhwimi river to Basoko, to be visited and show their papers; by forbidding a mission steamer to fly its national flag without permission from a local Government; by permitting the natives to carry on the slave-trade, and by engaging in the wholesale and retail slave-trade itself.

NINTH.—Your Majesty's Government has been, and is now, guilty of waging unjust and cruel wars against natives, with the hope of securing slaves and women, to minister to the behests of the officers of your Government. In such slave-hunting raids one village is armed by the State against the other, and the force thus secured is incorporated with the regular troops. I have no adequate terms with which to depict to your Majesty the brutal acts of your soldiers upon such raids as these.

The soldiers who open the combat are usually the bloodthirsty canni-balistic Bangalas, who give no quarter to the aged grandmother or nursing child at the breast of its mother. There are instances in which they have brought the heads of their victims to their white officers on the expeditionary steamers, and afterwards eaten the bodies of slain chil-dren. In one war two Belgian Army officers saw, from the deck of their steamer, a native in a canoe some distance away. He was not a com-batant and was ignorant of the conflict in progress upon the shore, some distance away. The officers made a wager of £5 that they could hit the native with their rifles. Three shots were fired and the native fell dead, pierced through the head, and the trade canoe was transformed into a funeral barge and floated silently down the river.

In another war, waged without just cause, the Belgian Army officer in command of your Majesty's forces placed the men in two or three lines on the steamers and instructed them to commence firing when the whistles blew. The steamers approached the fated town, and, as was usual with them, the people came to the shore to look at the boats and sell different articles of food. There was a large crowd of men, women and children, laughing, talking and exposing their goods for sale. At once the shrill whistles of the steamers were heard, the soldiers levelled their guns and fired, and the people fell dead, and wounded, and groaning, and pleading for mercy. Many prisoners were made, and among them four comely looking young women. And now ensued a most revolting scene: your Majesty's officers quarreling over the selection of these women. The commander of this murderous expedition, with his garments stained with innocent blood, declared, that his rank entitled him to the first choice! Under the direction of this same officer the prisoners were reduced to servitude, and I saw them working upon the plantation of one of the stations of the State.

TENTH.—Your Majesty's Government is engaged in the slave-trade, wholesale and retail. It buys and sells and steals slaves. Your Majesty's Government gives £3 per head for able-bodied slaves for military ser-vice. Officers at the chief stations get the men and receive the money when they are transferred to the State; but there are some middle-men who only get from twenty to twenty-five francs per head. Three hundred and sixteen slaves were sent down the river recently, and others are to follow. These poor natives are sent hundreds of miles away from their villages, to serve among other natives whose language they do not know. When these men run away a reward of 1,000 N'taka is offered. Not long ago such a re-captured slave was given one hundred "chikote" each day until he died. Three hundred N'taka-brassrod is the price the State pays for a slave, when bought from a native. The labour force at the stations of your Majesty's Government in the Upper River is composed of slaves of all ages and both sexes.

ELEVENTH.—Your Majesty's Government has concluded a contract with the Arab Governor at this place for the establishment of a line of military posts from the Seventh Cataract to Lake Tanganyika, territory to which your Majesty has no more legal claim, than I have to be Commander-in-Chief of the Belgian army. For this work the Arab Governor is to receive five hundred stands of arms, five thousands kegs of powder, and £20,000 sterling, to be paid in several instalments. As I write, the news reaches me that these much-treasured and long-looked for materials of war are to be discharged at Basoko, and the Resident here is to be given the discretion as to the distribution of them. There is a feeling of deep discontent among the Arabs here, and they seem to feel that they are being trifled with. As to the significance of this move Europe and America can judge without any comment from me, especially England.

TWELFTH.—The agents of your Majesty's Government have misrepresented the Congo country and the Congo railway. Mr. H. M. STANLEY, the man who was your chief agent in setting up your authority in this country, has grossly misrepresented the character of the country. Instead of it being fertile and productive it is sterile and unproductive. The natives can scarcely subsist upon the vegetable life produced in some parts of the country. Nor will this condition of affairs change until the native shall have been taught by the European the dignity, utility and blessing of labour. There is no improvement among the natives, because there is an impassable gulf between them and your Majesty's Government, a gulf which can never be bridged. HENRY M. STANLEY's name produces a shudder among this simple folk when mentioned; they remember his broken promises, his copious profanity, his hot temper, his heavy blows, his severe and rigorous measures, by which they were mulcted of their lands. His last appearance in the Congo produced a profound sensation among them, when he led 500 Zanzibar soldiers with 300 campfollowers on his way to relieve EMIN PASHA. They thought it meant complete subjugation, and they fled in confusion. But the only thing they found in the wake of his march was misery. No white man commanded his rear column, and his troops were allowed to straggle, sicken and die; and their bones were scattered over more than two hundred miles of territory.

Emigration cannot be invited to this country for many years. The trade of the Upper Congo consists only of ivory and rubber. The first is very old and the latter very poor. If the railway were completed now, it would not be able to earn a dividend for ten or twelve years; and as I have carefully inspected the line of the proposed road, I give it as my honest judgment that it cannot be completed for eight years. This is due to the stock-holders; they should be undeceived. I am writing a report on the Congo Railway, and will not present any data in this letter upon that subject.

Conclusions

Against the deceit, fraud, robberies, arson, murder, slave-raiding, and general policy of cruelty of your Majesty's Government to the natives, stands their record of unexampled patience, long-suffering and forgiving spirit, which put the boasted civilisation and professed religion of your Majesty's Government to the blush. During thirteen years only one white man has lost his life by the hands of the natives, and only two white men have been killed in the Congo. Major BARTTELOT was shot by a Zanzibar soldier, and the captain of a Belgian trading-boat was the victim of his own rash and unjust treatment of a native chief.

All the crimes perpetrated in the Congo have been done in *your* name, and *you* must answer at the bar of Public Sentiment for the misgovernment of a people, whose lives and fortunes were entrusted to you by the august Conference of Berlin, 1884–1885. I now appeal to the Powers, which committed this infant State to your Majesty's charge, and to the great States which gave it international being; and whose majestic law you have scorned and trampled upon, to call and create an International Commission to investigate the charges herein preferred in the name of Humanity, Commerce, Constitutional Government and Christian Civilisation.

I base this appeal upon the terms of Article 36 of Chapter VII of the General Act of the Conference of Berlin, in which that august assembly of Sovereign States reserved to themselves the right "to introduce into it later and by common accord the modifications or ameliorations, the utility of which may be demonstrated experience."

I appeal to the Belgian people and to their Constitutional Government, so proud of its traditions, replete with the song and story of its champions of human liberty, and so jealous of its present position in the sisterhood of European States,—to cleanse itself from the imputation of the crimes with which your Majesty's personal State of Congo is polluted.

I appeal to Anti-Slavery Societies in all parts of Christendom, to Philanthropists, Christians, Statesmen, and to the great mass of people everywhere, to call upon the Governments of Europe, to hasten the close of the tragedy your Majesty's unlimited Monarchy is enacting in the Congo.

I appeal to our Heavenly Father, whose service is perfect love, in witness of the purity of my motives and the integrity of my aims; and to history and mankind I appeal for the demonstration and vindication of the truthfulness of the charges I have herein briefly outlined.

And all this upon the word of honour of a gentleman, I subscribe myself your Majesty's humble and obedient servant.

GEO. W. WILLIAMS.

Stanley Falls, Central Africa,
    July 18th, 1890.

Appendix 2

A Report on the
Proposed Congo Railway, by
Colonel the Honorable Geo. W. Williams,
of the United States of America.

(This report was added to the "Open Letter
to the King of the Belgians.")

Stanley Falls,
(Central Africa,)
July 16th 1890.

I inspected the route of the proposed Congo Railway and the country through which it is to pass, in May and June, but I judged it wise to withhold my views, until I should examine the Congo River, country and commerce, from Leopoldville to the headwater of the navigable Congo River at the seventh cataract, a distance of 1,068 miles.

A Congo railway has always been one of HENRY M. STANLEY's favourite schemes, but the stalwart common sense and commercial wisdom of Englishmen rejected his wild estimates, as was also the fate of his two volume advertisement of the possessions of the State of Congo. His scheme, as presented to the Conference of Berlin, was rejected and disowned as an American enterprise. The Sovereign of the Congo State and a few Belgian capitalists fell under the spell of MR. STANLEY's figures, so fearfully and wonderfully made, and the railway scheme for the Congo took definite shape.

On the 26th March, 1887, the Independent State of Congo granted a charter to the "Compagnie du Congo pour le Commerce et l'Industrie" for the surveying and building of a railway in the Congo country. The life of the charter was for ninety-nine years, and its terms the most liberal. The survey was to be completed within eighteen months, and a copy of it, with the cost of the work, was to be furnished to the Government of the State of Congo. On the part of the Government it agreed to grant to the railway company 150,000 hectares (one hectare is equal to nearly two and one half acres) of land, to be selected by the company within one hundred days after filing its survey. The second paragraph, article three, conferred upon the railway company a most dangerous and doubtful power,—the company to be allowed provisionally to take possession of the lands, and to work the same to the best of their interests. I saw this done at Fuca Fuca, where the railway company entered the premises of the Dutch Trading House, and began to dig and carry away the soil without first requesting the State to purchase the land or the owners to sell it.

The railway company is allowed to withdraw, within three years after the completion of the survey, and the State reserves to itself the right to operate the road, or to issue a new charter to another company. The State grants to the railway company an annual subside of 20 per cent of the net produce of export-duties collected during each previous year, from the issuing of the charter to the end of its life, a period of ninety-nine years. The company is to keep strict accounts of the operation of the road, and the profits realised are to be divided between the State and itself as follows:

"Five (5) per cent to the legal reserve; six (6) per cent interest on sums spent on survey, construction of the railway, and for tools.

"The surplus to be divided between the State and the company, at the rate of forty (40) per cent for the State, and sixty (60) per cent for the company."

The railway company received 12,000 francs for the survey of the first year, 20,000 francs for the second year, and 28,000 francs for the third year. The road was to be completed within four years, at a cost of 25,000,000 francs = £1,000,000 = $5,000,000 Nearly three and one half years have passed, and not one mile of the road-bed has been made, and only twenty miles of the survey completed. Of course the time will be extended.

The Difficulties

with which the Congo Railway Company has to contend are almost insuperable. The first twenty miles of the proposed route present the real difficulties, while the remaining 250 miles furnish but comparatively slight obstructions. Matadi—in the Congo language *Stone*—richly deserves its name. It is but one aggregation of rocks piled one upon the other, in the wildest and most bewildering confusion. It is the most forbidding looking place in the Congo country. It occupies an important position at the head of the navigable waters of the lower Congo, and is situated about one hundred and ten (110) miles from the

Atlantic Ocean. Although it is claimed that the river is navigable from Boma or Matadi by sea-going steamers, only one has ever ventured to ascend to Matadi. On the 20th June, 1889, Captain J. W. Murray of the British steamship "Lualaba" went up, the Governor-General furnishing a bond covering the value of the vessel. I questioned Captain Murray on the 24th April last past, respecting the navigability of the thirty-five miles of river between Boma and Matadi; and while he admits that there are dangerous rocks, he also feels confident that there is water enough for European steamers, if they can once learn the channel. However, no other steamer has ventured to pass beyond Boma, where about one European steamer arrives each week. At present all supplies and goods for the railway company, the State stations and missions of the Upper Congo, are discharged at Banana or Boma and sent to Matadi by small draught steamers. This is an expensive and damaging system, since freight often remains exposed to the weather at Boma for weeks, there being no shelter; and the handling of it twice results in a great breakage. But this system, at present unavoidable, will, in my judgment, continue after the railway is completed, unless the State and the railway have the courage of their conviction, that the river *is* navigable between Boma, the Cape Salcity, and Matadi, the commercial entrepôt; and offer European steamers a guarantee of safe passage and free pilotage.

The terminal facilities at Matadi came under my observation first. Owing to the dangerous condition of the river bank, one or two large quays will be necessary for the transfer of freight to and from steamers and cars. After a careful study of all data bearing upon the question of tides there at Matadi, I conclude that the water rises from sixteen (16) to eighteen (18) feet, and that the volume and velocity of the river require works of unusual strength. And yet I saw a quay in process of construction at Matadi that would not endure one African season. It would be partially swept away and completely submerged.

I followed the surveyed route of the Congo railway from Matadi to the mouth of the Mpozo river,—about five miles. Every foot of this section is beset with difficulties: an ugly stream to bridge, cuts to dig, rocks to blast, a tunnel to bore, grades to make, culverts and masonry work to construct, nearly one thousand (1,000) feet above the bed of the River Congo, in sight of which the projected road is intended to pass until the river Mpozo, along whose left bank it is to pass for a short distance and then cross to the Mpalaballa-hill. This hill is 1,700 feet above sea level, and while the road may pass around or through it, it can never pass over it. The Mpozo is a turbulent stream, and it often rises from twelve to fifteen feet; and the bridge across its stormy bosom must be of ample size and strength. In the estimates of the Railway Company nine bridges are accounted for, and I have found twenty-six others of importance.

The young engineers who are employed upon the Congo railway have technical knowledge and zeal, but as Belgians they are deficient in that special experience of the weather phenomena of tropical countries, and there are many trials and disappointments awaiting them. A few years of experience might enable them to triumph over difficulties which no engineer unacquainted with African climate would master; but at the moment when experience is harvested, health fails or the term of service expires. New men come out to take the places of experienced men, and thus in the next eight years three distinct sets of engineers will have come and gone, sickness, death and expiration of term of service thinning their ranks.

Even after the road is completed it will require great care to keep it open during the rainy season.

The Labour System

is difficult of solution, and the more I have studied it the more I am convinced that the railway company is pursuing an unwise policy in the recruitment and treatment of their workmen. In the estimates printed at Brussels early last year, the managers of this project declare their ability to secure many labourers in the cataract region, through which the road is to pass; but the harsh policy of the State towards the natives has produced in them a dread and suspicion of the white man. Thus the Company has been compelled to import labourers, like the State of the Congo, from the East and West Coast of the African Continent. From the East Coast come Zanzibar slaves, from the West Coast free Kroomen; the former for a term of years, the latter for one year. The compensation for the slave-labour is paid to their Zanzibar master, and the Kroomen get one shilling per day. I personally examined the food and quarters of these man, and as to the first, I am compelled to say it is deficient, in both quality and quantity; and, as to the second, it is just to declare that they are worse quartered than the natives, and that is saying a good deal. The food consists of two articles only: rice and a venerable dry fish; and the most general sicknes is dysentry, of which malady a number die monthly. Added to bad food and poor quarters, the severe treatment bestowed upon these work-people is of such nature and frequency as to greatly impair their efficiency. They are beaten and kicked by their overseers upon the slightest provocation, and many run away. While I was carrying on my investigations near Matadi fifty

Kroomen ran away in one group, and every week these men are making desperate efforts to escape from the bondage of the railway company. The Kroomen belong to the sea; and when they no longer behold its blue bosom nor swell its sweet waters, they droop and die. They were not intented to dig in the earth; but whereever they appear along the African continent, in factories or upon steamers, their labour has proved invaluable and their reputation for fidelity is unquestioned. The Congo has seen the first and the last of the Kroomen. They will count the moons upon a string, making a knot each month. When the twelfth knot is tied, they will return home to boycott the Belgium-Congo. It was thus they treated the Portuguese for ill-treating them, and neither love nor money can ever induce them to enter their service again. These black Irishmen of the West Coast have no flag to cover them, no language, no Government, but every year 5,000 of their number go from home to work with a united determination to serve their friends and shun their enemies.

The Zanzibar slaves are not useful on a railway, and they fall to their tasks with bitter reluctance.

The mechanics are composed of Belgians and black men from Sierra Leone and Accra. They receive the usual pay of men of their various handicrafts, and food and quarters are furnished by the railway company. The black men endure the climate and do excellent work of a certain kind; and where the white men are more skilful they are less useful because of their inability to endure the climate under the full stress their trades require. The loss by death falls more heavily upon the whites, and from Matadi to Stanley Falls their loss is 50 percent.

The road is to be narrow-gauged, 29½-inch wide, and single track; and its length from Matadi to Stanley Pool about 270 miles. It is proposed to run two trains per week in each direction, and as there will only be a daily service, it will require two days to perform the journey from Matadi to Stanley Pool. The half-way halting station wil be at Kimpisi, with three other large stations, one at Loufou, Inkissi and Ntampa. There are to be five sections of little more than fifty miles each, with three halting places to each section for water and food.

The Estimates

for the construction of such a road in such a country as the Congo must have been made with precipitous haste, and based upon insufficient data. In the first place it was proposed to construct the road in four years, and I have already shown that, after more than three years, not one mile of the roadbed is prepared. In the next place the estimates for the cost of construction are based upon earth works, bridges and culverts, with iron superstructures, acqueducts of pressed beton, way ballasting and laying. For the first year the cost is estimated at francs 2,633,000; for the second year 4,434,000; for the third year 4,723,500; for the fourth year 4,790,000; making a total of 16,590,550 francs.

Estimates for salaries of surveyors, mechanics, engineers, clerks, instruments, engines, cars, water tanks, physician and medical stores, food, travelling expenses, contingencies ten per cent of the entire capital, bring the expenses up to 22,065,350 francs. The intercalary interest of 5 per cent, on the sums paid, during a avarage period of two years, upon a capital of 25,000,000 francs, and general contingencies 434,650 raise the expenses to the capital, 25,000,000 francs.

Even if these estimates were correct there is the vital question of the ability of the road to pay for itself. I know of no work, dealing along with the commerce of Africa, more unreliable and misleading than Mr. STANLEY's, "The Congo Free State." When he describes things and persons he displays the ability of an able correspondent. But the moment he attemps to deal with figures and trade, he becomes the veriest romancer. I cannot intrude upon the place I am permitted to occupy with this letter, a careful examination of the errors of Mr. STANLEY's estimates. I shall do that service later, but I must call attention to a few of his flights of imagination. "In my opinion," says Mr. STANLEY (Congo State, vol. II, page 355, English edition), "the ivory however, stands but fifth in rank among the natural products of the basin. The total value of the ivory supposed to be in existence in this region to day would but represent 170,000 tons of palm oil, or 30,000 tons of india-rubber. . . . At the same time, although limited, it is a valuable product, and as such will be an object of commerce. If 200 tusks arrived per week at Stanley Pool, or say £260,000 per annum, it would still require twenty-five years to destroy the elephant in the Congo basin. (vide page 356). Here the explorer has degenerated into the speculator, but what caputalists [sic] and business-men require are *facts*, not *fancies*. Now, what are the facts respecting the trade of Congo basin?

The *ivory* is the *first* article of commerce in the basin, and *rubber* the *second*. In fact, these are the only two articles of commerce exported from the Upper Congo. At present there are about 150 tons of ivory exported from the Upper Congo per annum, and each ton represents 100 elephants, or 15,000 elephants annually. Ivory brings in Europe about £800 per ton; 150 tons would bring £120,000, or about $600,000. About 30 tons of rubber are exported from the Upper Congo per annum; and it is dirty, poorly prepared, and often falsified. It brings in Europe about sixpence per pound, equal to £1,680, or $8,400. Or suppose, we allow that this inferior rubber would bring one shilling per pound, it would only amount to £3,360, or $168,000. This trade is not paying, and cannot pay for some time to come. So the total trade of the Upper River amounts to only £121,680 or $608,400

There are, however, other articles of commerce within the arms-length trade of the proposed Congo railway. But they are not yet placed in the market, nor will they be for many years to come, until the native is taught the gospel of compensated labour, and his wants increased.

But let us listen once more to Mr. STANLEY, the "Colonel MULBERRY SELLERS" of the Congo, and the chief advertising agent of a speculative king. "Supposing," says Mr. STANLEY (ibid. pp. 369–370), "a few factories were established on the Upper-Congo, a few at Isanghila, and a few at Manyanga, and judging from what is being done on the Lower-Congo, the following produce was shipped:

		£	Tons.
Isanghila	Groundnuts	370,000	25,000
Manyanga	"	370,000	25,000
Isanghila and Ma-nyanga	Palmoil	310,000	10,000
Stanley Pool &c.	Orchella Weed	450,000	10,000
"	Ivory	260,000	232
"	Hippo Teeth	11,200	20
Upper-Congo ...	Rubber	1,530,000	10,000
"	Skins	20,000	1,800
"	Palm Oil	1,240,000	40,000
"	Beeswax	5,000	50
"	Copal Gum	600,000	10,000
Over Lake Leo-pold II, and Matumba	Camwood	480,000	20,000
Kwa Mouth	Sesame Seed	20,800	4,000
	Total . . .	£5,667,000	156,102

"The tonnage thus adduced by the above estimate would be equal to 427½ tons per day, which would task the resources of such a railway. At one penny per ton per mile freight the gross revenue of the railway would be equal to £152,000, and if we estimate the revenue, derived from the freight of goods, going into the interior for commerce, State and missions, we may well conceive that the aggregate for up and down freight would amount to £300,000 per annum, exclusive of passengers."

Modern history records nothing equal to the speculations of Mr. STANLEY, who has heretofore been regarded as a practical man. And while I have an interest in the civilisation of Africa equal to any person's, I cannot be silent, or suffer to pass unchallenged statements calculated to mislead and deceive the friends of humanity and civilisation. Mr. STANLEY's speculations—for they are nothing else—concerning the Congo may be, in part, realised within the next fifty or seventy-five years, but they are not available for the present. His figures as regards the population, towns and areas of the Congo, are no more deserving of confidence than his calculations about the commerce of the country. It is not an agreeabl[e] task to have to say these things of a man whose valour, perseverance, sufferings and triomphs have sent a thril of admiration throughout the civilised world; but it is the stern duty of history to prevent error from being canonized instead of the truth, which must be written with an iron pen.

The plants of Mission stations and of tradinghouses and their steamers have already been or will be transported to the Upper Congo before the railway becomes a fact accomplished. By an organised industry for the preservation of Europeans, and the good of the natives, these Missions and tradinghouses will decr[e]ase the necessity of calling upon Europe for supplies; and the 40,000 native carriers in the zone, through which the railway is to pass, having once tasted the fruit of honest labour, will become suspicious and jealous of a railway, which would deprive them of those articles of European manufacture they now prize and enjoy. The result would become competition, and tradinghouses, which only receive goods every quarter, and make shipments in like periods of time, would find the transport system cheap enough and speedy enough to answer their business requirements. I examine all these questions knowing well that a successful financier, like a victorious soldier, must fight on both sides of his plans.

The projectors of the Congo Railway scheme have been too boastful and too profuse in their promises to the shareholders, and under these circumstances disappointment and confusion are sure to cover them, as heat follows light and the rising sun.

The Congo Railway ought to be built, and from the bottom of my heart I hope it will be. But capitalists and philantropists must remember what I have declared, that it cannot be built for less than 40,000,000 francs, nor in less than eight years. By skillful and practical management, and with all the machinery employed in the construction of European and American railroads, the time could be reduced by two or three years. Meanwhile Africa needs the blessing of a practical labor system which, while it adresses itself to the soul, will not ignore the body, its earthly temple; and, while inculcating spiritual truths, will not fail to teach the native the primal lesson of human history: *For in the sweat of thy face shalt thou eat thy bread.*

GEO. W. WILLIAMS.

Appendix 3

A Report upon the Congo-State and Country to the President of the Republic of the United States of America, by Colonel the Honorable Geo. W. Williams.

St. Paul de Loanda,
Province of Angola, (S. W. Africa).
October 14th 1890.

To the President of the Republic of the United States of America:

I have the honor to submit herewith a Report upon the condition of the State of Congo, and the country and people over which it claims jurisdiction.

During my interview with you at the Executi[ve] Mansion, Washington, D. C., Monday morning December 23d 1889, I promised to prepare for you a Memorandum of the International Law and sentimental reasons why the Government of the Republic of the United States should ratify the General Act of the Conference of Berlin, (1884–1885) recognizing *L'Etat Indépendant du Congo,* and assume certain obligations in regard to it, especially as to neutrality.

In an interview with the Honorable JOHN SHERMAN, Chairman of the Senate Committee on Foreign Relations, I learned that he entertained the same views as yourself, in regard to the danger of annulling the traditions of a century; of violation the Monroe Doctrine, and of approaching the stormy circle of European politics. The Senator seemed pleased that I was going to furnish a Memorandum on "l'Acte Général de la Conférence de Berlin," and promised to suspend action on the act until I had completed my investigations. Two days later I sailed for Europe, on my way to the Congo, (Southwest-Africa).

Upon my return to Brussels, early in January, I found the atmosphere about the Palace rather cool. Officials, who formerly greeted me cordially, now avoided me, and wrapped themselves in an impenetrable reserve. It had become known that I was going to visit the Congo, and every possible influence was exerted to turn me aside from my mission. An officer of the King's Household was dispatched to me for the purpose of persuading me not to visit the Congo. He dwelt upon the deadly character of the climate during the rainy seasons, the perils and hardships of travelling by caravans, and the heavy expenses of the voyage, which would cost, he said, £400 (Dollar 2,000). I simply replied, that I was going. — After this the King sent for me, and received me very cordially. I did not care to lead up to a conversation on the Congo, and consequently I strove to turn the conversation to other topics. But I soon saw that there was but one thing about which His Majesty cared to converse, and I made up my mind to allow him to do all the talking, as far as was possible. He said that STANLEY had told him the Congo would not be worth a shilling without a railway; that it was difficult to travel in the country, and more difficult to obtain wholesome food for white men; that he hoped I would postpone my visit to the Congo for at least five years; and that all necessary information would be furnished me in *Brussels*. In reply I told His Majesty that I was going to the Congo *now*, and would start within a few days. "Then you cannot go on the State-Steamers, and must rely upon the Mission-Steamers," responded His Majesty in an impatient tone of voice. I made no reply, but simply turned the conversation to the Anti-Slavery Conference of the Powers. At a convenient moment I took my leave of His Majesty and quitted the Palace. A young nobleman of Belgium with whom I had been on terms of good fellowship, and who knew all the political gossip of the Court, told me that Mr. HENRY S. SANFORD, an American citizen, who has resided in Belgium for twenty-five or thirty years, suspected one of two things in connection with my mission to the Congo, viz: that I came as the representative of an American company to open up trade and commerce in the Congo, or that I was the agent of his enemies in America who wished to prove the falsity of his statements in reference to the fertility of the country and the volume of trade.

I crossed the Channel to England on the night of the 21st day of January 1890, and arrived in London the following morning. I purchased my African travellers-outfit at the Army and Navy Store, and on the 28th of January I left for Liverpool, from which port I sailed for the Congo on the 30th of January, in the British and African Steam Navigation Co's steamer "Gaboon." I wrote you a brief letter from Liverpool, intimating the opposition my mission met with in Brussels.

The voyage from Liverpool to the capital of the State of Congo,

(Boma) occupied fifty three days; but I was afforded abundant time and opportunity of visiting all the important ports on the West Coast of the African Continent.

Permit me, at this point, to make a statement personal to my-self, but not irrelevant to this Report. I was among the very first of public men in America to espouse the cause of *l'Association Internationale du Congo*. I wrote a series of articles on African geography, during the winter of 1883–1884, in which I combated Portugal's claim to the Congo. In April 1884, I presented an argument before the Senate Committee on Foreign Relations, urging the passage of a resolution recognizing the flag of *l'Association Internationale du Congo*, as the flag of a friendly Government. The resolution passed on the 10th of April, and on the 22nd the` Secretary of State, the Honorable FREDERICK J. FRELINGHUYSEN, sent an order instructing the officers of the army and navy of the Republic to salute the flag of *l'Association Internationale du Congo* as the flag of a friendly Government.

Shortly after this I went to Belgium to place before the King certain plans for the perfection of the labor-system in the Congo; and they met the approbation both of the King and HENRY M. STANLEY. On the 21st of August 1889, I published an elaborate historical paper on the Congo; and a few weeks later, at the reunion of the *Anti-Slavery Leaders* at Boston, I offered a resolution, requesting the President of the Republic of the United States to accept the invitation of the King of the Belgians to be represented in an Anti-Slavery-Conference of the Powers of Europe, to unify action upon the land and sea looking towards the abatement of the slave-trade, around and upon the African Continent. Within a few days a representative was appointed, and I sailed for Europe to do whatever I could to promote the success of this notable Conference. I remained at Brussels two months.

Thus much to prove how deeply I have been interested in the success of the Congo State, the overthrow of the African Slave-Power, and the spread of civilization. I have never entertained any other than friendly feelings towards the King of the Belgians and his African State; and my report deals only with those matters *which have come under my personal observation*, or the truth of which has been established by the testimony of competent and veracious witnesses.

The establishment of a State in the Valley of the Congo is due to His Majesty Leopold II, King of the Belgians. On the 13th and 14th days of September 1876, he convened at his Palace at Brussels, a company of distinguished African travellers who represented Germany, Austria-Hungary, France, England, Italy, Russia and Belgium. The object of this Conference was to devise the best means of opening the Congo-country to commerce and civilization. On the 20th and 21st days of June 1877, another meeting was held at Brussels, when the Conference took definite shape, and *l'Association Internationale du Congo* was formed under the Presidency of the King of the Belgians. He employed HENRY M. STANLEY as his Chief-Agent to proceed to the Congo and secure the country as His Majesty's personal possession. MR. STANLEY was supposed to have made treaties with more than four hundred native Kings and Chiefs, by which they surrendered their rights to the soil. And yet many of these people declare that they never made a treaty with STANLEY, or any other white man; that their lands have been taken from them by force, and that they suffer the greatest wrongs at the hands of the Belgians. I have never met a chief or tribe or native, man, woman or child, from Banana, the mouth of the Congo River, to Stanley-Falls at its headwaters, who expressed any other sentiment towards the Congo State than that of hatred, deeply rooted in an abiding sense of injury, injustice and oppression. In Russia, Creta and Ireland the constituted authorities have some support from among the people; but in the Congo State there is not one solitary native who would put out his hand to aid the Congo State Government.

Although the majority of the treaties alleged to have been made by Mr. STANLEY, were only witnessed by his servantboy "Dualla," they were accepted as genuine in Europe and America. Having possessed itself of a vast tract of land in the Congo, *l'Association Internationale du Congo*, of which the King of the Belgians was President and treasurer, now sought to obtain recognition in Europe. Failing to secure the countenance of a single Power, the *Association* appealed to the Republic of the United States of America. Its representative was the Hon. HENRY S. SANFORD, a citizen of the United States, who had resided in Belgium for twenty-five or thirty years. Mr. SANFORD had been many years in the diplomatic service, and was well qualified for this delicate mission. He was fortunate to find at Washington a President who was the son of a Baptist clergyman, whose fame chiefly arose from his extreme anti-slavery sentiments and work for the slave in ante-bellum days. Moreover, the Secretary of State was the son of one of the earliest and most eminent of the Presidents of the American Colonization Society. Mr. SANFORD'S course was plain, he appealed to American sentiment and commercial interest; and the manner in which the flag of the *Association* was recognized, I have already described.

Germany and France now saw that it was the moment to call for a Conference of European Powers, engaged in the unseemly scramble for commerce upon the African Continent. But, after several private conferences between Germany and France, it was decided to invite the

Republic of the United States of America on account of its supposed relations to Liberia; and at length the programme was so extended as to include all the Great-Powers and the Scandinavian States. The Republic of the United States received an invitation to join the Congo Conference at Berlin on the 10th of October, 1884, presented by Baron VON ALVENSLEBEN, Envoy Extraordinary and Minister Plenipotentiary of His Majesty the Emperor of Germany. The invitation declared that "the Governments of Germany and France are of opinion, that it would be well to form an agreement on the following principles:

1st. Freedom of commerce in the basin and the mouths of the Congo;

2nd. Application to the Congo and the Niger of the principles adopted by the Vienna Congres, with a view to sanctioning free navigation on several international rivers, which principles were afterwards applied to the Danube;

3rd. Definition of the formalities to be observed, in order that new occupations on the coast of Africa may be considered effective.["]

On the 17th of October Mr. FRELINGHUYSEN, Secretary of State, adressed a reply to Baron VON ALVENSLEBEN's note of invitation, and said:

"The Government of the United States views in this announcement and invitation an expression of the wish of the German Government to recognize the importance of the unimpeded traffic of the Congo Valley and the West Coast of Africa, and to secure its free enjoyment to all countries. This Government, entertaining the same views, to which it has given effect by its recognition of the flag of the *International Association of the Congo,* will have pleasure in accepting the invitation of His Imperial Majesty's Government, and will instruct the representative of the United States at Berlin to take part in the proposed Conference, on the understanding (so far as this Government is concerned) that the business to be brought before the Conference is to be limited to the three heads mentioned in your note, dealing solely with the commercial interests of the Congo region and of Western Africa, and that while taking cognizance of such establishment of limits to international territorial claims in that region as may be brought before it as matters of fact, the Conference is itself not to assume to decide such questions. The object of the Conference being simply discussion and accord, the Government of the United States, in taking part therein, reserves the right to decline to accept the conclusions of the Conference."

This then was a clear statement of the views and attitude of the Government of the Republic of the United States in regard to the proposed Conference of Berlin upon Congo and West African affairs.

The Secretary of State never altered his views or position from first to last; and he never permitted his Government to become a party to a scheme of seizing and dividing the Congo-country among certain European Powers, one of the foulest crimes of modern diplomatic history! One plenipotentiary told me that when he went to a certain European Statesman, and asked that his Government be given more territory, this Chairman of the Committee on "Distribution" exclaimed: "I have given away all the territory that is on the map!" This was not in reference to the Congo-State alone, for there is the French Congo and the Portuguese Congo as well; and the amount of territory passed upon at Berlin was 2,400,000 square miles.

The Conference met at Berlin on the 15th of November 1884, and , under the Presidency of Prince BISMARCK, continued in session, excepting a few adjournments, until the 26th February 1885; and after signing the General Act, the august Conference adjourned.

L'Etat Indépendent du Congo was created and became the successor of *l'Association Internationale du Congo*. The King of the Belgians was now requested, or rather became the natural chief of the new State, as he had been of the *Association;* but there was a constitutional obstacle in the way of his Majesty assuming the legal headship of this African State. Article LXII (62) of the Belgian Constitution provides,—"The King cannot be at the same time chief of another State, without the consent of the two Chambers. Neither of the two Chambres can discuss this subject unless two-thirds at last of the members composing it be present, and the resolutions can only be passed providing it is supported by two-thirds of the votes." I translate and insert here the record of the proceeding by which LEOPOLD II became the Sovereign of the Congo State. "The Belgian Legislative Chamber, by a resolution, adopted in the Chamber of Representatives the 28th of April 1885, and in the Senate April 30th 1885, authorized His Majesty LEOPOLD II, King of the Belgians, to become the Chief of another State, in conformity with article 62 of the Belgian Constitution." The resolution is as follows: "His Majesty LEOPOLD II, King of the Belgians, is authorized to become the Chief of the State founded in Africa by *l'Association Internationale du Congo*. The union between Belgium and the new State shall remain exclusively personal."

On the 1st of August 1885, His Majesty notified the Powers that the possessions of *l'Association Internationale du Congo* would in the future constitute *l'Etat Indépendant du Congo;* that he had assumed, in accord with the *Association,* the title of "Soverain de l'État Indépendant du Congo;" that the relation between Belgium and this State was exclusively personal, and that it was to remain perpetually neutral.

On the 30th of October 1885, His Majesty, as Sovereign of the Congo State, issued a Decree creating three Departments for his new State Government, and naming three chiefs, 1st *Department of Foreign Affairs, including Justice,* with three Bureaux: *a.* Foreign Affairs, *b.* Postal and Maritime, *c.* Judicial affairs; 2nd *Department of Finance; a.* General taxes, *b.* Land Department, *c.* Pay and Auditor's Department; 3rd *Departement* [sic] *of Interior: a.* Administration, *b.* Roads and communications, *c.* Army and Navy.

The three heads of departments constituted a council, under the Presidency of the Sovereign, who is the absolute Ruler. His councelors may recommend but can never share his authority. He makes all the laws under the title of "Decrees," and from his decisions there is no appeal. His Government is denominated as local, the European portion of the Congo-State.

In the Congo there is a Governor-General, in charge of the State, who issues such laws as he feels are necessary under the title of *"ordonnances,"* but except they are reïssued as a "Decree" by the Sovereign within six months, they are *null and void.* There are an Inspector-General, Secretary-General, Procurer-General, Finance-General, Judges and Commissaires of Districts. There are postmasters, transport-officers and clerks of various kinds.

A small portion of the country, claimed by the *Independant State of Congo,* is divided into Military Districts; the rest is *dominated* by natives whose lawful possession it is. There are eleven Military Districts, viz: 1. Banana, 2. Boma, 3. Matadi, 4. Manyanga, 5. Lukunga, 6. Leopoldville, 7. The Kassai River, 8. Bangala, 9. Basoko, 10. Lumani, 11. Stanley Falls. There are two "Military and Commercial Expeditions" on the Itimberi and Welle Rivers, and a third has just started.

Each one of these military districts is commanded by an officer of the Belgian Army, supported by other officers and non-commissioned officers. The "Commissaire of District" is of one of three classes, and needs not always be an army officer, for he deals with civil affairs only. All disputes and native *palavers* are settled by the military commander, and sometimes by the commissaire of the district, and their decision is final. When an offence has been committed against the State, the native may be fined, emprisoned or enslaved. In the Upper-Congo the State officials generally demand slaves for settling natives palavers. They promise to liberate these people after seven years service. As far as I have been able to investigate, this system of Government is unjust, capricious and absolutely cruel. There is scarcely one percent of the State officials, military and civil, who know the native language; and frequently the interpreter, an uneducated negro from Zanzibar or the

East-Coast, knows little French, and puts questions indistinctly, or translates the testimony of the natives indifferently. I have seen this in the Supreme Court at Boma also. I called the attention of the Clerk of the Court to the poor French of the Interpreter, and he told me that, if that were all, it would not be so bad; but that the fellow was a *notorious liar* into the bargain! And yet upon this stammering patois hangs the bondage or liberty, the peace and property of many a native.

In addition to these military districts there are more than fifty (50) posts of from two to ten black soldiers in the Upper-Congo. They have no white commissioned officer, and act to suit their own fancy. They receive no supplies from the State, and are expected to levy tribute upon the natives. They seize fish, goats, fowls, eggs, vegetables &c. for their nourishment; and when the natives demur or refuse to be "spoiled," these black pirates burn their villages and confiscate their property. I have been an unwilling and mournfull witness to these atrocities. It is almost impossible for a traveller to buy food, [on] account [of] the ravages committed by these buccaneers of the State of Congo, who are guilty of murder, arson and robbery. Often the natives move their towns miles away rather than submit to the indignities inflicted by an unfeeling mercenary soldiery.

The entire military force of the State of Congo is less than three-thousand (3,000) men, and hundred of miles of the country is without a single soldier. In this country, distitute of a military police and semblance of constituted authority, the most revolting crimes are committed by the natives. They practice the most barbarous religious and funeral rites; they torture, murder and eat each other. Against these shocking crimes the State puts forth no effort; indeed it systematically abandons thousands of victims to the slaughter every year. Human hands and feet and limbs, smoked and dried, are offered and exposed for sale in many of the native village markets.

From the mouth of the Loumami-River to Stanley-Falls there are thirteen armed Arab camps; and in them I have seen many skulls of murdered slaves pendant from poles and over these camps floating their blood-red flag. I saw nowhere the Congo-State flag, and I know that it would be torn down if it were displayed among these ivory and slave raiders. Here the State has no authority, can redress no wrong, protect no life or property.

The tribes of the Congo are numerous and interesting people, and may be divided as follows: 1. The Mussurongo are on the Lower Congo River; 2. The Ki-Congo inhabit the Cataract Region; 3. The Ki-Têke or Batike people reside around Stanley-Pool and up as far as the mouth of the Kwa River; 4. Ki Bangi or Bobangi people extend from the mouth of the Kwa River to the mouth of the Mobangi River; 5. The Irebu (Kilolo?) or Balolo people occupy the banks of the Lulonga, Ruki and Ikelemba rivers; 6. The Lulanga, Bangala and Mekiba people speak the Bangala language; 7. The Upoto, N'Dobbe, Ebunda, Bumba and Jambinga people speak the Langa-Langa language, as far as the Itimberi River; 8. The Jalulema language is spoken as far as Basoko; 9. The Wakumu and Wakenia languages are spoken from Basoko to Stanley-Falls.

These various peoples are differentiated by their environs and occupations. In the Lower Congo, where the natives have been in contact with Europeans for centuries, felt the shock of the slave-trade and the degrading influence of rum, they are diminutive in form, obsequious, deceitful, untrustworthy, unmanly and unreliable. Their villages are the abodes of wretchedness, misery and common vice. Their huts, poorly constructed of bad material, and their uncleanness breed the most pestilential diseases, which often devastate whole communities of these hapless victims of their own filth.

Passing from the coast inland I found a slight improvement, a stronger and more active people, in the Cataract Region; and yet these pastoral people are surely falling under the destructive influence of poisonous liquor. Under the effect of this deadly liquor I found the old people looking older, and the young men weary and prematurely decaying; and villages, formerly the scenes of content and activity, at present rent by brawling disorders.

At Stanley-Pool, where the natives cannot obtain liquor, I found them an industrious and prosperous people. They are fishermen and traders, and live in neat and comfortable villages. And as I continued my journey up the river, I noticed the native type improving in feature, size, complexion and even in character. Among the people around Bolobo, Bangala and Equator I beheld the most splendid types of physical manhood I had seen in any land or among any people I have travelled; I found them brave, frank and generous; but how long they will be able to keep this character if rum is once introduced among them, I cannot say. They have only been in contact with the white men for a few years, and thus far they are eager for trade, industrious and peaceable. And with practical missionary work, or industrialism, these people would soon become civilized.

From Iringi until some distance above Upoto, the natives are in a deep state of degradation. Their villages are built in circular form of grass and small bamboopoles, and their food is scanty and almost entirely vegetable. They suffer from cutaneous diseases; their eyes are jaundiced, and by constant intermarriage heartdisease is a tribal affliction. The women wear nothing but a string of beads around their loins, and the loss of life among infants is great, from lack of proper nursing and nourishment. The faces and bodies of these people are covered with the most revolting looking scares [scars] made with sharp knives. There is not one half square inch of space upon the face that is not cut and scar[r]ed; and often a piece of Ivory or Iron is passed through a hole in the upper lip or nose, and is worne as an ornament. Holes are made in the ears large enough to run an ordinary walking stick through, and large pieces of rope tied in them. The arms and breast are cut and tattooed, and around the neck and ankles are worn large brass and iron rings. These people practise human sacrifices; and I have examined the skulls of their victims in their villages, where they display them with an almost f[ie]ndish pleasure. From the mouth of the Aruwimi to the mouth of the Lumani river, there is quite a different people from those I had previously met with. They were a people without a country or a village. I called them Water-gypsies, for they live in large boats with their families. They fish and trade along the river with the natives. They are a strong, healthy and contented people, taking pleasure in their work, and with spirit to fight, when assailed by the more warlike tribes inhabiting the rivertowns.

I have noticed that wherever the African has sufficient food and labor, he presents a splendid type of man, tall, well and closely knit, muscular, agil[e] and cheerful. He is also less cruel and superstitious.

I found a strange and striking variety of types. I have had among my carriers perfect types of the North-American Indian, the flat head, broad chin, large eyes, thin lips and wide mouth. Their hair is long, reaching below their shoulders, and which they always kcep plaited in long braids. Their voice is shrill and far-reaching, and they run with the same skill and speed of the Indians, I have served against in Southwestern and Western America and Mexico.

I have come across the Japanese type, the eyes, head, face and size of body, identical with those of our eastern neighbours. I have seen tribes, destitute of every negroid characteristic, being light copper-color, with pronounced European features, a gentle and generous people.

As to the population in the Valley of the Congo, I would say it is many millions less than the figures furnished by H. M. STANLEY or the State of Congo. These figures give a population of from 49,000,000 to 51,000,000, while I give it as my honest and candid judgment that there are not more than 15,000,000 people in the entire country. I have travelled over the same route Mr. STANLEY took, and stopped at the same towns. I had the same or as good facilities for finding out the population, and with his book in my hand I endeavoured to test his figures. First of all it must be understood that the towns are numerous but thinly populated; and where he found ten thousand, (10,000) I found only 4,000 people, and so on in proportion.

Many of the towns, mentioned in his book on the Congo, have been moved away or destroyed by war or small pox epid[e]mic. Nothing is so deceptive as estimating a population in a heathen country. The villages are often built along the river bank for miles, with small spaces between them. To see the people along the fronts of their villages creates the impression that the population is numerous; but when you begin your investigation you will find two hundred people in one village, one hundred and fifty in another, four hundred in another, and so on. In three miles of villages you may find two thousand (2,000) souls. Nothing concerning Africa is so constantly overestimated and exagerated as its population, and I must warn lexicographers and map-makers that the population of Africa, as set down at 250,000,000, is pure and simple fiction. I do not believe it is 100,000,000, and no one will even know, untill we shall be able to have a census by the European Powers occupying territory upon the African Continent, and then it will only be approximate. From Banana to Boma the Congo-country is composed of Islands, available for rice, coffee, and grazing; and from Boma to Matadi it is absolutely sterile. From Matadi to Leopoldville — the Cataract Region — there is but little good soil, and the vegetable life is small and precarious. Around Stanley-Pool there is some fertile land, and it is cultivated by the natives to some extent. From the Pool through the Channel, — as I have decided to call it, — three days steaming, the country is perfectly barren. From the mouth of the Pool to the mouth of the Kassaï River the banks are steep and of white clay, and the channel narrow, through which rushes a current at 4 knots an hour. At the mouth of the Kassaï the high bluffs give way to low lands, fertile, open, green, wide and beautiful. At Bolobo and Lokolela, tobacco, beans, corn-manioc, &c. are raised in large quantities. On the Equator and at Bangala, nearly every vegetable found in Europe can be grown. The country continues fairly good until the Lumani river, and from thence to the seventh cataract (Stanley-Falls) it is poor. The Congo-country has been overestimated and its fertility exagerated by the advertising agents of persons who wished to promote financial schemes. The commerce of the Congo has always been misrepresented. There are only two articles exported from the Upper-Congo, Ivory and Rubber, and these only in small quantities. I have no doubt but that many other valuable products of the country could be exported, and would find a ready market; but the native must be taught,—and he is a very conservative individual,—to bring other things to the white trader. And if it require labor to put the new products before the trader, it will be a long time before it will be forth-coming.

There are five houses of the Dutch Trading Company between Stanley-Pool and Stanley-Falls; the Belgians have five; the French three. All the goods and supplies for trading purposes, which these Companies use, are carried from Matadi and Loango, two hundrd and seventy and three hundred miles respectively, on the heads of natives. While it is true that the native does not care to work, that custom has made the African woman the producer while the man is the consumer, it should not be forgotten that within ten years or more seventy five thousand (75,000) blacks are engaged in the transport-system. This is one of the brightest and most significant pages in African history, and deserves our admiration and praise. These men make from three to four trips a year, 810 to 1,080 miles, and carry from 65 to 80 pounds burden. They are faithful and reliable, and without their service no trade could be conduced upon the Upper-Congo; neither missionary nor trader could exist. But while the transport system is admirable and adequate, it is also costly. Every load costs from £1- to £1.10.- from Matadi to the Pool, and from Loango to Brazzaville. The carriers take up to the Pool bales of cloth, salt, powder, brass rods, beads, and canned food for the European traders and missionaries. They carry back to the Coast ivory and rubber. The transport is the great burden to commerce and missions at present, for it costs from ten to fifteen percent of the cost-price of goods to get them from the Coast to the Upper-Congo River. After all that is said about the fertility of African soil there is very little at present that an European can rely upon as food. He must import lard, butter, sardines, ham, sausages, corned-beef, tea, coffee, sugar, condensed milk, pickles, peaches, pears, strawberries, salt, pepper, crackers, flour, cheese, rice, macaroni, tapioca, spices &c. Flour, rice and sugar are heavy articles, and cost the consumer dearly. In fact all the articles I have enumerated have to be packed securely and are consequently bulky.

Last year the State of Congo sent 35,000 loads from Matadi to Leopoldville across the Cataract Region. It is hoped that the Congo-railway will remedy the difficulties of the transport-system; but this road is not yet built, nor will it be for some eight years to come. Even when completed it will not pay for years, untill the native brings into the market some thing else besides Ivory and Rubber.

There must be organized industrialism by which cotton, rice, sugar, tobacco, coffee &c. can be cultivated for export.

In addition to the burdens of the transport system, the Congo-State has unwisely imposed burdensome taxes and duties upon the produce exported from the Congo. These duty on ivory of every quality is 2,000 francs = £80-/- per ton, enough to destroy the trade, and drive the trading companies into bankruptcy. The fact is, *the State of Congo is engaged in trade,* and while it taxes other traders exempts itself from all financial burdens, in direct violation of the provisions of the General-Act of the Conference of Berlin.

Timber is taxed to such an extent that a missionary cannot cut a stick three feet long without securing written permission, and even then a tax must be paid. The State steadfastly refuses to give a clear title to land; and every trader and missionary may be ousted by the railway company under the law of expropriation. Every servant, carrier and laborer, of whatsoever description, is taxed, and thus the State represses the spirit of progress and retards the development of the country. It is in a state of chronic controversy with the traders, and the most unfriendly relations subsist between them. No one has a voice in the Government. A carefully organized system of import-taxes has been established and goes into effect in Oct. 1890. Nothing in the history of political economy and tariff-legislation can equal these laws for their inequality, injustice and repressive character.

The State recruits its soldiers and employs its laborers on the East and West-coast of Africa; to transport them from the former coast costs £10 = $50 per capita, and to bring them from the latter coast costs £1 to £1. 10/- = $5 to $7.

The soldiers serve three years, the workmen one year; and the loss by desertion, sickness, death and reshipment is about £12,000 = $60,000 per annum. The natives of the Congo serve in the transport corps because there are no Belgians to cruelly treat them; but they will not enter the service of te State. Kindness, firmness and justice to the natives would soon secure a large and reliable native labor force. But violence and injustice drive these poor children of nature away from the white man. Emigration cannot be invited to the Congo for a quarter of a century, and then only educated blacks from the Southern United States, who have health, courage, morals and means. They must come only in small companies, not as laborers, but as landed proprietors. One hundred families in ten years would be quite enough and not for twenty five years yet. *White labor can never hope to get a foot-hold here.*

The climate is too severe for northern people. There are the dry and the rainy season in the Lower-Congo, but above the Equator there is no dry, no rainy season; it rains at intervals all the time. I rather enjoyed the climate of the Equator more than the West-Africa climate. The climate above the Lumani and at Stanley-Falls is the severest I experienced. I

have recorded a change of thirty degrees in the mercury of my ther-
mometre at Stanley-Falls in one day of sixteen hours; and I have noted
frequent changes of fifteen degrees. The rains fall frequently and the
mists from the Falls are very heavy morning and evening. I found the
five white men residing there either sick or convalescent.

Although the State of Congo promised the Powers of Europe to use
all its abilities to suppress the slave-trade, the traffic goes on beneath its
flag and upon its territory. At Stanley-Falls slaves were offered to me in
broad day-light; and at night I discovered canoe loads of slaves, bound
strongly together. When I complained of this I was told by the "Resident" of the Congo-State that he had no power to prevent it, which is
quite true, for he had a garrison of thirty men of whom only seventeen
were effectives.

But the State not only suffers the trade in slaves to continue, *it buys
the slaves of natives*, and pays to its military officers £3-/- per capita for
every able-bodied slave he procures. Every military post in the Upper-
Congo thus becomes a slave-market; the native is encouraged to sell
slaves by the State, which is always ready to buy them. This buying of
slaves is called "redemption," and it is said that after seven years the
slave may have his liberty. But it is my opinion that these hapless
creatures are the perpetual slaves of the State of Congo.

After thirteen years of occupation by the International Association
and State of Congo, no map has been made of the Upper-Congo River;
no school has been erected; no hospital founded and nothing contributed to science or geography. At first the Government was international in character, but of late years it has degenerated into a narrow
Belgian Colony, *with a determined purpose to drive all other nations
out of the Congo that are now represented by trade*. In a letter of
instructions to the representative of the Government of the Republic of
the United States at Berlin, the Secretary of State wrote on the 17th of
October 1884: "As far as the administration of the Congo-Valley is
concerned, this Government has shown its preference for a neutral
control, such as is promised by the Free-States of the Congo, the
nuclens of which has been already created through the organized efforts
of the International Association. Whether the approaching Conference
can give further shape and scope to this project of creating a great State
in the heart of Western Africa, whose organization and administration
shall afford a guarantee that it is to be held for all time, as it were, in trust
for the benefit of all peoples, remains to be seen."

This singularly lucid statement carries with it a prophetic influence,
and I clearly see how the promises and pledges of the Association and
State have been violated. It would be vain to endeavour to hide the fact

that the Congo-State is a Belgian colony as much as the Cape of Good Hope is an English Colony. The difference is that every body knew when England went to the Cape she intended to built a colony that should wear the British colonial stamp. Belgians invited the world to enjoy free-trade in the Congo, and now, after Englishmen, Frenchmen, Portuguese and Dutch have invested thousands of pounds in the venture, *they are to be taxed to death* by a purely Belgian Colonial Government. The mask is cast off and every provision of the General Act of the Conference of Berlin has been violated; and the written and sealed pledge made to the Government of the Republic of the United States, that no import- or export-duties would be levied, has long since been torn up and given to the winds. Please see Senate Executive Document No. 196, p. p. 348 and 355–357.

There is one ray of hope for the Congo, and that is in the character of the Christian Missions.

No foreign missionary field was ever so quickly occupied by Christian workers as the Congo. The American Baptist Missionary Union has eight stations, the English Baptists seven, and the Congo Bololo Mission three; Catholic missions three, one just abandoned, which made four, three Bishop-Taylor-missions, one "faithcure," "Simpson mission," two Swedish missions, twenty-seven (27) in all. Some of them are eminently useful, and several of them are conspic[u]ously helpless. The missionaries have great influence with the natives, and they go and come among the fiercest cannibalistic tribes without fear of being molested. Whenever the friends at home, who support and regulate these missions, will add an industrial feature to each one of them, their efficiency will be increased tenfold.

My travels extended from the mouth of the Congo at Banana, where it empties into the South Atlantic, to its headwaters at the Seventh Cataract, at Stanley-Falls; and from Brazzaville, on Stanley-Pool, to the South Atlantic Ocean at Loango, I passed through the French-Congo, via Comba, Bouenza and Loudima. In four months, or in one hundred and twenty five days I travelled 3,266 miles, passing from Southwestern Africa to East Central Africa, and back to the sea. I camped in the bushes seventy-six times, and on other occasions received hospitilaty of traders, missionaries and natives. Of my eighty-five natives I lost not a life, although we sometimes suffered from fatigue, hunger and heat.

Although America has no commercial interests in the Congo it was the Government of the Republic of the United States which introduced this African Government into the sisterhood of States. It was the American Republic which stood sponsor to this young State, which has disappointed the most glowing hopes of its most ardent friends and most zealous promoters. Whatever the Government of the Republic of the United States did for the Independent State of Congo, was inspired and guided by noble and unselfish motives. And whatever it refrains from doing, will be on account of its elevated sentiments of humanity, and its sense of the sacredness of agreements and compacts, in their letter and spirit. The people of the United States of America have a just right to know *the truth,* the *whole truth* and *nothing but the truth,* respecting the Independant State of Congo, an absolute monarchy, an oppressive and cruel Government, an exclusive Belgian colony, now tottering to its fall. I indulge the hope that when a new Government shall rise upon the ruins of the old, it will be simple, not complicated; local, not European; international, not national; just, not cruel; and, casting its shield alike over black and white, trader and missionary, endure for centuries.

GEO. W. WILLIAMS.

A Note on the Sources

In the Introduction I indicated some of the difficulties in locating manuscripts and other materials bearing on the life of George Washington Williams. In the notes I have provided details regarding the nature, extent, and location of specific sources. Consequently, here I shall only briefly point to the principal relevant manuscript and printed sources and indicate the ways that the secondary literature has taken notice of Williams.

The early life of Williams is difficult to trace. He was barely literate until he was in his early twenties. The only manuscripts in which he is mentioned by name before he was twenty are the decennial census records for 1850 and 1860. The first surviving document written by him is the letter seeking admission to Howard University, and the second is his commencement oration at the Newton Theological Institution. These documents, along with other important materials, are respectively at the Moorland-Spingarn Research Center at Howard University and the library of the Andover Newton Theological School. The records of Williams's service in the army during the Civil War must be used with caution since he served under an assumed name, presumably Charles Steward or William Steward. The record of his postwar service in the United States Army may be conveniently consulted in "Records Relating to the Regular Army, Registers of Enlistments, 1798–1914," Record Group 94, National Archives.

For the years after Williams became more active in religious, civic, and political affairs—in the District of Columbia in 1875 and in Ohio from 1876 to 1881—manuscript collections are generally more helpful. There are letters from prominent Americans to Williams, which he printed in various issues of *The Commoner* in September and October 1875. For this period there are letters from Williams in the Longfellow Papers at the Houghton Library of Harvard University, in the Rutherford B. Hayes Papers at the Hayes Library, in the John P. Green Papers at the Western Reserve Historical Society, and in the William Howard Taft Papers at the Library of Congress.

From the time that Williams began to write history, he was more active as a correspondent. There are Williams letters in the office of the Adjutant General, Record Group 94, National Archives; in the George Bancroft Papers and the George F. Hoar Papers at the Massachusetts Historical Society; in the Society Archives of the American Antiquarian Society; and in the Alexander Crummell Letters at the Schomburg Center for Research in Black Culture. This is the period in which he wrote several letters to his wife, Sarah. These were in the Henry P. Slaughter Collection, and I took notes from them when they were in Slaughter's possession. They were lost before the collection went to Atlanta University in 1947. I refer to them in the notes as Williams Papers.

For the later years there is an abundance of Williams letters, as well as other materials bearing on his appointment as United States minister to Haiti, in the Williams File, Box 103, in the General Records of the Department of State, "Applications and Recommendations for Public Office, 1797–1901," Record Group 59, National Archives. There are also Williams letters in the Benjamin Harrison Papers, the Grover Cleveland papers, and the Robert H. Terrell Papers at the Library of Congress; in the Lee and Shepard Papers at the American Antiquarian Society; in the Cable Collection at Tulane University; in the Henry S. Sanford Papers in Sanford, Florida; in the Collis P. Huntington Papers at the George Arents Library of Syracuse University; and in the William Mackinnon Papers at the School of Oriental and African Studies in London. Papers dealing with various aspects of Williams's activities in the final years of his life include the Huntington Papers; the Mackinnon Papers; correspondence in the British Foreign Office, 1889–91, at the Public Record Office; the George Grenfell Diary and Letters at the Baptist Missionary Society in London; and the Royal Archives in Brussels.

When Williams was in the Ohio General Assembly, his activities were reflected in various official records. Most important is the *Journal of the House of Representatives of the State of Ohio for the Regular Session of the Sixty-Fourth General Assembly*, 1880, and for the *Adjourned Session*, 1881. Regarding his activities in the Grand Army of the Republic, see George H. Thomas Post No. 13, *Proceedings of a Camp Fire*, and T. D. McGillicuddy, *Proceedings of the Annual and Semi-Annual Encampments of the Department of Ohio, Grand Army of the Republic* (Columbus, 1912). The fate of Williams's effort to secure a national monument to Negro veterans in the Civil War can be followed in the *Congressional Record, Forty-Ninth Congress, Second Session,* vol. 18 (Washington, D. C., 1887), and the *Fiftieth Congress, First Session,* vol. 19 (Washington, D. C., 1888).

Newspapers are an invaluable source in studying the career of Williams. He first appeared in the press in a letter in the *New National Era* in 1874. From that point on, items by or about Williams appear in the Afro-American press, including his *Commoner,* New York *Globe,* New York *Freeman,* Huntsville *Gazette,* Cleveland *Gazette,* Boston *Advocate,* Washington *Bee, People's Advocate,* and Indianapolis *World.* He received considerable attention in the predominantly white daily press, including the Boston *Evening Transcript,* Boston *Herald,* Washington *National Republican,* Cincinnati *Commercial,* Cincinnati *Enquirer,* Cincinnati *Daily Gazette,* Columbus *Dispatch,* Ohio *State Journal,* Worcester *Telegram,* New York *Sun,* New York *Daily Tribune,* New York *Times,* London *Times,* and the West Lancashire *Evening Gazette.*

Several works are important in providing context as well as specific information on Williams. Notable in this regard are Wendell P. Dabney, *Cincinnati's Colored Citizens, Historical, Sociological, and Biographical* (Cincinnati, 1926); John Daniels, *In Freedom's Birthplace: A Study of Boston Negroes* (Boston, 1914); David Gerber, *Black Ohio and the Color Line, 1860–1915* (Urbana, Ill., 1976); John P. Green, *Facts Stranger than Fiction: Seventy-Five Years of a Busy Life* (Cleveland, 1920); Sir Harry Johnston, *George Grenfell and the Congo* (London, 1908); and William J. Simmons, *Men of Mark: Eminent, Progressive, and Rising* (Cleveland, 1887).

In recent years scholars have accorded greater recognition to the work of Williams, especially his African journey. Examples of this are S. J. S. Cookey, *Britain and the Congo Question, 1885–1913* (London, 1968); Roger Anstey, *King Leopold's Legacy: The Congo under Belgian Rule, 1908–1960* (London, 1966); François Bontinck, *Aux origines de l'Etat Indépendant du Congo: Documents tirés d'archives Américaines* (Louvain, 1966); David Lagergren, *Mission and State in the Congo* (Uppsala, 1970); Edmund D. Morel, *King Leopold's Rule in Africa* (London, 1904); Paul McStallworth, "The United States and the Congo Question, 1884–1914" (unpublished Ph. D. dissertation, Ohio State University, 1954); William K. Parmenter, "The Congo and its Critics, 1880–1913" (unpublished Ph. D. dissertation, Harvard University, 1952); Ruth Slade, *King Leopold's Congo* (London, 1962); and Jean Stengers, *Rapport sur les dossiers, "Reprise du Congo par la Belgique"* et *"Dossier économique,"* Institut Royal Colonial Belge, *Bulletin des Séances,* XXIV (Brussels, 1953).

Notes

(George Washington Williams is abbreviated here as GWW)

Chapter 1

1. Daniel Rupp, *The History and Topography of Dauphin, Cumberland, Franklin, Bedford, Adams, and Perry Counties* . . . (Lancaster, 1846), p. 508.

2. Butler v. Delaplaine, 7S and R, 378, in Helen T. Catterall (ed.), *Judicial Cases Concerning American Slavery and the Negro*, 5 vols. (Washington, D.C., 1926–37), 4:279.

3. Winona Garbrick, ed., *The Kernel of Greatness: An Informal Bicentennial History of Bedford County* (State College, Pa., 1971), p. 76.

4. The only known account of the life of Thomas Williams is in a letter that his son wrote many years later. See GWW to General O.O. Howard, March 1, 1869, in the Archives of Howard University, Moorland-Spingarn Research Center, Howard University.

5. Population Schedules of the Seventh Census of the United States, 1850, Pennsylvania, Bedford County, National Archives and Records Service.

6. GWW to Howard, March 1, 1869; and Population Schedules of the Seventh Census, Bedford County, National Archives and Records Service.

7. Population Schedules of the Eighth Census of the United States, 1860, Pennsylvania, Lawrence County, National Archives and Records Service.

8. GWW to Howard, March 1, 1869. See also Archer Butler Hulbert, *The Great American Canals* (Cleveland, 1904), pp. 169-251.

9. GWW to Howard, March 1, 1869.

10. Population Schedules of the Eighth Census, Lawrence County.

11. GWW to Howard, March 1, 1869. When he enlisted in the regular army in 1867, he gave his occupation as a barber. See his Certificate of Disability for Discharge, September 4, 1868, United States Army, Headquarters, Department of the Missouri, National Archives, Record Group 94.

12. GWW to Howard, March 1, 1869.

13. Aristides [GWW], "The Last Campaign of the War," Cincinnati *Commercial*, February 10, 1877. GWW used the pseudonym "Aristides" when writing for the *Commercial*.

14. Record and Pension Office, 572 820, Case of George W. Williams, deceased, January 13, 1900, National Archives, Record Group 94.

15. Physical descriptions made by persons unfamiliar with or indifferent to the wide range of differences among Negro Americans may be wholly unreliable, especially when one is described as "complexion black, hair black, eyes black."

There were many variations in the description of GWW's physical appearance. In his military discharge papers in 1868, he was described as having a light, mulatto complexion and blue eyes. Certificate of Disability for Discharge, July 27, 1868, U.S. Pension Office, National Archives, Record Group 15. In a passport application of June 30, 1884, he was described as having a dark complexion with dark hazel eyes. Passport Application No. 12282, Department of State, National Archives, Record Group 59. Elsewhere he was described as "a man of large mould, standing about six feet high and weighing one hundred and eighty to two hundred pounds." William J. Simmons, _Men of Mark: Eminent, Progressive and Rising_ (Cleveland, 1887), p. 371. I believe the description in the military discharge papers is closest to the truth.

16. Case of George W. Williams (see note 13 above).

17. All information about the possible aliases of GWW is in Case of George W. Williams (see note 13 above).

18. Ibid.

19. GWW to Howard, March 1, 1869.

20. Ibid. For a vivid but impersonal account of the battle in which GWW was wounded, see his _History of the Negro Troops in the War of the Rebellion, 1861–1865_ (New York, 1887), pp. 251–53.

21. Aristides, "The Last Campaign of the War."

22. Aristides, "A Winter on the Rio Grande," Cincinnati _Commercial_, January 13, 1877.

23. Ibid.

24. The account of the Mexican military career of Williams is based on the article cited in note 22 above. All attempts to secure documentary materials from the Mexican military archives have been unsuccessful.

25. See James E. Sefton, _The United States Army and Reconstruction, 1865–1877_ (Baton Rouge, 1967), p. 261.

26. The shortage of defense funds later reduced the black infantry units from four to two. The Ninth and Tenth cavalry regiments remained. See Richard J. Stillman II, "Black Participation in the Armed Forces," in Mabel M. Smythe (ed.), _The Black American Reference Book_ (Englewood Cliffs, N.J., 1976), p. 893. See also Ulysses Lee, _The Employment of Negro Troops_ (Washington, D.C., 1966), pp. 23–25.

27. In one of his newspaper columns GWW gave a vivid description of his experiences with the Tenth Cavalry. See Aristides, "Military Life on the Plains," Cincinnati _Commercial_, January 6, 1877.

28. In the enlistment document GWW said he was twenty-two years and ten months old. See Recruitment Declaration, no. 1643, August 29, 1867, Record

Group 94, National Archives. See also the Records Relating to the Regular Army, Register of Enlistments, 1898–1914, vol. 67, Record Group 94. In fact, Williams was not twenty-two but would be eighteen on his next birthday, October 16, 1867. On November 4, 1850, his parents had listed him with the census enumerator as one year old. Population Schedules of the Seventh Census of the United States, November 4, 1850, Pennsylvania, Johnstown Township, County of Cambria.

29. Aristides, "Military Life on the Plains."

30. Ibid.

31. Ibid.

32. There is a good account of the duties and activities of the Tenth Cavalry in William H. Leckie, *The Buffalo Soldiers: A Narrative of the Negro Cavalry in the West* (Norman, Okla., 1967), pp. 19–44.

33. Special orders, Fort Arbuckle, May 19, 1868, Record Group 94.

34. Certificate of Disability for Discharge, July 27, 1868, filed in the Pension Office, National Archives, Record Group 94. Emphasis supplied.

35. R. H. Pratt, "Report of Training School at Carlisle, Pa.," in *Fifty-Ninth Annual Report of the Commissioner of Indian Affairs to the Secretary of the Interior* (Washington, D.C., 1890), p. 308.

36. George W. Ford to Mrs. Sarah Williams, September 26, 1900, Pension Office, National Archives, Record Group 94. See also the Certificate of Disability for Discharge, ibid.

37. Cleveland *Gazette*, December 24, 1887. The piece was based on a sketch by GWW originally published in the New York *Sun*, which the *Gazette* described as "one of the best, if not the best, portraits yet given to the public by Mr. Williams."

38. GWW to Howard, March 1, 1869. Andrew Pleasant was a well-to-do black Virginia-born farm laborer with a wife, four children, and real estate valued at $3,000.00. There is no record of how GWW met him, perhaps through the local Baptist church. Population Schedules of the Eighth Census of the United States, Quincy, Illinois, 6th Ward, August 17, 1870, p. 64.

39. To indicate his qualifications for part-time work, GWW said he had been employed as "Conductor" on a sleeping car as he worked his way back east. See Declaration for Invalid Pension, April 24, 1869, Bureau of Refugees, Freedmen, and Abandoned Lands, Record Group 105, National Archives. For more on the impact of the war on the aspirations of black soldiers, see Ira Berlin, Joseph P. Reidy, and Leslie S. Rowland, *The Black Military Experience* (Cambridge, Mass., 1982), pp. 32–33.

40. Declaration for Invalid Pension (see note 36 above).

41. Neither Howard nor Wayland has any record of GWW's matriculation.

42. Newton Theological Institution, Faculty Record Book, entry for September 9, 1870, in the Library of Andover Newton Theological School.

43. Richard Donald Pierce, ed., *General Catalogue of the Newton Theological Institution, 1826–1943* (Newton Centre, Mass.), p. xii.

44. Faculty Record Book (see note 39 above).

45. Pierce, *General Catalogue*, pp. 108–10.

46. *Annual Catalogue of the Newton Theological Institution at Newton Centre* (Boston, 1871), pp. 12–14.

47. Pierce, *General Catalogue*, pp. 25, 60, 63, 65, 98. There are sketches of Anderson and Hovey in the *Dictionary of American Biography* (New York, 1957), vol. 1, p. 264, and vol. 5, p. 270.

48. For brief biographies of the members of the class of 1874, see Pierce, *General Catalogue*, pp. 111–14.

49. On the commencement program itself, GWW's address was listed as "The Early Church in Africa," but the manuscript of the address, written in Williams's hand, is titled "Early Christianity in Africa." Both documents are in the Library of the Andover Newton Theological School.

50. GWW, "Early Christianity in Africa."

Chapter 2

1. Important surveys of Boston Negroes in the nineteenth century are John Daniels, *In Freedom's Birthplace: A Study of the Boston Negroes* (Boston, 1914), and James O. and Lois E. Horton, *Black Bostonians: Family Life and Community Struggle in the Antebellum North* (New York, 1979).

2. Boston *Evening Transcript*, November 28, 1873; *New National Era* (Washington, D.C.), December 4, 1873.

3. The Reverend J. Sella Martin, a long-time advocate of emancipation and racial equality, was editor of the *New National Era* from 1870 to 1874. James Monroe Trotter (1842–91), a civil war veteran and author, was the father of William Monroe Trotter, civil rights advocate and critic of Booker T. Washington. William Wells Brown, *The Rising Son; or the Antecedents and Advancement of the Colored Race* (Boston, 1876), pp. 535–36; Stephen R. Fox, *The Guardian of Boston, William Monroe Trotter* (New York, 1970), pp. 3–16.

4. *New National Era*, March 26, 1874.

5. Richard Edwards, comp., *Chicago Census Report*, 1871, p. 1061. See also New York *Globe*, May 26, 1883, for a brief account of Sterrett at the time of his death.

6. The marriage license of George W. Williams and Sarah A. Sterrett was filed in the office of the Clerk of Cook County on June 3, 1874. Copy in the U.S. Pension Office, File 651,476, widow of George W. Williams, November 24, 1902, National Archives and Record Service, Record Group 15. Little is known about Sarah's personality or appearance. In 1879 she was described as "small, ladylike, and refined" and "hardly as dark as her husband" (Cincinnati *Gazette*, October 17).

7. Boston *Evening Transcript*, June 12, 1874.

8. GWW gives an account of his ordination and of his regard for his Watertown friends in his *History of the Twelfth Baptist Church* (Boston, 1874), pp. 38–40. Blodgett was a well-to-do iron manufacturer; Delano March and George March were the wealthiest merchants in Watertown; and Royal Gilkey was a retired lumber and coal dealer with large real estate holdings. *Ninth Census of*

the United States, 1870, Middlesex County, Watertown, Microcopy 593, Reel 633, pp. 37, 53–54, 73, 75.

9. GWW, in his *History of the Twelfth Baptist Church*, gives a rather full account of the church and of Grimes's leadership. See also Daniels, *In Freedom's Birthplace*, pp. 64n, 452; and Benjamin Quarles, *The Negro in the Civil War* (Boston, 1953), pp. 26, 129, 173.

10. See Newton Theological Institution, Faculty Record Book, entry for October 9, 1870.

11. GWW, *History of the Twelfth Baptist Church*, p. 46. Unless otherwise indicated, the account of the installation and pastorate of Williams is taken from this source.

12. Shortly before he graduated, GWW accepted an invitation to deliver a sermon on blacks in the military service. See George W. Williams, *The Advent of the Colored Soldier: a Memorial Sermon Delivered before Robert A. Bell Post 134, G.A.R., Sunday, May 24, 1874* (Boston, 1874).

13. Boston *Evening Transcript*, June 23 and 25, 1874.

14. Ibid., October 21, 1874.

15. *Seventy-Second Annual Report of the Massachusetts Baptist Convention* (Boston, 1874), p. 37; and *Seventy-Third Annual Report of the Massachusetts Baptist Convention* (Boston, 1875). For a list of regular services and other activities sponsored by the church, see the *Boston Church Directory, 1874–75* (Boston, 1874).

16. Boston *Evening Transcript*, September 3, 1874. For a discussion of the conditions in the South, see *United States Congress, House Reports*, vol. 5, 43d Congress, 2d Session, 1874–75.

17. For a discussion of the lag in interest in the bill, see David Donald, *Charles Sumner and the Rights of Man* (New York, 1970), pp. 579–80. See also John Hope Franklin, "The Enforcement of the Civil Rights Act of 1875," *Prologue* 6 (Winter 1974): 225–35.

18. GWW to James M. Trotter, September 7, 1874, *New National Era*, October 1, 1874.

19. Boston *Evening Transcript*, November 14, 1874.

20. Ibid., January 5, 1875. Smith, a popular poet, was praised by William Wells Brown as having written more poetry than any other living Negro. *Rising Son*, pp. 552–55.

21. *Journal of the House of Representatives of the Commonwealth of Massachusetts, 1874 and 1875* (Boston, 1875), p. 9. See also Boston *Evening Transcript*, January 7, 1875.

22. Boston *Evening Transcript*, January 8, 1875. GWW may have been mollified that spring by his appointment as chaplain of the Second Battalion of Infantry of the Massachusetts State Militia. Boston *Evening Transcript*, May 28, 1875. For a brief biographical sketch of Seymour, see George W. Lasher (ed.), *The Ministerial Directory of the Baptist Churches* (Oxford, Ohio, 1899), p. 653.

23. See James M. McPherson, *The Abolitionist Legacy from Reconstruction to the NAACP* (Princeton, 1975), pp. 13–23.

24. *New National Era,* November 25, 1873.

25. See Franklin, "The Enforcement of the Civil Rights Act of 1875" (note 17 above); and chapter 7 below.

26. GWW, *History of the Twelfth Baptist Church,* pp. 48, 60–61.

27. Boston *Morning Journal,* July 2 and 3, 1875; Boston *Evening Transcript,* July 2, 1875.

28. GWW to Henry Wadsworth Longfellow, July 24, 1875, Longfellow Papers, Houghton Library, Harvard University.

29. Ibid. GWW also thanked Longfellow for sending his glove, which he had left at the Longfellow home.

30. *The Commoner,* September 1, 1875.

Chapter 3

1. *Freedom's Journal,* March 16, 1827.

2. *The North Star,* December 3, 1847.

3. Irvine Garland Penn, *Afro-American Press and Its Editors* (Springfield, 1891), pp. 112–14; reprinted 1969 by Arno Press.

4. *New National Era,* September 8, 1870.

5. Philip S. Foner, *Frederick Douglass* (New York, 1964), p. 311. This work contains a full account of the role of Douglass in the life of the *New National Era.* See especially pp. 276–80 and 311–12. The final issue of the paper appeared on October 22, 1874, not September 8, 1874, as asserted by Foner.

6. See, for example, *New National Era,* November 25, December 18, 1873; and March 26, October 15, 1874. In the last mentioned issue there was a lengthy front-page article by Williams reporting the death, funeral, and burial of Theodosia Louisa Elizabeth Brown Lewis.

7. In New York, John J. Freeman published *The Progressive American.* In Alexandria, Virginia, formerly a part of the District of Columbia, John W. Cromwell published the *People's Advocate,* but it was not launched until 1876.

8. Better known as the Colfax riot, the events that occurred in Grant Parish, Louisiana, in the spring of 1873, were fresh in the minds of Northerners, including GWW, for many months. In February 1874, nine white men accused of participating in the riot were tried in federal court in New Orleans. Four were acquitted, and the remainder were found guilty of conspiracy against peaceful assemblage, not of murder. The memory of the riot was kept alive for years through the trials, appeals, and other legal maneuvers. See U.S. Congress, *House Reports,* vol. 5, 43d Congress, 2d Session, 1874–75 (Washington, D.C., 1875), no. 261, pt. 1, pp. 12–14; Manie White Johnson, "The Colfax Riot of April, 1873," *Louisiana Historical Quarterly* 12 (July 1930: 391–427; Joe Gray Taylor, *Louisiana Reconstructed, 1863–1877* (Baton Rouge, 1974), pp. 267–73.

9. *The Commoner,* September 4, 1875.

10. Ibid., September 4, 1875. This first issue of *The Commoner* contains a lengthy piece on how GWW made the decision to launch a newspaper.

11. Rayford W. Logan, *Howard University: The First Hundred Years, 1867–1967* (New York, 1969), pp. 73–81.

12. *The Commoner*, September 4, 1875.

13. This account of the meeting is based on the detailed reporting of it in the *National Republican*, July 13, 1875. It was reprinted in *The Commoner*, September 4, 1875.

14. The account in *The Commoner* lists some contributors who were not named in the article in the *National Republican*.

15. William Lloyd Garrison to GWW, July 19, 1875, in *The Commoner*, September 4, 1875.

16. Detroit *Tribune*, August 23, 1875.

17. Frederick Douglass to GWW, *The Commoner*, September 4, 1875. The caption over the Douglass letter read, "The Duty of the Hour."

18. Detroit *Tribune*, September 14, 1875.

19. *The Commoner*, November 20, 1875. The reports from the South were in the form of letters to Wendell Phillips, subsequently published in *The Commoner*.

20. There are numerous accounts of the Clinton riots. See especially Herbert Aptheker, "Mississippi Reconstruction and the Negro Leader, Charles Caldwell," in *To Be Free: Studies in American Negro History* (New York, 1948), pp. 163–87.

21. *The Commoner*, December 11, 1875. This second of the Southern letters to Wendell Phillips had a Jackson, Mississippi, dateline of October 4, 1875.

22. Ibid., December 11, 1875.

23. *Daily Pilot* (Jackson, Mississippi), October 6, 1875.

24. *The Commoner*, December 11, 1875. The usual vote of thanks was passed unanimously.

25. *Daily Pilot*, October 6, 1875.

26. See, for example, the issues for December 4 and 11, 1875.

27. In the issue of December 4, 1875, for example, Williams was promoting Douglass or Langston for the position of Secretary of the Senate.

28. *The Commoner*, November 20, 1875.

29. *The Colored American* (Washington, D.C.), June 25, 1898. Smith was later editor of the Boston *Leader*. See Penn, *Afro-American Press*, p. 360.

30. *The National Republican*, September 6, 1875.

31. The meeting, held in the offices of *The Commoner*, took place on December 3, 1875. In attendance were Frederick Douglass, George T. Downing, Alexander Crummell, Robert Purvis, John W. Cromwell, and many other leading citizens of Washington, Virginia, Maryland, and Pennsylvania. *The Commoner*, December 4, 1875.

32. *The Commoner*, December 11, 1875.

33. Ibid., December 4, 1875.

34. Simmons, *Men of Mark*, p. 375. This sketch of Williams is presumably based on materials and information provided by Williams for Simmons, an intimate friend.

Chapter 4

1. *The New National Era and Citizen,* July 3, 1873.

2. Eighth Census of the United States, *Population of the United States in 1860* (Washington, 1864), p. 381; Ninth Census of the United States, *The Statistics of the Population of the United States* (Washington, 1870), p. 231.

3. David Gerber, *Black Ohio and the Color Line, 1860–1915* (Urbana, Ill., 1976), p. 146. This work provides an excellent background for understanding the society and conditions under which GWW lived from 1876 to 1882. I am indebted to Professor Gerber for permitting me to read his manuscript before it was published.

4. Wendell Phillips Dabney, *Cincinnati's Colored Citizens: Historical, Sociological, and Biographical* (Cincinnati, 1926), pp. 370–71.

5. Cincinnati *Commercial,* March 2, 1876.

6. Emery, a white city missionary, had been superintendent of the Union Baptist Sabbath School since 1850. He served as pastor of the church from 1881 to 1885. Joseph Emery, *Thirty-Five Years Among the Poor, and the Public Institutions of Cincinnati* (Cincinnati, 1887), pp. 265–68.

7. This account of the installation is from the Cincinnati *Commercial,* March 3, 1876.

8. Aristides, "The Colored Baptists of Cincinnati," *Commercial,* December 3, 1876.

9. Cincinnati *Commercial,* July 22, 1876.

10. Ibid., December 18, 1876.

11. Ibid., January 30, 1877.

12. Ibid., February 16, 1877.

13. GWW, *The American Negro, from 1776 to 1876 , Oration Deliverd July 4, 1876, at Avondale, Ohio* (Cincinnati, 1876). The role of GWW and other black Americans in the observance of the nation's centennial is discussed in Philip Foner, "Black Participation in the Centennial of 1876," in his *Essays in Afro-American History* (Philadelphia, 1978), pp. 134–53. The influence of this oration on GWW's subsequent career is discussed below.

14. Frank U. Quillen, *The Color Line in Ohio* (Ann Arbor, 1913), pp. 98–102. While this work has been superseded by Gerber's *Black Ohio and the Color Line,* it contains some useful information not found elsewhere.

15. Cincinnati *Daily Enquirer,* March 4, 5, 1875. See also Gerber, *Black Ohio and the Color Line,* pp. 58, 187–90.

16. Cincinnati *Commercial,* August 19, 1876.

17. Ibid., August 22, 1876.

18. Ibid., September 18, 1876. Later, GWW published an urgent appeal for support for the asylum. See Aristides, "The Colored Orphan Asylum," Cincinnati *Commercial,* May 20, 1877.

19. Cincinnati *Daily Enquirer,* October 23, 1876.

20. Frank Monaghan, "Murat Halstead," *Dictionary of American Biography* (New York, 1960), vol. 4, pt. 2, p. 163.

21. Emma Lou Thornbrough, *T. Thomas Fortune, Militant Journalist* (Chicago, 1972), pp. 96–97.

22. See note 8 above.

23. Cincinnati *Commercial,* June 10, 1877.

24. Ibid., May 19, 1878.

25. Aristides, "The President's Southern Policy," Cincinnati *Commercial,* March 12, 1877.

26. Gerber, *Black Ohio and the Color Line,* p. 213.

27. Cincinnati *Commercial,* April 20, 1876.

28. Ibid., August 6, 1876.

29. Ibid., August 10, 14, 1876.

30. Ibid., September 6, 7, 1876. In the following month, GWW urged the Republicans to get out the vote on election day, but, according to the *Commercial,* GWW was one of several of the "most intelligent and respectable citizens who did not vote in the October elections." Cincinnati *Commercial,* October 10, November 7, 1876.

31. Ibid., October 26, 1876.

32. Ibid., February 26, 1877.

33. GWW to Governor Rutherford B. Hayes (telegram), February 20, 1877, Hayes Papers, Rutherford B. Hayes Library.

34. GWW to Governor R.B. Hayes, February 21, 1877, ibid.

35. Joseph Emery, Supt. and Geo. W. Williams, Pastor, to President Hayes, May 6, 1877, ibid.

36. GWW and Alfred J. Anderson, "President Hayes' Southern Policy and the Colored Voters of the South," printed circular in the Hayes papers. The circular was reprinted in the Cincinnati *Commercial,* May 15, 1877. GWW had also sent a spirited defense of the Hayes policy to the Wendell Phillips Club of Boston. A clipping of the letter, taken from the Cincinnati *Gazette,* May 14, 1877, is in the Hayes papers.

37. Williams was still pastor of Union Baptist Church. He would not resign until December 1, 1877.

38. Among the white men who had supported GWW was the former governor of Ohio, Edward F. Noyes, soon to be United States minister to France. See the endorsement on GWW to Capt. Wm. K. Rogers, May 14, 1877, Hayes Papers.

39. GWW to R. B. Hayes, May 14, 1877, ibid.

40. Anderson had been cosigner with GWW of the circular letter "President Hayes' Southern Policy and the Colored Voters of the South."

41. Cincinnati *Daily Enquirer,* July 1, 1877.

42. Ibid., July 31, 1877; Cincinnati *Commercial,* July 21, 1877.

Chapter 5

1. Herbert Gutman, "Peter Clark: Pioneer Negro Socialist, 1877," *Journal of Negro Education* 34 (Fall 1965): 413–18.

2. Gerber, *Black Ohio and the Color Line,* p. 230. See also Lawrence Grossman, *The Democratic Party and the Negro: Northern and National Politics, 1868–92* (Urbana, Ill., 1976), p. 81.

3. Cincinnati *Daily Enquirer,* August 18, 1877.

4. Ibid., August 21, 1877. Presumably Jesse Fossett was a member of the very prominent Fossett family, the leading caterers of the city. Both he and William Jones were members of the Independent Colored Conservative Club. Cincinnati *Commercial,* September 7, 1877.

5. Ibid., August 23, 1877. A more sympathetic account of the convention appeared in the Cincinnati *Commercial,* August 23, 1877. There is no evidence to support the claim of the *Daily Enquirer* that GWW had been a janitor in the sheriff's office. In one place (p. 4), the *Enquirer* for August 23 described Williams as "a full-blooded negro"; in another (p. 8), it described him as "a mulatto with half or a predominance of white blood."

6. Cincinnati *Commercial,* August 23, 1877.

7. Ibid., August 28, 1877.

8. Ibid., September 6, 1877.

9. Ibid., September 9, 1877.

10. Cincinnati *Daily Enquirer,* September 17, 1877. The statement originally appeared in the *Commercial,* August 5, 1877.

11. Cincinnati *Daily Enquirer,* September 17, 1877.

12. The published letter from GWW to R. M. Bishop, September 18, 1877, appeared in the Cincinnati *Daily Enquirer,* September 19, 1877.

13. The second letter from GWW to Bishop appeared in the Cincinnati *Daily Enquirer,* September 19, 1877, and in the Cincinnati *Commercial,* September 20, 1877.

14. Cincinnati *Commercial,* September 19, 1877.

15. Even the hostile *Enquirer* conceded that GWW was "perhaps the ablest of the [Republican] candidates for the House," August 23, 1877.

16. Cincinnati *Commercial,* September 26, 1877.

17. Ibid., September 29, 1877.

18. Ibid., September 30 and October 7, 1877.

19. Ibid., October 7, 1877.

20. Cincinnati *Daily Enquirer,* October 9, 1877.

21. Ibid., October 4, 1877. Several GWW supporters from other parts of the state wrote letters in his behalf. See one from Alfred J. Anderson of Hamilton, Ohio, in the *Commercial,* October 3. Anderson had cosigned with GWW the open letter on Hayes's Southern policy. There was also one in the *Commercial,* October 9, from "A True Republican," urging Republicans to vote the straight ticket.

22. Cincinnati *Commercial,* October 13, 23, and 24, 1877.

23. John P. Green tells of his own defeat in his autobiography, *Facts Stranger than Fiction: Seventy-five Years of a Busy Life* (Cleveland, 1920), pp. 152–53. He was elected to the state senate in 1881 and introduced the bill that led to the designation of the first Monday in September as Labor Day. For

an excellent discussion of the politics of this period, see Gerber, *Black Ohio and the Color Line,* pp. 209–44.

24. Cincinnati *Commercial,* October 21, 1877. Williams had taken a brief holiday in Chicago. Chicago *Interocean,* quoted in the New Orleans *Weekly Louisianian,* October 20, 1877.

25. Ibid., September 18, 1877; Cincinnati *Daily Enquirer,* September 18, 1877.

26. Cincinnati *Commercial,* October 30, 1877.

27. Simmons, *Men of Mark,* p. 377.

28. Cincinnati *Commercial,* February 24, 1878. Dabney, in *Cincinnati's Colored Citizens,* p. 188, is in error in stating that GWW published *The Colored Citizen.* That was the name of the paper published in Cincinnati by John P. Sampson during the Civil War.

29. *Appleton's Cyclopedia of American Biography* (New York, 1889), p. 522; *Dictionary of American Biography* (New York, 1936), vol. 10, pt. 2, p. 264.

30. Louisville *Commercial,* March 10, 1889.

31. Cincinnati *Commercial,* January 8, 1878.

32. J. H. Hollander, *The Cincinnati Southern Railway: A Study in Municipal Activity* (Baltimore, 1894), p. 28. In 1875–76 Taft was a trustee of the railway. See the *Report of the Commission on the Affairs of the Trustees of the Cincinnati Southern Railway* . . . (Cincinnati, 1879), p 46.

33. Simmons, *Men of Mark,* p. 377.

34. Hollander, *The Cincinnati Southern Railway,* pp. 46–47.

35. Cincinnati *Commercial,* May 2, 1878.

36. Hollander, *The Cincinnati Southern Railway,* p. 47.

37. Cincinnati *Daily Enquirer,* March 26, 1878.

38. Ibid., March 27, 1878.

39. Ibid., March 28, 1878.

40. Ibid., June 12, 1878. This proved to be an accurate assessment of convention sentiment. The platform recognized in Hayes's administration "the highest integrity and patriotism, the most sincere effort to promote political purity and harmony and secure general business prosperity throughout the whole country." *The Ohio Platforms of the Republican and Democratic Parties from 1855 to 1881 Inclusive* (Columbus, 1881), p. 55.

41. Cincinnati *Daily Enquirer,* June 13, 1878. White had been appointed to the court to fill a vacancy in 1864. He was elected later that same year. From 1857 to 1864 he was a judge of the Court of Common Pleas. Edward Howard Gilkey, *The Ohio Hundred Year Book* (Columbus, 1901), pp. 473–74, 553.

42. GWW to R. B. Hayes, August 20, 1878, Hayes Papers.

43. Simmons, *Men of Mark,* p. 377.

44. Cincinnati *Commercial,* August 23, 1878.

45. GWW to John P. Green, August 28, 1878, Green Papers, Western Reserve Historical Society.

46. Cincinnati *Commercial,* September 10, 1878.

47. Ibid., September 20 and 21, 1878.

48. Ibid., October 2, 4, 6, and 8, 1878.

49. Ibid., September 29, 1878.

50. GWW to President Hayes, October 9, 1878, Hayes papers.

51. GWW to the President, October 14, 1878.

52. GWW to John P. Green, October 9, 1878, Green Papers. GWW's letters were on the stationery of the United States Internal Revenue.

53. GWW to Alphonso Taft, November 3, 1878, William H. Taft Papers, Series I, Microfilm Reel 13.

54. GWW's first biographer, who knew him, said that he studied at the Cincinnati Law School. W. J. Simmons, *Men of Mark: Eminent, Progressive, and Rising* (Cleveland, 1887), p. 557. In December, 1879, GWW stated that he had finished his law course. GWW to John P. Green, December 3, 1879. Green Papers.

55. Cincinnati *Daily Enquirer*, June 25, 1879. Earlier, GWW had referred to *one* war wound and one (nonwar) wound at Fort Arbuckle in 1868 (see chapter 1 above).

56. Cincinnati *Commercial*, March 30, 1879.

57. Cincinnati *Daily Enquirer*, April 7, 1879.

58. Cincinnati *Commercial*, April 7, 1879.

59. Ibid., April 9, 1879.

60. Ibid., April 10, 1879.

61. Ibid., May 29, 1879.

62. Even the *Commercial* recognized this as a problem. See the issue for June 28, 1879.

63. Cincinnati *Daily Enquirer*, July 17, 1879.

64. Cincinnati *Commercial*, June 27, 1879.

65. Ibid., June 29, 1879.

66. Ibid., June 28, 1879.

67. Ibid., June 29, 1879.

68. Ibid., July 1, 1879. Later, a Harlan supporter called the *Commercial* to task for its alleged inaccurate reporting of the meeting. He did not make a convincing case regarding the inaccuracies, however. Ibid., July 4, 1879.

69. Cincinnati *Daily Enquirer*, July 29, 1879.

Chapter 6

1. Cincinnati *Daily Enquirer*, July 30, 1879.

2. Ibid., July 31, 1879. Ben Eggleston, white, was a Republican candidate for the state senate.

3. Ibid., August 7, 1879.

4. Cincinnati *Daily Gazette*, August 1, 1879.

5. Columbus *Dispatch*, July 30, 1879.

6. Cincinnati *Commercial*, August 3, 1879.

7. Cincinnati *Daily Gazette*, August 5, 1879.

8. For an account of Clark's socialist interests and activities, see Herbert

Gutman, "Peter Clark: Pioneer Negro Socialist, 1877," *Journal of Negro Education* 34 (Fall 1965): 413–18; and Gerber, *Black Ohio and the Color Line*, p. 175.

9. Cincinnati *Daily Gazette*, August 9, 1879.

10. Cincinnati *Commercial*, August 9, 1879.

11. Cincinnati *Daily Gazette*, August 9, 1879.

12. Cincinnati *Commercial*, August 9, 1879.

13. Ibid., August 12, 1879.

14. Cincinnati *Daily Gazette*, August 15, 1879. The same report was carried in the Columbus *Dispatch*, August 15, 1879.

15. Cincinnati *Daily Gazette*, August 16, 1879.

16. Ibid., August 16, 1879. See also Cincinnati *Commercial*, August 17, 1879.

17. Cincinnati *Commercial*, August 22, 1879.

18. Cincinnati *Daily Gazette*, August 23, 1879. In the same issue there was a lengthy editorial in which editor Smith recounted the same charges against GWW that Handy had made.

19. Cincinnati *Commercial*, June 29, 1879.

20. Ibid., August 22, 1879. A similar editorial appeared the following day.

21. Cincinnati *Commercial*, August 24, 1879.

22. The lengthy letter from "A Friend of Geo. W. Williams" had estimated that 6,000 voters, including 500 blacks, would refuse to vote for GWW. Ibid.

23. Cincinnati *Commercial*, August 25, 1879.

24. Cincinnati *Daily Gazette*, August 26, 1879.

25. Cincinnati *Commercial*, September 9, 1879. In addition to Springfield, GWW spoke to a meeting of Negro Republicans at the Gallia Fairgrounds in Gallipolis on September 22. Cincinnati *Commercial*, September 23, 1879.

26. Ibid., August 27 and September 1, 1879.

27. Ibid., September 9, 1879.

28. Ibid., September 2, 1879.

29. The piece was reprinted from the Washington *Post* in the Cincinnati *Daily Enquirer*, September 16, 1879.

30. Cincinnati *Commercial*, October 9, 1879.

31. Ibid., September 24, 1879.

32. Cincinnati *Daily Enquirer*, September 24, 1879.

33. Cincinnati *Commercial*, September 29, 1879.

34. Ibid., October 11, 1879.

35. Cincinnati *Daily Enquirer*, October 2 and 11, 1879.

36. Cincinnati *Daily Gazette*, October 13, 1879.

37. Cincinnati *Enquirer*, October 14, 1879.

38. Cincinnati *Commercial*, October 13, 1879. The reference to Fort Wagner was, perhaps, based on an unsigned letter in the *Commercial*, August 24, 1879, written by a resident of Cincinnati who said that he had known Williams as the sole black lieutenant in the Fifty-Fourth Massachusetts Regiment. He had not seen Williams, he said, since 1863 until they met in Cincinnati in 1877 and "recognized in him the personage in my memory." On several occasions they

discussed the war and especially Fort Wagner. Cincinnati *Commercial*, August 24, 1879. There was a George W. Williams in the 54th Massachusetts. See Luis F. Emilio, *A Brave Black Regiment: History of the Fifty-Fourth Regiment of Massachusetts Volunteer Infantry*, 1863–1865 (Boston, 1891). GWW was not yet fourteen years old and not only was not an officer and not at Fort Wagner, but was not in the army at the time of the assault on Fort Wagner, July 16, 1863. See chapter 1 above.

39. See the official vote for Hamilton County, Cincinnati *Commercial*, October 22, 1879. The *Commercial* for October 27, 1879, said that GWW received 2,587 votes more than his nearest Democratic rival. The Chicago *Tribune* for October 16, 1879, reported that GWW's margin over Blair was 886, doubtless a premature estimate.

40. GWW to R. B. Hayes, October 15, 1879, Hayes Papers.

41. The reference is to John Brough, Ohio's wartime governor, who was elected in 1863 by a majority of 100,099, which remained the national record for forty years. *Dictionary of American Biography*, vol. 2, pt. 1 (New York, 1958), pp. 94–95.

42. Cincinnati *Commercial*, October 15, 1879. The *Daily Gazette* of the same date, reporting the same proceedings, said that at the beginning of his speech GWW was hissed, "but the crowd cried, 'Order, Order,' in very positive tones, and very soon perfect quiet was restored." There was also a victory meeting at the Union Baptist church. Cincinnati *Daily Enquirer*, October 16, 1879.

43. Cincinnati *Commercial*, October 17, 1879.

44. The *Enquirer*, October 16, 1879, insisted that Harlan's rejoicing over the election of GWW "is not deep."

45. Cincinnati *Commercial*, October 17, 1879; see also Cincinnati *Daily Gazette*, October 17, 1879.

46. *People's Advocate*, October 18, 1879.

47. *The Louisianian*, October 18, 1879.

48. Topeka *Colored Citizen*, October 18, 1879.

49. David M. Ellis and others, *A Short History of New York State* (Ithaca, 1957), pp. 364–66.

50. I.e., the "bloody shirts" waved by the victims of Southern Democratic violence. The Republicans used the expression as a slogan against the Democrats. GWW then called upon his hearers to reject the Democrat's bid for office.

51. New York *Times*, October 26, 1879.

52. Cincinnati *Daily Enquirer*, October 24, 1879.

53. Ibid., December 3, 1879. At the time of the alleged incident, GWW had been in Columbus for several days. Columbus *Dispatch*, November 28, 1879.

54. Cincinnati *Daily Enquirer*, December 4, 1879. The *Enquirer* had apparently picked up the story from the Columbus *Dispatch*, which had carried it on December 2.

55. Cincinnati *Daily Enquirer*, December 4, 1879.

56. Columbus *Dispatch,* December 30, 1879.

57. Cincinnati *Commercial,* December 30, 1879.

Chapter 7

1. In June 1880, the census enumerator in Columbus recorded GWW's age as thirty-three. Tenth Census of the United States, Franklin County, Ohio (Columbus), Reel 1017, p. 22. The 1850 Census, which lists him as being in his first year, seems more reliable for the purpose of determining his age. See chapter 1, note 5, above.

2. *Journal of the House of Representatives of the State of Ohio, for the Regular Session of the Sixty-Fourth General Assembly, Commencing Monday, January 5, 1880* (Columbus, 1880), pp. 4, 6, hereafter cited as *House Journal, 1880.* At the end of the legislative session GWW took the Ohio bar examination but did not pass. Columbus *Dispatch,* May 6, 1880. The Cincinnati *Daily Enquirer,* ever determined to discredit GWW, complained on December 30, 1879, that he was absent from a caucus of Hamilton County members of the legislature, implying that the group was ignoring him. It did not complain that others, such as Peter Stryker of the House and Charles Fleischman of the Senate, were also absent or that they too were being ignored by their colleagues.

3. *House Journal,* 1880, pp. 34–36, 566; Cincinnati *Commercial,* January 21, 23, 1880.

4. House *Journal,* 1880, p. 16.

5. Cincinnati *Daily Enquirer,* January 7, 1880.

6. Columbus *Dispatch,* February 3, 1880.

7. *House Journal,* 1880, p. 50.

8. Cincinnati *Commercial,* February 25, 1880. For an anti-GWW version of the debate in which his speech was referred to as "wind-work" and the bill as bringing, in his view, the millenium, see the Cincinnati *Daily Enquirer,* February 25, 1880.

9. GWW to John P. Green, December 24, 1879, Green Papers.

10. *House Journal,* 1880, p. 49.

11. Gerber, *Black Ohio and the Color Line,* pp. 27–28.

12. Columbus *Dispatch,* January 12, 1880; Cincinnati *Commercial,* January 13, 1880.

13. Cincinnati *Daily Enquirer,* January 12, 1880.

14. Cincinnati *Commercial,* February 3, 1880.

15. Cincinnati *Daily Enquirer,* January 6, 1880.

16. Ibid., January 12, 1880.

17. The facts in the case as presented here are from the report of the select committee of the house that was appointed to investigate the matter. The text of the report appeared in the Cincinnati *Daily Enquirer,* January 16, 1880. See also the Columbus *Dispatch,* January 15, 1880.

18. The text of the report of the Select Committee is in *House Journal*, 1880, pp. 982–84. Newspaper accounts are in Cincinnati *Daily Enquirer*, and Cincinnati *Commercial*, January 16, 1880.

19. For a discussion of the difficulties in enforcing the law, see John Hope Franklin, "The Enforcement of the Civil Rights Act of 1875," *Prologue: Journal of the National Archives* (Fall, 1974), pp. 225–35.

20. Cincinnati *Daily Enquirer*, January 13, 14, and 22, 1880.

21. James Poindexter to the editor, Columbus *Dispatch*, January 10, 1880. Beck's business is said to have declined because of his continued discrimination against blacks even after the Williams incident. See Gerber, *Black Ohio and the Color Line*, pp. 54–55. There was discussion in Cincinnati of GWW's visit to Washington in early March, where he stopped at the Ebbitt House. Although he was not ejected, "with the Civil Rights Law at hand and LAWRENCE BECK as an example," the *Daily Enquirer* (March 2 and 3, 1880) reported that many guests were offended by his presence.

22. *House Journal*, 1880, p. 278; Cincinnati *Commercial*, February 18, 1880.

23. Columbus *Dispatch*, April 17, 1880; see also Cincinnati *Commercial*, March 17, 1880.

24. *House Journal*, 1880, pp. 144, 644.

25. Cincinnati *Daily Enquirer*, January 27, 1880.

26. *House Journal*, 1880, p. 582. See excerpts of GWW's speech on the Stryker bill in the Cincinnati *Commercial*, February 27, 1880.

27. Ibid., pp. 467, 584, 636–37.

28. Ibid.

29. Cincinnati *Commercial*, March 15, 1880.

30. *House Journal*, 1880, p. 827.

31. Dabney, *Cincinnati's Colored Citizens*, p. 193.

32. The *Daily Enquirer*, April 13, 1880, said that the letter was received with derisive laughter.

33. The account of the meeting at Allen Temple was reported in great detail in the Cincinnati *Commercial*, April 13, 1880. A somewhat less detailed account is in the *Enquirer* of the same date. A second meeting was held at Allen Temple, April 15, 1880. Cincinnati *Commercial*, April 16, 1880. A formal resolution went to the legislature, April 13, 1880. Cincinnati *Daily Enquirer*, April 14, 1880.

34. The Board of Health of Avondale also sent to the legislature a message requesting it to grant the petition of the citizens at the present session, "inasmuch as the evil is a growing one, and that the warm weather is approaching, with the possibility of more sickness prevailing than in ordinary seasons." GWW included this communication with his letter of explanation.

35. This was House Bill 491, which GWW introduced on April 10, 1880. There is no record of the House having taken action. *House Journal*, 1880, p. 835. On the same day the Senate gave the bill three readings and passed it by a vote of 22-0. *Senate Journal*, 1880, p. 587.

36. Cincinnati *Commercial*, April 13, 1880.

37. Ibid., April 14, 1880.

38. Cincinnati *Enquirer,* April 15, 1880.

39. Columbus *Dispatch,* April 14, 1880.

40. Cincinnati *Commercial,* April 14, 1880.

41. Ibid., April 18, 1880.

42. Ibid., April 13, 1880.

43. GWW to John P. Green, New York, March 16, 1883, Green Papers.

44. *House Journal,* 1880,p. 585.

45. Cincinnati *Daily Enquirer,* March 6, 1880.

46. Columbus *Dispatch,* April 15, 1880.

47. *Ohio State Journal,* February 12 and March 11, 1880; Cincinnati *Commercial,* January 27, 1880.

48. Cincinnati *Commercial,* September 9 and October 15, 1879.

49. Cincinnati *Daily Enquirer,* March 1, 1880.

50. Cincinnati *Commercial,* April 11, 1880.

51. Cincinnati *Enquirer,* April 23, 28, 1880.

52. Huntsville *People's Advocate,* May 1, 1880.

53. For a discussion of Ohio and the presidential election of 1880, see Philip D. Jordan, *Ohio Comes of Age: 1873–1900* (Columbus, 1943) , pp. 168–73. See also *Proceedings of the Republican National Convention, Chicago, 1880.*

54. Jordan, *Ohio Comes of Age,* p. 170.

55. The Cincinnati *Daily Enquirer* took particular interest in GWW's political activities, noting when he was not met by local party leaders, when candidates rejected his offer of assistance, and when he was insulted or heckled by his audience. See the issues for July 29; August 21, 25, and 27; September 4, 14, and 17; and October 4, 1880.

56. Frederick Douglass, R. B. Elliott, Blanche K. Bruce, Richard Greener, and George W. Williams were among those who had done "effective work in the Northern states. . . . President Garfield will remember them." Huntsville *People's Advocate,* November 6, 1880.

57. Cincinnati *Enquirer,* November 25, 1880.

58. Ibid.

59. *Journal of the House of Representatives of the State of Ohio for the Adjourned Session of the Sixty-Fourth General Assembly commencing Tuesday, January 4, 1881* (Sandusky, 1881), p. 3.

60. Cincinnati *Commercial,* January 5, 1881; and *House Journal,* 1881, p. 785.

61. *House Journal,* 1881, pp. 201–2.

62. Ibid., p. 713. See also Columbus *Dispatch,* April 1, 1881; and Cincinnati *Daily Enquirer,* April 2, 1881.

63. *House Journal,* 1881, pp. 228, 315, 358, 378.

64. Ibid., pp. 408, 449, 999, 1031. See also Columbus *Dispatch,* April 6, 1881.

65. *House Journal,* 1881, p. 97.

66. Cincinnati *Commercial,* February 3, 1881.

67. *House Journal*, 1881, p. 1134.

68. Ibid., pp. 1031–32.

69. Ibid., pp. 215, 275. See also the Columbus *Dispatch*, February 3, 1881.

70. *House Journal*, 1881, pp. 40, 300.

71. Cincinnati *Commercial*, February 10, 1881.

72. *House Journal*, 1881, p. 839.

Chapter 8

1. For a convenient summary of the activities of historians during these years, see Michael Kraus, *A History of American History* (New York, 1937), chapters 6–8. See also J. Franklin Jameson, *The History of Historical Writing in America* (Boston, 1891), pp. 122–60; William A. Dunning, "A Generation of American Historiography," *Annual Report of the American Historical Association for the year 1917* (Washington, 1920), pp. 347–54; and John Hope Franklin, "The New Negro History," *Journal of Negro History* 43 (April, 1957): 89–97.

2. See chapter 4 above, and Philip S. Foner's essay, "Black Participation in the Centennial of 1876," in his *Essays in Afro-American History* (Philadelphia, 1978), pp. 134–53.

3. GWW, *The American Negro from 1776 to 1876* (Cincinnati, 1876).

4. Reginald C. McGrane, "Robert Clarke," *Dictionary of American Biography,* vol. 2, pt. 2 (New York, 1958), p. 162.

5. There is some discussion of GWW's use of libraries and other repositories in the preface of his *History of the Negro Race in America from 1619 to 1880: Negroes as Slaves, as Soldiers, and as Citizens* (New York, 1882), 1:v–x.

6. Ohio State Library Records, "Delivery Ledger, 1875–1889," p. 122, Rare Book Room of the State Library of Ohio, Columbus. I am grateful to Mildred Vannorsdall for calling these borrowings to my attention.

7. Cincinnati *Daily Enquirer,* July 29, 1880.

8. Cincinnati *Commercial*, June 20, 1880. For an account of Chester A. Arthur's role in the Lemmon case, see Paul Finkelman, *An Imperfect Union: Slavery, Federalism, and Comity* (Chapel Hill, 1981), pp. 303–10.

9. *People's Advocate* (Washington, D.C.), September 17, 1881; and Williams, *History of the Negro Race*, vol. 1, p. ix.

10. *People's Advocate* (Washington, D.C.), August 27, September 10, and September 17, 1881.

11. Huntsville *Gazette*, November 5, 1881, and *People's Advocate*, October 29, 1881.

12. GWW, *History of the Negro Race*, vol. 1, p. viii.

13. GWW to General W. T. Sherman, November 7, 1881; R. C. Drum, Adjutant General, to GWW, November 12, 1881. Letters Received, 1805–1889, Record Group 94, Records of the Adjutant General's Office, National Archives and Record Service.

14. The interview, reported by GWW several months after his return, was concerned largely with an attempt by the general to vindicate his conduct at

Shiloh because the orders from General U. S. Grant had been reproduced inaccurately by the messenger who brought them. Cincinnati *Commercial*, January 17, 1882.

15. Cincinnati *Commercial*, December 7, 1880. See chapter 12 below.

16. GWW, *History of the Negro Race*, vol. 1, p. viii.

17. For example, in his chapter on "Negroes as Soldiers," Williams made extensive use of three New York papers: the *Herald*, the *Times*, and the *Tribune. History of the Negro Race*, vol. 2, pp. 310–49.

18. GWW to George Bancroft, June 27, 1881, Bancroft Papers, Massachusetts Historical Society.

19. George Bancroft to GWW, July 1, 1881, Bancroft Papers. Bancroft was seeing his *History of the Formation of the Constitution of the United States* through the press.

20. GWW to George Bancroft, October 21, 1881, Bancroft Papers.

21. GWW to George Bancroft, September 1, 1882, ibid.

22. George Bancroft to GWW, September 9, 1882, ibid.

23. GWW, *History of the Negro Race*, vol. 1, p. ix.

24. Justin Winsor to George H. Moore, December 9, 1882, Lenox Library Correspondence, New York Public Library.

25. GWW, *History of the Negro Race*, p. 173 n. 1, and p. 174 n. 2.

26. GWW, *A History of the Negro Troops in the War of the Rebellion, 1861–1865* (New York, 1887), p. xiii.

27. GWW, *History of the Negro Race*, vol. 2, p. 50.

28. Ibid., p. 59.

29. GWW, *The American Negro*, pp. 13–14.

30. GWW, *History of the Negro Race*, vol. 1, pp. 316–17.

31. Ibid., p. 385n.

32. Ibid., vol. 2, p. 58n.

33. Ibid., vol. 1, p. x.

34. GWW to George F. Hoar, September 20, 1887, Archives of the American Antiquarian Society.

35. GWW, *History of the Negro Race*, vol. 2, p. iii.

36. Ibid., pp. 132–33.

37. Ibid., vol. 1, p. vi. The first volume was entered at the copyright office on November 12, 1882, and the second volume on February 3, 1883. Stephen G. Soderberg, United States Copyright Office, to the author, December 7, 1981.

38. GWW, *History of the Negro Race*, vol. 1, pp. vi, 22.

39. Ibid., pp. 116–19.

40. John Henderson Russell, *The Free Negro in Virginia, 1619–1865* (Baltimore, 1913).

41. GWW, *History of the Negro Race*, vol. 1, pp. 172, 179, 180.

42. Ibid., vol. 1, p. 369; vol. 2, pp. 27, 349.

43. Ibid., vol. 2, p. 274.

44. Ibid., vol. 2, pp. 311, 314, 323, 334.

45. Ibid., p. 377n.

46. Subsequent statements by GWW indicate that he completed the work on Reconstruction, but I have found no evidence that it was ever published. See chapter 9 below.

47. GWW, *History of the Negro Race*, vol. 2, pp. 433, 438. See chapter 9 below.

48. Ibid., vol. 2, pp. 527, 397.

49. Ibid., pp. 423, 478.

50. Ibid., vol. 1, p. 114; vol. 2, p. 552. While William Toll correctly suggests that GWW believed black people had a special example of freedom to bring to the world, he is not correct in saying that GWW went to Africa "to preach the gospel in the Congo." Toll, *The Resurgence of Race: Black Social Theory from Reconstruction to the Pan-African Conferences* (Philadelphia, 1979), p. 26. For a discussion of GWW's activities in the Congo, see chapters 13 and 14 below.

51. Cincinnati *Commercial*, June 20, 1880.

52. Cincinnati *Daily Enquirer*, August 3, 1880.

53. There was no reply to the author's letter to the editor-in-chief, January 8, 1974.

54. Columbus *Daily Dispatch*, August 3, 1882. Putnam's Sons has retained no records of correspondence "older than twenty-five years." William Targ to the author, January 11, 1974.

55. GWW to Mrs. S. R. Putnam, February 28, 1883. Alexander Grummell letters, Schomburg Center for Research in Black Culture. In the course of his researches, GWW had acquired books, pamphlets, government documents, manuscripts, and other historical materials. Presumably there was a problem of housing them, especially since he no longer lived in Cincinnati and was in the process of leaving Ohio altogether, and apparently Mrs. Putnam had given him some assistance in this matter. Mrs. Putnam had written a fictitious narrative discussing the plight of black Americans in *Record of An Obscure Man* (Boston, 1861) and was very active in the abolitionist movement. Joseph Adelman, *Famous Women* (New York, 1926), p. 177.

56. GWW to Mrs. S. R. Putnam, June 1 and 9, 1883, Crummell Letters. The Schomburg Center incorrectly refers to Mrs. Putnam as "wife of the publisher." "Crummell Letters," *Calendar of the Manuscripts of the Schomburg Collection of Negro Literature* (New York, 1942), pp. 92–93.

57. When GWW wrote George Bancroft September 15, 1882, he was in New York and was using the letterhead of G. P. Putnam's Sons. Bancroft Papers.

58. At the meeting of the Massachusetts Historical Society on February 8, 1883, the president, Robert C. Winthrop, called attention to the recent publication of the "very able and interesting" *History of the Negro Race* by George W. Williams. Boston *Transcript*, February 10, 1883.

Chapter 9

1. Cincinnati *Commercial*, December 23, 1882; New York *Independent*, December 22, 1882; New York *Times*, January 22, 1883.

2. Cincinnati *Commercial,* December 23, 1882.

3. New York *Times,* January 22, 1883.

4. Boston *Transcript,* April 2, 1883.

5. *Magazine of American History* 9 (April 1883): 299–300. See also A. L. Chapin's review in *The Dial* 3 (March 1883): 252–54.

6. *Kansas City Review of Science and Industry* 6 (April 1883): 733–34.

7. *Atlantic Monthly* 51 (April 1883): 564–68.

8. *Nation,* vol. 36 (April 12, 1883), pp. 325–326.

9. For some details on the publisher's London operations, see George Haven Putnam, *Memories of a Publisher, 1865–1915* (New York and London, 1915), pp. 44–79.

10. *Spectator,* June 23, 1883: 808–10; *Athenaeum,* no. 2905 (June 30, 1883: 826; *Academy* 24 (August 18, 1883): 107–8; *Westminster Review* 120 (July 1883): 254–56.

11. See I. Garland Penn, *The Afro-American Press and Its Editors* (1891; repr. New York, 1969). The Afro-American periodicals, especially newspapers, have been so poorly preserved that it is difficult to locate and examine them. See, for example, Library of Congress, *Negro Newspapers on Microfilm* (Washington, 1953).

12. Huntsville *Gazette,* January 6, 1883.

13. Washington *Bee,* February 24, 1883.

14. GWW, *History of the Negro Race,* vol. 2, pp. 438, 433.

15. Washington *Bee,* February 24, 1883.

16. GWW, *History of the Negro Race,* vol. 2, pp. 424–38; see especially p. 438.

17. Washington *Bee,* January 16, 1883. See also the account of the banquet and of the speech by GWW, in the New York *Globe,* January 6, 1883.

18. The *Bee* for January and February 1883 contain several attacks on Fortune and Purvis, provoking the Philadelphian to sue Chase for libel. There is a contemporary sketch of Chase in Penn, *The Afro-American Press and Its Editors,* pp. 287–90.

19. Washington *Bee,* February 24, 1883.

20. New York *Globe,* March 3 and 10, 1883. The review extended over two issues of the weekly newspaper.

21. New York *Globe,* March 17, 1883.

22. Washington *Bee,* May 5, 1883.

23. Ibid.

24. Ibid.

25. New York *Globe,* May 12, 1883.

26. Ibid., May 19, 1883.

27. Frederick Douglass, Jr., insisted that his father did not promise anyone that he would discuss the exodus with Greener at the Saratoga meeting. Nevertheless he does not explain why Dean Wayland read a paper prepared by his father. New York *Globe,* May 26, 1883.

28. New York *Globe,* May 19, 1883. GWW sent his letter to the *Globe* from

Plymouth Rock House in Massachusetts. For a commendation of the reply by GWW and an affirmation that the exodus was good for black Americans, see *The Western Recorder* (a newspaper published in Lawrence, Kansas), May 24, 1883.

29. Washington *Bee,* May 26, 1883.

30. Ibid., May 19, 1883.

31. Williams, *History of the Negro Race,* vol. 2, pp. 249–50, 287.

32. Washington *Bee,* November 24, 1883.

33. For a discussion of the rise of historical societies in the United States, see Michael Kraus, *A History of American History* (New York, 1937), pp. 175–76.

34. New York *Globe,* June 16, 1883. The manuscript copy of this letter is in the James Weldon Johnson Collection, Yale University Library.

35. Ibid., June 23, 1883. In the same issue see the enthusiastic letter of approval from Albro Lyons of Plainfield, New Jersey.

36. Ibid., June 30, 1883. For an explanation of the title "Col.," see chapter 12 below.

37. Quoted in ibid.

38. Washington *Bee,* July 21, 1883.

39. New York *Globe,* February 17 and May 5, 1883.

40. Ibid., June 7, 1884.

41. New York *Freeman,* April 4 and 25, 1885.

42. Ibid., August 15, 1885, and June 14, 1890.

43. Ibid., January 17, 1885, and February 20, 1886.

44. See Benjamin Quarles, *The Negro in the Civil War* (Boston, 1953).

45. GWW, *History of the Negro Troops,* p. 328.

46. GWW, *The Advent of the Colored Soldier* (Boston, 1874).

47. An example of his recalling his own experiences during the war is his discussion of the occasion when General Birney was relieved of his command because he refused to march his division, containing Negro troops, "in the rear of all the white troops." GWW, *History of the Negro Troops,* vol. 2, p. 344 n. 1.

48. Ibid., pp. x–xii.

49. Ibid., pp. ix–x.

50. Ibid., pp. 262, 359–61, 375.

51. Ibid., p. 61.

52. Ibid., pp. 272, 319.

53. Ibid., pp. 320–25.

54. Ibid., pp. 327–28.

55. New York *Freeman,* September 11, 1886. In 1884 the name had been changed from *Globe* to *Freeman,* and in 1887 to *Age.* For a discussion of the various transformations of the paper, see Emma Lou Thornbrough, *T. Thomas Fortune: Militant Journalist* (Chicago, 1972).

56. Boston *Advocate,* September 25, 1886; Cleveland *Gazette,* December 11, 1886; Washington *Bee,* July 31, 1886.

57. Quoted in Huntsville *Gazette,* August 21, 1886.

58. Washington *Bee,* December 10, 1887.

59. New York *Sun,* November 16, 1887; Boston *Evening Transcript,* May 29, 1888.

60. Boston *Post,* November 21, 1887.

61. See GWW, *History of the Negro Troops,* pp. 181–303, for his detailed discussion of the role of Negro soldiers in battle.

62. *New Englander and Yale Review* 51 (November 1889): 362; *Literary World* 19 (February 18, 1888): 85; *The Dial* 8 (February 1888): 253.

63. There is a brief sketch of Wilson's career in Penn, *The Afro-American Press and Its Editors,* pp. 174–80.

64. *Nation* 46 (March 1, 1888): 180.

65. For a discussion of the controversy surrounding GWW's appointment as United States minister to Haiti, see chapter 11 below.

66. New York *Age,* March 10, 1888 and August 24, 1889.

67. Penn, *The Afro-American Press and Its Editors,* p. 179.

68. In 1883, GWW said that if he ever got a position he would "give the country a work on Reconstruction." GWW to John P. Green, February 27, 1883, Green Papers.

69. New York *Freeman,* January 17, 1885.

70. Boston *Advocate,* June 27, 1885.

71. GWW to George F. Hoar, January 9, 1888. The George F. Hoar Papers, Massachusetts Historical Society. Williams was apparently quite anxious to see these documents. Later that day he complained to Senator Hoar that a man in the Senate Documents Room kept the Williams messenger waiting all afternoon and then told him to come back the following day between noon and four. By mid-January the matter was settled. See the second letter of GWW to Hoar, January 9, 1888, and the one of January 14, 1888. Hoar Papers.

72. GWW to George Bancroft, February 1, 1888, Bancroft Papers.

73. Indianapolis *World,* June 9, 1888.

74. GWW to Samuel A. Green, January 25, 1887, Massachusetts Historical Society. See also chapter 8, note 46, above.

75. Indianapolis *World,* March 31, 1888.

76. New York *Age,* February 4, 1888.

77. *Fisk Herald* 5 (January 1888): 8.

78. W. E. B. Du Bois, "The Negro in Literature and Art," *Annals of the American Academy of Political and Social Science* 49 (September 1913): 235.

79. Indianapolis *World,* December 24, 1887.

Chapter 10

1. GWW to John P. Green, New York, March 16, 1883. Green Papers.

2. Ibid.

3. New York *Globe,* January 13, February 17, March 3, April 28, 1883.

4. New York *Globe,* March 31, 1883.

5. New York *Globe,* April 14, 1883; New York *Daily Tribune,* April 10, 1883.

6. New York *Daily Tribune,* April 10, 1883. See also New York *Times,* April 10, 1883, and Columbus *Dispatch,* April 11, 1883.

7. Quoted in New York *Globe,* April 21, 1883.

8. New York *Globe,* May 26, 1883.

9. Boston *Evening Transcript,* September 28, 1883.

10. Ibid., October 3, 12, 18, 25, 26, and 30, and November 2 and 5, 1883. New York *Globe,* November 3, 1883.

11. For the election results, see Boston *Evening Transcript,* November 7, 1883. For the role of blacks in the election of Robinson, see New York *Globe,* November 10, 1883.

12. Boston *Evening Transcript,* November 12, 1883. New York *Globe,* November 17, 1883.

13. GWW to George L. Ruffin, November 19, 1883. GWW wrote two letters to Ruffin on November 19, one regarding the action of the Commonwealth Council and the other proposing the dinner in Ruffin's honor. George L. Ruffin Papers, Moorland-Spingarn Research Center, Howard University.

14. GWW to Judge George L. Ruffin, November 19, 1883. Ruffin Papers.

15. Boston *Evening Transcript,* November 23, 1883. See also the account of the dinner in the New York *Globe,* December 1, 1883.

16. Cincinnati *Commercial,* June 9, 1881.

17. The papers dealing with the admission of GWW to the Massachusetts bar, including his petition, Ruffin's affidavit, and the report of the Board of Examiners, are in the files of the Supreme Judicial Court of Massachusetts. These proceedings attracted considerable attention in the public press. See, for example, the New York *Globe,* November 24, 1883; Boston *Evening Transcript,* December 5, 1883; Cleveland *Gazette,* December 8, 1883; and Huntsville *Gazette,* February 9, 1884.

18. Boston *Evening Transcript,* December 5, 1883 and New York *Globe,* December 8, 1883.

19. New York *Globe,* December 8, 1883 and February 16, 1884.

20. Ibid., March 29, 1884.

21. Robert H. Farsen, *The Cape Cod Canal* (Middletown, Conn., 1977), p. 22.

22. Boston *Evening Transcript,* May 5, 1884.

23. E. W. Gilliam, "The African in the United States," *Popular Science Monthly* 22 (February 1883):433–44.

24. Boston *Evening Transcript,* January 25, 1884.

25. Cleveland *Gazette,* October 6, 1883.

26. Boston *Evening Transcript,* April 4, 1884. GWW was present a few months earlier but apparently did not speak when the Boston Odd Fellows celebrated their tenth anniversary. New York *Globe,* February 9, 1884.

27. Boston *Evening Transcript,* September 30, 1884.

28. Cleveland *Gazette,* April 26, 1884. One report said that 50,000 "colored people thronged the streets on the 16th. They have an esprit de corps and undaunted cheerfulness. . . . They have made at least a surface showing of

progress from their condition of servitude to that of equality in the march of life."
Boston *Evening Transcript*, April 19, 1884.

29. GWW to George F. Hoar, Washington, D.C., April 16, 1884. Hoar Papers.

30. Cleveland *Gazette*, April 26, 1884.

31. Boston *Evening Transcript*, April 17, 1884. While GWW was in Washington, a group of men tendered him a sumptuous banquet at John Gray's, "one of the best caterers in the city." The host of the evening was Professor Richard T. Greener of Howard University. Several of the sixteen present made remarks that were highly complimentary of the honored guest. On the same visit to Washington, GWW also gave a lecture at Howard University. New York *Globe*, April 26, 1884.

32, Boston *Evening Transcript*, April 26, 1884. Of twenty-nine votes cast, GWW received twenty. New York *Globe*, May 3, 1884.

33. New York *Globe*, June 21, 1884.

34. Boston *Evening Transcript*, December 19 and 22, 1884; January 17, 1885.

35. GWW to Sarah Williams, S.S. *Egypt*, July 14, 1884. George W. Williams Papers. Last seen in the possession of Henry P. Slaughter, Washington, D.C.; see "A Note on the Sources" above.

36. GWW to Sarah Williams, Heidelberg, Germany, August 11, 1884, ibid. See also GWW's account of his European travels in his centennial oration before the African Lodge of the Free and Accepted Masons, September 29, 1884. Boston *Evening Transcript*, September 30, 1884. For other aspects of his trip, see chapter 11 below.

37. Boston *Evening Transcript*, September 29, 1884.

38. GWW, *History of the Negro Race*, vol. 2, pp. 518–19.

39. Washington *Bee*, September 13, 1884; Cleveland *Gazette*, October 25, 1884; New York *Freeman*, March 7, 1885, and November 22, 1884.

40. Washington *Bee*, October 30, November 13, 1886; Cleveland *Gazette*, November 27, 1886.

41. New York *Freeman*, April 23, 1887.

42. Washington *Bee*, April 30, 1887; Cleveland *Gazette*, April 30, 1887.

43. T. Thomas Fortune's *Black and White: Land, Labor, and Politics in the South* (New York, 1884).

44. Worcester *Sunday Telegram*, June 16, 1889.

45. William B. Shaw, "James A. Pond," *Dictionary of American Biography*, vol. 8, pt. 1 (New York, 1935), pp. 60–61; and Major J. B. Pond, *Eccentricities of Genius* (New York, 1900).

46. Williams File, Box 164, Department of State. When GWW wrote Hoar requesting an endorsement, he said that Pond planned to send out 2,000 circulars to his correspondents. GWW to George F. Hoar, Worcester, September 14, 1888. Hoar Papers.

47. GWW, *The Advent of the Colored Soldier* (Boston, 1874). Many of GWW's other orations received extensive coverage in the press. See, for

example, the full text of his "The Distinctive Features of American Patriotism" in the Salem (Ohio) *Republican,* June 1, 1882.

48. GWW, *The American Negro from 1776 to 1876* (Cincinnati, 1876).

49. GWW, *The Negro as a Political Problem* (Boston, 1884).

50. GWW, *The Constitutional Results of the War of the Rebellion* (Worcester, 1889).

51. GWW gave the Worcester lecture on the Congo on April 8, 1889. GWW to George F. Hoar, Worcester, April 6, 1889, Hoar Papers. For GWW's earlier writings on Africa, see the Worcester *Evening Gazette,* July 27, 1889.

52. Washington *Bee,* April 2, 1887. See also the Huntsville *Gazette,* June 11, 1887. There is no record of GWW's having written the piece. Another writing project that apparently got nowhere was the invitation from Funk and Wagnalls, as he told Senator Hoar, to write "a life of our dear dead friend William Lloyd Garrison." GWW to George F. Hoar, Worcester, April 13, 1889. Hoar Papers.

53. Editor of *Magazine of American History* to GWW, New York City, July 19, 1889, Hoar Papers.

54. Cleveland *Gazette,* February 4, 1888.

55. Huntsville *Gazette,* January 21, 1888; Washington *Bee,* February 25, 1888.

56. Cleveland *Gazette,* June 6, 1885.

57. GWW to Lee and Shepard, Washington, D.C., April 16, 1886, Lee and Shepard Papers, American Antiquarian Society.

58. GWW to Lee and Shepard, Washington, D.C., May 27, 1886, ibid.

59. Indianapolis *World,* December 24, 1887. There was an extensive biography of GWW in the same issue.

60. Ibid.

61. New York *Freeman,* September 8, 1888.

62. London, 1837.

Chapter 11

1. New York *Freeman,* December 6, 1884.

2. Ibid., January 17, February 7, 1885.

3. Washington *Bee,* February 28, 1885; New York *Freeman,* March 14, 1885.

4. George W. Williams File, Box 103, Applications and Recommendations for Public Office, 1797–1901, Record Group 59, General Records of the Department of State, National Archives and Record Service (hereafter called Williams File, Box 103, Department of State).

5. Since the session was entirely off the record, all that is reported in the *Congressional Record* is that the Senate met in executive session on that date at eight o'clock in the evening. *Congressional Record,* 48th Congress, 2d Session, vol. 16, pt. 2 (Washington, D.C., 1885), p. 2360. There is therefore no mention of GWW in the *Record* or in the index. The U.S. Court of Claims, however, accepted as a fact that GWW was confirmed by the Senate on March 2, 1885. *Cases Decided in the Court of Claims of the United States, 1887–1888,* vol. 23

(Washington, D.C., 1889), p. 46. And the Boston *Evening Transcript,* March 3, 1885, in its column on proceedings in Congress, reported that the Senate had confirmed GWW's appointment in executive session the previous day.

6. *The National Republican,* March 16, 1885.

7. Boston *Evening Transcript,* March 3, 1885.

8. New York *Freeman,* March 7, 1885; Washington *Bee,* March 7, 1885. See also the New York *Times,* March 3, 1885.

9. GWW to George F. Hoar, January 9, 1886, Hoar Papers.

10. New York *Freeman,* March 7, 1885.

11. Cleveland *Gazette,* March 14, 1885.

12. GWW to Thomas F. Bayard, Washington, D.C., March 12, 1885, Williams File, Box 103, Department of State.

13. *National Republican,* April 16, 1885.

14. GWW to Grover Cleveland, April 13, 1885, Washington, D.C., Williams File, Box 164, Department of State. This lengthy letter to the president is a convenient summary of GWW's version of the appointment imbroglio.

15. Ibid.

16. *National Republican,* April 16, 1885.

17. GWW to George F. Hoar, Washington, D.C., March 16, 1885, Hoar Papers.

18. Charles B. Purvis, graduate of the College of Medicine of Western Reserve University, was a member of a prominent Philadelphia family. A professor of materia medica and medical jurisprudence at Howard University, he was, at the time he treated Williams, surgeon in charge of Freedman's Hospital. Simmons, *Men of Mark,* pp. 477–79.

19. GWW to Sarah Williams, Washington, D.C. March 23, 1885. Williams Papers.

20. GWW to George F. Hoar, Washington, D. C., April 30, 1885, Hoar Papers.

21. The letter read, "At the request of the President, I take pleasure in introducing Mr. George W. Williams of Boston, who is about departing for Europe and in whose behalf I bespeak your friendly consideration." It was signed by Frederick T. Frelinghuysen. Williams File, Box 103, Department of State.

22. Department of State memorandum, April 15, 1885. Williams File, Box 103, Department of State.

23. GWW to Lyell Adams, Geneva, Switzerland, July 26, 1884; GWW to Lyell Adams, Stuttgart, Germany, August 11, 1884; GWW to Ferdinand Gehrung, Brussels, Belgium, August 15, 1884; Telegram: GWW to Ferdinard Gehrung, Brussels, Belgium, n.d., 1884; GWW to Ferdinand Gehrung, London, England, August 26, 1884; Ferdinand Gehrung to George L. Catlin, Stuttgart, September 15, 1884; Receipt, from Ferdinand Gehrung to George Catlin, Stuttgart, September 16, 1884; Lyell T. Adams to Frederick T. Frelinghuysen, Geneva, October 9, 1884; George L. Catlin to F. O. St. Clair, Stuttgart, September 18, 1884; all in Williams File, Box 103, Department of State.

24. This comment was scribbled in red ink across the bottom of a copy of GWW's letter of introduction from the Secretary of State, Williams File, Box 103, Department of State.

25. See, for example, the Washington *Bee's* support of Logan and Blaine in the spring of 1884 and of Blaine and Logan following the Republican National Convention that summer.

26. Washington *Bee,* March 14, 1885.

27. Boston *Advocate,* April 25, 1885; Cleveland *Gazette,* May 9 and 16, 1885.

28. Washington *Bee,* March 14, 1885.

29. GWW to Sarah Williams, Washington, D.C., March 23, 1885, Williams Papers.

30. Peter Clark to Thomas F. Bayard, Cincinnati, Ohio, n.d., 1885; J. Lundy Brotherton to Thomas Bayard, Philadelphia, March 11, 1885; J. Lundy Brotherton to Peter H. Clark, Philadelphia, March 12, 1885; J. Lundy Brotherton to Hon. Secretary of State, Philadelphia, March 21, 1885; Henry L. Bryan to Robert Purvis, Washington, March 20 [1885]; Robert Purvis to Henry L. Bryan, Philadelphia, March 22, 1885; all in Williams File, Box 103, Department of State.

31. S. R. Scottron to Grover Cleveland, Buffalo, April 29, 1885. Williams File, Box 103, Department of State.

32. William Means to George H. Pendleton, New York, March 10, 1885; George H. Pendleton to Thomas F. Bayard, Washington, April 1, 1885; William Birney to Henry L. Bryan, Washington, March 13, 1885; R. B. McCrory to [Secretary of State Bayard], Mansfield, Ohio, April 15, 1885; Alfred Harrison to Thomas F. Bayard, Indianapolis, April 16, 1885; all in Williams File, Box 103, Department of State. See also the editorial in the Newport *Daily News,* April 20, 1885, supporting George Downing for the post, and the letter from S. S. Bloom to Thomas Bayard, Shelby, Ohio, May 1, 1885. Bloom was a Democratic lawyer who as a Democrat sought the Ohio House Speakership and lost when GWW was in the legislature in 1880. He said that for many reasons GWW "ought *not* to represent the United States anywhere." Williams File, Box 103, Department of State.

33. Middletown *Daily Argus,* April 22, 1885. The editor sent the clipping to the Secretary of State, and declared that the statements in the article "are exactly true and are easily susceptible to proof." George H. Thompson to [Secretary of State Bayard], Middletown, New York, April 22, 1885, Williams File, Box 103, Department of State.

34. New York *Tribune,* April 18, 21, 24, 1885.

35. GWW to Grover Cleveland, Washington, April 20, 1885, Williams File, Box 103, Department of State.

36. New York *Tribune,* April 20, 1885.

37. GWW to Thomas F. Bayard, Washington, April 26, 1885 (the letter, apparently misdated, was received at the Department of State on April 25,

1885), Williams File, Box 164, Department of State. See also New York *Tri-bune*, April 26, 1885.

38. New York *Freeman*, April 18, 1885; Boston *Evening Transcript*, April 17, 21, 1885.

39. Cleveland *Gazette*, April 18, 1885.

40. GWW to John Sherman, Washington, D.C., December 23, 1885, Legislative Papers, Record Group 46, Committee on Foreign Relations, National Archives and Record Service. This is an eight-page letter with numerous accompanying documents. Doubtless, GWW hoped that Republican Sherman would assist him in his fight against a Democratic administration.

41. Thompson received a recess appointment in May. Cleveland sent his name to the Senate in December, where it was promptly confirmed. For a sketch of Thompson's life, see Rayford W. Logan and Michael R. Winston, eds., *Dictionary of American Negro Biography* (New York, 1983), pp. 588–89.

42. Boston *Evening Transcript*, May 12, 1885; New York *Freeman*, May 16, 1885; Washington *Bee*, May 16, 1885.

43. *Cases Decided in the Court of Claims of the United States, Term 1887–1888*, vol. 23 (Washington, 1889), pp. 46–53.

44. GWW was in Europe during June and July, 1888. In August he was vacationing in Plymouth. In September he was placed on the roster of speakers for the Republican State Committee. Robert A. Southworth to George F. Hoar, Boston, Mass., September 15, 1888, Hoar Papers.

45. George F. Hoar to GWW, Washington, D.C., March 23, 1889, Benjamin Harrison Papers, Series 1, Reel 19.

46. New York *Age*, March 30, 1889.

47. New York *Freeman*, May 30, 1885.

48. New York *Age*, March 30, 1889.

49. GWW to Benjamin Harrison, Worcester, Mass., April 9, 1889, Williams File, Box 164, Department of State.

50. Ibid; GWW to James G. Blaine, Worcester, Mass., April 10, 1889, Williams File, Box 164, Department of State.

51. James G. Blaine to GWW, Washington, D.C., April 22, 1889; GWW to James G. Blaine, Worcester, Mass., April 24, 1889; all in Williams File, Box 164, Department of State.

52. George F. Hoar to Benjamin Harrison, Worcester, Mass., April 12, 1889; Henry W. Blair to Benjamin Harrison, Washington, D.C., June 12, 1889; all in Williams File, Box 164, Department of State.

53. For several months the Harrison administration made no appointments of blacks, and the black press expressed impatience and fear that none would be forthcoming. See Washington *Bee* and Cleveland *Gazette* for April and May 1889. The New York *Freeman*, which had become anti-Republican as early as 1884, expressed no surprise. GWW's anxiety about the appointment was reflected in a telegram concerning their own strategy that he sent to Senator Hoar: "Is it safe to defer action any long[er]. Urgency." GWW to George F.

Hoar, Worcester, Mass., March 23, 1889, Hoar Papers. The leading authority on Haitian-American relations makes it clear that Harrison and Blaine had no intention of appointing GWW or any other Negro to the post in Haiti. Rayford W. Logan, *The Diplomatic Relations of the United States with Haiti, 1776–1891* (Chapel Hill, 1941), pp. 426–28.

54. GWW to George F. Hoar, Worcester, Mass., December 24 and December 27, 1888, February 20, 1889, Hoar Papers.

55. *Congressional Record,* 51st Congress, 1st Session, vol. 21 (Washington, D.C., 1889), pp. 127, 222.

56. GWW to Frederick Douglass, Worcester, Mass., June 29, 1889, Douglass Papers, Reel 5.

57. GWW to George F. Hoar, Worcester, Mass., July 3, 1889. GWW was also having difficulty placing his articles in places that would pay him for them. GWW to George F. Hoar, Worcester, Mass., August 12, 1889, Hoar Papers.

58. Harry Smith, Cleveland leader and editor, was especially critical of the Douglass appointment on the ground that Republicans should encourage young blacks by appointing them to office. Cleveland *Gazette,* July 6, 1889. See also George Sinkler, *Racial Attitudes of American Presidents from Abraham Lincoln to Theodore Roosevelt* (New York, 1971), pp. 265–72.

Chapter 12

1. The account of GWW's entire experience with the New York Land League appears in a lengthy interview by a New York reporter with GWW. New York *Daily Tribune,* December 19, 1880. His trip was well reported in the press. See Washington *People's Advocate,* December 4, 1880; Huntsville *Gazette,* December 11, 1880; Columbus *Dispatch,* December 6, 1880; and Cincinnati *Commercial,* January 10, 1881.

2. New York *Daily Tribune,* December 19, 1880.

3. The entire text of the chief justice's letter was reproduced in the New York *Daily Tribune,* December 19, 1880.

4. Washington *People's Advocate,* December 25, 1880. GWW gave an account of his trip to New Mexico to a gathering of blacks in Cincinnati early in January. Cincinnati *Commercial,* January 10, 1881.

5. For a brief history of the Negro convention movement, see August Meier, *Negro Thought in America, 1880–1915* (Ann Arbor, 1963), pp. 4–10; and Rayford W. Logan, *The Betrayal of the Negro from Rutherford B. Hayes to Woodrow Wilson* (New York, 1965), pp. 332–35.

6. New York *Globe,* May 12, 1883. The text of the call is printed in the Huntsville *Gazette,* May 12, 1883.

7. New York *Globe,* May 19, 1883.

8. Washington *Bee,* June 9, 1883.

9. Huntsville *Gazette,* August 18, 1883.

10. Quoted in ibid., September 1, 1883.

11. Boston *Evening Transcript,* September 18, 1883; Huntsville *Gazette,* September 29, 1883.

12. New York *Globe,* September 29, 1883. See also Huntsville *Gazette,* September 29, 1883.

13. Huntsville *Gazette,* September 29, 1883.

14. New York *Globe,* September 29, 1883.

15. Huntsville *Gazette,* October 6, 1883.

16. Cleveland *Gazette,* October 6, 1883.

17. Cincinnati *Commercial,* September 19, 1879.

18. George H. Thomas Post No. 13, *Proceedings of a Camp Fire Oct. 5, 1880,* n.p.

19. T. D. McGillicuddy, comp., *Proceedings of the Annual and Semi-Annual Encampments of the Department of Ohio, Grand Army of the Republic* (Columbus, 1912), pp. 162–64. See also Cincinnati *Commercial,* January 21, 1880. The extent of involvement of members of the GAR in politics and related matters is discussed in Mary R. Dearing, *Veterans in Politics: The Story of the G.A.R.* (Baton Rouge, 1952).

20. Cincinnati *Commercial,* January 22, April 15, 1880.

21. *Proceedings of the Fourteenth Annual Meeting of the National Encampment, Grand Army of the Republic, 1880* (n.p., n.d.); and Cincinnati *Commercial,* June 9, 1880.

22. *The Ohio State Journal,* January 27, 1881. See also Columbus *Dispatch,* February 3, 1881. and Cincinnati *Commercial,* February 3, 1881. One authority suggested that it was not uncommon for a department officer "to be showered indiscriminately with such titles as 'general,' 'colonel,' or 'captain' " even though the person has been a private in the army. Elmer Edward Noyes, "A History of the Grand Army of the Republic in Ohio from 1866 to 1900," Ph.D. Dissertation, Ohio State University, 1945, pp. 30–31.

23. Grand Army of the Republic, *Proceedings of the Sixteenth Annual Encampment, Department of Ohio* (Toledo, 1882), pp. 47–48.

24. GWW, *History of the Negro Troops,* pp. 328–29.

25. GWW to George F. Hoar, Washington, D.C., August 14, 1886, Hoar Papers. (For an example of news media involvement, see the Washington *Bee,* August 7, 1886.)

26. GWW to George F. Hoar, Washington, D.C., December 7, 1886, Hoar Papers.

27. *Congressional Record,* 49th Congress, 2d Session, December 8, 1886, Senate Bills, vol. 10, n.p.

28. Ibid., January 13, 1887, vol. 18, p. 598.

29. Ibid., December 20, 1886, vol. 18, p. 287.

30. GWW to George F. Hoar, Washington, D.C., December 9, 1886, Hoar Papers.

31. GWW to George F. Hoar, Washington, D.C., January 5, 1887, ibid.

32. Cleveland *Gazette,* January 22, 1887.

33. There is no report of the Senate Library Committee in the committee reports of the 49th Congress, 2d Session.

34. *Congressional Record,* 49th Congress, 2d Session, vol. 18, pt. 1, p. 598. See also Huntsville *Gazette,* February 26, 1887.

35. GWW to George F. Hoar, Plymouth, Mass., July 6, 1887, Hoar Papers.

36. J. M. Addeman to George F. Hoar, Providence, R.I., October 22, 1887, Hoar Papers.

37. Ibid. See also the Providence *Journal,* October 19, 1887.

38. *Congressional Record,* 50th Congress, 1st Session, vol. 19, pt. 1, p. 214.

39. GWW to George F. Hoar, Washington, D.C., March 21, 1888, Hoar Papers.

40. *Congressional Record,* 50th Congress, 1st Session, vol. 19, pt. 1, p. 214.

41. I am indebted to Professor Philip Butcher's writings and conversations with him for this discussion of the Williams-Cable relationship. See especially his "George W. Cable and George W. Williams: An Abortive Collaboration," *Journal of Negro History* 53 (October 1968): 334–44.

42. GWW to George W. Cable, Worcester, Mass., November 5, 1888, Cable Collection, Tulane University.

43. Diary entry, January 8, 1889, Cable Collection, Tulane University.

44. George W. Cable to Adelene Moffat, Northampton, Mass., January 9, 1889, Cable Collection, Columbia University Library.

45. GWW, *The Constitutional Results of the War of the Rebellion* (Worcester, 1889), p. 18.

46. GWW to George W. Cable, Worcester, Mass., June 11, 1889, Cable Collection, Tulane University.

47. GWW to Mrs. George W. Cable, Worcester, Mass., June 18, 1889, ibid.

48. See Philip Butcher, *George W. Cable* (New York, 1962); and Arlin Turner, *George W. Cable: A Biography* (Baton Rouge, 1966).

49. He wrote his wife from Deming that he was not well yet. "I will write again soon, if I live." GWW to Sarah Williams, Deming, New Mexico, May 9, 1881, Williams Papers.

50. Boston *Evening Transcript,* September 30, 1884.

51. Cincinnati *Commercial,* June 4, 1879.

52. GWW to Sarah Williams, Deming, New Mexico, May 9, 1881; GWW to Sarah Williams, Heidelberg, August 11, 1884; GWW to Sarah Williams, ss. *Egypt,* July 14, 1884; all in Williams Papers.

53. GWW to Sarah Williams, Heidelberg, August 11, 1884; GWW to Sarah Williams, Washington, March 23, 1885; both in Williams Papers.

54. Washington *Bee,* July 24, 1886; Cleveland *Gazette,* August 7, 1886; Boston *Advocate,* August 14, 1886 (the newspaper commented that the news of a divorce was not unexpected to Bostonians); Huntsville *Gazette,* August 21, 1886.

55. Washington *Bee,* July 24, July 31, 1886.

56. Cleveland *Gazette,* August 7, 1886.

57. Boston *Advocate,* October 23, 1886.

58. A search of the records of the Superior Court of the District of Columbia, of those of the United States District Court for the District of Columbia, and those at the National Archives failed to yield any information about the divorce proceedings. Thomas A. Duckenfield, Clerk of the Superior Court of the District of Columbia, to the author, April 13, 1982. When GWW died, Sarah Williams still regarded him as her husband. Sarah Williams to John P. Green, Washington, D.C., August 24, 1891, Green Papers.

59. Louisville *Courier-Journal,* May 18, 1887.

60. *American Baptist,* May 5, 13, 20, 1887.

61. Cleveland, 1887.

62. James Johnston, *Report of the Centenary Conference on the Protestant Missions of the World Held in Exeter Hall (June 9–19th), London 1888* (New York, 1888), vol. 1, pp. 135, 217, 593.

63. Ibid., vol. 2, pp. 316–17.

64. Worcester *Sunday Telegram,* September 29, 1889.

65. GWW, "The African Slave Trade," Worcester *Evening Gazette,* July 27, 1889. An editorial in the same issue supported the statement GWW had made.

66. GWW to James G. Blaine, Worcester, Mass., August 3, 1889. Williams File, Box 164, Department of State.

67. Worcester *Telegram,* October 15, 1889. A similar account appeared in the Huntsville *Gazette,* October 26, 1889, and the Washington *Bee,* October 19, 1889. The story of the romance came out, it was said, when the young lady went to the U.S. Legation in London to inquire if there would be any legal difficulties in contracting to marry a Negro American. It is not known what advice she received. New York *Age,* October 19, 1889.

68. Worcester *Telegram,* October 17, 1889.

69. Worcester *Sunday Telegram,* November 24, 1889.

70. His mother had died in January 1881, when he was in the legislature. Presumably his father was already deceased.

Chapter 13

1. The commission itself, dated September 26, 1889, was in the Williams Papers.

2. Peter Lyon, *Success Story: The Life and Times of S.S. McClure* (Deland, Fla., 1963), pp. 59, 76, 86–98.

3. Boston *Herald,* November 17, 1889. See also the account of the *Herald* article in the New York *Age,* November 23, 1889, on the letter from Brussels by GWW "purporting to give a talk had by him with the King of the Belgians."

4. Sanford's ideas are set forth in his "American Interests in Africa," *The Forum* 9 (June 1890): 409–29. See also Joseph A. Fry, *Henry S. Sanford: Diplomacy and Business in Nineteenth-Century America* (Reno, 1982), pp. 133–63.

5. GWW to Henry S. Sanford, Brussels, October 31, 1889. Henry S. San-

ford Papers, Box 28, Sanford, Florida; and Henry S. Sanford to Count Outre-
mont, Brussels, n.d., Royal Archives, Brussels.

6. *L'Indépendance Belge,* November 1, 1889.

7. Department of State, "Notes to the Belgian Government," September
25, 1889, December 5, 1889, Record Group 59, National Archives and Record
Service.

8. Huntington told Chicagoan Lambert Tree that he had subscribed £10,000
to the railroad scheme but was too busy to take an active role in the project.
Lambert Tree to Henry S. Sanford, Chicago, July 16, 1889, Sanford Papers.

9. The conversations that GWW had with Huntington, presumably in London, were not a matter of record, but they may be easily assumed from
subsequent correspondence between the two that is in the Collis P. Huntington
Papers, George Arents Research Library, Syracuse University.

10. Collis P. Huntington to GWW, London October 11 and 24, 1889 (The
Congo Book), Huntington Papers, Arents Research Library, Syracuse University.

11. For a discussion of the general problems taken up by the Conference,
see Arthur B. Keith, *The Belgian Congo and the Berlin Act* (Oxford, 1919),
pp. 77 ff.

12. Department of State, "Instructions to the U.S. Minister" (Brussels), vol.
11, p. 525, September 24, 1889, Record Group 59, National Archives and
Record Service.

13. Collis P. Huntington to GWW, New York, November 12 and 13, 1889
(The Congo Book), Huntington Papers.

14. Lord Vivian to Lord Salisbury, Brussels, May 31, 1890, Proceedings of
the Slave Trade Conference, no. 156, FO 84/2103, Public Record Office.

15. See Ruth Slade, *King Leopold's Congo* (London, 1962), pp. 105–6.

16. The New York *Age,* September 21, 1889, reported that GWW was about
to visit the Congo Free State.

17. For a full discussion of Sanford's views on this matter, see James Patrick
White, "Henry Shelton Sanford and Africa," unpublished M.A. thesis, Vander-
bilt University, 1963; and Fry, *Henry S. Sanford,* pp. 138–39.

18. Henry S. Sanford to the editor, New York *Herald,* July 17, 1886.

19. New York *Daily Tribune,* March 2, 1890.

20. GWW to Collis P. Huntington, New York, December 9, 1889, Huntington Papers.

21. Collis P. Huntington to S. C. Armstrong, New York, December 6, 1889,
Huntington Papers. For another, quite similar account of how the two men met,
see Collis P. Huntington to William Mackinnon, New York, March 18, 1890, Sir
William Mackinnon Papers, School of Oriental and African Studies, London.

22. S. C. Armstrong to Collis P. Huntington, Hampton, Va., December 16,
1889; GWW to Collis P. Huntington, New York, December 18, 1889; both in
Huntington Papers.

23. M. E. Strieby to Collis P. Huntington, New York, February 4, 1890,
Huntington Papers.

24. GWW, *A Report upon the Congo-State and Country to the President of the Republic of the United States of America* (1890; reprinted as Appendix 3 below), pp. 3–4.

25. GWW to Collis P. Huntington, Loango, French Congo, September 6, 1890, and Zanzibar, December 1, 1890, Huntington Papers.

26. GWW, *Report upon the Congo-State and Country*, pp. 4–5.

27. White, "Henry Shelton Sanford and Africa," pp. 97, 101.

28. Cerinda W. Evans, *Collis Potter Huntington* (Newport News, 1954), pp. 658–59. See also the San Francisco *Call*, August 15, 1895. The official documents regarding Huntington's investment in the Congo Railway are in the Huntington Papers. See especially Berryman and Turnbull to Balser and Co., New York, December 5, 1889, and "Memorandum in respect to subscription to Congo Railway Company by C. P. Huntington." The amount of the subscription was listed as $50,000.

29. GWW to C. P. Huntington, Brussels, January 7, 1890; telegram: C. P. Huntington to GWW, New York, January 8, 1889 [1890]; C. P. Huntington to GWW, New York, January 7, 1890; all in Huntington Papers.

30. In London, Williams purchased arms, ammunition, medicine, a tent, and camp furniture. GWW to Robert H. Terrell, Cameroons, March 13, 1890, Robert H. Terrell papers, Library of Congress.

31. GWW to Collis P. Huntington, Zanzibar, East Africa, December 1, 1890, Huntington Papers.

32. GWW to Robert H. Terrell, Cameroons, March 13, 1890, Terrell Papers. The New York *Tribune*, June 8, 1890, carried an account of his trip from Liverpool to Boma. The *Tribune* was one of the subscribers to the Associated Literary Press, for which Williams was writing. GWW to Collis P. Huntington, Las Palmas, February 6, 1890, Huntington Papers.

33. GWW to Collis P. Huntington, Boma, Congo State, April 14, 1890, ibid.

34. GWW to Henry S. Sanford, Sierra Leone, February 12, 1890, Box 28, Sanford Papers.

35. GWW to Collis P. Huntington, Las Palmas, February 6, 1890, Huntington Papers.

36. GWW to George F. Hoar, Boma, April 12, 1890, Hoar Papers. This letter was marked "Confidential." In a letter to Huntington a few days later, GWW repeated the comment about a man of war, saying that its presence would have a "splendid moral effect and might save me from assassination." GWW to Collis P. Huntington, Boma, April 14, 1890, Huntington Papers.

37. François Bontinck, *Aux Origines de l'État Indépendant du Congo* (Louvain, 1966), pp. 58–73, 399–403.

38. GWW to Collis P. Huntington, Boma, April 14, 1890, Huntington Papers.

39. GWW to Collis P. Huntington, Tunduwa, May 12, 1890, ibid.

40. See chapter 14 below for GWW's criticisms of Stanley's railway estimates.

41. GWW to Robert H. Terrell, St. Paul de Loanda, Angola, October 14, 1890, Terrell Papers.

42. GWW to Collis P. Huntington, Boma, Congo State, April 14, 1890; GWW to Collis P. Huntington, Tunduwa, S. W. Africa, May 12, 1890; GWW to Collis P. Huntington, Stanley Falls, Central Africa, July 16, 1890; GWW to Collis P. Huntington, Loango, French Congo, September 6, 1890; all in Huntington Papers.

43. George Grenfell to A. H. Baynes, Bolobo, Congo State, June 23, 1890, Baptist Missionary Society Papers, London.

44. George Grenfell, Diary, March 2, 1889 to August 1, 1890; George Grenfell to A. H. Baynes, Bolobo, Congo State, June 23, 1890; both in Baptist Missionary Society Papers. On the reluctance of Grenfell to criticize Leopold, see Sir Harry Johnston, *George Grenfell and the Congo*, 2 vols. (London, 1908), vol. 1, pp. 467–68.

45. Johnston, *Grenfell*, vol. 1, p. 445.

46. George Grenfell to A. H. Baynes (see note 43 above).

47. GWW *Report upon the Congo State*, pp. 11–13, 16–17, 20.

48. Ibid., p. 16. For Stanley's discussion of the population figures and other demographic features of the Congo basin, see Henry M. Stanley, *The Congo and the Founding of Its Free State*, 2 vols. (New York, 1885), vol. 2, chap. 37, esp. p. 364.

49. GWW to Collis P. Huntington, Stanley Falls, Central Africa, July 16, 1890, Huntington Papers.

50. Grenfell Diary, July 29, 1890, Baptist Missionary Society papers.

51. GWW to Robert H. Terrell, St. Paul de Loanda, Angola, October 14, 1890, Terrell Papers; GWW to Collis P. Huntington, Loango, French Congo, September 6, 1890, Huntington Papers; GWW to Robert H. Terrell, St. Paul de Loanda, Angola, October 14, 1890, Terrell Papers.

52. GWW to Collis P. Huntington, Loanda, S. W. Africa, September 18, 1890; GWW to Collis P. Huntington, Zanzibar, East Africa, December 1, 1890; both in Huntington Papers.

53. GWW to Robert H. Terrell, St. Paul de Loanda, Angola, October 14, 1890, Terrell Papers.

54. Ibid.

55. GWW to Collis P. Huntington, Zanzibar, East Africa, December 1, 1890, Huntington Papers.

56. Ibid.

57. Ibid.

58. Ibid. Mackinnon had already warned Euan Smith about GWW (see chapter 15 below).

59. GWW to Robert H. Terrell, Cairo, Egypt, March 7, 1891, Terrell Papers.

60. GWW to Collis P. Huntington, Cairo, Egypt, January 23, 1891, Huntington Papers.

61. The partition of Africa had resulted in Zanzibar's loss of its independence

and the establishment in November 1890 of a British protectorate over the country. The sultan's emancipation edict three months earlier doubtless resulted from pressure brought on him by the British government. See Robert Nunez Lyne, *Zanzibar in Contemporary Times* (London, 1905), pp. 174–75.

62. See Edward Francis Russell, "Charles Alan Smythies," *Dictionary of National Biography* (Oxford, 1917), vol. 18, pp. 609–10.

63. GWW to Collis P. Huntington, Zanzibar, East Africa, December 1, 1890, Huntington Papers.

64. GWW to Collis P. Huntington, Cairo, Egypt, January 23, 1891, ibid.

65. GWW to Robert H. Terrell, Cairo, Egypt, March 7, 1891, Terrell Papers.

66. GWW to Collis P. Huntington, Cairo, Egypt, January 23 and February 11, 1891, Huntington Papers.

67. "Charles George Gordon," *Dictionary of National Biography* (Oxford, 1917), vol. 8, pp. 169–76; and Georg Schweitzer, comp. *Emin Pasha: His Life and Work* (New York, 1969), vol. 1, pp. 138–40.

68. GWW to Collis P. Huntington, Cairo, Egypt, January 23, 1891, Huntington Papers.

69. GWW to Collis P. Huntington, Cairo, Egypt, February 11, 1891, ibid.

70. Ibid. The reference to Huntington's "circular" was to a widely circulated statement by Huntington on slavery and the slave trade in Africa. See, for example, a copy of the statement, "A Few Words to Americans on the Slave Trade in Africa," in *The American,* September 21, 1889.

71. GWW to Collis P. Huntington, Cairo, Egypt, April 25, 1891, Huntington Papers.

Chapter 14

1. New York *Daily Tribune,* June 8, 1890. This was one of the letters that GWW sent to the Associated Literary Press. Although it is not signed, internal evidence leaves no doubt that GWW wrote it.

2. George Grenfell to A. H. Baynes, Bolobo, June 23, 1890, Baptist Missionary Society Papers.

3. Unless otherwise indicated, the charges against Leopold and the discussion of them are from GWW, *An Open Letter to His Serene Majesty Leopold II* (1890; reprinted as Appendix 1 below).

4. The discussion of the proposed railway is based on GWW's *Report on the Proposed Congo Railway* (1890).

5. GWW's observations were confirmed the following year when investors conceded that "difficulties connected with the labour question have done much to delay the works." William Mackinnon to Collis P. Huntington, Balinmakill, Argyllshire, Scotland, March 14, 1891, Huntington Papers.

6. Williams wrote a third report some weeks later, while at St. Paul de Loanda, Angola. It was *A Report upon the Congo-State and Country to the*

President of the Republic of the United States of America (reprinted as Appendix 3 below). This formed the basis of much of the discussion of GWW's view of the Congo and its people.

7. GWW to Collis P. Huntington, Cairo, January 23 and February 11, 1891, Huntington Papers. The third report was the one to the president (see note 6 above).

8. GWW to Collis P. Huntington, Cairo, April 25, 1891, Huntington Papers.

9. William Mackinnon to Collis P. Huntington, Liverpool, October 27, 1890, Huntington Papers.

10. Collis P. Huntington to William Mackinnon, New York, September 20, 1890, Mackinnon Papers.

11. New York *Herald,* April 14, 1891.

12. A. Le Ghait to Monsieur le Directeur du "Herald," Washington, April 14, 1891; A. Le Ghait to Baron Lambermont, Washington, April 14, 1891; both in Correspondence, Baron Lambermont, Belgian Royal Archives.

13. Martin Gosselin to Lord Salisbury, Brussels, June 24, 1891, British Foreign Office Files, Fo84/2118, no. 48, Africa, Confidential, Public Record Office. By "private" circulation, Gosselin presumably meant the proofs referred to above.

14. Lord Vivian to Lord Salisbury, Brussels, April 4, 1891, British Foreign Office Files, Fo84/2118, no. 23, Africa, Confidential, Public Record Office. The United States minister to Belgium, Edwin H. Terrell, made no mention of GWW in his dispatches to the secretary of state.

15. *Report of the Proceedings of the Conference of African Merchants on the Congo Free State and Import Duties* (London, 1890), pp. 33–34. The copy used here is in U.S. Department of State, Dispatches from U. S. Ministers to the Netherlands, Microfilm M-42, Roll T33, National Archives. See also E. D. Morel, *Affairs of West Africa* (London, 1902), p. 320.

16. Ibid. A more recent student of the Congo question saw in the king's effort to brand GWW as a blackmailer merely a maneuver to discredit him in advance. S. J. S. Cookey, *Britain and the Congo Question, 1885–1913* (London, 1968), pp. 35–36.

17. A near-verbatim version of the introductory paragraphs of "Un Colonel noir" was reproduced in 1952 in the Belgian Colonial Biography. In the account of the 1891 article, it was claimed that GWW recruited six students at Hampton. *Mouvement Geographique,* June 14, 1891. In the 1952 piece, his recruits had increased to ten. *Biographie coloniale belge,* vol. 3 (Brussels, 1952), p. 926.

18. *Mouvement Géographique,* June 14, 1891.

19. *La Réforme,* June 9, 10, 12, 1891.

20. *Journal de Bruxelles,* June 12, 13, 14, 1891.

21. Ibid., June 12, 1891.

22. Ibid., June 14, 1891.

23. *La Réforme,* June 18, 1891.

24. *La Nation,* June 14, 1891.

25. *Le Jour,* June 14, 1891.

26. Quoted in *La Nation,* June 14, 1891.

27. *Le Temps,* June 18, 1891.

28. *Le Patriote,* June 19, 1891.

29. Parlement, Chambre des Représentants, *Annales Parlementaires* (Brussels, 1891), pp. 1351–52.

30. Martin Gosselin to Lord Salisbury, Brussels, July 19, 1891, British Foreign Office Files, Public Record Office.

31. *Bulletin Officiel de L'Etat Indépendant du Congo, no. 7 bis, Rapport au Roi-Souverain* (Brussels, 1891).

32. GWW, *Open Letter,* p. 9. While the government report made no reference to this case, the *Journal de Bruxelles,* June 14, 1891, discussed it and exonerated the servant and the governor-general of any wrongdoing.

33. Roger Casement to the Foreign Secretary, the Marquis of Landsdowne, London, December 13, 1902, British Foreign Office Files, Africa, Confidential, Public Record Office.

34. Brian Inglis, *Roger Casement* (New York, 1973), pp. 28–31.

35. Ibid., February 15, 1903.

36. *Correspondence and Report from His Majesty's Consul at Boma Respecting the Administration of the Independent State of the Congo* (London, 1904), p. 23, 26, 34, and passim.

37. Quoted in Inglis, *Roger Casement,* p. 56.

38. Ibid., pp. 75–76.

39. Morel, *Affairs of West Africa,* p. 320. See also his *King Leopold's Rule in Africa* (New York, 1905), p. 104. The account of the reading from the *Open Letter* in a London meeting is repeated in his *Red Rubber,* 4th ed. (London, 1919), p. 40.

40. Quoted in Inglis, *Roger Casement,* p. 79. See also a memorandum by E. D. Morel, "Origin of British Interest in Congo Reform," a manuscript in the Morel Collection, London School of Economics.

41. "The Congo Diary," in Joseph Conrad, *Tales of Hearsay and Last Essays* (London, 1955), p. 161.

42. Joseph Conrad, *Heart of Darkness* (London, Penguin edition, 1973), p. 48.

43. The problem of inefficiency in the Congo is discussed in Hunt Hawkins, "Conrad's Critique of Imperialism in *Heart of Darkness,*" *PMLA* 94 (March 1979): 286–99.

44. In his article "The Issue of Racism in *Heart of Darkness,*" *Conradiana* 14, no. 3 (1982): 163–71, Hunt Hawkins argues that Conrad was not a racist. For an opposing view, see Chimea Achebe, "An Image of Africa," *Massachusetts Review* 18 (Winter 1977): 782–94.

45. Conrad's letter to Casement is quoted in Inglis, *Roger Casement,* p. 92. Conrad continued to be sympathetic and even wrote a letter for publication. For

a discussion of his role in Congo reform, see Hunt Hawkins, "Joseph Conrad, Roger Casement, and the Congo Reform Movement," *Journal of Modern Literature* 9, no. 1 (1981): 65–80.

46. Johnston, *George Grenfell*, vol. 1, pp. 467–68.

47. Roger Casement, "Diary, Wednesday August 5, 1903," British Home Office; in custody of the Public Record Office.

48. Johnston, *George Grenfell*, vol. 1, p. 467. During these years the *Baptist Missionary Magazine* did not mention GWW's criticisms and "remained a steady admirer of both the Congo country and its government." David Lagergren, *Mission and State in the Congo* (Uppsala, 1970), p. 106.

49. See, for example, the monthly issues of the *Official Organ of the Congo Reform Association* for the years 1905–7.

50. William K. Parmenter, "The Congo and Its Critics, 1880–1913," unpublished Ph.D. dissertation, Harvard University, 1952, p. 149.

Chapter 15

1. See Collis P. Huntington to William Mackinnon, New York, September 20, 1890, Mackinnon Papers.

2. William Mackinnon to Collis P. Huntington, Liverpool, October 27, 1890, Huntington Papers.

3. Smith Mackenzie to William Mackinnon, Zanzibar, November 27, 1890, Mackinnon Papers.

4. Collis P. Huntington to William Mackinnon, San Francisco, April 17, 1891, Mackinnon Papers.

5. GWW to Collis P. Huntington, Cairo, April 25, 1891, Huntington Papers.

6. William Mackinnon to Collis P. Huntington, London, June 11, 1891, Huntington Papers.

7. Ibid., and Francis William Fox to Collis P. Huntington, London, July 6, 1891, Huntington Papers.

8. B. F. Stevens to General Henry S. Sanford, London, June 5, 1890; Alvey A. Adee, Second Assistant Secretary, Department of State to Senator George F. Hoar, July 1, 1890; both in Hoar Papers.

9. Samuel Pelling to Mrs. L. A. Staples, Blackpool, September 3, 1891, Williams Papers. Pelling said that Miss Fryer was traveling in the company of her mother. No one on the passenger list of the ship on which Miss Fryer was traveling can possibly be identified as her mother. Other women were traveling either with their husbands, their children, or both. There was no other unattached woman traveling under the name of Fryer or, indeed, under any other name. Form of passenger list, SS *Golconda*, 95098, of the British India Steam Navigation Company, Ltd., Public Record Office, Kew, England. In subsequent reports to the Department of State, Alice Fryer was usually referred to as GWW's "intended wife." See, for example, Thomas M. Sherman to William F. Wharton, Liverpool, August 27, 1891, Dispatch No. 135, General Records of

the Department of State, Consular Dispatches, Liverpool, vol. 51, National Archives.

10. Excerpts of letter, GWW to Herbert Hall, Worcester, December 13, 1888, May 18, 1889. Hoar Papers. Hall, an officer in the Public Record Office, was representing GWW's creditors there.

11. Francis William Fox to Collis P. Huntington, London, July 6, 1891, Huntington Papers.

12. Thomas H. Sherman to Mrs. C. M. Hubbard, Liverpool, August 19, 1891, Department of State, General Correspondence, Outward, vol. 44 (June 12, 1891 to Nov. 12, 1891), National Archives.

13. Thomas H. Sherman to William F. Wharton, Assistant Secretary of State, Liverpool, August 27, 1891. Dispatch no. 135, General Records of the Department of State, Consular Dispatches, Liverpool, vol. 51, National Archives; *General and Commercial Directory of Preston, Blackpool . . . and Adjacent Villages and Townships* (Preston, 1895), pp. 562, 613.

14. Immediate accounts of GWW's death are in the *Blackpool Times and Fylde Observer*, August 5, 12, 1891; *Blackpool and Fleetwood Gazette*, August 7, 14, 1891; Samuel Pelling to Mrs. L. A. Staples, Blackpool, September 3, 1891, Williams Papers; and Thomas W. Sherman to William F. Wharton, Liverpool, August 27, 1891, Dispatch no. 135, General Records of the Department of State, Consular Dispatches, Liverpool, vol. 51, National Archives. The death certificate indicates that an Ann Cox was also present at the death. One can presume that she was a nurse, since the hotel later presented a bill which included the services of a nurse. *Register of Deaths in the County of Lancaster, Sub-district of Blackpool*, 1891, no. 302; Thomas Sherman to T. T. Partington [manager of the Palatine Hotel], Liverpool.

15. In section F, grave 123. "Register of Burials in the Burial Ground of the Blackpool Burial Board," Blackpool, 1891, p. 68. Manuscript records in the office of the Warden of Layton Cemetery, Blackpool, February 23, 1892. See also Department of State, General Correspondence, Outward, vol. 45, National Archives.

16. Samuel Pelling to Mrs. L. A. Staples, Blackpool, September 3, 1891, Williams Papers. This is the only communication in the Williams Papers held by Mrs. Williams until her death in 1945 that mentioned Miss Fryer. The Department of State was exceedingly careful in withholding from Mrs. Williams all information about Miss Fryer.

17. J. C. Sherman to Miss Alice Fryer, Liverpool, August 10, 1891, Department of State, General Correspondence, Outward, vol. 44, National Archives.

18. Thomas H. Sherman to Miss Alice M. Fryer, Liverpool, August 24, 27, 1891, Department of State, General Correspondence, Outward, vol. 44, National Archives. At times the consulate varied the spelling of Miss Fryer's first name, calling her Alyce on August 24 and Alice on August 27.

19. Thomas H. Sherman to Thomas D. Crawford, Liverpool, February 10, 1892. Department of State, General Correspondence, Outward, vol. 45, National Archives.

20. J. C. Sherman to Thomas D. Crawford, Liverpool, August 10, 24, 1891, Department of State, General Correspondence, Outward, vol. 44, National Archives.

21. Greenway (Justice of the peace) to R. T. Lincoln, American Minister, Darwen, Lancashire, August 4, 1891; Robert T. Lincoln to John C. New, London, August 4, 1891; John C. New to Thomas Sherman, London, August 4, 1891; all in Department of State, General Correspondence, Outward, vol. 44, National Archives.

22. John C. New to Thomas H. Sherman, London, August 7, 1891, Official Letter Book, London Consul General's Office, vol. 35, Record Group 84, National Archives. Additional information is in an interim report of Thomas H. Sherman to the assistant secretary of state, William F. Wharton, Liverpool, August 27, 1891. Consular Dispatches to the Department of State, Liverpool, vol. 51, National Archives.

23. W. J. Sulis to Mrs. L. A. Staples, Liverpool, August 11, 1891; Thomas H. Sherman to Mrs. L. A. Staples, Liverpool, September 18, 1891; both in Department of State, General Correspondence, Outward, vol. 44, National Archives.

24. Samuel Pelling to Mrs. L. A. Staples, Blackpool, September 3, 1891, Williams Papers. As late as April of the following year, Mrs. Staples was still attempting to retrieve her letters. At that time the consul informed her that the estate had been settled and that all materials, including manuscripts and letters, had been sent to the widow. "If you were to request Mrs. Williams to send you such of your letters to the Colonel as were found among his effects, I have no doubt that she will promptly respond." Thomas H. Sherman to Mrs. Lois A. Staples, Blackpool, April 5, 1892, Department of State, General Correspondence, Outward, vol. 45, National Archives. Mrs. Staples died in 1912 at eighty-four years of age. Worcester *Evening Gazette*, February 8, 1912.

25. Thomas H. Sherman to Harry F. Williams, Liverpool, August 27, 1891; Thomas H. Sherman to Lola Williams, Liverpool, September 8, 1891; Thomas H. Sherman to Mrs. C. M. Hubbard, Liverpool, August 19, 1891; all in Department of State, General Correspondence, Outward, vol. 44, National Archives.

26. Thomas H. Sherman to Mrs. Sarah A. Williams, Liverpool, August 27, 1891, ibid.

27. Thomas H. Sherman to William F. Wharton, Liverpool, August 27, 1891, Consular Dispatches to the Department of State, Liverpool, vol. 51, National Archives.

28. Sarah A. Williams to William F. Wharton, Washington, September 16, 1891, General Records of the Department of State, Miscellaneous Letters, September, 1891, National Archives. Her letters of administration arrived in Liverpool, November 7, 1891. W. J. Sulis to Mrs. Sarah A. Williams, Liverpool, November 27, 1891, Department of State, General Correspondence, Outward, vol. 45, National Archives.

29. Thomas H. Sherman to Messrs. James Bros., Liverpool, February 6,

1892, Department of State, General Correspondence, Outward, vol. 45, National Archives.

30. Thomas H. Sherman to Miss Alyce Fryer, Liverpool, February 8, 1892; Thomas H. Sherman to Thomas D. Crawford, Liverpool, February 10, 1892; Thomas H. Sherman to T. T. Partington, Liverpool, February 16, 1892, February 23, 1892; Thomas H. Sherman to George C. Kinsbury, M.D., Liverpool, February 19 and March 19, 1892; Thomas H. Sherman to W. C. Richardson, Chemist, Liverpool, March 17, 19, 1892; all in Department of State, General Correspondence, Outward, vol. 45, National Archives.

31. Thomas H. Sherman to R. C. Phillips, Liverpool, January 18, 1892. Department of State, General Correspondence, Outward, vol. 45, National Archives; R. C. Phillips to Mrs. Sarah A. Williams, Manchester, January 21, 1892. Williams papers. For the appraisal by Phillips of Williams's strictures against King Leopold, see above, chap. 14.

32. When Mrs. Williams died in 1945, the diaries were still in her possession.

33. B. F. Stevens, representing GWW's creditors at the British Museum, was in regular touch with U. S. officials in an attempt to collect for his clients. Thomas H. Sherman to B. F. Stevens, Liverpool, August 28, 1891, February 6, 1892, Department of State, General Correspondence, Outward, vols. 44 and 45, National Archives.

34. One of the posters was in the possession of Sarah Williams at the time of her death.

35. Francis W. Fox to Collis P. Huntington, London, July 6, 1891, Huntington Papers.

36. Thomas H. Sherman to Sarah Williams, Liverpool, March 29, 1892, Department of State, General Correspondence, Outward, vol. 45, National Archives.

37. Ibid.

38. New York *Tribune*, August 5, 1891; Worcester *Telegram*, August 6, 1891.

39. New York *Age*, August 8, 1891. On the same day the Cleveland *Gazette* carried an account of GWW's death, together with a portrait, which it pronounced "a splendid one." See also the *Gazette's* editorial, August 15, 1891, and the St. Paul *Appeal*, August 8, 1891.

40. Indianapolis *Freeman*, August 15, 1891.

41. Cleveland *Gazette*, August 22, 1891. The same piece appeared in the Huntsville (Alabama) *Gazette*, September 5, 1891.

42. Boston *Herald*, August 5, 1891; Springfield *Republican*, August 5, 1891.

43. Kenneth L. Kusmer, *A Ghetto Takes Shape: Black Cleveland, 1870–1930* (Urbana, Ill., 1976), p. 118.

44. Sarah A. Williams to John P. Green, Washington, August 24, 1891, Green Papers. Although Green and GWW had been friends and political associates in Ohio for years, Green does not mention GWW in his autobiography, *Facts Stranger than Fiction*.

45. Indianapolis *Freeman,* September 20, 1890. See also New York *Age,* September 27, 1890.

46. Denver *Statesman,* quoted in the Cleveland *Gazette,* October 25, 1890. Cooper, incidentally, was the only one on the list, with the exception of L'Ouverture, of course, who did not appear in the recently published *Dictionary of American Negro Biography,* edited by Rayford W. Logan and Michael Winston (New York, 1983).

47. Cleveland *Gazette,* October 4, 1890.

48. George F. Hoar, *Autobiography of Seventy Years,* 2 vols. (New York, 1903).

49. Kraus, *A History of American History;* Harvey Wish, *The American Historian: A Social-Intellectual History of the Writing of the American Past* (New York, 1960); H. Hale Bellot, *American History and American Historians* (Norman, Okla., 1952).

50. Frederick Douglass, *Life and Times of Frederick Douglass* (New York, Centenary edition, 1941); John Mercer Langston, *From the Virginia Plantation to the National Capitol* (Hartford, 1894); and Green, *Facts Stranger Than Fiction.*

51. John Hope, "Col. George Williams' Service to the Race as a Historian," Ms. in the John Hope papers, Moorland-Spingarn Research Center, Howard University.

52. Booker T. Washington, *The Story of the Negro,* 2 vols. (New York, 1909), vol. 1, pp. 91, 93, 258, 312, 325.

53. W. E. Burghardt Du Bois, *The Gift of Black Folk: Negroes in the Making of America* (Boston, 1924), pp. 101, 104, 107, 117–18, 124, 164, 187, 301.

54. Carter G. Woodson, *The Negro in Our History* (Washington, 1945), p. 469.

55. Carter G. Woodson, "George Washington Williams," n.d., manuscript in the Carter G. Woodson Papers, Association for the Study of Afro-American Life and History, Washington, D.C. I am grateful to Charles H. Wesley for making the manuscript available to me.

56. John Hope Franklin, "George Washington Williams, Historian," *Journal of Negro History* 31 (January 1946): 60–90.

57. Vernon Loggins, *The Negro Author: His Development in America to 1900* (New York, 1931), p. 278.

58. Benjamin Brawley, *A Social History of the American Negro* (New York, 1921), p. ix.

59. Rayford W. Logan, *The Negro in American Life and Thought: The Nadir, 1877–1901* (New York, 1954), p. 332.

60. Earl E. Thorpe, *Negro Historians in the United States* (Baton Rouge, 1958), p. 38.

61. François Bontinck, *Aux Origines de l'État Indépendant du Congo: Documents tirés d'archives américaines* (Louvain, 1966), pp. 441–49.

62. By the Arno Press, a subsidiary of the New York *Times.*

63. The program of the banquet, in the possession of the author, has line drawings by Ernest Crichlow of Aldridge, Douglass, and GWW.

64. New York *Times,* September 21, 1970.

65. *Carolina Times,* November 16, 1974. The same feature reappeared in the *Carolina Times* for September 4, 1982.

66. Morrie Turner, "Soul Corner," January 11, 1981.

67. Parmenter, "The Congo and its Critics, 1880–1913."

68. Paul McStallworth, "The United States and the Congo Question, 1884–1914" (Ann Arbor: University Films, 1973), pp. 186–187, 196.

69. Ruth Slade, *King Leopold's Congo: Aspects of the Development of Race Relations in the Congo Independent State* (London, 1962), p. 178. See also her *English Speaking Missions in the Congo Independent State, 1878–1908* (Brussels, 1959), pp. 240–41.

70. S.J.S. Cookey, *Britain and the Congo Question, 1885–1913* (London, 1968), pp. 35–36. For a similar statement on GWW's dismay over what he saw in the Congo, see Stanley Shaloff, *Reform in Leopold's Congo* (Richmond, 1970), p. 24, n. 7.

George Washington Williams
A Chronology

October 16, 1849: Born in Bedford Springs, Pennsylvania
1864: Enlisted in United States Colored Troops
December 1865: Discharged from United States Colored Troops
December 1865: Enlisted in Mexican Revolutionary Army
1867: Discharged from Mexican Revolutionary Army
August 29, 1867: Enlisted in Tenth Cavalry, United States Army
July 27, 1868: Discharged for disability
1869: Enrolled at Howard University
1870: Enrolled at Wayland Seminary
September 9, 1870: Entered Newton Theological Institution
June 2, 1874: Married Sarah A. Sterrett of Chicago
June 10, 1874: Graduated from Newton Theological Institution
June 11, 1874: Ordained into the Baptist ministry in Watertown, Massachusetts
June 24, 1874: Installed as pastor of Twelfth Baptist Church, Boston
1874: Published *History of the Twelfth Baptist Church*
October 1, 1875: Resigned as pastor of Twelfth Baptist Church
September 4–December 18, 1875: Editor of *The Commoner*, Washington, D.C.
March 2, 1876: Installed as pastor of Union Baptist Church, Cincinnati, Ohio
July 4, 1876: Delivered oration, "The American Negro from 1776 to 1876," Avondale, Ohio
December 3, 1876–November 24, 1878: Columnist for the Cincinnati *Commercial*
October 9, 1877: Defeated as candidate for the House of Representatives of the Ohio General Assembly
December 1, 1877: Resigned as pastor of Union Baptist Church
January 1878: Began the study of law in the office of Alphonso Taft
October 14, 1879: Elected to the House of Representatives of the Ohio General Assembly—served one term, 1880–81

January 26, 1881: Appointed judge advocate, with the rank of colonel, in the Ohio Encampment of the Grand Army of the Republic—served for one year

June 8, 1881: Admitted to the practice of law in Ohio

December 1882: Published *History of the Negro Race in America*

November 15, 1883: Admitted to the practice of law in Massachusetts

Summer 1884: Traveled in Switzerland, Germany, France, and Great Britain

March 2, 1885: Appointed United States minister to Haiti by President Chester A. Arthur

April 15, 1885: Was refused clearance to leave for Haiti by Secretary of State, Thomas Bayard

July 1886: Unsuccessfully sought divorce from Sarah A. Williams

1887: Published *History of Negro Troops in the War of the Rebellion*

May 17, 1887: Received honorary degree of Doctor of Laws from the State University of Louisville

January 3, 1888: Lost suit against United States in U.S. Court of Claims regarding salary for his appointment to the Haitian post

June 1888: Attended Centenary Conference of Protestant Missions in London

January–June 1888: Published installments of *The Autocracy of Love* in the Indianapolis *World*

October–December 1888: Undertook research trip to England, France, and Spain

September 28, 1889: Sailed for Europe to attend antislavery conference in Brussels

December 9, 1889: Returned to United States

December 23, 1889: Called on President Benjamin Harrison

January 30, 1890: Sailed from Liverpool for the Congo

July 18, 1890: At Stanley Falls, wrote *Open Letter to . . . Leopold, King of the Belgians*

September 17, 1890: Arrived at Loanda, Angola, to begin tour of Africa

January 21, 1891: Completed African journey at Cairo, Egypt

May 1891: Met Alice Fryer aboard SS. *Golconda* en route from Ismailia

June 1, 1891: Arrived in London from Africa

July 7, 1891: Went to Blackpool with Alice Fryer

August 2, 1891: Died in Blackpool, England

August 5, 1891: Funeral; burial in Layton Cemetery, Blackpool

George Washington Williams
A Bibliography

The following, with the exception of the newspaper columns, are the principal writings of Williams and were published separately as books or pamphlets. Numerous speeches and other pieces that were published in whole or in part in the daily press are not listed here.

The Advent of the Colored Soldier: A Memorial Sermon Delivered before Robert A. Bell Post 134, G.A.R., Sunday, May 24, 1874. Boston, 1874.
History of the Twelfth Baptist Church, Boston, Mass. from 1840 to 1874. Boston, 1874.
The American Negro, from 1776 to 1876: oration Delivered July 4, 1876, at Avondale, Ohio. Cincinnati, 1876.
Columns in the Cincinnati *Commercial*
   "The Colored Baptists of Cincinnati," December 3, 1876.
   "John Brown," December 23, 1876.
   "Military Life on the Plains," January 6, 1877.
   "A Winter on the Rio Grande," January 13, 1877.
   "The Last Campaign of the War," February 10, 1877.
   "Business Colored Men of Cincinnati," February 11, 18, and 25, and March 4, 1877.
   "Colored Chicagoans," March 11, 1877.
   "The President's Southern Policy," March 12, 1877.
   "The Colored Orphan Asylum," May 20, 1877.
   "Hope for Africa," May 31, 1877.
   "Our Colored Fellow Citizens," June 10, 1877.
   "The Louisiana Native Guards," June 17, 1877.
   "Music Among the Colored People," May 19, 1878.
   "The Soldiers' Home, Its Officers and Men," November 24, 1878.
History of the Negro Race in America from 1619 to 1880: Negroes As Slaves, as Soldiers, and as Citizens. 2 vols., New York, 1882, 1883; 2 vols. in one, New York, 1885.

The Negro as a Political Problem, Oration . . . at the Asbury Church, Washington, D.C., April 16, 1884. Boston, 1884.

The Ethics of War, Oration . . . at Newton, Massachusetts, May 30, 1884. Delivered before Charles Ward Post 62, G.A.R. Newton, 1884.

A History of the Negro Troops in the War of the Rebellion, 1861–1865. New York, 1887.

The Constitutional Results of the War of the Rebellion, An Oration . . . Memorial Day, May 30th, 1889 at Millbury, Mass. Worcester, 1889.

An Open Letter to His Serene Majesty Leopold II, King of the Belgians and Sovereign of the Independent State of Congo. 1890.

A Report on the Proposed Congo Railway. 1890.

A Report upon the Congo-State and Country to the President of the Republic of the United States of America. 1890.

Index

(George Washington Williams is abbreviated here as GWW)